KOREAN STUDIES OF THE HENRY M. JACKSON
SCHOOL OF INTERNATIONAL STUDIES

Clark W. Sorensen, Editor

KOREAN STUDIES OF THE HENRY M. JACKSON SCHOOL OF
INTERNATIONAL STUDIES

Over the Mountains Are Mountains: Korean Peasant Households and Their Adaptations to Rapid Industrialization, by Clark W. Sorensen

Cultural Nationalism in Colonial Korea, 1920–1925, by Michael Edson Robinson, with a new preface by the author

Offspring of Empire: The Koch'ang Kims and the Colonial Origins of Korean Capitalism, 1876–1945, by Carter J. Eckert, with a new preface by the author

Confucian Statecraft and Korean Institutions: Yu Hyŏngwŏn and the Late Chosŏn Dynasty, by James B. Palais

Peasant Protest and Social Change in Colonial Korea, by Gi-Wook Shin

The Origins of the Chosŏn Dynasty, by John B. Duncan

Protestantism and Politics in Korea, by Chung-shin Park

Marginality and Subversion in Korea: The Hong Kyŏngnae Rebellion of 1812, by Sun Joo Kim

Building Ships, Building a Nation: Korea's Democratic Unionism under Park Chung Hee, by Hwasook Nam

Japanese Assimilation Policies in Colonial Korea, 1910–1945, by Mark E. Caprio

Fighting for the Enemy: Koreans in Japan's War, 1937–1945, by Brandon Palmer

Heritage Management in Korea and Japan: The Politics of Antiquity and Identity, by Hyung Il Pai

Wrongful Deaths: Selected Inquest Records from Nineteenth-Century Korea, compiled and translated by Sun Joo Kim and Jungwon Kim

The Emotions of Justice: Gender, Status, and Legal Performance in Chosŏn Korea, by Jisoo M. Kim

Buddhas and Ancestors: Religion and Wealth in Fourteenth-Century Korea, by Juhn Y. Ahn

BUDDHAS & ANCESTORS

RELIGION AND WEALTH IN FOURTEENTH-CENTURY KOREA

JUHN Y. AHN

UNIVERSITY OF WASHINGTON PRESS
Seattle

Buddhas and Ancestors was supported by the Nam Center for Korean Studies at the University of Michigan, and by the Korea Studies Program of the University of Washington in cooperation with the Henry M. Jackson School of International Studies.

A Study of the Weatherhead East Asian Institute Columbia University
The Studies of the Weatherhead East Asian Institute of Columbia University were inaugurated in 1962 to bring to a wider public the results of significant new research on modern and contemporary East Asia.

The Korea Foundation has provided financial assistance
for the undertaking of this publication project.

Copyright © 2018 by the University of Washington Press
Printed and bound in the United States of America
Design by Katrina Noble
Composed in Minion, typeface designed by Robert Slimbach
Cover illustration: Anonymous, *Kshitigarbha*, first half of fourteenth century. Hanging scroll; ink, color, and gold on silk, 33¼ x 14½ in. H.O. Havemeyer Collection, Gift of Horace Havemeyer, 1929, Metropolitan Museum of Art.
22 21 20 19 18   5 4 3 2 1

All rights reserved. No part of this publication may be reproduced or transmitted in any form or by any means, electronic or mechanical, including photocopy, recording, or any information storage or retrieval system, without permission in writing from the publisher.

UNIVERSITY OF WASHINGTON PRESS
www.washington.edu/uwpress

LIBRARY OF CONGRESS CATALOGING-IN-PUBLICATION DATA
Names: Ahn, Juhn Young, author.
Title: Buddhas and ancestors : religion and wealth in fourteenth-century Korea / by Juhn Y. Ahn.
Description: Seattle : University of Washington Press, 2018. | Series: Korean studies of the Henry M. Jackson School of International Studies | Includes bibliographical references and index. |
Identifiers: LCCN 2017049031 (print) | LCCN 2017050622 (ebook) | ISBN 9780295743400 (ebook) | ISBN 9780295743387 (hardcover : alk. paper) | ISBN 9780295743394 (pbk. : alk. paper)
Subjects: LCSH: Korea—Religious life and customs. | Wealth—Religious aspects—Buddhism. | Wealth—Religious aspects—Confucianism. | Buddhism—Korea—Customs and practices. | Buddhist funeral rites and ceremonies—Korea. | Confucianism—Korea—Customs and practices. | Funeral rites and ceremonies, Confucian—Korea. | Korea—Civilization—935–1392.
Classification: LCC BL2236.R58 (ebook) | LCC BL2236.R58 A39 2018 (print) |
    DDC 294.309519/09023—dc23
LC record available at https://lccn.loc.gov/2017049031

To Se-Mi and Dojin

CONTENTS

Acknowledgments   ix
Author's Note   xiii
Koryŏ Kings and Reign Periods   xv

INTRODUCTION   3

1. Sowing the Seeds of Salvation with Wealth   15
2. Dark and Mysterious Ways   35
3. This Way of Ours   59
4. All the King's Men   81
5. Buddhas and Ancestors   105

CONCLUSION   133

Notes   143
Glossary of Chinese Characters   197
Bibliography   211
Index   227

ACKNOWLEDGMENTS

This book owes its existence to many generous and kind individuals. First and foremost, I am grateful to Don Lopez for his continued support and encouragement, which have allowed me to develop what was nothing more than an accidental discovery into a full-blown research project and eventually a book.

The bulk of the research that led to the production of this book was done while I was a member of the School of Historical Studies at the Institute for Advanced Study at Princeton University on a Mellon Fellowship and, later, a Kyujanggak Fellow at Seoul National University's International Center for Korean Studies. At Princeton, I benefited immensely from the company of Nicola DiCosmo, Caroline Walker Bynum, Tomoko Masuzawa, and new friends John Herman, Norman Kutcher, and Micah Muscolino. At the International Center for Korean Studies, I was able to develop my research in new directions thanks to the warm hospitality of Pak Sŏngch'ang, Kim In'gŏl, Park T'aegyun, Sŏ Yŏngch'ae, and Sem Vermeersch.

While I was still struggling to render my thoughts on Korean Buddhism and history, I was fortunate enough to receive guidance and support from John Duncan and Robert Buswell at a manuscript workshop sponsored by my home department at the University of Michigan. Without their feedback and encouragement, this book would certainly have been nothing more than a half-baked thought experiment.

I would also like to thank James Benn, Eunsu Cho, Griff Foulk, Luis Gómez, Greg Levine, Alex von Rospatt, Bob Sharf, and Duncan Williams for patiently guiding me through the labyrinth of Buddhist Studies. I am most indebted to Bob for introducing me to not only the study of Buddhism but also the wonders of being a critical intellectual, an ideal that I still struggle to live up to. I would also like to express my sincerest gratitude to Paul Chang, Henry Em, Judy Han, Jisoo Kim, Helen Lee, Eugene Park, Janet

Poole, Andre Schmid, Jesook Song, and the late Nancy Abelmann for kindly sharing their wisdom and passion for Korean studies with me.

The opportunity to present my research at the Religious Identities in Asia Seminar series hosted by the Center for the Study of World Religions at Harvard Divinity School and the Harvard University Asia Center was particularly helpful during the final stages of preparing this book for publication. I would like to thank my host, Sun Joo Kim, and the staff at Harvard's Korea Institute for making this visit possible. I would also like to thank Carter Eckert, Francis Clooney, James Robson, and others present at the talk for their valuable criticisms and suggestions.

Finally, I would like to thank my friends and colleagues, who, despite all my shortcomings, have continued to show me enthusiastic support. Rather than list everyone here, I would like to give special recognition those who offered help at critical moments when I thought all was lost: Ben Brose, Miranda Brown, Paul Copp, Reggie Jackson, Kenneth Koo, Andy Quintman, Mark Rowe, Youngju Ryu, and Dominic Steavu-Balint. Miranda deserves a special word of thanks for finding ingenious ways of dragging me repeatedly out of the proverbial academic gutter. I am particularly indebted to my former office neighbors Varuni Bhatia and Jonathan Zwicker, with whom I shared many delightful, encouraging, and insightful conversations and moments that temporarily elevated me above the burdens of academia. I am also deeply indebted to the Nam Center for Korean Studies, center director Nojin Kwak, Do-Hee Morsman, Adrienne Janney, and the Nam family. The Asian Languages and Cultures department staff and my students at the University of Michigan also deserve a special word of appreciation for creating an environment in which I could comfortably complete my manuscript.

This book also owes its existence to a few others who deserve special mention here. At the most critical moment of its production, Theodore Jun Yoo and Ted Hughes miraculously appeared and turned the source of much anxiety and despair into hope. For that, I am eternally grateful. I am also grateful to the three anonymous readers who provided valuable feedback and comments. All remaining errors, needless to say, are my own. This book would have never seen the light of day had it not also been for the Weatherhead East Asian Institute at Columbia University. I want to offer a special word of gratitude to the institute's publications coordinator Ross Yelsey for his superhuman speed, efficiency, and kindness. I also want to thank the series editor, Clark Sorensen, and my editor at the University of Washington Press, Lorri Hagman, for making the publication process the most pleasant and rewarding experience possible. The book benefited immensely from their constructive feedback and the assistance of others at the press. I am especially indebted to my copy editor, Laura Iwasaki, for all the miracles she performed to render my prose readable and presentable.

Parts of chapters 3 and 5 were previously published as "The Merit of Not Making Merit: Buddhism and the Late Koryŏ Fiscal Crisis," in *Seoul Journal of Korean Studies* 23, no. 1 (2010), and "This Way of Ours: Buddhist Memorial Temples and the Search for Values during the Late Koryŏ Dynasty," in *Han'guk pulgyohak* 54 (2009). I sincerely thank the editors for granting me permission to use this material here.

Although my name adorns the cover of this book, the people who actually deserve credit for all that is good in it are my parents, Se-Mi, her mom, and our big boy, Ben Dojin Ahn. *Buddhas and Ancestors* is the product of all the sacrifices they made. I dedicate this book to them.

AUTHOR'S NOTE

Romanization of Korean follows the McCune-Reischauer system, and pinyin is used for standard Chinese (Mandarin). Pronunciations are Korean unless labeled as Chinese (C), Japanese (J), or Sanskrit (S). Following standard practice for Korean and Chinese names, the surname is placed before the given name, and the two are not separated by a comma. Biographical dates and dates for rituals are provided in the traditional form "X day of the X lunar month." Lunar calendar dates that cannot be readily converted into Western calendar dates are also identified as "lunar month." All other dates follow the Western calendar.

KORYŎ KINGS AND REIGN PERIODS

T'aejo	918–43	Ŭijong	1146–70
Hyejong	943–45	Myŏngjong	1170–97
Chŏngjong	945–49	Sinjong	1197–1204
Kwangjong	949–75	Hŭijong	1204–11
Kyŏngjong	975–81	Kangjong	1211–13
Sŏngjong	981–97	Kojong	1213–59
Mokchong	997–1009	Wŏnjong	1259–74
Hyŏnjong	1009–31	Ch'ungnyŏl	1274–1308
Tŏkchong	1031–34	Ch'ungsŏn	1298, 1308–13
Chŏngjong	1034–46	Ch'ungsuk	1313–30, 1332–39
Munjong	1046–83	Ch'unghye	1330–32, 1339–44
Sunjong	1083	Ch'ungmok	1344–48
Sŏnjong	1083–94	Ch'ungjŏng	1348–51
Hŏnjong	1094–95	Kongmin	1351–74
Sukchong	1095–1105	U	1374–88
Yejong	1105–22	Ch'ang	1388–89
Injong	1122–46	Kongyang	1389–92

BUDDHAS AND ANCESTORS

INTRODUCTION

ON SEPTEMBER 1, 1352, THE FIRST YEAR OF KING KONGMIN'S REIGN, the kingdom of Koryŏ (918–1392) lost one of its most affluent and influential officials. After battling an acute illness for several months, assistant chancellor (*ch'ansŏngsa*) and royal-in-law Kwŏn Chun passed away at the age of seventy-one. Following established court protocol, the grieving family quickly notified the king of the assistant chancellor's death. The king accordingly had the "office of royal sacrifices" (*taesang*) grant the assistant chancellor the posthumous title Ch'anghwa. With due financial support from the office of royal sacrifices, the grieving family also began making preparations for the assistant chancellor's funeral. His body was first cleaned, dressed, and placed inside a coffin. It was then installed in a temporary resting place where mourners and condolence visitors could pay their last respects. At this time, a talented literatus named Yi Inbok was also asked to furnish Kwŏn Chun, his former examiner (*chigonggŏ*), with an elegant funerary inscription. A month later, on October 2, the coffin was carefully moved to an auspicious site located less than a day's journey from the capital for burial.[1] There, in keeping with his wishes, the assistant chancellor was finally laid to rest on the grounds of his own memorial monastery (*wŏndang*), Chahyo-sa, and given what was no doubt a splendid Buddhist funeral.[2]

Eighteen years later, a drastically different kind of funeral was performed for an equally high-ranking Koryŏ official. Although he nominally held the same title, Assistant Chancellor, at the time of his death, the former "academician of the security council" (*chehak*, also *milchik haksa*) Yun T'aek saw no need to replicate the practice of men like Kwŏn Chun and restore a lavish memorial monastery near the capital to prepare for death.[3] Having emerged from relatively humble origins, the academician possessed no wealth and could not lay claim to a pedigree. But he did not regard this as a source of shame. On the contrary, the academician took the impoverished state of his household as proof of moral rectitude and righteousness. Determined to preserve this stoic attitude toward affluence and wealth as the legacy of his family, the ailing academician summoned his children and grandchildren to his bedside. The eighty-one-year-old academician explained to them that he owed both his extraordinarily long life and his successful career to the hidden virtue (*chamdŏk*, also *ŭmdŏk*) of his own grandfather, who, in spite of his impoverished background, had been honest and morally principled at all times. Concerned, perhaps, that his descendants would not know how to put this lesson into practice immediately, the academician added the following final instructions on his deathbed: "When I die, do not have scruples about not using Buddhist customs. Do not be wasteful."[4]

The academician passed away a few weeks later, on October 9, 1370. His body was cleaned, dressed, and placed inside a coffin that very same day. The king was also duly notified of his passing. The office of royal sacrifices granted Yun T'aek the posthumous title Munjŏng, an honor that he was due as assistant chancellor. The funerary process thus began to take what at first appeared to be a predictable path. However, in keeping with Yun T'aek's final instructions, his sons, daughters, and their spouses made no effort to copy a Buddhist sutra, cremate his body, or sponsor a Buddhist memorial service every seven days after his passing as other elite families in Koryŏ were inclined to do.[5] The grieving family also did not wait for condolence visitors to pay their last respects and contribute to the funerary expenses. Instead, they kept the funeral simple, modest, and discreet, limiting the wake to just three days.

At the end of this short wake, they also performed what their social peers may have considered a burial unbecoming someone of Yun T'aek's high social standing. Deviating from the strong trend among the central office-holding elite of securing an auspicious burial site inside the capital district with the help of a yin-yang specialist or geomancer, the grieving family members kept his remains on their rural estate in Kŭmju and buried him next to his mother, Lady Kim.[6] Their deviation from established norms did not end there. Rather than endow or build a memorial monastery, Yun T'aek's eldest son, Kusaeng, chose to convert the graveside mourning shed that his father had temporarily built for mourning his mother into a more permanent family shrine (*kamyo*). There, Kusaeng performed seasonal sacrifices for his father and ancestors according to the instructions found in the manual *Family Rituals* (C. Jiali), attributed to the renowned Chinese classicist Zhu Xi (1130–1200).[7]

Examined side by side, the differences between Kwŏn and Yun and their methods of managing death may seem more apparent than their commonalities. Kwŏn chose to take the costly route of building a memorial monastery; Yun deemed this practice wasteful and instructed his children to abandon Buddhist methods. Kwŏn was buried near the capital; Yun's body was relocated to what appears to be a clan gravesite in his mother's rural ancestral seat (*pon'gwan*).[8] These differences between Kwŏn and Yun stand out even more, perhaps, because of their seemingly trivial commonalities. Both men officially held the title Assistant Chancellor. This meant that they belonged to an exclusive class within Koryŏ's officialdom known as ministers of the chancellery (*chaesin* or *chaesang*).[9] Because Kwŏn and Yun held ministerial titles, they were both entitled to privileges reserved for men of their high social standing, such as posthumous titles, financial support from the state for their funerals, and funerary inscriptions written by renowned scholar-officials.[10] Both also belonged to families with multiple generations of men who had passed the much-respected literary examination (*chesul kwa*) and served in key bureaucratic posts.[11] But these commonalities obviously did not prevent them from making some remarkably different choices at the end of their lives. How, then, should we make sense of their divergence in attitude toward the management of death?

This divergence could conceivably be read as a simple matter of opposing personal tastes. But this reading would be persuasive only if the intimate relationship between mortuary customs and elite identity in Koryŏ could be ignored.[12] In Koryŏ, mortuary customs were too essential to the process of establishing elite family credentials to be changed on a whim. Earlier studies of fourteenth-century Korea therefore tend to regard Kwŏn and Yun not as examples of men who exercised their unique personal tastes but as representatives of two contradictory sociopolitical impulses.[13] On one side, these studies claim, were officials like Kwŏn's brother-in-law Yi Chehyŏn and his student Yi Saek, who sought to preserve earlier customs, which included the old territorial status system and Buddhist ways of managing death.[14] On the other side were scholar-officials such as Chŏng Tojŏn, Cho Chun, and Yun T'aek's grandson Yun Sojong, who attributed the many problems of their age to these same customs and pushed for comprehensive socioeconomic reform.[15] Hoping to reform society along Neo-Confucian lines, the reformists and their supporters also exerted considerable effort in denouncing Buddhism as an "abnormality" (*koe*) and urged their peers and the populace at large to follow the guidelines in Zhu Xi's *Family Rituals* instead.

Although it is now widely accepted as the scholarly consensus, this neat account of the ideological divisions that led to the so-called anti-Buddhist movement (*ch'ŏkpul undong*) of the late Koryŏ and early Chosŏn periods can be misleading.[16] Upon closer examination, it becomes clear that this emphasis on differing levels of ideological commitment to Neo-Confucianism can create more interpretive problems than solutions. Kwŏn Chun's father, Kwŏn Pu, for instance, was born to a devout Buddhist family, but he is known to have been the first person to attempt the publication of Zhu Xi's commentaries on the Four Books—*Analects* (C. Lunyu), *Mencius* (C. Mengzi), *Doctrine of the Mean* (C. Zhongyong), and *Great Learning* (C. Daxue)—in Korea.[17] At the request of his father, Kwŏn Chun himself is said to have collected the stories of sixty-four filial sons and, with the editorial assistance of his brother-in-law Yi Chehyŏn, published the collection as a single volume, *Record of Filial Deeds* (Hyohaeng rok). Kwŏn Chun's family, the Andong Kwŏn, and their affinal kin were clearly no strangers to Neo-Confucianism. On the contrary, they saw fit to boldly declare themselves the fountainhead of Tohak (learning of the Way) or Neo-Confucian learning in Korea.[18]

Kwŏn Chun's decision to build a memorial temple for himself may strike us as odd, if not incoherent, for precisely this reason. But Kwŏn and Yun may not, in fact, be all that different. Kwŏn's decision to build a lavish memorial monastery and Yun's decision to rely on a humble mourning shed to manage death may well have been different responses to the same underlying problem, namely, the problematization of wealth in fourteenth-century Korea.

This concern about wealth can be glimpsed in Yun's final instructions for his family, when he repeatedly emphasized the virtue of not being wasteful. The same concern also informs Yi Inbok's reflections on the praiseworthy qualities of his examiner Kwŏn Chun:

> I think that the five blessings [*obok*] in the *Great Plan* [C. Hongfan] are things that human beings desire, but those who can enjoy them are usually few in number.[19] How could it not be the case that Heaven waits for the [right] person to grant that which it [otherwise] will not grudge? The people whom the world calls "noble and affluent" [*kwibuga*] acquire [nobility and wealth] through merit but lose them through [lack of] virtue, gain them at the beginning [of their careers] but lose them at the end, and enjoy them with their bodies but are unable to rid their minds of sorrow. Speaking of them, how can we not feel pity? The [assistant

chancellor] was rich and noble, but he did not possess these numerous concerns. And, though he attained a long life, his descendants became noble and illustrious.[20]

Yi here appears to be showering Kwŏn with unconditional words of praise. Kwŏn, Yi claims, must be the kind of person who deserves extremely rare blessings from Heaven. Otherwise, how could he have enjoyed longevity, nobility, and wealth his entire life without a worry in the world? There is no denying that Kwŏn was a blessed man. He did live to be more than seventy years of age, and there is no record of him becoming seriously ill before 1352, the year of his death. Kwŏn was also undeniably wealthy.[21] This allowed him to do some extraordinary things. He could, for instance, make offerings to ten monks every morning for more than thirty years.[22] He could also restore a memorial monastery (i.e., Chahyo-sa) once owned by the Kyŏngwŏn Yi, arguably the most affluent and powerful family of early Koryŏ.

Was Yi Inbok's short but piercing reflection on wealth meant to be nothing more than a glorifying confirmation of the obvious? This does not seem to be case. There is something quite novel about the way Yi praises the late assistant chancellor. Funerary inscriptions (*pimyŏng*) and prefaces (*sŏ*), that is, tomb epitaphs from earlier periods, seldom, if ever, problematized wealth.[23] Wealth was simply a privilege that noble (*kwi*) families were entitled to enjoy. It was an organic part of their identity as hereditary elites, or *sejok*, who continued to produce high-ranking ministers generation after generation. *Sejok* families were expected to be able to enjoy professional end-of-life care at a Buddhist monastery in their final moments of life, purchase a burial site near the capital, commission a funerary portrait (*chinyŏng*), and make generous endowments to a Buddhist monastery in order to ensure perpetual prayers for their souls and the souls of their loved ones after death. Extremely affluent *sejok* families could even emulate the royal family and build their own memorial monasteries near the capital.[24]

Yi Inbok, however, offered his reflection on wealth in a drastically different sociocultural environment: elite families of the fourteenth century disagreed as to whether they should continue to aspire to old *sejok* ideals. There were some, like Kwŏn Chun, who blatantly emulated these ideals in order to build *sejok* credentials.[25] Their newly acquired affluence made this possible. In contrast, there were others, like Yun T'aek, who possessed neither wealth nor *sejok* credentials. They did not consider this a source of shame. Rather, they chose to purposefully demonstrate their indifference to wealth, in the belief that this attitude made them bona fide members of the elite.

The disagreement between Kwŏn and Yun should not, however, be understood along class lines as a disagreement between *sejok* and non-*sejok* families. Both Kwŏn and Yun aspired to be part of the *sejok*, but they held different assumptions about Buddhism and wealth. Before the fourteenth century, *sejok* families in Koryŏ did not hesitate to make generous donations to the Buddhist establishment. This is because they expected their donations to function like seeds and mysteriously (*hyŏn*) transform into something qualitatively different, namely, salvation. Like the small seed that grows into a giant tree, this transformation was mysterious in the sense that the cause (wealth) and the effect (merit and salvation) were not proportional or obviously related. Wealth donated to a Buddhist monastery or a field of merit (*pokchŏn*) grew exponentially into perpetual merit, and perpetual merit eventually guaranteed salvation. This transformation was not only mysterious but also seamless. No one questioned it, and no one had to.

Kwŏn's decision to restore Chahyo-sa was rooted in this old assumption that wealth could still mysteriously transform into perpetual merit and hence postmortem salvation. But this does not mean that we can take Kwŏn and his memorial monastery as evidence of the continuing vitality of the *sejok* aristocracy and their customs in late Koryŏ. Kwŏn and his monastery were, in fact, anything but. According to the preface of his funerary inscription, Kwŏn chose to restore the monastery Chahyo-sa because it once belonged to Yi Chayŏn (1003–1061), a Koryŏ nobleman who enjoyed unrivaled status as the father of no fewer than three royal consorts (*pi*).[26] Kwŏn, as the preface to his funerary inscription also duly notes, did not hesitate to suggest out loud that he might be the reincarnation of Yi. He had good reason to believe this to be true. His own brother became the adopted son of King Ch'ungsŏn, and two of his granddaughters became royal consorts.[27]

But if Kwŏn's *sejok* credentials were evident and could be taken for granted, there would have been no need for him to go to the extent of establishing this explicit connection between himself and Yi Chayŏn by restoring Chahyo-sa. The author of his funerary inscription and preface, Yi Inbok, was aware of this problem. Yi tried to find a way to praise Kwŏn, who clearly had established his nobility (*kwi*) with wealth acquired through unconventional means, as a man whose nobility did not depend solely on his wealth. As he was expected to do, Yi portrayed the assistant chancellor as a noble man worthy of the five blessings, but he made sure to add the important caveat—which one would not expect to see in the tomb epitaphs of members of the old *sejok* elite like Yi Chayŏn and the Kyŏngwŏn Yi—that nobility and blessings from Heaven had little to do with wealth. For Yi Inbok, wealth could not be expected to perpetually produce merit, even if sown in the field of a memorial monastery. Wealth was something that could be acquired one day through merit but lost another day because of the lack of virtue. It was a fickle and unreliable thing. Although it could please the body, this did not necessarily translate into happiness and peace of mind. Wealth could be cause for respect. It could also as easily be cause for pity.

Yun T'aek and Yi Inbok were not alone in being concerned about the relationship between nobility and wealth, a concern they shared with their peers in Koryŏ's central bureaucracy. Consider, for instance, the following lines from the funerary inscription for Yun Sŏnjwa, the husband of Yun T'aek's paternal aunt:

> People consider poverty to be misery; Yun considered wealth a disgrace.
> Some flatter their sovereign; Yun acquired a reputation for being upright.
> Who are the personators with high-ranking titles? High-ranking titles are subordinate to virtue.
> Mature in both virtue and age, what need is there to discuss Yun's nobility?[28]

Lest this appear to be nothing more than empty praise, the author of the inscription, Yi Saek's father, Yi Kok, made sure to note in the inscription's preface that Yun "had never managed the family's estate." As evidence of Yun's indifference to wealth, the preface also notes the final lesson he offered to his children: "Brothers today are not on good terms with each other because they fight over [inheritance].... Be harmonious, do not fight, and instruct your children and grandchildren [accordingly]." Yun then had his son draw up a will (*mun'gye*) wherein he specified the even distribution of the patrimony (*kaŏp*).

More than ever before, the Koryŏ elite emphasized the virtue of being "honest and upright" (*ch'ŏngnyŏm*), as Yun T'aek and his uncle Yun Sŏnjwa did in their final will and testament to their children and grandchildren. It also became quite common for members of the elite class to question the nature of giving to the Buddhist establishment. By the middle of the fourteenth century, it became necessary to problematize wealth and its relation to religion.

A THEORY OF CORRUPTION

Three prevailing assumptions have guided earlier studies of late Koryŏ Buddhism and wealth. First, there are those who argue that criticisms of the Buddhist establishment, which became more vocal in the late fourteenth century, were products of an "anti-Buddhist movement," a movement motivated primarily by the desire to respond to the Neo-Confucian call for comprehensive social reform. The anti-Buddhist movement was ostensibly led by scholars who "were infected with this call to action and strove to determine and implement a reform program that would Confucianize Korean society."[29] The problem with this Confucianization argument, however, is its reliance on the unfounded assumption that historical change is orchestrated by conscious or ideologically driven human agents. This assumption mistakenly confuses agent with subject: the actions of an agent do not necessarily have to stem from subjective knowledge or intention in order to effect meaningful and sustainable change.[30] A momentous shift did take place in the fourteenth century, but those responsible for this shift were not all trying to advance a specific ideological cause.

Second, there is the assumption that the anti-Buddhist movement was driven less by ideology than by concrete social concerns.[31] According to this argument, *sejok* families abandoned Buddhist methods of managing death and adopted Neo-Confucian rituals because they felt threatened by the growing prominence of non-*sejok* families, or what late Koryŏ sources call the "gates of power" (*kwŏnmun*) or the "powerful" (*kwŏn*, also *kwŏnse*). As one recent study puts it, "The display of reformed ritualism was an excellent means of demonstrating opposition to the *kwŏnmun*'s lavish self-aggrandizement with Buddhist trappings."[32] Buddhist methods of managing death were abandoned, in other words, because they were exploited by the powerful for private gain and therefore ceased to function as compelling strategies of distinction.[33] There is no denying that concerns about the rise of new social elements were at work in the changing attitude toward Buddhism in the fourteenth century, but what needs to be made more explicit is how the *sejok* worked out and made sense of these concerns.[34] Without this clarification, there is the danger of taking the capacity to conceptually distinguish private motives from religious ones (or what Martina Deuchler calls the "political" from the "social") for granted. There is also the danger of rendering religion irrelevant by turning it into a simple instrument of social, political, or economic gain.

Third, there are those who tend to assume that the so-called anti-Buddhist movement was a legitimate and much needed reaction to the corruption of the Buddhist establishment. The management of large landed estates (*nongjang*, also *chŏnwŏn*) by Buddhist monasteries and the extensive involvement of Buddhist monks in politics during this period are often cited as evidence of corruption.[35] The growth of landed estates, however, is not a problem unique to the Buddhist establishment, and Buddhist monks had maintained close relationships with kings and ministers since the beginning of the dynasty. The political and economic activities of the late Koryŏ Buddhist establishment do not, in other words, support the view that the establishment had become corrupt.

The greatest weakness of the corruption argument, however, is the very notion of corruption itself. Earlier studies of Buddhism and wealth tend to assume that corruption comes about when the unthinkable mixture of wealth and religion takes place. This assumption has already been taken to task by Jacques Gernet in his influential study of the economic history of Chinese Buddhism. Gernet demonstrated that Buddhism and wealth had always been inseparable, since before Buddhism arrived in China.[36] What allowed wealth and salvation to remain inseparable, he claims, was religious fervor. It was the lack thereof that led to the decline of Buddhism. As Gernet explains:

> Loans and rents had to serve the same purpose as offerings. The functioning of these heterogeneous arrangements relied entirely on religious fervor. Furthermore, the secular promoters of the Buddhist movement, great families that were hostile to the Confucian tradition, imperial princesses and eunuchs, constituted a social group that had an interest in the acquisition of riches and commercial power. From the moment these milieus became aware of the private ends, political and economic, that their adherence to Buddhism enabled them to pursue—as soon as their detachment from the religion became more apparent—Buddhism began its decline in China.[37]

Gernet's point is well taken, but he leaves unexplained exactly how private ends become detached from religious ones. The vague notion of "religious fervor" assumes more than it explains. An explanation of how offerings became wealth and how religion became otherworldly through the conceptual separation of wealth and religion is precisely what this book intends to offer, thereby demonstrating that the epistemological separation, rather than the mixture, of wealth and religion is what makes it possible to speak of corruption and decay.

What, then, caused the separation of wealth and religion in fourteenth-century Korea? Critical to answering this question are the novel issues that the Koryŏ elite began to raise about their identity under Mongol rule, which lasted roughly from the middle of the thirteenth to the end of the fourteenth century. These issues emerged under a set of unique historical circumstances. A sudden influx of men from nontraditional backgrounds (slaves, butchers, merchants, soldiers, interpreters, falconers, eunuchs, and so on) into the elite stratum forced members of the regular bureaucracy—officials in the civil and military branches of the central government who established their identities on their commitment to the ideals of bureaucratic service (*sa*)—to try to redefine the stratum in more exclusivist terms.

Problems deepened as the newcomers tried to conform to the cultural expectations and ritual decorum of the *sejok*. Like the *sejok* of early Koryŏ, some of the newcomers began to build and restore lavish memorial monasteries and give generously to the Buddhist establishment in order to honor their beloved dead. Consequently, at the level of ritual practice, the boundary between the regular bureaucracy and these newcomers began to blur. It thus became necessary for members of the regular bureaucracy and their families to offer a more refined explanation of the relationship between giving and greatness—a quality that many of the affluent newcomers, who tended to acquire their wealth through unconventional and unscrupulous means, were not expected to possess. Their solution was to separate the moral substance of giving generously to the Buddhist establishment from its material form. Leaders of the regular bureaucracy, such as Yi Chehyŏn and Yi Saek, argued that moral substance, rather than wealth, was what really mattered and what made a family "great." Even newcomers who lacked great-family (*taejok*) credentials (e.g., a long family history of producing officials) could claim greatness if they could demonstrate this moral substance.

This redefinition of giving and greatness silently led to the separation of salvation from wealth. Behind the vitriolic criticisms of the wastefulness of Buddhist practices in fourteenth-century Korea was this assumption that the ritual expenditure of wealth could no longer translate seamlessly into salvation and family prestige. This change in the grammar of concepts, which came about because religious giving lost its ability to function smoothly as an element of distinction, made it possible for elite families of this period to speak of the decadence and corruption of Buddhism.[38] Contrary to conventional scholarly narratives about the decline of Buddhism in Korea, the "corruption" of the Buddhist establishment—understood as the *mixture* of wealth and religion—was not what led some outspoken elite families from this period to abandon Buddhist methods of managing death. The decision made by officials such as Yun T'aek to abandon Buddhism and seek a new identity for the elite was the consequence of the *separation* of wealth and religion into two independent spheres of human activity and thought.

However, as wealth and religion went their separate conceptual ways, reform-minded court officials began to voice criticisms of the Buddhist establishment more frequently. They drafted and then put into effect new legislation to limit the influence of the Buddhist establishment. This is commonly assumed to be a turning point in the history of Korean Buddhism. It is at this critical moment that the Buddhist establishment ostensibly began its precipitous "decline." We must, however, question this notion of the decline of Buddhism in Korea. Admittedly, the new Chosŏn (1392–1910) state did try to impose a limit on the number of Buddhist monasteries in the major population centers.[39] The state also tried to limit the monasteries' control over taxable and alienable resources like land and labor (i.e., slaves).[40] But monasteries continued to amass large landed estates and receive financial support from elite patrons such as the new Chosŏn royal family. If there was decline, then it did not consist of a radical change in the pattern of patronage.

More devastating to Buddhist institutions located in well-populated areas were the Mongol invasions of the thirteenth century and the Red Turban occupation of the capital in the mid-fourteenth century.[41] Reconstruction efforts made in the aftermath of these devastating events naturally channeled wealth into the Buddhist establishment.[42] Accusations of the corruption of Buddhism were made in this context. These accusations, however, should not be taken literally. They were part of the reformists' agenda of keeping religion and wealth apart. A century of Mongol rule followed by the collapse of the Yuan paper currency bloc, limited state-level trade with China, and repeated Red Turban and Japanese pirate incursions left the Koryŏ court in dire financial circumstances.[43] The reformists believed that they could overcome this crisis by establishing stronger state control over alienable and taxable resources. As part of this plan, the reformists tried to prevent these resources from flowing into lavish Buddhist restoration projects and becoming privatized.

The execution of this plan through legislation did not amount to a suppression of Buddhism as some earlier studies claim, but it did allow the new state established by the reformists (i.e., Chosŏn) to push Buddhism into the margins of public authority in Korea.[44] Buddhism and especially the monasteries that had once been officially recognized as "places of aid and remedy" (*pibo chi so*) could no longer make the state's presence known to the public through its power to convert wealth into salvation, protection, and aid. This was a prerogative that was to belong only to the state and its central bureaucracy. Wealth had to be wealth. Religion had to be religion. The two could not be brought together to perform the mysterious (*hyŏn*). What the Buddhist establishment in Korea experienced, then, was not so much decline or decay as relocation: it was relocated from the center to the margins of public authority, where it continued to thrive, albeit in new ways, for centuries.

1 SOWING THE SEEDS OF SALVATION WITH WEALTH

THROUGHOUT THE FOURTEENTH CENTURY, ELITE FAMILIES IN THE Koryŏ capital Kaegyŏng built monasteries, made handsome monastic endowments, and sponsored Buddhist services both large and small to pray for the salvation of their beloved dead. As the academician of the security council Yun T'aek was willing to admit on his deathbed, it had become customary for families of high standing like his own to respond to death in this way. Other than unsanctioned monastery building, there were no statutory regulations for officialdom that either mandated or prohibited the use of Buddhist methods at the time of death in Koryŏ. Nevertheless, Buddhist sermons, prayers, and stone inscriptions that date as far back as the eleventh century provide evidence that the capital-based elite—kings, queens, high-ranking officials, and their families—had continued to manage death with a combination of pious devotion and large outlays of money and land for centuries.[1]

What motivating forces allowed this pattern of behavior to persist over time? Key to Buddhism's success in the management of death was its ability to provide those willing to convert their impressive wealth into prayers for the dead with the possibility that those prayers would miraculously continue in perpetuity. Elite families were keenly aware of the fact that their fame and fortune were ultimately unreliable things that could not withstand the vicissitudes of time, but they also knew that their earthly possessions could become an inexhaustible source of salvific power and prayer if placed in the care of an enlightened Buddhist master or the *saṅgha* (monastic community). It was this promise of postmortem salvation and eternal remembrance through unending prayer that drew the wealthiest families in Koryŏ to Buddhist methods of managing death. How, then, was this promise made?

CHAPTER ONE

LEGITIMACY AND FILIAL PIETY

In 1021, a magnificent stele was prepared to commemorate the completion of a monastery named Hyŏnhwa-sa, or Monastery of Mysterious Transformation. It informed all those who gazed upon it of the circumstances that had led a charismatic patron to commission the monastery and of the generous endowments that the monastery received from this patron.[2] Commemorative steles prepared for Buddhist monasteries in honor of parents and loved ones during the late Koryŏ period provide similar information. The virtuous actions of the patrons and their generous offerings to the *saṅgha* were meticulously recorded for posterity. Some scholars argue that such steles are products of a veiled effort to justify the ostentatious display of wealth, status, legitimacy, and power.[3] Others argue that the individuals and families involved in ambitious building projects were genuinely motivated by filial piety and devotion to Buddhist teachings rather than by the desire to display their fame or fortune.[4] What these interpretations have in common is the assumption that socioeconomic and religious actions are incommensurables. The evidence, however, does not support this assumption. The case of Hyŏnhwa-sa is useful for comparison.

The rise of Hyŏnhwa-sa's main patron, King Hyŏnjong, to the throne was unusually complex. His mother and maternal aunt were both consorts of their cousin King Kyŏngjong.[5] After Kyŏngjong's death, Hyŏnjong's mother formed a close relationship with her agnatic uncle Wang Uk, Hyŏnjong's father. When King Sŏngjong learned about the relationship in 993, he had Wang Uk exiled to Sasu County, located far from the capital in the southernmost reaches of the Korean peninsula. Wang Uk died shortly thereafter in 996. Sŏngjong himself died the following year, and Kyŏngjong's son King Mokchong ascended the throne. The new king, however, did not attend to the affairs of government himself. The king's mother—Hyŏnjong's maternal aunt—ruled in his stead as regent from Ch'ŏnch'u Hall.[6] But the queen mother's ascendance to power did not bode well for the child of her sister, Hyŏnjong.

Fearing that her nephew could one day try to seize the throne, the queen mother had him become a monk and removed from the capital.[7] In 1009, Hyŏnjong's fate would change drastically for the better thanks to Kang Cho, the chief inspector of the northwestern circuit, who marched to the capital and deposed King Mokchong. With the support of Kang and several high-ranking civil officials at court, Hyŏnjong was installed as the new king. But his life would soon be turned upside down again on January 7,

1010, when the invading Khitan forces, four hundred thousand strong, defeated the Koryŏ border defense troops, captured their commander Kang Cho, and made it all the way to the Koryŏ capital.

The Khitan campaign left the king with a host of security-related issues that required his immediate attention, but, according to earlier scholarship, something else weighed heavier on his mind.[8] As the illegitimate son of a long-forgotten prince and former royal consort, Hyŏnjong was ostensibly preoccupied with the task of painting a new image of himself as a virtuous monarch who was born with the right to rule. As soon as he ascended the throne, Hyŏnjong granted his parents new honorary titles.[9] In the summer of 1012, a year after the Khitan invasion, the king also made what appears to be his first trip to his mother's tomb on Mount Kŭmsin, located a few miles to the north of the capital.[10] Four years later, in 1016, the king relocated and paid due respects to the remains of T'aejo in order to strengthen his relationship to the dynastic founder and bolster his image as a legitimate heir to the throne.[11] The following year, the king also had his father's remains relocated from Saju, the place of his exile, and reburied next to his mother's tomb on Mount Kŭmsin.[12] The king paid his first official visit to his father's new tomb later that same year.[13] There was, however, one more step that the king had to take in order to properly honor his late parents according to the conventions of Koryŏ.[14] The king had to find an ideal place in which to install their funerary portraits.[15] With this in mind, the king ordered the construction of the monastery Hyŏnhwa-sa the very next year. Placed in the context of this sequence of events, the construction of this monastery, as some scholars contend, seems to be another clear instance of building legitimacy and political authority, but the contents of the stele that commemorated its completion do not support this interpretation.

MYSTERIOUS TRANSFORMATION

Under the supervision of the special commissioner Ch'oe Sawi, construction of the monastery began on August 7, 1018, almost exactly a year after the king had his father's remains relocated to the capital district, and ended officially three years later on October 1, 1021 with the installation of a commemorative stele inscribed with a title written in the king's own hand.[16] The main text of the commemorative stele—an inscription and preface—was composed by the Hallim academician recipient of edicts Chu Chŏ, and the calligraphy was done by the state councilor Ch'ae Ch'ungsun, who also prepared the monastery record inscribed on the reverse side of the stele.[17]

Chu's preface opens with lavish praise of the virtues of the sage-kings of the past. Many rulers, he claims, have aspired to be like the sage-kings Yao and Shun, but few were able to perfect their cultivation of benevolence (*in*) and practice of filial piety (*hyo*) as Yao and Shun once did. Most rulers just give up midway for a rather simple reason, according to Chu: "Is this not because the mystery of Yao's Principle is difficult to carry on and the Way of Shun's filial piety is difficult to maintain?"[18] But Chu claims that the one ruler who did not give up is, of course, Hyŏnjong. Not only did the king never fail to fulfill his filial duties while his parents were alive, but he also continued to think about the gratitude and debt he owed his late parents, which grew day by day. He therefore honored his parents with posthumous titles and the performance of sacrifices on their behalf in the grand ancestral shrine (*t'aemyo*), but he apparently did not consider these classicist, or Confucian, customs (*yujŏn*) to be enough. As soon as he relocated his father's remains to the capital area, the king began work on a new monastery and a portrait hall (*chinjŏn*, also *yŏngdang*) in which to house funerary portraits of his parents. There, the king could pray for the spiritual well-being of his late parents, have their souls accumulate good karma, and help them attain enlightenment more quickly. Although he does not state it explicitly in the preface, the main thrust of Chu's argument here seems to be that Buddhism is what made it possible for Hyŏnjong to become a sage-king like Yao and Shun and to not give up as the rest did.

Chu's stele inscription reiterates the preface's claims in lyrical form. The inscription begins with the example of Yao and Shun, who "brought Principle to the country with the Way and virtue and morally transformed the people with benevolence and filial piety."[19] This summary of the sagely accomplishments of Yao and Shun anticipates the argument that follows: King Hyŏnjong should also be considered a sage-king because he "practices good governance with virtue, pacifies the elite and brings Principle to the lives of commoners, honors ancestors and respects parents, brings all things under control with compassion, and places filial piety above all practices."[20] In what way did the king place filial piety above all practices? The king built a new Buddhist monastery for his parents on Vulture's Peak (Yŏngch'wisan), where he installed a set of Buddhist scriptures imported from China.[21] As Chu explains in the preface to his inscription, the king had furnished the monastery with a new set of Buddhist scriptures that he requested and eventually received from the Song emperor Zhenzong.[22] Installing these scriptures at the monastery allowed the king to frequently read aloud from the scriptures himself and enabled the spread of the Buddha's teachings throughout the kingdom. As a consequence, "the merit [thus accrued] reached the living and the dead, and the good work done moved the gods and spirits." Chu therefore declares with confidence, "One man upholds filial piety and everyone follows."

This seems to be Chu's take on the name of the monastery, Hyŏnhwa-sa, or the Monastery of Mysterious Transformation. Like Yao and Shun the king morally transforms (*hwa*) his people by setting a good example (one that "everyone follows"), and he sets a good example by performing profound or mysterious (*hyŏn*) acts of filial piety. Chu then explains why the construction of a grand monastery for the king's late parents should be regarded as a profound or mysterious act of filial piety:

> Paying back debt [to one's parents] while alive moves August Heaven above;
> Praying on behalf of the dead reaches the Yellow Springs below.
> Perform great Buddhist services, and the ancestors' legacy/good karma will last forever;
> Virtue will certainly grow thicker—there is no greater [instance of] filial piety.
> For a land to plant merit, this [monastery] is a good field;
> No other method of mourning produces better karmic conditions.
> Eons pass, oceans dry up, valleys change, and hills move,
> [But] the filial Way of our sovereign will be known for ten thousand generations.

Chu's argument here may at first appear to be nothing more than literary embellishment. How could donations toward building a monastery, a "field of merit/good fortune" (*pokchŏn*) as he puts it, guarantee that the legacy/good karma of one's ancestors (*choŏp*) and that of one's own filial actions will last forever? Chu does not share this skeptical attitude toward the mixing of the economic and the religious—an attitude that surely tells us more about our own assumptions than about the assumptions of Koryŏ Buddhists. His reliance on the notion of a field of merit, an old Buddhist metaphor, shows that he meant his argument to be taken seriously.

"Field of merit" is an appellation reserved for things that can miraculously (*pulgasaŭi*) turn something fleeting and insignificant (i.e., wealth) into something spiritually and temporally substantial (i.e., infinite merit). Well-managed Buddhist monasteries could perform these miracles on two intricately related levels. First, they could use their corporate wealth—the monastery's permanent property (*sangju*) and endowments (*po*) created for specific purposes—to maintain or even increase that wealth for many generations and, theoretically, forever. Before the fourteenth century, this was something that no other private institution in Koryŏ could do. In Koryŏ, charitable funds or estates (C. *yitian*), like the kind the famed Song statesman Fan Zhongyan (989–1052) founded for his lineage, were first established in the early fourteenth century.[23] In fact, the concept of lineage as an institution played no apparent institutional role until this period. Instead, Koryŏ had Buddhist monasteries that knew how to use their permanent property and special endowments as fixed inalienable capital with which to generate interest-bearing loans.[24] Second, Buddhist institutions also knew how to keep earthly wealth and spiritual wealth indistinguishable. Metaphors—here understood as articulations not of conscious strategies but of cultural competencies—such as the field of merit were critical in this regard. The unification of these two levels (i.e., the management of wealth and metaphors) made it possible for Buddhist monasteries to promise eternal prayers and merit/good fortune (*pok*) for patrons and their beloved dead.

Hyŏnhwa-sa was meant to function precisely this way as a field of merit. What it clearly was not meant to do was function simply as a political tool for legitimation. Reducing the monastery to an instrument for realizing the king's practical need to put legitimacy and power on ostentatious display fails to consider the power of metaphors and Buddhist rituals in giving shape to the needs, desires, and even sociocultural tastes of the people who relied on these rituals and metaphors.[25] It also fails to take into account the power of metaphors to infuse the act of giving "with a sense of drama."[26] Indeed, the "legitimation" thesis does not explain why donating an incredible amount of wealth—an act undoubtedly infused with a sense of drama—would be considered virtuous (and, needless to say, without virtue there could not be legitimacy).

Virtue could be established in a field of merit, for it was a sacred place that possessed the much-desired power to render socioeconomic and religious actions indistinguishable. The field of merit was also a sacred place where patrons could expect the (spiritual) return to be far greater than the initial (monetary) investment. When King Hyŏnjong decided to embark on the costly project of building a grand monastery for his late parents, he did so with the expectation that this project would produce something even more substantial (i.e., infinite merit) that would also stand the test of time. This is why he tried to donate 1,240 *kyŏl* of military support land (*tunjŏn*) in the Ansŏ protectorate (*tohobu*) region to Hyŏnhwa-sa.²⁷ Not surprisingly, the bold plan met great opposition at court.²⁸ This sizable donation, if it was in fact made, would have constituted the bulk of the new monastery's permanent property, and a permanent property of this size would presumably have set the monastery on a firm financial footing. Under proper management, this permanent endowment would sustain itself and even grow, which would in turn allow the prayers for the king's parents—the condition of the endowment—to continue on an impressive scale in perpetuity. For precisely this reason, the king had the metropolitan controller of monks (*tosŭngt'ong*), royal preceptor, and abbot of Samch'ŏn-sa on Mount Samgak (present-day Mount Pukhan in Seoul), Pŏpkyŏng, installed as the new abbot of Hyŏnhwa-sa.²⁹ According to Chu's preface, after Pŏpkyŏng was installed as abbot, the king donated 2,000 *sŏk* of grains, 2,000 *kyŏng* of land, 100 slaves, cows, horses, and tools to work on the land as the monastery's permanent property.³⁰ It would certainly have been imperative to secure an endowment of this size to support the livelihood of the thousand or so monks who, Chu notes, came from all four corners of the country to study under the new esteemed abbot.

What made the monastery commissioned by Hyŏnjong profound or mysterious, however, was not its immense wealth and prowess as an economic institution. It was the ability to use this wealth to sustain a beautiful legacy "for ten thousand generations." This was a task too important to entrust to descendants who could easily forget the debt they owed to their ancestors or squander their inheritance.³¹ This is what Chu suggests when he claims that many simply give up on the task of perfecting filial piety. But a field of merit such as Hyŏnhwa-sa was mysterious for other reasons as well. As Ch'ae Ch'ungsun notes in his monastery record, donations to a field of merit also yield miracles. In 1020, just before the monastery's completion, relics of the Buddha miraculously appeared in the sky, emitting rays of light, in his mother's hometown of Hwangju, and the Buddha's tooth miraculously appeared in the monastery Pomyŏng-sa located next to his father's tomb. Later, these relics were enshrined in a seven-story stupa constructed at Hyŏnhwa-sa. More Buddha relics appeared in the sky the following year in Sangju's Chungmo County, North Kyŏngsang, and were placed inside the monastery's main icon. A dark and a light crystal pearl were also discovered while digging the foundation of the monastery's lecture hall and main hall respectively. The light pearl was placed on the main icon's forehead, to function as its *ūrṇā* (an infinitely long strand of hair located between the eyebrows of a buddha). All these miracles, Ch'ae explains, are "sympathetic responses" (*kamŭng*) to the king's profound reverence for the dead and Buddhism.³²

In explaining the chain of miracles that occurred at the time of the monastery's completion, Ch'ae relies on an old metaphor borrowed from Chinese cosmology. "Sympathetic resonance" or "stimulus and response" (C. *ganying*) refers to the situation wherein two spatially distant phenomena spontaneously and miraculously (*pulgasaŭi*), to use Ch'ae's own words, affect each other. The same metaphor was at work when Hyŏnjong blamed himself for the frequent drought and earthquakes that occurred during his reign. Ch'ae similarly uses the metaphor to underscore the intricate relationship between the king's actions and larger forces at work in the world. More specifically, he uses the metaphor to paint the relationship between the economic actions of the king and the religious actions of the truth or truth-body (*chinsin*) of the Buddha as one of interdependence: there cannot be one without the other. This allows Ch'ae to seamlessly transfer the sense of wonder evoked by the miraculous appearance of holy relics to the filial actions of the king. It also allows him to lend further support to the assumption Chu Chŏ expresses in his inscription on the stele, that the economic and the religious are truly indistinguishable.

PRAYERS FOR THE DEAD

More evidence of the combination of piety and wealth in the management of death can be found in Buddhist eulogies and sermons for the dead. Eulogies or sacrificial orations (*chemun*)—a genre that originated in China—were in use in Korea at least as early as the Unified Silla period (668–935).³³ The oldest surviving examples of this genre in Korea were written by the famed scholar-official Ch'oe Ch'iwŏn (b. 857) and can be found in his *Plowing the Cassia Grove with a Writing Brush* (Kyewŏn p'ilgyŏngjip) and the *Anthology of Korean Literature* (Tongmunsŏn) compiled by Sŏ Kŏjŏng in 1478.³⁴ Buddhist eulogies (often labeled "*ch'ŏn X so*") differ slightly from sacrificial orations used in non-Buddhist contexts. Both tend to follow distinctive formulaic patterns (e.g., they contain short biographical information about the deceased and use stock phrases such as "Oh, how great the grief [of your loss]! Please come back and enjoy these offerings"), but whereas sacrificial orations refer only to the offering of wine, Buddhist eulogies tend to mention other, more substantial offerings such as vegetarian feasts (*chae*) and food offerings for hundreds of monks. Buddhist eulogies and the ritual context in which they are used thus assume wealth.³⁵

The earliest known example of a Buddhist eulogy, a "native song" (*hyangga*) composed by the monk Wŏlmyŏng (fl. 742–65), is preserved in Iryŏn's (1206–1289) *Memorabilia of the Three Kingdoms* (Samguk yusa). This elegantly worded eulogy, or elegy to be more precise, illustrates well how ritual occasioned the coupling of wealth and piety in the management of death.

> The road of life and death is here [in purgatory and this feast],
> So [rebirth] has yet to be.
> Before finishing the words "I will leave [this world],"
> You left,
> Like leaves falling here and there
> In the winds that arrived early one autumn;
> Born on the same branch,
> [But] I know not where you go.
> Ah, I will wait for you while cultivating the Way
> And meet you [again] in Amitābha's *kṣetra*.[36]

Along with a vegetarian feast, Master Wŏlmyŏng is said to have offered this native song as a sacrifice (*che*) for his late sister. During the performance of this rite, a whirlwind suddenly appeared and blew away the paper money that was also offered as a sacrifice.[37] But the money, Iryŏn relates, flew in the direction of the west, that is, in the direction of Amitābha's buddha-land (S. *buddhakṣetra*), otherwise known as his Pure Land.

The rich symbolism that all too apparently informs the story of Wŏlmyŏng's prayer for his sister has received much deserved attention. A particularly relevant aspect of this story is that as early as the eighth century, wealth, both literal and symbolic, played an important role in postmortem salvation.[38] Vegetarian feasts cost money, but with the ritual presentation of an elegant and pious prayer, this money could shape "the road of life and death" and magically help the wind of destiny blow in the direction of Amitābha's Pure Land. Literary mediations—metaphors and prayers—were critical to the Buddhist art of salvation after death. Ritual was equally important. It provided the context in which patrons such as Master Wŏlmyŏng could expect wealth and salvation to work as one. Without this context, wealth was wealth. It was something that even monks like Wŏlmyŏng could accumulate for various purposes, including the accumulation of more wealth or, as in the case above, providing a vegetarian feast for his late sister.

Little changed in this regard during the Koryŏ. Buddhist eulogies continued to mediate the power to translate wealth into postmortem salvation. Like Wŏlmyŏng's elegy, Buddhist eulogies achieved this end by using a voice that was distinctively personal and charged with emotion. Sadness and grief were often explicitly expressed, as in this example from the late Koryŏ period:

> The enlightened realm is a mirror of compassion. It is neither partial nor biased. But the opportunity for rebirth has both a beginning and an end. I therefore rely on [the Buddha's] wisdom to deliver my wife from the darkness of purgatory. I recall that my late wife so-and-so married into a poor family at a young age. She acquired the deference and grace of a housewife and never caused my parents any grief. We had made the earnest pledge to grow old together, but I now unexpectedly find myself blaming the dead for the sadness of life and death. I am like the phoenix that laments its now lonesome shadow and the pig or dog that guards its lone pen by itself. Facing the hundredth day [anniversary of her death], I again exhaust myself with sorrow. What was prepared may be insignificant, but may the sympathetic response be near at hand. I [humbly] bow down and wish for my late wife to transcend the [three evil] destinies in the six realms, be reborn at the highest stage in the pond of unsurpassed enlightenment, have a personal audience with the Tathāgata [Amitābha], and mingle with the accomplished on the path of nirvana.[39]

The scholar-official Yi Ch'ŏm (1345–1405) wrote this Buddhist eulogy at the request of a certain Superintendent U. It was read or offered as sacrifice during a ritual, namely, the hundredth-day rite for the superintendent's late wife. One of its purposes was to translate wealth into postmortem salvation: "modest" or "insignificant" offerings were made, but sympathetic responses (*kamt'ong*) that were nothing short of a miracle were expected in return. The assumptions that guided Ch'ae Ch'ungsun as he wrote the Hyŏnhwa-sa monastery record were clearly still at work in the late fourteenth century.

It was metaphor and also ritual that made this possible. Following an old Chinese custom, Buddhists in Koryŏ made sacrifices to buddhas, bodhisattvas, and powerful spirits on three auspicious occasions in attempts to alter the fates of the dead. These occurred on the hundredth day after death, a month after the first full year had passed after death, and not long after two full years had passed after death. The second and third sacrifices were also known as the *sosang* (C. *xiaoxiang*) and *taesang* (C. *daxiang*) respectively.[40] In Koryŏ, as in China, sacrifices were also prepared for rites performed every day for a total of seven weeks after death. These are typically known as the "seven seven" (*ch'ilch'il*) rites. They mark critical moments in the "intermediate existence" (S. *antarābhava*, *chungyu*) between death and rebirth. The average person was expected to experience this intermediate existence as a kind of purgatory. Like a criminal or prisoner, the deceased, who lacked good karma or merit, was expected to undergo a trial administered by a judge every day for seven weeks.[41] During these trials, the mourning family could try to affect the judgment with offerings made in the name of the dead. Eulogies were also offered on such an occasion. Yi Ch'ŏm wrote one, for instance, for a literatus named Yi Hye who wished to offer prayers and sacrifices at the end of his father's seven weeks in the intermediate existence.[42]

The intermediate existence provided ritual context, and ritual context, in turn, provided an opportunity for miracles. For a former royal preceptor named Ch'unggyŏng (1191–1271), also known as Honwŏn, Sŏn master Ch'ungji (1226–1293) composed a moving eulogy, which he presented with other offerings at a vegetarian feast held forty-nine days after the royal preceptor's death.[43] In the eulogy, Ch'ungji wrote: "May all the lamps lit [at the feast] turn into a tower of radiant illumination and shine all over the Dharma realm, and may all the grains of rice transform into a sublimely fragrant dish and fill our inherent emptiness."[44] This miraculous transformation of offerings was meant to ensure not only the royal preceptor's enlightenment but also the fulfillment of his bodhisattva vow to save all living beings: "May you quickly ascend the path of enlightenment and mingle with all the accomplished ones. [After that,] may you once again enter the gate of the patriarchs and leave not a single living being unsaved." Lest his wish go unheard, Ch'ungji made sure to sponsor another vegetarian feast and make more offerings to the Three Jewels—the Buddha, the Dharma (the Buddha's teachings), and the Saṅgha—at the royal preceptor's first death anniversary sacrifice (*sosang*). For this rite, he composed another eulogy and wished again for the royal preceptor to ascend the path of enlightenment but not forget his original vow to reenter the path of saving others.[45]

Prayers for the dead in Buddhism were not limited to these ritual occasions. Another important date for Buddhists was the fifteenth day of the seventh lunar month. On this day, the *sangha* formally ended its three-month summer retreat, and its members ritually "released themselves" (S. *pravāraṇa*, *chaja*). This made it the most advantageous day for patrons, both lay and monastic, to take advantage of the merit and ascetic powers that the *sangha* had accumulated during the retreat.[46] Given the time of year, this day also served as the perfect occasion for ritually marking the transition into a new season—autumn—and pray for a good harvest. Inspired also by the heroic attempt made by the Buddha's legendary disciple Maudgalyāyana to save his mother from hell, Buddhists organized prayer assemblies, such as the Uran (C. Yulan) Bowl assembly or Ghost Festival, to make offerings to the *sangha* on this auspicious day and transfer the merit thus accrued to their deceased parents or beloved dead.

Evidence suggests that Koryŏ Buddhists celebrated this day as well. To pray for the salvation of his parents, King Hyŏnjong had the monks at his new monastery Hyŏnhwa-sa hold Amitābha assemblies for three days and three nights beginning on the fifteenth day of the seventh lunar month every year.[47] There is also evidence from the late Koryŏ period. Not long after the Red Turban invasion in 1361, the eminent Korean Sŏn master Hyegŭn (1320–1376) offered a general sermon (*posŏl*) on the day of the Ghost Festival at the request of a certain Minister Cho.[48] In keeping with the spirit of the day, the minister wished to pray for the salvation of his late parents. As one would expect from a Sŏn master, Hyegŭn opened his sermon with antinomian words that seemed to undermine the very premise of the occasion. How could there be a heaven or a hell, he asked, when in reality everything is empty? How could there be rebirth as animals or hungry ghosts when in reality the Buddha's body of truth fills the universe? "Regardless of whether [we] call [ourselves] a monk, a layperson, a man, or a woman, from birth to death, whatever [we] do in [our] daily activities—be it good or evil—is, in fact, the Dharma."[49] These words, however, were not addressed exclusively to the minister and those in the master's presence that day. They were also addressed to the minister's deceased parents and ancestors. For the minister whose handsome donations to the monastery occasioned the sermon, the master had something else to say, no doubt more soothing to the donor's ears: "Mister Cho, the donor who made today's assembly possible, prepared various Buddhist services for his deceased father and mother. With this merit, what sin could not be made to disappear, what karma could not be made to go away, what merit could not be produced, and what good [roots] could not be made to grow? This being the case, it is indubitably certain that [your parents] will be reborn in the buddha-land [of Amitābha]."⁵⁰ By invoking a familiar metaphor, the master was saying that the minister could rest assured knowing that the seeds of merit he has sown with the help of his wealth will grow roots and eventually bear the sweet fruit of salvation for his late parents. This seems to have been the promise that continued to attract the wealthy in Koryŏ to monasteries for centuries.

FIELD OF MERIT

Buddhist teachers in Koryŏ often relied on metaphors to explain how earthly gifts to the *saṅgha* could create otherworldly benefits. Wealthy patrons were told that their generous gifts were seeds. Like seeds, if sown, their gifts would grow in the fertile fields of the monastic community and eventually bear the fruit of infinite merit and good karma.

Scholar-officials of the fourteenth century were well aware of this metaphor and its wide acceptance in Koryŏ.⁵¹ In a stone tablet he prepared for Hŭngbok-sa, a monastery built by fellow Koryŏ patrons in the Yuan capital Dadu, the renowned scholar-official Yi Chehyŏn wrote: "According to the Buddhist teaching of cause and effect, if one cultivates kindness, then one obtains [good] karmic reward. This is like watering the roots and eating the fruit. [This teaching] can help the deluded attain merit."⁵² Similarly, Yi Sungin once wrote: "The Way of the Buddhists is pure, lofty, and sublime. It is not tainted by even a single speck of dust. It transcends all worldly things. The wise had always enjoyed it. Among their [i.e., Buddhists'] sayings there is also the so-called benefits of a field of merit. Because of this [teaching,] loyal ministers and filial sons who wish to repay the debt to their sovereign and parents use every means possible [to make offerings to the Three Jewels]. One cannot help but take refuge therein."⁵³ This passage is from a record that Yi wrote for a new monastic library built on the grounds of the monastery Sillŭk-sa.⁵⁴ The seeds of this project, as Yi duly notes in his record, were sown by the great scholar-official Yi Saek, who used the project to honor his late father, Yi Kok, and the recently deceased sovereign King Kongmin.

By no means, however, are husbandry metaphors unique to Koryŏ Buddhist texts written on behalf of the dead. The use of husbandry metaphors to extol the virtues of good actions, giving (S. *dāna*) in particular, is also well attested in Buddhist scriptures. The Mahāparinirvāṇa Sutra, for instance, declares that humans and gods who make offerings to the Buddha will all attain the fruit of the "immovable" (i.e., liberation from all afflictions and defilements) and permanently enjoy happiness and bliss. This, the Buddha explains, "is because I am a good field of merit for living beings."[55]

This declaration appears at the end of an episode in the Mahāparinirvāṇa Sutra that retells the Buddha's fateful encounter with a layman named Cunda, who is usually remembered as the person who served the Buddha his last meal. During their encounter, Cunda uses agriculture and poverty as metaphors to explain why the Buddha should accept a final offering before entering nirvana. Cunda first states that pure deeds in body and speech can be likened to a trained ox, wisdom to a fertile field, illusion to weeds, and the Dharma, or the Buddha's teachings, to rain. Cunda then claims that he is in possession of a trained ox and a good field devoid of weeds, but he still needs rain if he is to save himself from poverty, a metaphor for a state of impurity and also the loss and despair that would follow the Buddha's nirvana. Using these metaphors, Cunda finally exhorts the Buddha to accept his paltry food offering and, in exchange, offer rain, that is, the Dharma. When the time finally comes to make the offering, however, Cunda is overtaken by grief at the prospect of losing the Buddha forever. In response, the Buddha reminds the devoted layman that his nirvana is an expedient means and therefore not a cause for grief and sorrow. To help the layman liberate himself from samsara, grasp the true meaning of nirvana, and become a field of merit, the Buddha ultimately accepts his food offering. At this moment, the Buddha explains the benefits of making offerings to a good field of merit such as himself.[56]

Why is the Buddha a good field of merit? The *Commentary on the Greater Perfection of Wisdom Sutra* (C. Da zhidu lun) attributed to Nāgārjuna explains that buddhas, *pratyekabuddhas* (solitary buddhas), and arhats are fields of merit because they have exhausted all afflictions or defilements (S. *kleśa*, C. *fannao*).[57] In addition to these three categories of enlightened beings, the commentary also identifies the *saṅgha* as an unsurpassed field of merit in the sense that it can spiritually reward both the wealthy and the poor for their gifts.[58] This is possible because in the case of the *saṅgha*, the plow of wisdom is used to dig up the root of fetters (S. *saṃyojanamūla*) and the soil is cultivated with the four limitless qualities (S. *apramāṇa*), namely, loving kindness (S. *maitrī*), compassion (S. *karuṇā*), empathetic joy (S. *muditā*), and equanimity (S. *upekṣā*). Naturally, when donors sow the seeds of faith and generosity and irrigate this field with the water of reverence, pure mind, and mindful recollection of generosity, the harvest is bound to be plentiful. The *saṅgha*, the commentary adds, is also an unsurpassed field of merit in the sense that the faithful can obtain a great amount of good karmic fruit with even the smallest seed. The commentary supports this claim with the example of Bakkula, who, in the time of the Buddha Vipaśyin, offered the *saṅgha* the gift of a single fruit from the Myrobalan tree (S. *harītakī*). As a result, Bakkula lived in the heavens for ninety-one eons and reaped the fruits of bliss and good fortune in the realm of human beings—more specifically, he never suffered from illness. After many fortunate rebirths, Bakkula met the Buddha Śākyamuni, left home to become a monk, and eventually became an arhat.[59]

But the most revered field of merit was undoubtedly the Buddha.[60] The same commentary, for instance, cites the story of an old woman who is given the prediction of future *pratyekabuddhahood* when she offers the Buddha a bowl of foul broth that she was about to throw away. A Brahmin who witnessed the scene admits that he finds it difficult to understand how such an insignificant gift could be rewarded so handsomely. The Buddha then asks him if he has ever witnessed anything rare and difficult to imagine. The Brahmin answers that he has seen a banyan tree so big that its shade could easily cover five hundred chariots. In response, the Buddha asks him how big the seed of this giant tree is, and the Brahmin answers that the seed is extremely small, merely a third the size of a mustard seed. The Buddha reminds him that this, just like the prediction he made for the old woman, would be impossible for others to believe. The story ends with the Buddha's explanation that the old woman's food offering can produce the fruit of *pratyekabuddhahood*, just like the extremely tiny seed can produce an unbelievably giant tree. Besides, the Buddha adds, "the Tathāgata's field of merit is the utmost in fertility and beauty."[61]

These are but a few of the many examples of the use of the field of merit to extol the virtues of giving in Buddhism. One thing that they emphasize is the magical power of gifts to generate counter-gifts that seem to far exceed the size, scope, and significance of the original gift.[62] Even a gift that gives the impression of being small and insignificant, like the fruit from the Myrobalan tree or a bowl of inedible foul broth, has the power to bless the giver with many eons of life in heaven and, eventually, enlightenment. Buddhist texts from Koryŏ tend to emphasize this magical ability of a field of merit to transform something paltry and insignificant into something spiritually substantial when they wish to praise the faithful for their gestures of generosity.

THE PARADOX OF CAUSALITY

Buddhist sources seldom, if ever, offer a clear explanation of what makes this transformation possible. Although the field of merit is frequently used as a metaphor in Buddhist literature, explanations of the metaphor are rare and typically focus on why someone or something deserves to be called a "field of merit." The metaphor of sowing seeds and reaping fruit was far more common as an explanation of how generosity works. To cite another example, Zongmi (780–841), in his commentary on the Yulan Bowl Sutra (C. Yulan pen jing), makes the following analogy:

> It is like worldly people who want to obtain a granary so abundantly stocked with the five grains that they are never in want. They must gather the seeds from grain, use an ox and plow to till the fields, and plant the seeds. If they do not plant them, they will run out. It is the same with the Dharma. The heart of compassion, the heart of respect, and the heart of filiality are the seeds. Food, clothing, and valuables are the ox and plow. The destitute and the sick, the Three Jewels, and parents are the field.
>
> There are disciples of the Buddha who want to obtain a store consciousness with all kinds of merit so splendid that it is never exhausted. They must pull together the heart of compassion, respect, and filiality; take food, clothing, valuables, and their own lives; and donate them respectfully for the support and aid of the destitute and sick, the Three Jewels, and parents. This is called "planting merit." If they do not plant merit, they will be poor; lacking merit and wisdom, they will enter the dangerous path of birth-and-death. Just as the field where grain is planted is called a "grain field," the field where merit is planted is called the "field of merit."[63]

Here, Zongmi offers no explanation of the husbandry metaphor itself, but he does use the metaphor to establish two important points. First, if seeds are not sown, then there is no fruit to reap, and this is not desirable because it means the person who niggardly refuses to practice generosity has to remain in samsara. Second, seeds sown in the right fields (i.e., fields of merit) produce such an abundant harvest that the giver (or "cultivator") is, to use Zongmi's own words, "never in want."

What Zongmi does not make clear here is the fact that both points assume knowledge of the rich history of the seed-and-fruit metaphor in Buddhism. This is knowledge that Zongmi himself possessed.[64] In

Buddhist scriptures and commentaries, as Zongmi knows all too well, seed and fruit are commonly used as metaphors for cause and effect or, more generally, karma. In the Mahāparinirvāṇa Sutra, the Buddha makes use of seed-and-fruit metaphors to explain why the *śrāvaka* (followers of the Hīnayāna or Lesser Vehicle) do not know anything about the great final nirvana, or *mahāparinirvāṇa*: "I sent down the great rain of the Mahāparinirvāṇa Sutra. If all living beings sow good seeds, then they will obtain the sprout and fruit of wisdom. Those who do not have good seeds do not have anything to reap."[65] The Buddha, in other words, did not conceal the teachings from the *śrāvaka*. The fault lies with the *śrāvaka* who failed to sow the proper seeds. Even worse, according to this scripture, are the *icchantika*, beings without buddha nature or the seed of buddhahood, who have cut off all wholesome roots (S. *kuśalamūla*, C. *shangen*). In the Mahāparinirvāṇa Sutra, their fate is similarly explained with the help of the seed metaphor: "A burned seed will not produce a sprout even if rain falls on it for a hundred thousand million eons."[66] This, the scripture claims, is just like the *icchantika*. No matter how many teachings of the Buddha (rain) they encounter, the *icchantika* (burned seed) cannot germinate the thought of enlightenment (sprout).[67] But the notion that there are beings permanently cut off from the possibility of attaining buddhahood never gained much currency. This was true especially in East Asia, where the view that all living beings and even insentient objects possess the seed of buddhahood became the orthodox position.[68]

The seed metaphor is also often used when one must avoid falling into extreme views of existence and nonexistence—something that all Buddhists were encouraged to do. To cite but one example, the *Treatise on the Middle* (C. Zhong lun) or *Mūlamadhyamakakārikā* attributed to Nāgārjuna, someone with extreme views raises the following doubt:

> If karma dwells until [one] receives its consequences, this karma is permanent;
> If it ceases to exist, then there is no karma—how, then, will karmic fruit arise?[69]

In response, a corrective was offered in the form of a verse:

> [Parts] of a continuum, like the sprout, all arise from a seed;
> From this arises the fruit—without the seed there is no continuum.]

> From the seed there is continuum, and from the continuum there is fruit;
> First there is the seed, and then there is the fruit—there is neither annihilation nor permanence.[70]

In lieu of a straightforward answer, the text presents a metaphor, which was regarded as self-explanatory: the seed is obviously not the fruit, and the fruit not the seed, but the two *must* be related. Otherwise, there would be no continuum. This seems to be the gist of what the verse is trying to tell the person with extreme views.[71]

Similar concerns about causality can be found in later scriptures produced in East Asia. In China, for instance, Chan masters—monks who claimed the status of living buddhas—used their knowledge of these earlier scriptural metaphors and related debates about causality and buddha nature to bring much-needed clarity to an important notion that defined the entire Chan tradition. That notion was transmission. If it cannot be said that the truth exists or does not exist, then what, they asked, did the legendary first patriarch, Bodhidharma, transmit to China?

In the Dunhuang version of the famous Platform Sutra, there is a series of verses attributed to the first six patriarchs of Chan.[72] The first verse, attributed to Bodhidharma, claims that the Indian patriarch transmitted "the teaching" (C. *jiao*) in order to save deluded beings. As a result, the verse continues, "one flower opens five petals and the fruit ripens of itself."[73] Here, Bodhidharma uses a familiar metaphor to emphasize the fact that seeds from one flower (cause) produced more flowers (effect), but the fruit is not therefore identical to the seed. It ripens of itself (C. *ziran cheng*). The five petals, that is, the next five patriarchs, offer what appear to be responses to this verse, using the same metaphor. The second patriarch, for instance, states: "Because originally there is earth, from this earth seeds bring forth flowers. If from the outset there were no earth, from where would the flowers grow?"[74] The flower, in other words, is as much a product of what is inherently there in the second patriarch (the earth) as it is something that was implanted in him by Bodhidharma. The verses of the third and fourth patriarchs make similar claims. The fifth patriarch's cryptic verse, which seems to have confused later generations of Chan authors, elaborates on the metaphor of earth or ground. He argues that the seed of truth can produce something only if they are sown in *sentient* beings, or what he calls the "mind-ground" (C. *xindi*).[75] The last verse, attributed to the sixth patriarch, synthesizes the teachings of the preceding five verses and brings this discussion of transmission to a close: "The mind-ground contains the seed of living things. When the rain of the Dharma falls, the flowers are brought forth."[76] The sixth patriarch here seems to be claiming that Bodhidharma did not actually transmit anything, not even a "seed." He simply gave nourishment to what was already there (i.e., the seed in the mind-ground). The verse thus concludes that when one realizes this for oneself, "the fruit of enlightenment matures of itself."[77]

However we may wish to make sense of the ultimate soteriological message of these verses, it is clear that in Buddhism the seed and fruit continued to function as powerful metaphors for the paradox of causality.[78] Are they one and the same thing, or are they two independent entities? Can we say that the fruit is in the seed? At what point in the continuum, then, does the seed cease to be itself? Can good actions (fruit) arise from more than one kind of intention (seed)? Can they arise from two different "seeds"?[79] When Koryŏ Buddhists used the analogy of sowing seeds in a field of merit, they were, willingly or not, making sense of their actions as paradox and miracle. Like the Christian notion of a treasure in heaven, the seed sowed in a field of merit "was thought to be instantly magnified out of all proportion in an other world."[80] Something fleeting and insignificant (wealth) magically becomes something eternal and substantial (merit and salvation), just as a seed magically comes to produce fruit. They are neither different nor identical.

These examples challenge a widely held assumption about the relationship between wealth and religion. The two are commonly assumed to occupy related but ultimately incommensurable spheres, implying that the massive wealth that Buddhist monasteries accumulated in the fourteenth century is a sign of corruption and decay. But when patrons made offerings to monasteries to pray for their beloved dead, the rituals and metaphors used in this context to frame this act of generosity showed that it was no longer clear where the offerings ended and infinite merit began. As long as Koryŏ Buddhists could keep the two indistinguishable in this way, they could remain confident in their ability to secure salvation and honor (or esteemed family legacy) with wealth even in death.

2 DARK AND MYSTERIOUS WAYS

DURING THE KORYŎ DYNASTY, GIVING TO A FIELD OF MERIT WAS critical to practicing filial piety and paying dutiful respect after the loss of a family member. What made a grieving son or daughter filial (and the same goes for dutiful husbands and wives and respectful brothers and sisters) were not so much their motives as their actions, and actions were filial and virtuous when they were performed in the ritual context of giving. Giving to a field of merit was more than just another means for the wealthy and powerful to seek legitimacy and social recognition. It was a virtuous act that could mysteriously transform ephemeral wealth in the earthly realm into timeless treasure in a spiritual one. Like a tiny seed that grows into a giant tree, in a field of merit, wealth had the potential to transform itself into eternal salvation. In this context, it therefore made little sense to speak of greed and ostentation. The more one gave, the better.

This was no longer true by the early fourteenth century. Wealthy and powerful members of the Koryŏ elite continued to honor their deceased parents or loved ones with newly restored Buddhist monasteries and generous offerings to the Buddhist establishment, but these well-established demonstrations of love and respect for the dead did not always meet with the usual acclaim. Wealth and salvation were no longer assumed to be commensurable, even in the context of giving to a field of merit. This change in attitude toward Buddhist methods of managing death has been attributed either to the political rise of reform-minded Confucian (or Neo-Confucian) scholar-officials and their commitment to the idea of an activist government or to a fiscal crisis fueled or exacerbated by the supposed decadence and corruption of a bloated Buddhist establishment. Another interpretation, however, is that a crisis of identity was responsible for this change in attitude in the first few decades of the fourteenth century.

CHAPTER TWO

OUTSIDER

On August 14, 1328, the scholar-official Ch'oe Hae completed a commemorative text for the grand Sŏn monastery Sŏnwŏn-sa on Kanghwa Island.¹ The text was in fact a record (*ki*) of the donations made to the monastery by Ch'oe Sŏngji, the retired assistant chancellor and Lord of Kwangyang.² The record was meant to serve, it seems, as a kind of contract between the lord and the monastery. It contained not only the expected words of praise but also specific instructions on how to use the lord's generous gift. The record specifies, for instance, that the monastery had to add the lord's gift of 150 bushels (*sŏm*) of rice to its permanent property and use it to generate interest.³ Every year, the interest accrued from this endowment had to be further divided into three so that it could be used to hold vegetarian feasts and produce merit for three different people: the lord's late wife Lady Kim (d. 1327), their late son Munjin, and the lord himself.⁴ The record also specified the days on which the feasts were to be held every year. Vegetarian feasts had to be offered to the *saṅgha* to observe the anniversary of Lady Kim's death on the third day of the seventh lunar month, the anniversary of their son's death on the first day of the first lunar month, and the lord's birthday on the nineteenth day of the first lunar month. The record also made sure to note that the lord was making this endowment to pray for his wife and son only after he had already fulfilled his filial duties. To repay the debt to his parents, the lord had already carried out the formidable task of restoring a Sŏn monastery named Ch'ŏnhwa-sŏnsa. In the process of building this "grand place of worship" (*taedoryang*), the record declares, "there is nothing that the lord did not exhaust."⁵

The Sŏnwŏn-sa record also contains the author's own thoughts on the practice of supporting vegetarian feasts to feed the *saṅgha*. As any good writer of a stele inscription would do, Ch'oe Hae opens his record with a general reflection on the subject that he had been asked to commemorate. It begins with the anodyne statement that every living thing must eat in order to live. Food, he observes, comes from farming. Those who do not farm must labor in other ways to eat. This is because those who farm (lay patrons) and those who do not (Buddhist monks) "mutually nurture and do not harm each other."⁶ Although Ch'oe does not mention the Tang dynasty Chinese scholar-official Han Yu (768–824) by name in this short reflection on eating, farming, and mutual nurturing, it would have been apparent to any learned reader in Koryŏ that these concepts were unmistakable allusions to a passage from Han's famous essay "Origins of the Way" (*Yuandao*).⁷

Before he could offer the Lord of Kwangyang praise for financing vegetarian feasts at Sŏnwŏn-sa, Ch'oe seems to have felt it necessary to respond to Han's famous critique of Buddhism as a religious tradition that rejects "the way of mutual nurturing" (C. *xiangyang zhi dao*). Ch'oe's defense of Buddhism continues with an explanation of this ideologically charged concept. As he points out, Buddhist monks outnumber the entire nonordained population consisting of the four occupations (scholar, farmer, artisan, and merchant), but wherever monks go, people compete to give them better offerings. Even when no request for offerings is made, people voluntarily gather to give to the *saṅgha*. This is why monks can "live together as a group and leisurely eat," that is, eat without having to farm.[8] What do monks offer in return? Ch'oe surmises that they offer "hidden virtue" (*ŭmdŏk*). Otherwise, he asks, "how could they live like this [in leisure]?"[9]

In this halfhearted defense of Buddhism, Ch'oe purposefully speaks from the perspective of an outsider. He makes no attempt whatsoever to offer an insider's take on the practice of supporting vegetarian feasts. Unlike the commemorative stele inscriptions from earlier periods in Korea, Ch'oe's record contains, for instance, no scriptural passages and no traditional metaphors. Instead, he appeals to knowledge commonly shared among scholar-officials like himself: "I think the teachings of the Buddha are obscure and not something that people can see. However, if one enjoys making offerings with a heart of sincerity, one will obtain beautiful karmic rewards in dark and mysterious ways. This principle is beyond doubt."[10] Here, Ch'oe surreptitiously presents the argument that the merit of supporting vegetarian feasts can be understood without the help of the "dark and mysterious" (*myŏngmyŏng*), that is, the obscure (*mae*) teachings of Buddhism. Regardless of what the Buddha had to say about the matter, there can be no doubt that the practice of making offerings to the *saṅgha* is legitimate if the person doing it is sincere (*sŏngsim*), and sincerity, Ch'oe knows, is something that any of his potential readers—scholars and learned officials—can readily identify.

Elsewhere, Ch'oe uses a remarkably different tone to distance himself and his learned readers from the "dark and mysterious" promises made by Buddhism to those who donate their wealth. On May 4, 1329, less than a year after the completion of the above-mentioned Sŏnwŏn-sa record, Ch'oe wrote a letter to a monk named Sŏnji, who was about to depart for the famous Mount Kŭmgang.[11] Ch'oe wanted to inform the monk, presumably a close friend, of some things that he should know about the mountain before he left. Although many go to the mountain to enjoy its otherworldliness, Ch'oe informs his friend that the mountain may be problematic for precisely that reason. He explains that extraordinary things (*imul*) gather in deep mountain valleys where the traces of human beings are hard to find. That is why people who follow the teachings of Zhang Daoling—the Way of the Celestial Masters (C. Tianshi Dao)—often take permanent refuge in this mountain. There, they abandon the world, abstain from the consumption of grains, and attain the Way. But, as Ch'oe admits frankly to Sŏnji, "I detest the fact that they distance themselves from human relationships. I reckon there is a difference between me and them, so there seems to be no need to pursue this issue any further."[12]

Ch'oe does, however, dig deeper into the issue. He reminds Sŏnji that monks refer to Mount P'ungak—the local name of the mountain—as Mount Kŭmgang because the Avataṃsaka Sutra (C. Huayan jing) contains a reference to such a mountain as the abode of the bodhisattva Dharmodgata.[13] Ch'oe has not seen the sutra himself, so he refrains from drawing hasty conclusions about the veracity of the sutra's account, but he does offer harsh criticism of the baseless claims made in a text known simply as the *Mount Kŭmgang Record* (Kŭmgangsan'gi). Ch'oe goes to the trouble of debunking these claims (e.g., about the arrival of Buddhist icons on Mount Kŭmgang in ancient times) because he wants the monk Sŏnji to realize that the mountain's popularity is largely unfounded.[14] In his opinion, the only legitimate reason for going to the mountain is to practice asceticism. As he explains, the mountain used to be so rugged, uncultivated, and remote that, once there, the only way to satisfy one's hunger was to eat grass and trees. Buddhists should embrace this as the reason for going to the mountain because their teachings require them to endure hardship and suffering as a means of attaining the ultimate goal of enlightenment. In support of this claim, Ch'oe even cites the example of the Buddha, who practiced asceticism for six years in the Himalayas.

Ch'oe also admits that he has heard of ancient learners of emptiness (i.e., Buddhists) who earnestly applied themselves to their ascetic practices and attained their own (Buddhist) Way on this mountain. But what Ch'oe says next seems to imply that this is no longer possible:

> In recent years, the situation is different. Monastic dwellings on the mountain have increased in number year after year, and now there are a hundred. Among them, there are great monasteries such as Podŏk-sa, P'yohun-sa, and Changan-sa. They were all constructed by the state. Their halls and towers stand as tall as the sky and fill the mountains and

valleys. The brilliant decorations [on their walls] dazzle the eye. As for their permanent property and operating expenses, they have treasuries and officials who manage their wealth and fertile land as large as cities spread throughout the various districts and prefectures. Moreover, the annual prebends from the two circuits, Kangnŭng and Hoeyang, are submitted directly to the state, which transports them all to [the monasteries] on the mountain. Even in times of famine, they have never seen [the prebends] decline. Every year, an emissary is sent [to the monasteries] to check the clothing, food, oil, and salt that they need for the year and make sure there is nothing lacking. In general, the monks there are not attached to [any state service], so they are exempt from corvée duties. Commoners who flee from corvée duties, peacefully sit, and wait to be fed [at these monasteries] always number in the tens of thousands. And yet I have not heard of a single person who diligently cultivated himself or herself like [the Buddha] in the Himalayas and was able to realize the Way. There are even worse examples of those who deceptively entice people with the promise that a single visit to this mountain will prevent one from falling into the evil destinies.[15] The nobles above and the commoners below all take their wives and children [to the mountain] and compete to pay obeisance there. Except when the road is blocked by snow and ice in the winter or floodwaters in the summer, the crowds of people traveling to the mountain form a continuous line on the road. Among them, there are widows and virgins who follow others [to the mountain]. Because they spend the night on the mountain, ugly rumors are frequently heard, but people do not regard this as strange. By royal command, palace attendants use post stations [to travel to the mountain] and burn incense [to offer prayers] all year-round without end. Fearing their power, local officials busily run around, following their orders. The expenses they incur in the process require large amounts of cash. The commoners who live on the mountain suffer so much from the receptions they have to prepare that they curse out of anger and say, "Why can't this mountain be somewhere else?" Ah, people love this mountain because it is the abode of a bodhisattva, and the bodhisattva is respected because he can grant merit/good fortune to people in dark and mysterious ways. This merit/good fortune that works in dark and mysterious ways is already something that cannot be understood, but [to make things worse] monks take advantage of this mountain and seek to fill their own bellies. But it is the commoners who are harmed as a consequence. Need I say more?[16]

For his friend Sŏnji, Ch'oe paints a lucid picture of a mountain corrupted by wealth, power, and empty promises. The letter is clearly meant to shatter any fantasies that Sŏnji may have had about the mountain. Ch'oe wants Sŏnji and his readers to know that there may no longer be any room for asceticism and spiritual attainment in a space as spiritually bankrupt as Mount Kŭmgang.

Using this occasion to offer advice to a friend in the *saṅgha*, Ch'oe also takes a brief moment to reflect on his own kind, the scholar-official. In his letter to Sŏnji, Ch'oe confesses that he is secretly ashamed of the scholar-officials who travel to Mount Kŭmgang. How could they go when the commoners there suffer so? Scholar-officials should know that merit/good fortune cannot be accrued this way. To drive this point home, Ch'oe again assumes the position of an outsider. People go to Mount Kŭmgang with the intention of producing merit, but merit, he claims, works in "dark and mysterious ways" and cannot be understood. What *can* be understood, however, is the subterfuge that perniciously draws people to the mountain and beguiles them into wasting their wealth. Scholar-officials, Ch'oe implies, should know better.

There is more evidence to suggest that what matters to Ch'oe is less the issue of corruption and decadence than the issue of what scholar-officials should use to judge the appropriateness of making offerings to the Buddhist establishment. In 1323, a scholar-official named Yi Yŏnjong visited his friend Ch'oe to request a commemorative stele inscription for a monastery that his two older brothers had restored to honor their late father.[17] As Yi explained to Ch'oe, the monastery was originally built by his father, the palace censor Yi Sŭnghyu. Disappointed by the king's refusal to heed his advice, the palace censor had decided to leave his post and retire to the pleasant environs of his wife's hometown in Samch'ŏk County, Kangwŏn.[18] There, on a mountain named Tut'a, he built a private villa (*pyŏlsŏ*) and spent the rest of his years reading Buddhist scriptures borrowed from a nearby monastery, Samhwa-sa.[19] Eventually, the retired palace censor donated the private villa to a monk and named it Kanjang-am (Hermitage for Reading the Tripiṭaka). He also donated some land nearby as the new monastery's permanent property.

A year earlier, in 1322, while visiting their mother, Yi Yŏnjong's second brother, the Sŏn monk Tamuk, noticed that the monastery had become seriously dilapidated. He brought this to the attention of the eldest of the three, Yi Imjong, and the decision was made to restore the monastery. During the decision-making process, the two older brothers agreed that it would be appropriate to make some alterations. Although their father had lived frugally in his humble abode, that same abode was now a place for benevolent sacrifice (i.e., a Buddhist monastery), and surely, they reasoned, such a place deserved to be honored with upgrades. With some help from a family friend who happened to be serving as the local circuit inspector, they were able to expand the halls and hallways and adorn the walls with exquisite colors in less than a year. Yi Yŏnjong therefore proudly declared to his friend Ch'oe Hae that the monastery was now "more luxurious than what it used to be."[20]

Ch'oe includes all this information in his record for Kanjang-am because he wants to make a point. More specifically, he wants to offer some thoughts on what it means for scholar-officials to donate their wealth to Buddhism. He states his point bluntly in the following manner:

> In my personal opinion, the way the world worships the Buddha is far too excessive. Wherever a boat or cart can reach, there are rows of monasteries staring at each other. Their kind all attach themselves to the powerful and hoard wealth. They harm and poison our commoners and treat scholar-officials like slaves. For this reason, we Confucians do not accept [Buddhism]. But how could this be the fault of Buddhism? Buddhists like to practice kindness and dislike unkindness. If you look at their theory of illuminating the mind and seeing one's nature, it looks as if they had modeled it after our own Confucian [teachings]. Perfected beings and gentlemen find their Way tasteful. They enjoy and do not abandon it. There must be a reason for this as well.[21]

Ch'oe once again makes the disjunctive rhetorical move of pairing criticism with praise. This no doubt had something to do with his respect for the palace censor Yi Sŭnghyu. If a gentleman like Yi, who has contributed so much to Confucian learning, can find something tasteful in the teachings of Buddhism, then there must be a good reason. Ch'oe, however, does not explain what this reason is. Instead, he explains that it is only natural for sons to want to restore the place where their late father sought comfort for a long time. "This," he states, "is worth recording."[22]

As these examples illustrate clearly, Ch'oe was willing to offer some reserved words of praise for his scholar-official peers who made generous religious offerings to honor their beloved dead. Always assuming the role of the outsider, he made a point of praising these actions for their conformity to general moral ideals such as filial piety and sincerity rather than their conformity to the "dark and mysterious" claims made by the Buddhist establishment. Evidently, Ch'oe did not assume this role in his writings because he thought there was something inherently wicked about Buddhism, as in the case of Han Yu, who treated Buddhism as a moral aberration and social parasite. On the contrary, Ch'oe seems to have believed that Buddhism, itself potentially good, was corrupted by ignorant patrons who made offerings on the wrong grounds. It is for this reason that Ch'oe advised his scholar-official peers (and also his friends in the *saṅgha*) to distinguish themselves from "the powerful" (*kwŏn*) who thoughtlessly use their generous gifts to acquire things that work in dark and mysterious ways.[23] The criticism of Buddhism in Ch'oe's writings was intended, in other words, to serve as a wake-up call for fellow scholar-officials who were suffering from a crisis of identity.[24]

IDEOLOGY AND CRISIS

This, however, is not how the arguments about Buddhism presented by Ch'oe Hae and like-minded contemporaries are usually understood. Modern scholars tend to take his critical attitude toward Buddhism as evidence of the growing influence of Neo-Confucianism in Korea or of a fiscal crisis exacerbated by the corruption and decadence of the Buddhist establishment.[25] Most notable among the shortcomings of these interpretations is their reading of his arguments about Buddhism against the backdrop of later historical events. In 1390, new legislation was enacted to require the office-holding class to rebuild its identity around the practice of Confucian-style ancestor worship at the offering hall (*sadang*).[26] The following year, scholars in the Royal Confucian Academy (Sŏnggyun'gwan), most notably Kim Ch'o and Pak Ch'o, submitted vitriolic memorials that openly criticized the king for supporting the wasteful and deleterious practices of Buddhism and demanded that these practices be banned for good.[27] In an effort to make sense of these legislative measures and memorials against Buddhism, modern scholars looked for the conditions that had necessitated their creation. Some concluded that these were political actions taken by a class of new scholar-officials (*sinhŭng sadaebu*) whose shared ideological goal was to restructure society along Neo-Confucian lines.[28] Others, however, concluded that these were actually practical measures taken to address a fiscal crisis exacerbated by the profligate ways of Buddhism and had little to do with an ideological transformation. But these legislative measures and vitriolic memorials appeared almost fifty years after Ch'oe

Hae's death. Too much had happened between the beginning and end of the fourteenth century to reduce the historical significance of the many arguments made about Buddhism during this period, including Ch'oe's, to their relationship to events that took place in the 1390s.

The "new scholar-officials" thesis has its own shortcomings. The old ruling stratum, the great *yangban* descent groups of the capital, remained largely intact and in power after the founding of the Chosŏn dynasty.[29] They were not displaced by new social forces. Moreover, the reforms that took place at the end of Koryŏ and beginning of Chosŏn reflected the interests not of a new social class but of the old central *yangban* descent groups who had begun to redefine themselves as hereditary office-holding elites or "a central bureaucratic aristocracy" by the thirteenth century.[30] Although a new ideology—Neo-Confucianism—has been held responsible for spurring reformists like Cho Chun and Chŏng Tojŏn to action, this argument fails to explain why some of the most prominent scholars of Neo-Confucianism such as Yi Saek and Chŏng Mongju chose to adamantly oppose the overthrow of Koryŏ.[31]

It has also been argued that the main aim of the late Koryŏ reformist vanguard at court was to establish an activist government, an ideal more likely rooted in ancient style rather than Neo-Confucian or Cheng-Zhu learning. This revisionist view of the reformists' ideological orientation is not, however, without its own potential problems. If the desire to establish an activist government stems from revitalized interest in ancient-style learning after the *yangban*-dominated civil branch of government returned to political authority in the second half of the thirteenth century (i.e., under Mongol overlordship), then it needs to be explained why this desire manifested itself in the radical form of dynastic change late in the fourteenth century and not earlier. Moreover, if ancient-style learning reflected the concrete social and political interests of the *yangban*, then it also needs to be explained why the *yangban*, whose aim as a social group had always been to perpetuate the Koryŏ system, would advocate an ideology that would reform and perhaps even overthrow this system.[32] One possible explanation is that a persistent financial problem combined with the bloating of the central official class in the late Koryŏ led the *yangban* to try to realize the ancient-style ideal of an activist government.[33] But this seems to imply that socioeconomic crisis—not ideology—was what really motivated the *yangban* to act. All in all, it seems safe to say that the growing influence of a new ideology cannot adequately explain the late Koryŏ scholar-officials' changing attitude toward Buddhist methods of managing death.

This, in fact, is not an original observation. The tendency to interpret the actions of the late Koryŏ reformists as a reflection of their adherence to a particular ideology was subjected to systematic critique as early as the late 1930s.[34] In terms of their sense of urgency and reluctance to compromise with a pro-Buddhist king, the memorials submitted by Chŏng Tojŏn and fellow scholars in the Royal Confucian Academy in 1391 were deemed by these earlier studies to be qualitatively different from earlier criticisms of Buddhism voiced by such renowned Confucian scholar-officials as Ch'oe Sŭngno, Ch'oe Hae, Yi Saek, and Chŏng Mongju. The late Koryŏ anti-Buddhist movement therefore must have been motivated by something other than Confucianism. These studies use repeated references to the wastefulness of Buddhism in the memorials submitted by Kim Ch'o and Pak Ch'o in 1391 as evidence that this motivation must have come not from ideological but from political and economic concerns.

Corroborative evidence for this conclusion was found in the biography of Assistant Chancellor Yi Sŏngsŏ. According to his biography, monks from the well-funded royal memorial monastery Unam-sa—endowed with no less than 15,293 bolts of cloth, 2,240 *kyŏl* of land, and forty-six slaves—once submitted a formal request for further financial assistance to the privy council (*todang*, also *tobyŏngmasa*).[35] The additional funds, the monks explained, would be used for the purpose of serving guests. The privy council reluctantly approved the request, but Yi Sŏngsŏ refused to sign the order to release the funds. As grounds for his refusal, Yi noted that severe drought in 1359 and the Red Turban invasion of 1361 had left the state treasury depleted. The situation was so dire that officials were not able to receive their regular salaries. Even in such dire circumstances, Yi was willing to admit that it is reasonable for the state to feed monks and laborers at a royal memorial monastery, but how, he complained, could the privy council approve the releasing of funds to help the monastery entertain guests?[36]

This story was taken as evidence of a serious financial crisis that was exacerbated by a corrupt, decadent, and bloated Buddhist establishment. But Yi Sŏngsŏ's moderated critique was interpreted as qualitatively different from the late Koryŏ anti-Buddhist movement's thorough and complete rejection of Buddhism. Key to the emergence of this movement was the political rise of General Yi Sŏnggye, who famously turned his troops around at Wihwa Island and staged a successful coup d'état in 1388. With the help of reformist supporters at court, Yi Sŏnggye quickly moved to eliminate political enemies and gain control of both the government and the military.[37] As soon as Yi and his supporters accomplished this task, they immediately set out to fill the empty state treasury. To that end, they enacted the rank land law in 1391.[38] According to this "fiscal crisis" thesis, the late Koryŏ anti-Buddhist movement spearheaded by Yi Sŏnggye's supporters was part of the larger effort to seize political control and address the financial problems of the beleaguered Koryŏ state.

Like the "new scholar-officials" thesis, the "fiscal crisis" thesis also has some serious shortcomings.[39] Most notably, before anyone can argue that the Buddhist establishment had become decadent, corrupt, or too big to ignore during a serious state-level fiscal crisis, there must be reliable information about the size and scope of monastic landholdings and permanent property from different points in Koryŏ history. Such an argument also requires information that can help us understand the relationship between the monastic and commercial economies, but relevant sources of this kind of information are lacking. Supporters of the "fiscal crisis" thesis therefore rely on anecdotal evidence such as Ch'oe Hae's critique of Mount Kŭmgang and the anti-Buddhist memorials submitted by Kim Ch'o and Pak Ch'o in 1391, which speak of the bloated Buddhist establishment of late Koryŏ, but given its sensationalistic, impressionistic, and polemic nature, this evidence is far from reliable.

Perhaps less problematic in this regard is the rank land law of 1391. Even this law, however, does not support the "fiscal crisis" thesis. The rank land law, outlined earlier in two memorials submitted by Cho Chun in 1388, limited the land or land rents that a monastery could own to its original endowments as specified in official "land registers" (*chŏnjŏk*).[40] If a monastery had increased its landholdings beyond what was recorded in the registers, then the newly acquired land was confiscated. But if there was any loss of land, then the lost land was restored to the monastery. The law also prohibited private individuals or families from making donations of land to monasteries and made it illegal for monks and their descendants to own land.[41] The primary objective of these provisions in the rank land law, it seems, was not to strip the Buddhist establishment of its wealth and power but to prevent alienable and taxable resources from escaping state control. This could be done by bringing the increasing privatization of land and human resources to a halt.

It should also be noted that official land registers were incomplete and carelessly recompiled under the problematic leadership of Ch'ae Hongch'ŏl in 1313, the first year of King Ch'ungsuk's reign.[42] If these new registers (and newer registers that relied on these registers) were used during the rank land law reform, then the provisions concerning monastic property would probably have affected only those monasteries that received large private donations after Ch'ae carried out the cadastral survey. The rank land law, however, was not particularly effective in keeping alienable and taxable resources under state control.⁴³ In 1395, a remonstrance official named Han Sanghwan, for instance, had to remind King T'aejo (i.e., Yi Sŏnggye) that preventing monasteries from receiving additional land is an effective means of strengthening the army and increasing state revenue.⁴⁴ This advice was not heeded.⁴⁵ Using the frequent lawsuits launched by monasteries against one another as a political excuse, the state carried out a careful survey of monastic property (slaves, structures, inhabitants, and land) in 1397.⁴⁶ If the rank land law had satisfactorily settled the size and scope of monastic property in 1391, then, needless to say, this new survey would have been unnecessary. It also seems doubtful that the state could conduct such an ambitious survey only five years after the Koryŏ-Chosŏn transition.

The limits of monastic property reform were again made apparent during the reign of Chosŏn's King T'aejong. On March 17, 1402, the Censor General (Saganwŏn) recommended the collection of taxes from merit subject land (31,240 *kyŏl* in the capital district) and monastery land (4,680 *kyŏl* in the capital district), but there is no evidence that this recommendation was ever put into effect.⁴⁷ Indeed, it seems highly unlikely that the young and fractured Chosŏn court could force powerful, armed merit subjects such as the royal in-laws, the Yŏhŭng Min, to pay taxes. A few months later, on June 1, the office of astronomy and geomancy (*sŏun'gwan*) recommended the confiscation of land that belonged to monasteries not mentioned in the monk Tosŏn's *Record of Secrets* or *Secret Record* (Milgi).⁴⁸ The state council (*ŭijŏngbu*) accepted this recommendation but granted exemptions to monasteries with more than one hundred permanent residents.⁴⁹ To some monasteries, the state council offered more than exemptions, determining that if any of the seventy monasteries mentioned in Tosŏn's record were in financial need, then they had to be granted more land and cultivators. This attempt at the redistribution of monastic property was, however, short-lived. A few months later, T'aejo convinced his son T'aejong to return the monastic property that had been confiscated (or was in the process of being confiscated), safeguard the property of defunct monasteries until they were restored, allow anyone who so desired to receive ordination, and permit women to visit monasteries up to the one hundredth-day anniversary of a parent's death.⁵⁰

On December 25, 1405, the state council once again asked for monastic reform, and T'aejong approved the memorial.⁵¹ The reform proposal still relied on the *Record of Secrets*, but the information it contained was supplemented with information about local monasteries that provincial officials had recently collected. All this information was used to place a limit on the number of monasteries in areas that were significant from a politically administrative standpoint, including the new and old capitals, prefectures, and districts.[52] The reform proposal also focused on limiting the number of male slaves that the monasteries could use each year. Monasteries with 100 male slaves could use only 20 each year, those with 50 male slaves were limited to 10 each year, and those with 10 male slaves could make use of only 2 each year. The male slaves who were not working at the monasteries had to perform corvée duties and transfer their harvests to the state. The proposal also recommended using these male slaves in rotation and allowing them to live off fields located not too far from the monasteries. In addition, the proposal asked that the clergy's access to female slaves be limited.[53] A month later, on January 9, 1406, the office of the inspector general (*sahŏnbu*) recommended that monastic slaves who were transferred by monks to their disciples or family members be confiscated and made public slaves.[54] The office also recommended placing a permanent ban on the privatization of monastic slaves (i.e., the conversion of monastic slaves into private property).

Although supporters of the "fiscal crisis" thesis tend to treat these reform proposals as simply evidence of the state's efforts to fill the empty royal treasury with the wealth of the Buddhist establishment, the proposals may also be understood as steps taken to protect the Buddhist establishment's moral and financial integrity. By evenly redistributing the wealth of the entire Buddhist establishment among monasteries that received state recognition, the state council could meet the needs of the monasteries in the new capital (present-day Seoul) and elsewhere that lacked land and slaves, and it could do so without having to reach into the state treasury. But the state council also wanted to ensure that the other, better-endowed monasteries could continue to function properly without too much financial trouble after the redistribution of monastic wealth. This is precisely what is reflected in the addendum that the state council submitted on April 24, 1406.[55] The state council proposed granting one Sŏn and one Kyo monastery in the old and new capitals 200 *kyŏl* of land, 100 slaves, and 100 permanent monks (*sangyang*). The rest of the monasteries in the capitals were to be granted exactly half that amount. In the other major cities, one monastery chosen from either the Sŏn or Kyo school was to be similarly granted 100 *kyŏl* of land and 50 slaves. The Chabok-sa monasteries in the towns were each to be granted 20 *kyŏl* of land, 10 slaves, and 10 permanent monks.[56] All the monasteries on the outskirts of towns were to be granted 60 *kyŏl* of land, 30 slaves, and 30 permanent monks. These generous endowments practically guaranteed the continued operation of these monasteries. The state council also proposed taking the land and slaves needed by the new monasteries in the capital from monasteries that did not have state recognition. In total, the proposal identified 242 monasteries from twelve schools as beneficiaries of state recognition and therefore shares of the redistributed monastic wealth.[57] The attempted monastic reform of 1406 was, in effect, a zero-sum game.[58]

The king approved the reform measures but asked that the grand monasteries Hoeam-sa, P'yohun-sa, and Yujŏm-sa be exempted from the confiscation of land and slaves. In fact, the king granted these monasteries an additional one hundred *kyŏl* of land and fifty slaves. He also granted one or two *kyŏl* of woodlands to those monasteries that did not receive state recognition.[59] The reform proposal of 1406 did not, as supporters of the "fiscal crisis" thesis assume, entail the removal of these monasteries,[60] meaning that King T'aejong did not preside over a suppression of Buddhism, as these supporters mistakenly conclude. If anything, T'aejong and his officials tried to accomplish an even redistribution of the wealth of the Buddhist establishment. Some of this wealth surely made its way into the royal treasury, but the majority of it was clearly meant to be used to support the ongoing operations of Buddhist monasteries, both large and small. These efforts, however, ultimately proved to be as ineffective as the reform measures proposed in earlier periods: the Buddhist establishment found ways to once again possess large landed estates during the early Chosŏn period.[61] The evidence from this period clearly shows that the "state financial crisis and Buddhist corruption" thesis is more modern myth than premodern history.

THE MYTH OF CORRUPTION

Evidence from the Koryŏ period is no different. What is actually known about the endowments granted to Koryŏ monasteries also does not support the myth that Buddhism had grown decadent, corrupt, or too big for the state to ignore. The Buddhist establishment provided the state and the ruling house with the possibility of overcoming earthly limitations (death, bad weather, astronomical portents, shape of the land, unpredictable future, and so on), and, in exchange, it became the beneficiary of remarkable gestures of royal largesse beginning with the founding of the Koryŏ dynasty.[62] For instance, the dynastic founder, T'aejo, is said to have granted five hundred *kyŏl* of land to the monasteries Haein-sa and Unmun-sŏnsa and one thousand *kyŏl* to Chikchi-sa for their ability to provide aid and remedy (*pibo*) to the state in its efforts to overcome earthly limitations.[63] Generous endowments to Buddhist monasteries were not unique to the reign of King T'aejo. His successors continued to shower Buddhist monasteries with large gifts and donations. In 975, King Kwangjong furnished the monastery Powŏn-sa, for instance, with one thousand *kyŏng* of land and fifty slaves. This lavish gift was meant to show respect to the royal preceptor T'anmun, who chose the monastery as his place of retirement.[64] King Sŏngjong, best known perhaps for his close relationship with the renowned Confucian scholar Ch'oe Sŭngno, similarly made the generous gift (or, more likely, gave official recognition) of 1,050 *kyŏl* of land to the monastery Changan-sa on Mount Kŭmgang.[65] The king, royal clan members, and high-ranking officials seem to have granted the grand monastery Hyŏnhwa-sa, which housed the funerary portraits of King Hyŏnjong and his parents, an even more impressive endowment consisting of 2,000 *kyŏng* of land, 100 slaves, and 2,000 *sŏk* of grains to be used as principal for generating interest-bearing loans.[66] An equally large endowment was also probably granted to the grand monastery Hŭngwang-sa, which housed the funerary portrait of Hyŏnjong's son King Munjong.[67] The specific size of the landholdings or properties of the monasteries that housed royal funerary portraits for subsequent Koryŏ kings are not known, but the monasteries Kukch'ŏng-sa (completed in 1097) and Ch'ŏnsu-sa (completed in 1116), for example, were no doubt furnished with handsome endowments as well.[68]

If the preceding information about endowments to the monasteries is reliable, then just these monasteries alone could have possessed more than 1 percent of the total amount of arable land that was officially recorded in the Koryŏ tax registers (620,000 *kyŏl*).[69] But the impressive scale of the financial support that these Buddhist monasteries received from the throne does not necessarily imply that these grand institutions were decadent, bloated, or even economically threatening. In fact, the reason these monasteries received such impressive grants, as noted earlier, is because they performed the vital service of providing a means of overcoming earthly limitations for the state. Indeed, as the late Koryŏ official Cho Chun notes in one of his famous land-reform memorials, since the time of T'aejo, there had been a custom of officially granting financial support to Buddhist monasteries that functioned as "places of aid and remedy" (*pibo chi so*) for the state.⁷⁰ It was this official status that made it possible for the king to bestow not just slaves and grains but also *kongjŏn*—land reserved for "public" state-related institutions such as the throne, government offices, and so on—on Buddhist monasteries.⁷¹ The close relationship that the state maintained with Buddhist monasteries can also be seen in their use as alternative palaces, field offices that inspected the markets in the capital, and diplomatic-ritual spaces for showing respect to the sovereign of China.⁷² To argue, then, that these monasteries posed a financial threat to the state amounts to contending that the state posed a threat to itself.

This is not to say, however, that the above monasteries were always well received by officialdom. Hŭngwang-sa is a good example. King Munjong's proposal for construction of the grand monastery in 1055 met with strong opposition from the chancellery, but its opposition was based on the grounds that new construction would place an unnecessary burden on commoners and disturb the terrestrial force. The chancellery did not voice any concerns about the large landholdings, endowments, or even the practice of using state funds to support Buddhist monasteries.⁷³ That the state had to respect monasteries that provided aid and remedy was simply taken for granted. But in exchange for this respect, the Buddhist establishment was expected to remain pure. It is for this reason that, in 1056 (a year after he proposed building Hŭngwang-sa), Munjong issued an order to purify the *saṅgha* of "fake" clerics. By this, he meant those who did not follow the monastic rules but simply pretended to be Buddhist clerics so that they could avoid corvée duties and accumulate wealth through farming and commercial trade.⁷⁴ It also included those who accumulated wealth by collecting donations to build unsanctioned monasteries. Munjong's attempt to purify the *saṅgha* was not, however, an attempt to deal with a crisis, fiscal or political. It was an attempt to preserve the sanctity and hence the spiritual efficacy of the Buddhist establishment, an institution that served as the spiritual double of the throne and the state. Legal measures were implemented against frivolity, excess, wine making, and commercial activity in the Buddhist establishment for similar reasons at various points throughout the Koryŏ period.⁷⁵ These measures were clearly intended to manage the image of the Buddhist establishment—they were all instituted during the reign of kings who enthusiastically supported Buddhism—and not to manage a financial crisis or address endemic corruption.

It should also be noted that royal gifts to monasteries were not always as large or massive as those bestowed on the monasteries mentioned above.⁷⁶

There was an understanding that some monasteries deserved more, and others deserved a bit less. Giving to monasteries, in other words, was not indiscriminate. While restoring the monastery Taeun-sa, for instance, King Munjong determined that the original *kongjŏn* land grants did not generate enough wealth to provide for the monastery. He therefore granted the monastery an additional 100 *kyŏng* of fertile land.[77] The size of the original endowment is unclear, but the extra 100 *kyŏng* of land was apparently enough to help the monastery perform the important and undoubtedly expensive state ritual of praying for the long life of the Song emperor (*ch'uksu chae*).[78] This seems to have been possible because 100 *kyŏng* of fertile land could theoretically produce prebend rents of between 200 to 700 *sŏk* of grains.[79]

THE MYTH OF REFORM

Evidence from the age of military rule (1170–1259) also does not support the "fiscal crisis" thesis and myth of corruption. Endowments of all sizes and shapes continued to be made during this turbulent period without producing any signs of abuse or anomalous growth. This is well demonstrated in the famous example of Susŏn-sa, in South Chŏlla, arguably the most important and influential monastery of this period. Before it received an official plaque bearing that name, the monastery was known as Kilsang-sa. Kilsang-sa was a dilapidated monastery that could accommodate no more than thirty to forty resident monks.[80] Nevertheless, the monk Chinul (1158–1210) and his disciples chose it as an ideal site for their *samādhi* and *prajñā* (concentration and wisdom) retreat society, which had outgrown its original home, Kŏjo-sa on Mount P'algong, North Kyŏngsang. Kilsang-sa was restored and expanded with support from *hyangni* (hereditary local elites), a woodworker monk from a nearby monastery, and commoners of various economic backgrounds. The monastery's restoration record notes that "the rich donated their wealth and the poor exhausted their strength" to help with the restoration.[81] When the work was completed in 1205, the monastery was almost twice its original size.[82]

It is unclear how much land or prebend rents Kilsang-sa originally possessed and what sort of financial support it received at the time of its restoration, but in less than two decades Susŏn-sa acquired a remarkably large source of permanent income. Under the leadership of Hyesim (1178–1234), who succeeded his teacher Chinul as the second abbot of

Susŏn-sa, the retreat society apparently grew even more, and King Kangjong approved another expansion of the monastery.[83] Existing records indicate that Hyesim had acquired eleven branch monasteries and more than 10,000 *sŏk* in prebend rents from various sources including his own private assets to support the growing community at Susŏn-sa.[84] Some prebend rents came from large donations made by private individuals, many of whom were associated with the powerful statesman and military government leader Ch'oe U (alt. Ch'oe I).[85] Ch'oe himself, for instance, donated about 10 *kyŏl* of state-owned land to pray for the long life of the king.[86] He also donated a little over 126 *kyŏl* of his own privately owned land as a "death anniversary treasury" (*kiilbo*) that would ensure the regular performance of memorial rites for his late mother and younger sister on the anniversaries of their deaths. The same kind of endowment was also made by Supreme General Kim Chunggu and the acting director of the directorate for armaments Sŏ Ton'gyŏng, who donated 17 *kyŏl* and 35 *kyŏl* respectively for their late parents.

One could, perhaps, argue that the substantial support Susŏn-sa received from military officials is unusual and hence evidence of a corrupt and bloated Buddhist establishment, but studies of this monastery tend to make the exact opposite case. The construction of Susŏn-sa, they maintain, was a reaction *against* a Buddhist establishment corrupted by the influence of capital-based aristocratic families who used their wealth and power to try to take control of large monasteries and even entire Buddhist sects such as Hwaŏm and Pŏpsang.[87] One widely cited study that advances this argument contains two particularly noteworthy interpretations of Ch'oe U's support of Susŏn-sa. These interpretations focus on the "social function" (*sahoejŏk kinŭng*) of the Buddhist establishment.[88]

First, rejecting (and rightly so) the tendency to draw an unfounded connection between the proclivities of military men and the simplicity and radicalism of Sŏn Buddhism, the study claims that Ch'oe U supported Susŏn-sa because he needed a new ideological foundation, which he found in the monastery's emphasis on the joint cultivation of concentration and wisdom (*chŏnghye ssangsu*) and sudden awakening followed by gradual cultivation (*tono chŏmsu*). Ch'oe was attracted to Susŏn-sa's eclectic teaching because it could accommodate not only earlier forms of Sŏn learning popular among pro-military civil officials but also the conservative doctrinal sects that resisted military rule in order to protect the interests of their patrons, the capital-based aristocracy.[89] Susŏn-sa therefore represents not a rejection but an accommodation of the aristocratic Buddhist establishment in the capital.

Second, the study also claims that Susŏn-sa appealed to military leaders because it ostensibly provided them with an opportunity to win over two important social groups: *hyangni* and peasants. These two marginalized social groups faced some serious problems in the twelfth century. Growing tension between aristocratic families of the capital and new recruits to the central bureaucracy from *hyangni* backgrounds—a "contradiction inherent to Koryŏ society"—had developed into bloody purges at court.[90] Frustrated *hyangni*, the study surmises, must therefore have sought an alternative to the aristocratic Buddhist establishment in the capital. They found this alternative in the spirit of critical internal reflection (*pansŏng*) that gave rise to the retreat societies, which offered them a viable means of overcoming their frustrations with Confucian learning as it became increasingly difficult to carve out successful careers in the central bureaucracy.[91] Revising the "new scholar-officials" thesis, the study even goes so far as to suggest that the spread of this reformist spirit among educated *hyangni* (and the eventual failure of Buddhism to address the contradictions inherent to Koryŏ society) is what laid the foundations for the rise of Neo-Confucianism in the late Koryŏ period.[92] But the *hyangni* was not the only social group that faced serious problems during this period. There was also the problem of the illegal appropriation (*kyŏmbyŏng*) of land by aristocratic families and the consequent formation of large landed estates in the countryside, which threatened the livelihood of peasants.[93] Like the *hyangni*, the peasants must have also sought an alternative spiritual outlet. The study argues that retreat societies such as Chinul's Susŏn-sa and Yose's Paengnyŏn-sa on Mount Mandŏk in South Chŏlla provided an alternative for both the *hyangni* and the peasants.

These arguments, however, are based on an assumption that extant sources reveal to be groundless. It is assumed that the retreat societies of the thirteenth century were the product of a self-awakening, reformist movement within Buddhism led by frustrated men from the *hyangni* or scholarly class, most notably Chinul, Hyesim, and Yose. It was this reformist spirit that supposedly set the retreat societies apart from the conservative Buddhist establishment in the capital and attracted peasants and commoners.[94] However, there is nothing particularly novel about the leadership role played by monks from *hyangni* backgrounds.[95] There is also nothing particularly "reformist" about the size and pattern of financial support that Susŏn-sa received from wealthy patrons. The monastery's most important patrons (i.e., those who were remembered and honored in its steles and official records) were still high-ranking officials from the capital, and the endowments that Susŏn-sa received from these patrons were not qualitatively different from the endowments granted to other grand monasteries in or near the capital. The endowments—the monastery's main means of production—still consisted of large sums of grains and prebend rents, which were used to generate interest-bearing loans.

Even the kind of Sŏn learning promoted at Susŏn-sa cannot be so easily characterized as reformist or self-critical in character. There is no evidence to suggest that the teachings and practices that informed earlier Sŏn masters such as Tamjin (fl. late eleventh and early twelfth century), who taught at two important monasteries associated with the royal cult, Kwangmyŏng-sa and Yŏnbok-sa, were qualitatively different from the teachings and practices that informed Chinul and Hyesim. The Sŏn learning that Tamjin, Chinul, and Hyesim explored remained largely the same for all three Sŏn masters. It was the kind of learning that dominated the public monasteries (C. *shifangcha*) of Song dynasty China.[96]

All this necessarily leads to the conclusion that the rise of Susŏn-sa should not be used as evidence of a reform movement or a radical break from the past. Participants in Chinul's *samādhi* and *prajñā* retreat society may have explicitly shared an aspiration to pursue a path they perceived as more spiritually authentic than what was currently available in Koryŏ, but this path was cleared by relying on the same financial and institutional methods that made it possible for the grand monasteries in the capital to become such formidable economic and religious institutions. If anything, the example of Susŏn-sa demonstrates that wealth and Buddhism were still very much compatible in the thirteenth century. As always, the faithful were willing to donate large shares of their wealth to Buddhist monasteries that they regarded as the most efficacious fields of merit, and the Susŏn-sa community took advantage of this fact. The abbots of Susŏn-sa and its sister monastery on Kanghwa Island, Sŏnwŏn-sa (established in 1245), imported the style of Chan learning that was most popular in Song dynasty China and made this the defining characteristic of their monasteries.[97] This predictably attracted the wealthy and powerful. It is precisely for this reason that Sŏnwŏn-sa was chosen as Ch'oe U's memorial monastery and Susŏn-sa as the memorial monastery for his mother and sister.[98] Susŏn-sa, then, was not a reaction against a corrupt, decadent, and degenerate Buddhist establishment. Rather, it *was* the establishment, but newer and more up-to-date.

There is another important reason why the myth of reform and corruption cannot be accepted as valid. It relies on a widely shared but false dichotomy: if a monastery was associated with the aristocracy, it was corrupt, but if it was patronized by *hyangni*, scholars, and peasants, then it was reformist and self-critical. This dichotomy relies on the false assumption that the aristocracy's motivation for donating to monasteries was a desire for fame, fortune, and power, whereas the marginalized social groups were driven to do the same by what can only be described as genuine class struggle. In addition to the lack of corroborating evidence, one particularly notable problem with this assumption is that it misleadingly suggests that socioeconomic actions and religious ones are incommensurables.[99] This notion, however, does not apply in the context of giving to a field of merit. The faithful, regardless of whether they were from aristocratic or *hyangni* families, gave to the *saṅgha* with the same expectation that their earthly wealth would miraculously transform into timeless spiritual treasure (i.e., merit), which they could then transfer to the dead.

IDENTITY CRISIS

Little changed in this regard after the Koryŏ court surrendered to the Mongols and moved the capital back to Kaegyŏng in 1270. The wealthy, the powerful, and the morally upright continued to make handsome monastic donations to pray for their dead, as did Ch'oe Sŏngji and the palace censor Yi Sŭnghyu. What the supporters of the myth of corruption want to say about the Buddhism of this period, however, is predictably different. They contend that the spirit of reform that characterized the Buddhist establishment of the early thirteenth century gave way to deep and systemic corruption. The establishment came under the control of a lineage of monks who served as the abbots of a monastery named Myoryŏn-sa, and the monastery and its abbacy, in turn, came under the control of the P'yŏngyang Cho, an aristocratic family that colluded with the Mongol court to gain power and wealth. Buddhism consequently failed to address the contradictions inherent to Koryŏ society, making it possible for Neo-Confucianism to eventually take its place as the reigning ideology in Korea.[100]

This bold claim correctly rejects the "new scholar-officials" thesis and the tendency to see the growing influence of Neo-Confucianism as the outcome of ideological conversion or transformation. The rise of Neo-Confucianism in Korea was not, in other words, the consequence of an ideological battle with Buddhism. It was the consequence of a development internal to Buddhism itself. This insightful claim nevertheless neglects some important changes that began to take place under Mongol rule. For instance, it neglects to explain why the aforementioned Ch'oe Hae, who was active during this period, felt it necessary to distinguish between the values that guided the actions of scholar-officials and the dark and mysterious ways of Buddhism. Ch'oe Hae believed that the Koryŏ elite, if guided by the right values (e.g., sincerity and filial piety), could use Buddhist methods of managing death for the right reasons. But by the same token, those who lacked such values—the powerful—were prone to thoughtlessly use their generous gifts to acquire things that work in dark and mysterious ways. Ch'oe Hae made it clear in his writings that there is no virtue in such behavior. It was this behavior, in fact, that caused the decline of Buddhism in Koryŏ. Despite its decline, Ch'oe was ultimately reluctant to deny the efficacy of Buddhist methods of managing death. Rather than deny these methods, he wanted his peers to know that their moral content, rather than the ritual form, was what mattered. Clearly, much had changed since the early Koryŏ.

Ch'oe Hae, however, was not alone in worrying about the right and wrong ways of using Buddhist methods of managing death. Similar concerns are expressed in the restoration record for a monastery named Kŏndong-sŏnsa written by Ch'oe's good friend Yi Chehyŏn.[101] In his restoration record, Yi similarly voices his concern about mistaking the magnificence of the form of giving for the magnificence of its content. Like Ch'oe, Yi also notes this precarious relationship between the form and the content of giving so as to better define the identity of the scholar-official elite.

According to Yi, in 1304, while hunting in a mountain near his hometown of Kyŏngwŏn (present-day Inchon), the general of the royal guards (*siwi hogun*; rank 4a) Ha Wŏnsŏ—a man from a local *sajok* (family of officials), according to Yi—happened on the remains of a dilapidated monastery.[102] Moved by what he saw, the general vowed to restore it. The general funded the restoration with his own wealth, more than twenty years' worth of savings and money he saved by wearing and eating less. Rather than entrust the work to others, the general is said to have personally moved the construction materials himself. If there was something about the construction that did not please him, he did not hesitate to fix it. He neglected no detail in the reconstruction efforts. The central icon was placed in a large and beautiful hall with splendid decorations, and the monks were housed in an open and secluded room. The monastery's halls were tall and the hallways wide. From the windows, one could see the rugged mountains, and from its front gate, the big waves of the ocean. Materially, the general also made sure the monastery had everything it needed, including slaves and productive fields cultivated on reclaimed land.

Surely, Yi's description of the restoration process at Kŏndong-sŏnsa indulges in some hyperbole, as such a record naturally should. But the praise that Yi showers on the general is focused and its purpose clear. Yi wants to paint an image of the general as a virtuous man from a *sajok* background. He wants to show that the restoration of Kŏndong-sŏnsa supports this image. Yi underscores this point with a telling anecdote. On his way back to Mount Hua in China in the tenth lunar month of 1327, the Indian monk Chigong (d. 1361), who spent thirty-one months in Koryŏ from 1326 to 1328, stopped at Kŏndong-sŏnsa. During his visit, he expressed his "great amazement" at what he saw. He was so impressed by the monastery that he decided to spend some time there with more than a thousand of his followers. But the Indian monk's reaction to the monastery is said to have prompted a guest to ask Yi Chehyŏn this rhetorical question: Why would Chigong praise the general for restoring a single monastery if someone like Emperor Wu of Liang (r. 502–49), who built innumerable stupas and shrines, received only ridicule from Bodhidharma? Yi Chehyŏn offered this telling response:

> The outward appearance of their good work (*sase*) may be identical, but the [underlying] principles (*ri*) are not the same. If you do not possess skill in means (*kwŏndo*) within your breast, you will not be able to discern this difference. The ancient sage possessed all things under Heaven, but he did not consider what had no relation to him to be his possession. If one improperly takes all that which is not one's possession and considers it [his own] merit, then this is not as good as not doing this and taking this not doing as merit. As I see it, Ha did his utmost and did not rely on others. His aim was to benefit [all] things and not himself. The merit of a single fist of earth [that was used to build the monastery] is higher than Mount Meru, and the benefits created by the incense and candles [lit at the monastery] are greater in number than the sand of the Ganges River. Is this not a case of having the same outward appearance but different principles?[103]

Simply put, Yi's point is that the good work done by the general is morally principled (*ri*) and therefore legitimate, whereas the good work done by the emperor is unprincipled and therefore illegitimate. Unlike the emperor, who made the contrived effort to have the right outward appearance, the general's concern was only to benefit others, and this demonstration of moral principle inevitably manifested itself in the impressive outward appearance of Kŏndong-sŏnsa. Though noted only in passing, Yi clearly suggests that all this was possible because the general came from a *sajok*. But this suggestion may be masking a growing fear. It may be possible that Yi's brief reference to the general's family background was actually meant to hide his silent concerns about the general's elite family credentials.[104] Whatever the case may be, one thing is clear: like Ch'oe, Yi wanted his writings to serve as a wake-up call for fellow scholar-officials or those from families of officials who were suffering a crisis of identity.

In the writings of Ch'oe Hae and Yi Chehyŏn, one readily senses their unease with the material riches of the Buddhist establishment. What troubled both Ch'oe and Yi were the contributions that fellow scholar-officials and their families made to the expansion of the establishment's wealth. But rather than denounce the Buddhist establishment as irrevocably corrupt, Ch'oe and Yi chose to focus instead on redefining the efficacy of Buddhist methods of managing death. In the stele inscriptions they prepared for elite families and their monasteries, Ch'oe and Yi therefore argued that only those who were principled in their actions could derive merit from giving so generously to the Buddhist establishment. Even in the context of giving to a field of merit, one could no longer simply assume that wealth and salvation were commensurable. They were considered commensurable only if the giving was done by someone who possessed moral principle.

Ch'oe and Yi, however, were not trying to make a simple claim about the need to inject moral principle back into Buddhism. By redefining the relationship between wealth and salvation, they sought to address an urgent historical problem. They wanted to be able to say that there was a difference between true and ersatz elites. The urgency of this issue became apparent under Mongol rule. It became increasingly difficult in Koryŏ during this period to maintain the thin line that separated true elite families from ersatz elite families, those whom Ch'oe preferred to call "the powerful" (*kwŏn*). The meteoric rise of powerful families such as the P'yongyang Cho and their unmatched interest in Buddhist methods of managing death were a clear demonstration.

3   THIS WAY OF OURS

THE BUDDHIST ESTABLISHMENT POSSESSED THE ABILITY TO seamlessly transform wealth into salvation and "aid and remedy" (*pibo*), and this ability enabled it to maintain a large economic presence in Koryŏ for centuries. Under Mongol rule, however, renowned scholar-officials such as Ch'oe Hae and Yi Chehyŏn cautiously began to voice their reservations about the efficacy of the establishment's methods. For wealth to become a source of salvation and aid and remedy, Ch'oe and Yi were convinced that the act of showing generosity to the *saṅgha* had to first be consistent with moral principles such as sincerity and filial piety. This novel conviction was born of a deeper concern about the identity of the Koryŏ elite, which Ch'oe and Yi expressed in their reflections on Buddhism and the construction or restoration of monasteries. Others also showed interest in the problem of how to better distinguish "great families" (*taejok*) and "respected families" (*mangjok*) from simply powerful (*kwŏn*) ones.

Yi Kok and his son Yi Saek claimed, for instance, that greatness was not an inherent quality of those who made generous donations to a field of merit but was something that had to be established, maintained, and demonstrated. This, however, was a claim that would have made little sense to elite families from earlier periods. They would not have felt it necessary to *prove* their greatness. Giving generously to the *saṅgha* was just an extension of who they were. But there was something different about the historical circumstances under which Yi Kok and his son Saek made their claim about the need to demonstrate great-family credentials. Father and son made this claim as the presence of wealthy arrivistes and parvenu families among the Koryŏ elite grew stronger under Mongol domination.

Although it has become common to argue that the heavy involvement of parvenu families such as the P'yŏngyang Cho in Buddhist construction projects resulted in the corruption of Buddhism, Buddhist methods of managing death actually continued to serve as a legitimate means of establishing great-family credentials during the late Koryŏ, even for parvenu families. But the nontraditional background of these families—in particular their lack of a long history of producing officials—forced skilled writers like Yi Kok and his son to break from the conventions of the funerary inscription genre and look for innovative ways of supporting their claim that even families like the P'yŏngyang Cho were great. A key innovation was their reflection on the relationship between the (material) form and (moral) substance of giving to a field of merit. They advanced the novel claim that the efficacy of the ritual act of giving is a property of moral substance rather than material form.

This resulted in a change in the grammar of concepts and practices. In the writings of Yi Kok and other contemporary scholar-officials, the efficacy of ritual action was now defined in dichotomous terms. This dichotomy made it possible to separate wealth from religion. Wealth, it was assumed, could affect only the *form* of the gift. Its *substance* had to be guided by religion and moral values. This separation of wealth from religion would eventually turn both into conceptual incommensurables even in the context of giving to a field of merit in the late fourteenth century. It was this separation of wealth from religion, rather than their mixture, that made it possible to speak of corruption, decline, and decay.

THE P'YŎNGYANG CHO

The political success of the P'yŏngyang Cho marks the beginning of the reconstitution of the Koryŏ ruling elite stratum under Mongol domination.[1] Unlike the aristocratic families of early Koryŏ, who tended to perpetuate their high social status through regular bureaucratic channels—*ŭm* (protection) privilege or the civil service examinations—and marriage alliances with other Koryŏ elite families, the P'yŏngyang Cho relied heavily on its ties with the Mongol court to quickly become one of the most influential families in Koryŏ. Using this connection, the P'yŏngyang Cho maintained its prominence from the time it entered the ruling elite stratum in the latter half of the thirteenth century and well into the Chosŏn dynasty, which was founded in 1392.[2] However, in the early half of the fourteenth century, when the family had yet to produce a third generation of high-ranking officials in the central government, the P'yŏngyang Cho did not receive unconditional respect from its peers. Despite the family's elevated political status, peers were willing and able to publicly accuse prominent members of greed, corruption, and self-aggrandizement.[3]

The poor public reputation of this family stems in part from its obscure and humble origins. In spite of his high official status, the family head, Cho In'gyu, is known to have been continuously mocked and ridiculed as someone who began his illustrious career as an interpreter. Late in his career, when he served as chancellor on the left (*chwa chungch'an*), he had but one superior, the chancellor on the right Hong Chabŏn. Just below Cho was the junior chancellor Yŏm Sŭngik, who, like Cho, gained notoriety for his unscrupulous methods of acquiring wealth and his close relationship with the Mongol rulers.[4] According to one well-known anecdote, Cho is said to have once complained to Yŏm that people mockingly referred to him as the "old interpreter" (*noyŏk*) and Yŏm as the "old wizard" (*noju*).[5] In contrast, Hong, the scion of a well-established elite family, was called a "true minister." Yŏm is said to have retired that very day.[6]

The difference between Cho and Hong was obvious in the eyes of their peers and the public. Hong was the son of an acting royal secretary. Like his father and grandfather, he tried to enter the central bureaucracy by passing the much-respected literary examination.[7] His family had resided continuously in the capital for generations. In contrast, Cho was the son of a low-ranking military officer in the capital police (*kŭmowi*). His grandfather and father were neither *hyangni* nor slaves, which seems to imply that they were of commoner status. Indeed, Cho In'gyu's biography in the *History of Koryŏ* states that he "rose from low status" (*ki ŏ mich'ŏn*).[8]

Whatever Cho In'gyu's true social status may have been, his family's decision to settle down in Sangwŏn, which was located near the western capital P'yŏngyang, proved to be an important one.[9] Six years before Cho was born, the Mongols launched their first attack against Koryŏ, and by the time Cho turned thirty-three, in 1270, their conquest of the Korean peninsula was complete. Sangwŏn's proximity to the border and to the military garrison in P'yŏngyang meant that its inhabitants, Cho In'gyu included, would have borne the brunt of the Mongol attacks. Cho In'gyu, in other words, had grown up under the shadow of Mongol influence. Not surprisingly, perhaps, he ended up studying Mongolian and later found himself accompanying the heir apparent Prince Sim, the future King Ch'ungnyŏl, to the Yuan capital Dadu as his interpreter in 1269.

This was undoubtedly the opportunity of a lifetime. As the crown prince's interpreter, Cho In'gyu was able to quickly form close relations not only with the heir apparent himself but also with his Mongol consort, Qutlugh Kelmish (the Qiguo Imperial Princess), and her father, Qubilai Khan (temple name Shizu). For his role in arranging the marriage, Cho was promoted to senior colonel (*chungnangjang*; rank 5a). His close relationship with the Mongol imperial princess enabled him to quickly move up the bureaucratic ranks.¹⁰ In 1278, Cho In'gyu, now a great general (*taejanggun*; rank 3b), was promoted to a key post in the *p'iljajŏk*, or *bichēchi* ("secretaries" or "scribes"), a new state institution that temporarily took over some of the key functions of the secretariat-chancellery and personnel authority (*chŏngbang*).¹¹ A year later, he was appointed transmitter on the right (*u sŭngji*; rank 3a), followed by a promotion to royal undersecretary (*chi milchiksa sa*; rank 2b). He became censor-in-chief (*ŏsa taebu*; rank 3a) in 1286, received concurrent appointments as finance commissioner (*samsa sa*; rank 3a) and assistant state councilor (*chi munhasŏng sa*; rank 2b) in 1287, and was promoted to assistant chancellor (*ch'ansŏngsa*; rank 2a) in 1288.¹² Four years later, in 1292, Cho In'gyu eventually received the highest bureaucratic post of chancellor (*munha sijung*; rank 1b). As he neared retirement, the Koryŏ court also granted Cho a title of nobility, Lord of P'yŏngyang. From the Mongol court, Cho received senior third-grade titles, Grand Master of Excellent Counsel (C. Jiayi Dafu) and Darughachi of the Princely Appanage of Koryŏ (C. Wangfu Duanshiguan).¹³

This was quite an accomplishment for someone who had emerged from relatively humble circumstances, especially considering that the old, distinguished descent groups of Koryŏ had monopolized the high-ranking posts at the secretariat-chancellery for centuries.¹⁴ But the lord's greatest accomplishment, perhaps, was the marriage of his daughter to the crown prince, the future King Ch'ungsŏn, in 1292. Proof of this accomplishment appeared shortly after King Ch'ungsŏn reclaimed the throne after a brief hiatus. The court had produced a list of great families or "ministerial families" (*chaesang chi chong*) who could exchange brides with the royal family, and the P'yŏngyang Cho made it onto the list.¹⁵

By the end of the thirteenth century, the P'yŏngyang Cho could thus claim to have few equals. They had become one of the most accomplished families in the Koryŏ capital. The successful careers of Cho In'gyu's sons, who all held key posts in the secretariat-chancellery and finance commission, made the elevated status of his family all the more evident. Among his five sons—Sŏ, Ryŏn, Yŏnsu, Ŭisŏn, and Wi—two, Sŏ and Ryŏn, acquired high-ranking posts in the secretariat-chancellery while Cho In'gyu was still alive.¹⁶ As was expected of the sons of a high-ranking official, Sŏ used the literary examination to enter the central bureaucracy and Ryŏn took advantage of *ŭm* privilege. At the time of Cho In'gyu's death, however, the P'yŏngyang Cho still lacked one important qualification that was expected of a great family in Koryŏ—a respectable history of office holding. Cho In'gyu's death therefore presented the P'yŏngyang Cho with a serious challenge. A new history had to be written for the family, but this history had to conform to the expectations of elite tradition. It had to be written with the help of eloquent stele inscriptions prepared by renowned scholar-officials and, if possible, a grand memorial monastery where the stele could be prominently displayed. These two things were therefore coveted by the late Koryŏ elite who wished to build great-family credentials. Naturally, at the moment of Cho In'gyu's death, the P'yŏngyang Cho made what appears to have been an unprecedented effort to secure both.

THE DEATH OF CHO IN'GYU

The process of securing inscriptions and memorial monasteries (or, more precisely, portrait halls) began in earnest when Cho In'gyu passed away on the twenty-fifth day of the sixth lunar month of 1308.[17] According to his funerary inscription, a small sore appeared on Cho In'gyu's neck.[18] Having received a grim diagnosis, he refused medical treatment and began to devote his attention to Buddhism. As he approached the moment of death, Cho took a bath, changed his clothes, and passed away on his knees facing west and chanting the name of the Buddha Amitābha.[19] His funeral took place three days later at Unggok, a location in the capital. Following custom, the king granted the late chancellor the posthumous name Chŏngsuk. Before the funeral, his eldest son, the royal undersecretary Cho Sŏ, visited a close family friend, the director of guest affairs (*p'anye pinsisa*) and drafter of proclamations Pang Usŏn, with his father's record of conduct (*haengjang*) in hand and politely requested a funerary inscription.[20] The learned official Pang respectfully complied with Cho Sŏ's request. This, however, was just the beginning of the elaborate effort that the family made to honor the esteemed chancellor.

Almost three decades later, in 1341, with the family record (*kajŏn*) in hand, Cho Sŏ's younger brother Ryŏn and his nephew, Cho Ch'ungsin, visited the renowned scholar Yi Kok in Dadu and requested another inscription for their late father and grandfather, Cho In'gyu.[21] Although the Lord of P'yŏngyang already has a funerary inscription, he does not yet have a stele inscription for his "path of spirits" (*sindo*), that is, his offering hall, they implored Yi Kok. The late lord, they explained, used to spend his time in a structure behind his house that he named Kiwŏn or Jetavana. His descendants would now like to hang the late lord's funerary portrait in this hall and place a stone stele in front of it so that the lord's example would be available for all future descendants to see and follow. Unfortunately, Yi Kok was too busy—he had to rush back to the Yuan capital—and could not comply with their request. But Cho In'gyu's fourth son, the monk Ŭisŏn, also happened to be in the Yuan capital at the time and, apparently, continued to pester his friend Yi Kok about this matter.[22] Yi Kok eventually gave in to the persistence of the P'yŏngyang Cho and wrote the inscription.

The inscription was placed, as intended, before the offering hall located behind Cho In'gyu's private villa on Mount Ch'ŏnggye near the southern capital (present-day Seoul).[23] In the new offering hall, Cho In'gyu's descendants installed a funerary portrait for their distinguished ancestor, as they had promised Yi Kok, and a portrait for his late wife as well. The offering hall seems to have eventually become the property of a monastery known as Ch'ŏnggye-sa, which Cho In'gyu himself had established (or, more likely, restored) "to pray for the king."[24] Although there is no way to know for sure, the monastery may initially have consisted of a few buildings within or located near Cho In'gyu's villa, but the entire villa seems to have been converted into the monastery's permanent property after his death. This allowed Cho In'gyu's children and grandchildren to provide the monastery with land and slaves, ensuring the continued performance of ancestral sacrifices (*sasa*) in perpetuity. And that is exactly what it did. The offering hall eventually came to house the portraits of Cho In'gyu's prominent descendants, namely, his sons Sŏ, Ryŏn, Ŭisŏn, Ryŏn's son Cho Tŏgyu, Tŏgyu's son Cho Chun, and all of their spouses. If we are to trust an inscription prepared in 1689 by an eleventh-generation scion of the P'yŏngyang Cho, the monastery and its offering hall remained in the possession of his family for almost four hundred years.[25]

THE VIRTUES OF RESTORATION

For the P'yŏngyang Cho, the task of writing a respectable family history thus began with Cho In'gyu's funerary inscription, the construction of Ch'ŏnggye-sa, and the stele inscription that Yi Kok prepared for its path of spirits. This was consistent with the ritual conventions of the time. Elite Koryŏ families had relied on Buddhist methods of managing death to provide their beloved dead with unending prayers and the hope of salvation for centuries. Lest these virtuous deeds be forgotten, the same families sought the assistance of renowned scholar-officials who knew how to craft eloquent words of eternal praise in encomiums inscribed on stone. Few, if any, contemporaries would have considered this shallow and superficial. Like greatness, eternal praise was a privilege that the generous and virtuous elite were expected to enjoy.

Little changed in this regard under Mongol rule. Offering gifts of great material wealth to the *saṅgha* for the purpose of praying for the dead was still deemed a legitimate religious enterprise. As in the case of Ch'oe Sŏngji, powerful ministers and their families were expected to donate their wealth to the Buddhist establishment in as many ways as possible. But just as Ch'oe Sŏngji chose one of the most prominent monasteries in Koryŏ (i.e., Sŏnwŏn-sa on Kanghwa Island) to pray for his family, Cho In'gyu and his family exercised prudence in their selection of Buddhist projects. Befitting their status as royal and imperial in-laws, this family chose to contribute to Buddhist causes that were state-level projects, such as the restoration of the aid-and-remedy monastery Manŭi-sa and the royal memorial monastery Myoryŏn-sa. It was through these high-profile projects that the P'yŏngyang Cho hoped to establish great-family credentials.

There is good reason to believe that the restoration of Manŭi-sa, a monastery located, not coincidentally, just a few miles south of Ch'ŏnggye-sa, was a family affair.[26] The project was started by Cho In'gyu's older brother, the great Sŏn master (*taesŏnsa*) Hon'gi.[27] Destroyed perhaps during the Mongol invasions, the dilapidated remains of Manŭi-sa were left buried in a forest of thick vegetation, but Hon'gi decided to restore it sometime during the Huangqing era (1312–13).[28] Hon'gi was probably able to make this bold decision because Manŭi-sa, as an aid-and-remedy monastery, still owned sizable land grants. After the restoration, Hon'gi naturally served as the restored monastery's first abbot. His tenure as abbot was followed by the appointment of his nephew Ŭisŏn as the monastery's second abbot, and three generations later, the abbacy was handed over to another member of the P'yŏngyang Cho named Myohye, the grandson of Ŭisŏn's elder brother Ryŏn and the brother of the famous Cho Chun.[29] Manŭi-sa was thus a project that involved several generations of the P'yŏngyang Cho.[30] This and the fact that prayers for Myohye's father, Cho Tŏgyu, were performed at this monastery have led the historian of Korean Buddhism Ch'ae Sangsik to conclude rightly that Manŭi-sa was a memorial monastery that effectively belonged to the P'yŏngyang Cho.[31]

With the interest and support of the P'yŏngyang Cho, Manŭi-sa was able to acquire a considerable amount of slaves and landed wealth. This seems to have happened after Ŭisŏn received the king's approval to make it a branch monastery of Myoryŏn-sa, where he also served as abbot.[32] Like

Myoryŏn-sa, Manŭi-sa thus became an important center of Ch'ŏnt'ae learning, but its wealth and status as an aid-and-remedy monastery inevitably drew the attention of rival sects. During the reign of King U, the Ch'ŏnt'ae and Chogye sects—the two Sŏn sects in Koryŏ—alternately controlled the abbacy of Manŭi-sa. Eventually, the two sects found themselves in a legal dispute over the right to appoint someone from their own sect as abbot. With the reprimand that a monastery's land and slaves do not belong to the abbot and are not meant to be used for personal gain, the court decided in favor of the Ch'ŏnt'ae sect. Manŭi-sa's wealth, however, soon fell into private hands. In 1390, the Ch'ŏnt'ae monk Sinjo became the monastery's new abbot. Sinjo, a close ally and adviser to the dynastic founder, Yi Sŏnggye, had played a key role in the famous Wihwa Island coup d'état of 1388. As a reward for his role in the coup, Yi Sŏnggye gave Sinjo a merit subject's grant ordinance that officially turned Manŭi-sa, its land, and slaves into the private property of Sinjo and his disciples.[33]

In all likelihood, it was Ŭisŏn who made Manŭi-sa such a desirable object. Ŭisŏn seems to have been particularly skilled at (or was at least perceived to be skilled at) managing the finances of large construction projects and turning the fortunes of derelict monasteries around. His continued demonstration of these talents in monastic administration would, however, lead some, such as State Councilor (Ch'ŏmŭi Chamni) Pak Hŏjung, to accuse him of illegally seizing (t'alchŏm) monasteries.[34] Citing this as evidence, scholars argue that Ŭisŏn and his family did in fact engage in Buddhist construction projects purely for personal financial gain.[35] This reading of Ŭisŏn and his family is misleading. It must be borne in mind that Ŭisŏn's talents as an administrator and fund-raiser were precisely what made him so appealing to powerful patrons in China and Korea. If there was a high-profile monastery in need of restoration, time and again, imperial and royal patrons entrusted this work to Ŭisŏn.

The Mongol court, for instance, granted him the title Tripiṭaka Dharma Master (C. Sanzang Fashi) and installed him as the abbot of the grand monastery Tianyuan Yansheng Monastery in the Yuan capital.[36] In 1333, Ŭisŏn was also invited to serve as the abbot of Baoen Guangjiao Monastery, which had been built just outside Beijing's Zhangyi Gate by the retired king Ch'ungsŏn in 1317.[37] This invitation was offered by Ch'ungsŏn's son King Ch'ungsuk and the Sim Prince, Wang Ko.[38] According to a record prepared for the monastery by Yi Kok, Baoen Guangjiao Monastery had originally been furnished with a sizable endowment to ensure that the merit produced therein would be "inexhaustible" (*mugung*), but less than a decade after it was built, poor management left the monastery in bad financial shape.³⁹ King Ch'ungsuk and the Sim Prince were willing to entrust Ŭisŏn with the difficult task of restoring it to good financial health. Their faith in Ŭisŏn's ability was also shared by the restoration record's author, Yi Kok, who was certain that Ŭisŏn would not follow in the footsteps of the previous abbots of the monastery. On the contrary, Yi Kok was certain that Ŭisŏn would "make firm the foundation of what people call the field of merit."⁴⁰

The faith that the Koryŏ king placed in Ŭisŏn enabled him to occupy important abbacies in Korea as well. After serving as the abbot of Tianyuan Yansheng Monastery in the Yuan capital Dadu, Ŭisŏn returned to Koryŏ and began the process of restoring the royal memorial monastery Myoryŏn-sa. Ŭisŏn was entrusted with this important task because he had already earned the trust and support of the throne. But his relationship with the throne was not the only reason Ŭisŏn assumed the abbacy of Myoryŏn-sa. He also had his own personal reasons to be interested in the monastery's restoration. Ŭisŏn had spent some time at the monastery as a youth while training as the disciple of the monk Kyŏngi, a renowned monk from the Ch'ŏnt'ae monastery Paengnyŏn-sa.⁴¹ In the early 1280s, Kyŏngi, also known as the state preceptor Wŏnhye, participated in the construction of Myoryŏn-sa as the leader of its first retreat society (*kyŏlsa*).⁴² He was assisted by a senior monk named Hongsŏ, who became the monastery's founding abbot (*kaesan*).⁴³ In 1302, Hongsŏ was succeeded by Kyŏngi's younger brother in the Dharma and Paengnyŏn-sa lineage-holder Chŏngo.⁴⁴ It was here, under the tutelage of Kyŏngi and Chŏngo, that Ŭisŏn seems to have learned how to do large-scale fund-raising for the purpose of constructing monasteries. And it was here that Ŭisŏn learned the practical benefits of possessing this knowledge.

Chŏngo's career offers more evidence to support this view of Ŭisŏn's training.⁴⁵ For Chŏngo, the abbacy of Myoryŏn-sa became a steppingstone to an illustrious career. Five years after he assumed the abbacy, he was named royal preceptor (*wangsa*). The following year, in 1308, King Ch'ungsŏn granted him a new bureaucratic title and put him in charge of the joint deliberation bureau (*kongŭisa*), which seems to have overseen all matters concerning the Sŏn and Kyo sects.⁴⁶ The very next year, the king installed Chŏngo as abbot of Kukch'ŏng-sa—a grand monastery in the capital established by the famous monk Ŭich'ŏn—and granted him five new branch cloisters (*hawŏn*).⁴⁷ He was also put in charge of a directorate (*togam*) overseeing the restoration of Kukch'ŏng-sa.⁴⁸ Rather than rely on state funds,

Chŏngo is said to have sacrificed his own salary (talch'in, S. dakṣiṇā;) to rebuild the golden hall and furnish it with three new gilded icons.⁴⁹ In 1310, Chŏngo was appointed abbot of another important monastery named Yŏngwŏn-sa (in present-day Miryang, South Kyŏngsang). Citing the long history of this monastery's use as a place of retirement for state preceptors, Chŏngo politely tried to decline the appointment (which all appointees were expected to do), but he eventually accepted. While serving as abbot, he restored the monastery's golden hall and its portico. Three years later, Chŏngo was named State Preceptor Muoe.⁵⁰ In 1314, he retired and moved to a monastery named Yongam-sa (in present-day Chinju, South Kyŏngsang).⁵¹ Not surprisingly, he spent the remainder of his career restoring the monastery.

Ŭisŏn built a remarkably similar career. Like Chŏngo, he was repeatedly entrusted with the management of important monasteries and restoration projects, such as Manŭi-sa, Baoen Guangjiao Monastery, and Myoryŏn-sa. He was even granted the abbacy of Yŏngwŏn-sa, which Chŏngo restored. Yŏngwŏn-sa had fallen into the possession of the Mount Kaji branch of the Sŏn sect after Chŏngo's death, but Ŭisŏn reclaimed the monastery and made it once again a center of Ch'ŏnt'ae learning.⁵²

In addition to these projects, Ŭisŏn was also entrusted with the task of restoring a monastery named Purŭn-sa in the Koryŏ capital Kaegyŏng. According to the restoration record prepared by Yi Kok, the project continued for more than twenty years.⁵³ Ŭisŏn had embarked on this restoration project in 1314 as thanks to the Medicine Buddha at Purŭn-sa for curing him of an illness that year. To show his gratitude, Ŭisŏn is said to have funded the casting of three gilded icons, a new Buddha hall, and a new *saṅgha* hall with his private wealth. Yi Kok believed this was praiseworthy behavior:

> In my opinion, the Way of the Buddhists is utmost. What they say is grand and potent. Their theories of sin and merit can move the minds of people. Their teachings therefore flourish throughout the world. The worship of these teachings in the East [i.e., Koryŏ] is particularly sincere. Regardless of whether one is foolish or wise and young or old, everyone knows the Buddha. When troubled by the calamity of death, they often call out his name. They think that they cannot live even a single day without the Buddha. [The numerous] Buddhist monasteries therefore stand facing each other. They account for almost half of all the people's homes.⁵⁴ However, everyone prefers to establish new monasteries. When

flags and cornerstones fall apart, people do not show concern. This monastery [i.e., Purŭn-sa] has served as a place for worshipping the Medicine Buddha and a place for the state to depend on since the time of King Kwangjong. It was later lost in a fire during war and rebuilt just to the east [of its original location]. It continued to use its original name. A few hundred years have passed, and the lord [i.e., Ŭisŏn] was able to clear the old site and rebuild the monastery there. But when people build stupas and shrines, they either beg government offices for money or rely on the labor of commoners. By doing so, they sicken the state. The lord was not like this. He exhausted all the money he saved and everything he personally possessed. He diligently toiled away for many years until he could complete the project. This is record-worthy.[55]

Yi also added that people tend to forget their original intention (*chi*) after they acquire what they desire, but Ŭisŏn, despite having already acquired the good graces of the rulers of China and Korea, had not even for a single day forgotten his pledge to restore Purŭn-sa. This, Yi noted, is also record-worthy.

Yi Kok's record thus paints the restoration of Purŭn-sa as the virtuous action of a pious individual, but that image is a bit misleading. Purŭn-sa was, in fact, no ordinary monastery. On March 9, 1298, King Ch'ungnyŏl stepped down from the throne and retired to the personal residence of Chang Sunyong, a Uighur retainer of Qutlugh Kelmish, the imperial princess.[56] Chang's residence was quickly renamed Tŏkcha Palace. However, a week later, on March 16, the newly enthroned King Ch'ungsŏn had his father, the retired king, move to Purŭn-sa, which was renamed Tŏkcha Palace.[57] Nine months later, Ch'ungsŏn was dethroned by the Mongols, and his father, Ch'ungnyŏl, reclaimed the throne. Shortly thereafter, on October 13, King Ch'ungnyŏl moved out of Purŭn-sa and took up residence in Myŏngsun Palace.[58] This, however, does not mean that Purŭn-sa returned to being an ordinary monastery. In his restoration record, written sometime after 1338, Yi Kok continues to refer to Purŭn-sa as a "public" (*kwan*) space.[59] It is clear, then, that Ŭisŏn's decision to restore this monastery was a decision to come to the aid of the state. It was not, in other words, a private endeavor, as Yi Kok's restoration record would have its readers believe.

Like all the other major monasteries that he either managed or restored, Purŭn-sa was a project that allowed Ŭisŏn to represent the interests not only of himself as an individual but also of the throne and the state. These projects were also extraordinary opportunities to demonstrate virtuous behavior. As Yi notes in his restoration record for Purŭn-sa, people tend to prefer building new monasteries to restoring old ones. People also tend to rely on the wealth and labor of others. Ŭisŏn resisted these temptations, and that is what makes him virtuous and praiseworthy. Given the hyperbolic nature of commemorative stele inscriptions, it would be imprudent to take Yi Kok's praise of Ŭisŏn at face value, but the many stele inscriptions that Yi wrote for Ŭisŏn and his family make it abundantly clear that old assumptions about wealth and religion were still at work in the early fourteenth century. In the context of giving to a field of merit, wealth and religion were still expected to be commensurate. A field of merit was still a site where one could legitimately write a story of virtue and greatness. Ŭisŏn, however, chose his fields of merit with care. As a member of the illustrious P'yŏngyang Cho, Ŭisŏn deemed it only appropriate to write his story and the story of his family in the most spectacular and extraordinary way possible.

MYORYŎN-SA

Nowhere was this demonstrated more clearly than in the restoration of Myoryŏn-sa. According to a commemorative stele inscription prepared by Yi Chehyŏn, King Ch'ungnyŏl and his Mongol queen, the Qiguo Imperial Princess, commissioned the construction of this new monastery for the purpose of generating and rededicating merit to the princess's late father, Qubilai Khan, in 1283.[60] On November 9, 1302, a portrait hall (*yŏngdang*) was built for the imperial princess herself.[61] Later, the monastery came to house the funerary portraits of her husband, Ch'ungnyŏl, and their son, Ch'ungsŏn.[62] The latter's son King Ch'ungsuk is also known to have moved the funerary portrait of his Mongolian mother, the royal consort Ŭibi, from the monastery Ch'ŏngun-sa in the capital to Myoryŏn-sa, and eventually, like those of his father and grandfather, Ch'ungsuk's own portrait was enshrined at the monastery as well.[63] Under Mongol rule, memorial rites for Koryŏ kings and their Mongol queens were thus performed primarily at this new monastery. Myoryŏn-sa was thus arguably one of the most important memorial monasteries of the late Koryŏ period.

By King Ch'ungsuk's time, however, this important monastery was apparently in need of some repair. Shortly after his return from the Yuan capital Dadu in 1336 (i.e., after serving as the abbot of Baoen Guangjiao Monastery), the monk Ŭisŏn advised the king to restore Myoryŏn-sa as a way of demonstrating his filial affection and respect for his grandfather and father, whose portraits still hung in the monastery. Deeply moved, the king furnished the monastery with several million valuable utensils made of gold and silver to be used as its permanent property and made upgrades and repairs where necessary. The king also made sure that the rites for installing the icons were "extravagant" (*ch'i*) and the funds to pay for the vegetarian feasts sufficient.[64]

The monk and the king each had his own reasons for taking such a deep interest in Myoryŏn-sa. As noted earlier, Ŭisŏn is known to have spent some time when young at the monastery. This was presumably during his training as the disciple of Kyŏngi, who served as the head of Myoryŏn-sa's first retreat society. While this may explain Ŭisŏn's interest in restoring the monastery, there is another possible reason worth considering. Ŭisŏn had to witness his family, the P'yŏngyang Cho, undergo public disgrace after two anonymous letters accused his mother of hiring a shaman to curse King Ch'ungsŏn's Mongol bride, Buddhaśrī (the Jiguo Imperial Princess) (d. 1351).[65] The letters alleged that the shaman tried to turn the king's affection away from the imperial princess and toward his Korean consort, Lady Cho. In response, the imperial princess had Lady Cho's family—Ŭisŏn's father, mother, brothers, sisters, and brothers-in-law (Ŭisŏn himself seems to have been spared)—imprisoned, tortured, and exiled to a remote province in China.

Modern scholars agree that there was probably more at stake here than mere jealousy. The accusations leveled against the P'yŏngyang Cho may have actually been an attempt to thwart King Ch'ungsŏn's short-lived attempt to restore power to regular bureaucratic institutions, which were potentially in conflict with the interests of the Mongol court and the princess's prerogatives.[66] Whatever the true reasons for his exile, Ŭisŏn's father, Cho In'gyu, was able to once again prove his loyalty to the Mongol rulers and return triumphantly to Koryŏ, where he was assigned to the chancellery.[67] Although the P'yŏngyang Cho had thus been vindicated and handsomely rewarded for its close ties to the Mongol court, it may have been the case that Ŭisŏn was trying to forge an even closer relation with the Yuan imperial family and the Koryŏ king by playing a leading role in the restoration of the imperial and royal memorial monastery Myoryŏn-sa.

There is yet another possible reading of Ŭisŏn's actions. The P'yŏngyang Cho seem to have been involved in an incident that forced King Ch'ungsuk to return to the Yuan capital and surrender the royal seal in 1322. This humiliating incident is said to have been staged by supporters of the Sim Prince Wang Ko with the backing of the Yuan emperor Shidebala (temple name Yingzong).⁶⁸ Shidebala's assassination in 1323, however, temporarily squashed any hope of replacing Ch'ungsuk with the Sim Prince, and for his involvement in this affair, Ŭisŏn's brother Cho Yŏnsu was imprisoned and then exiled in 1324.⁶⁹ With the memory of this affair fresh in the minds of many, it may have made sense for Ŭisŏn to erase all ties between his family and the Sim Prince by taking charge of restoring a monastery that symbolized the legitimacy of Ch'ungsuk.

This may undeniably be one possible way of interpreting the following remark in Yi Chehyŏn's stele inscription for Myoryŏn-sa:

> I personally think that the difficulty of constructing [a monastery] does not compare to the difficulty of preserving it, and the difficulty of preserving it does not compare to the difficulty of restoring it. This monastery is King Ch'ungsŏn's grand realization of King Ch'ungnyŏl's vow. It was restored by King Ch'ungsuk. [State preceptor] Muoe followed in the footsteps of Wŏnhye, and [their work] was restored by Ŭisŏn. Is this not what *The Classic of Poetry* [Shijing] meant by "[they are possessed of the ability to move properly], and right is it that their movements should indicate it"?⁷⁰ If children and grandchildren are able to not forget the legacy of their late grandfather and father, fix it if it becomes dilapidated, and raise it if it falls, in the way it has been done for this monastery, then even after a hundred generations it will not perish.⁷¹

Yi's remark seems to reflect the need of both the monk (Ŭisŏn) and the king (Ch'ungsuk) to demonstrate that loyalty is the legacy of their respective families. That is to say, Ŭisŏn needed to demonstrate that the legacy of his family was undiminished loyalty to the Koryŏ throne, and Ch'ungsuk needed to demonstrate that the legacy of his family was undiminished loyalty to the Yuan throne. The restoration of Myoryŏn-sa was ideal in that it could serve both purposes.

There is no reason to doubt that political pressures were at play in the restoration of Myoryŏn-sa, but Yi Chehyŏn's carefully worded remark should not be reduced to the sublimation of such pressures. Yi did not portray the restoration of Myoryŏn-sa as a clever political ploy. He portrayed it as a virtuous and praiseworthy act. But Yi's praise of the restoration of a field of merit is not therefore unconditional. He wanted his readers to know that both the king and the monk are praiseworthy because they did something extraordinary: rather than build a new monastery, they restored one. As noted earlier, a similar claim had been made by Yi Kok in the restoration record for Purŭn-sa in which he also stated that "everyone prefers to establish new monasteries. When flags and cornerstones fall apart, people do not show concern." Claims like this were rare in the early Koryŏ period but are quite common in the writings of Yi Chehyŏn, Yi Kok, and other authors active in the fourteenth century. Something clearly had changed.

One notable change was the social makeup of the Buddhist establishment's greatest patrons. This posed an interesting problem to authors of commemorative stele inscriptions. For instance, in his stele inscription for the offering hall at Cho In'gyu's memorial monastery Ch'ŏnggye-sa, Yi Kok offered words of praise that curiously contained subtle hints of the criticism that the P'yŏngyang Cho received from other elite families:

> [The Lord of P'yŏngyang] was stern in the management of his household and righteous in the education of his sons. Before the lord became old, many of his sons and grandsons had already become established officials and famous scholar-officials whose posts are spread across the capital and the countryside. After the lord passed away, they all honored the family rules and remained filial, kind, and caring to each other. People cannot talk behind their backs about [the P'yŏngyang Cho].[72]

Respect was apparently not something that Cho and his family could just expect to receive from their peers. They had to prove that they had earned it, and this is presumably why it was necessary for Yi Kok to underscore the family's virtuous behavior in his commemorative record for Ch'ŏnggye-sa. There is, however, something quite novel about this rhetorical gesture. Observations on the virtuous behavior of children were uncommon in earlier funerary epitaphs and inscriptions, which were more likely to emphasize the family's long history of producing high-ranking officials and their marriage relations with other families of high social standing. Needless to say, this was not possible for the P'yŏngyang Cho, who emerged as an elite family only in the late thirteenth century under unusual circumstances. Yi therefore chose to focus on the present, namely, the P'yŏngyang Cho's *demonstration* and *maintenance* of a family legacy.[73] Yi's nervous remark about the impossibility of talking about the family behind one's back only highlights the novelty of this rhetorical move.

Yi Chehyŏn's analogy between the rise and fall of a great family and that of a monastery in his commemorative inscription for Myoryŏn-sa establishes a similar point: what makes a family great is less its origins than the legacy created by the effort to demonstrate, restore, and maintain it. Or, as

Yi put it, "if children and grandchildren are able to not forget the legacy of their late grandfather and father, fix it if it becomes dilapidated, and raise it if it falls, in the way it has been done for this monastery, then even after a hundred generations it will not perish." Greatness as a legacy, in other words, is not given. It has to be made, remade, and maintained.

GREAT-FAMILY CREDENTIALS

The notion of greatness articulated in Yi Kok's and Yi Chehyŏn's writings would have struck elite families from the early Koryŏ period as odd and perhaps even ludicrous. But even for Yi Kok and Yi Chehyŏn, some things remained the same. To be a great family, a family had to possess a few things, among them, a family record known as *kajŏn*, *sebo*, *karok*, *kabo*, *kach'ŏp*, *kajang*, *poch'ŏp*, or *po*. This record could attest to the family's ability to produce officials, be it through *ŭm* privilege, civil service examinations, or merit subject status.[74] More important, a family with such a record had to procure from a reputable scholar-official an inscription that rendered this record into stylish prose. This family also had to have this inscription set in stone on a monumental stele that could forever stand as testimony to the family's greatness. This stele alone, however, was often not enough. A great family also required a formal structure wherein to house this stele and perform memorial rites to thank and remember its illustrious ancestors.

This formal structure was almost always the portrait hall or offering hall located within the walls of a grand Buddhist monastery. Once the hall was built, the family had to look for a way to fund the memorial rites. These rites were expensive, relatively time- and labor-intensive, and also required a permanent staff of experts who could perform them for, in theory, an indefinite period of time. There were many different ways of pulling this off. Some families had a few of their own private slaves become monks, built a small structure for them to live in near the tomb, and had the slaves regularly perform simple memorial rites and guard the tomb.[75] The more honorable and ideal method was to furnish a grand monastery with a special endowment for memorial rites and, of course, a portrait of one's ancestors so that the monastery could continue to offer memorial rites for those ancestors annually on their behalf.

Elite families continued to rely on these methods during the late Koryŏ period. Among them were officials and families from traditional backgrounds, such as Ch'oe Sŏngji, who restored the monastery Ch'ŏnhwasŏnsa for his parents, the palace censor Yi Sŭnghyu, who turned his private villa into the monastery Kanjang-am, and the second assistant master of the Royal Confucian Academy Pak Ching, who restored an abandoned monastery named Yŏmyang-sŏnsa in his ancestral seat of Kangnŭng for his late mother.[76] But in the fourteenth century, officials and families from nontraditional backgrounds tried to use the same methods of seeking salvation for themselves and their ancestors. For instance, Senior Colonel Pak Kyŏn and his son the palace eunuch Pak Swaenooldae restored the monastery Sinbok-sŏnsa in their ancestral seat Kwangju, in Kyŏnggi); Chancellor Yu Ch'ŏng-sin and his grandson Chancellor Yu T'ak restored the monastery Chinjong-sa for use as their family's memorial monastery; and the palace eunuchs and inner palace favorites Ko Yongbo and Pang Sinu restored the monasteries Pogwang-sa, in Chŏnju, North Chŏlla, and Sŏnhŭng-sa respectively for similar reasons.[77]

For the late Koryŏ elite, the method of establishing great-family credentials remained unchanged from methods used in earlier periods, but the definition of greatness in the stele inscriptions for their monasteries showed signs of change. The Sinbok-sŏnsa restoration record by Yi Kok, for instance, relates that Pak Swaenooldae and his wife donated a sizable sum of land (15 *kyŏl*) from a nearby town and a considerable amount of movable wealth (500 *guan* in paper money) to the monastery because his father used to visit the monastery to pray for his well-being.[78] According to the record, Pak is said to have made the following argument to secure an inscription for his monastery: "the restoration of Sinbok[-sŏnsa] does not yet have a record—this is the worst case of an unworthy son neglecting his parents."[79] Pak went on to tell Yi Kok that he wished to have a monastery restoration record carved in stone so that future generations of his family, the Kwangju Pak (a *hyangni* descent group), might forever remember the loving kindness of his father and the names of his brothers in his ancestral seat of Kwangju.[80] Yi Kok, as he candidly admitted in the record he prepared, found this demonstration of filial piety and care for home and family very moving, especially since, in his opinion, men who seek wealth, prestige, and high office seldom seem to give any thought to their parents let alone their extended family members and their hometowns. Yi Kok implied here that Pak was not someone who just sought wealth, prestige, and high office. He was a virtuous person who possessed moral principles such as filial piety. One would, however, not expect to see this kind of distinction expressed in a stele inscription from earlier periods in Koryŏ. Something about the patron was clearly of enough concern to Yi that he considered it necessary to make this peculiar claim.

Similar, if not identical, concerns fill the space of the inscription for the monastery Chinjong-sa. According to the inscription, the monastery was originally restored by Yu Ch'ŏngsin, who, despite the restrictions against men of *pugok* origin like himself rising above the fifth grade in rank, was able to become chancellor with his Mongolian-language skills.[81] After the restoration was complete, Yu had his tomb constructed on a hill just to the west of the monastery. Naturally, his descendants visited the monastery every year to pay their respects. Noticing that the monastery was in a state of disrepair, Yu Ch'ŏngsin's grandson the chancellor Yu T'ak decided to restore the monastery once again. While he was at it, the chancellor also decided to add a portrait hall where he eventually hoped to install the funerary portrait of his grandfather. Yu T'ak's reasoning behind the second restoration was not unlike that provided by Pak Swaenooldae. "An unworthy grandson," as Yu T'ak himself put it, "was only able to follow in the footsteps of his ancestors truly because of their diligent effort to set a good example. Among the sons and grandsons, I am the eldest. If I cannot continue [to set a good example by restoring this monastery], how could I be excused from being punished for it?"[82] Yi Saek, the author of the inscription for Yu T'ak's monastery, boldly declared that it was the chancellor's unwavering adherence to the family legacy (*kabŏp*) that won him the respect he deserved. Filial piety, he continued, is the foundation of moral principle. The chancellor's decision to carry on the will of his ancestors and repay the debt of the king with the monastery Chinjong-sa is, therefore, Yi Saek argued, completely in agreement with the Way (*ki to tangyŏn*). How, he asked, could this compare to those who construct opulent monasteries and thereby exhaust the royal treasury and harm the people in the name of praying for good fortune, driving away the inauspicious, and inviting the good? "Those who call themselves men of influence (*hogŏl*)," Yi lamented, "usually tend toward this and do not consider this Way of ours."[83]

THIS WAY OF OURS

There is a subtle shift in the attitude toward Buddhist methods of managing death in the stele inscriptions for late Koryŏ monasteries. First, there is an emphasis on demonstrating, rather than assuming or taking for granted, filial piety through the active restoration of memorial monasteries. The practice of restoring monasteries, as shown in the records left by Yi Kok and his son Saek, had become an important means of demonstrating the Way. Second, there clearly was a concern about mistaking material prosperity for the Way, evident in the effort to distinguish those who know only the opulence of monasteries and not the moral principle that made them an efficacious field of merit.

At the root of this shift in attitude is a crisis of identity precipitated by the growing influence of parvenu families in Koryŏ. As wealthy families from nontraditional backgrounds made the earnest attempt to build greatfamily credentials by restoring monasteries, it became necessary in the early fourteenth century for scholar-officials to ask what distinguished the true from the ersatz elite. They addressed this question by taking note of the growing gap between the form and the content of greatness and argued that greatness was a property of the latter. This new awareness can also be witnessed in the following encomium written by Yi Kok for the monk Ŭisŏn's funerary portrait:

> That idle man of the Way
> has completed his learning and is left with nothing to do.[84]
> This great field of merit
> is called "tripiṭaka master."
> Embroidered robes and red hat,[85]
> why wear the black robes [of a monk]?
> His conduct was not abnormal
> and did not go against the times.
> A favorite of the emperors and princes
> and a disciple of the buddhas and patriarchs.
> What you see here is his outward appearance,
> [but] who understands what is inside?
> Ha![86]

Yi's thoughtfully worded encomium contains not only praise as one would expect but, curiously, rebuttals of the kind of criticism that Ŭisŏn and his family seem to have received from their peers. Perhaps even in his portrait, Ŭisŏn dressed like the son of a prosperous and prominent family and not, as a representative of the Buddhist establishment was supposed to do, like a monk. Counterintuitively, Yi Kok asserted that this was not abnormal. In fact, he insisted this kind of behavior was in perfect keeping with the practices of the day. But Yi's assertion belies the concern that he clearly felt about the incongruity of Ŭisŏn's appearance and what he possessed inside in his mind-and-heart (*sim*). Ŭisŏn, in other words, was a great and morally principled man favored by the Mongol emperors and princes, but his appearance, Yi seems to be arguing, may leave one with the wrong impression.

Changing historical circumstances exacerbated these concerns about the form and content of greatness and virtue. These concerns gained a sense of urgency as state support for monastery construction and restoration dwindled. With a few exceptions, most monasteries constructed during the early Koryŏ seem to have received financial support from the king or central government.[87] Naturally, they were almost always dedicated to the king. For instance, after the official Kim Yŏngŭi who lived in the Southern Song capital restored the monastery Sorim-sa in Kongsŏng County in 1177, he reported this to the king and requested a royal endowment of 1,500 *sŏk* of rice.[88] Interest from lending the rice, he explained, would be used annually to pay for Buddhist services that also included prayers for the long life of the king. Requests of this kind were not uncommon during the early and mid-Koryŏ periods. This was no longer true in the fourteenth century. Consider the following words of an abbot found in Yi Chehyŏn's inscription for the monastery Kaegug-nyulsa, which was restored in 1323: "The present [state] of our country is unlike that of former times. It is difficult to expect [the king] to follow old custom and repair our hut. Besides, it is not righteous to expect our neighbors to mend the holes in our fence and not wise to expect others to remove the weeds from our fields."[89] Witnessing this effort, Yi Chehyŏn himself tellingly remarked: "Material things cannot always remain in a state of disrepair. When the time is right, they will flourish [again]. The Way cannot indefinitely remain impoverished. When the right person [comes along,] it will rise [again]."

In the fourteenth century, one could no longer take it for granted that the state and its customs would, as it once did, provide the means for maintaining stability (or aid and remedy) and enduring values.[90] Those who sought greatness for themselves and their families therefore had to assume a more active role in embodying these values. Renowned scholars and writers argued that like the greatness of an old but dilapidated monastery, the greatness of a family had to be maintained and reestablished, not expected or presupposed. This, at least, is how they made sense of the affluent parvenu families who tried to demonstrate their greatness in distinctly material ways. But the identity crisis that resulted from the steady influx of nontraditional elements into the elite stratum under Mongol rule forced the moral economy of Buddhism to change in an irreversible way. A gap opened up between the form and the substance of greatness in the minds of stele inscription authors. What once seemed to be a simple conversion of wealth into greatness was now a question of how to define this greatness or legacy—the Way—for one's family. As wealth thus began to lose its ability to serve as an element of distinction, some within the elite stratum began to ask if it was *necessary* to follow old customs, that is, lavish Buddhist customs to define family values. Their answer, as we shall see, was "no."

4 ALL THE KING'S MEN

THE SEPARATION OF WEALTH AND RELIGION THAT TOOK PLACE under Mongol rule in Koryŏ Korea was done publicly with inscriptions on the smooth stone surface of steles on prominent display in front of restored Buddhist monasteries. In these carefully executed inscriptions, renowned scholars such as Ch'oe Hae, Yi Chehyŏn, Yi Kok, and Yi Saek continued the tradition of showing support for fellow officials who built or restored monasteries to generate merit for themselves and their beloved dead. But their support was not unconditional. Unlike such inscriptions from earlier periods, those written during the period of Mongol rule made the novel rhetorical gesture of distinguishing the magnificence of a new monastery's material form from the magnificence of its moral substance, emphasizing that wealth could no longer translate seamlessly into salvation.

A unique set of historical circumstances made this transformation of wealth and religion into incommensurables possible. First, Buddhist construction projects resumed after decades of continued armed conflict with the Mongols, which came to an end when Koryŏ surrendered in 1259. The war-torn kingdom had lost many of its monasteries in the flames of war, and individuals and families with the means to do so took it upon themselves to support the work of restoration. Second, wealth was unmoored from the ideals of bureaucratic service (*sa*). Critical to the separation of wealth from these ideals was the rise of men from nontraditional backgrounds (e.g., slaves, eunuchs, interpreters, and special district residents) to political and economic prominence during the reign of King Ch'ungnyŏl. Taking advantage of his dual status as Koryŏ king and imperial son-in-law, Ch'ungnyŏl attempted to build a network of supporters who could work outside the boundaries of the recalcitrant central bureaucracy. This often entailed the employment of men from nontraditional backgrounds. Third, frequent clashes between these newcomers and the regular bureaucracy—officials in the civil and military branches of the central government—gave birth to a deeply divided court. Divisions within the Koryŏ court grew deeper as Ch'ungnyŏl repeatedly relied on unsustainable measures to reward his nontraditional supporters: they were granted the authority to acquire alienable and taxable resources without going through normal bureaucratic channels.

Fame and fortune, which had been reserved for elite families with long histories of producing high-ranking officials, consequently lost their air of nobility and exclusivity, and a crisis of identity ensued among the Koryŏ elite. Members of the regular bureaucracy were compelled, not by ideological conversion, but by the problematization of wealth, to redefine themselves as a social group that valued the ideals of bureaucratic service above all else.

THE REGULAR BUREAUCRACY

The term *sadaebu*, translated here as "regular bureaucracy," has already received much scholarly attention. Earlier studies used the term to refer not to the regular bureaucracy but to the ideologically motivated agents of historical change who toppled the corrupt aristocratic social order of late Koryŏ, namely, the new scholar-officials. The targets of the new scholar-officials' attack were believed to have been the "powerful hereditary elites" (*kwŏnmun sejok*) who came to possess large landed estates during this period.[1] An effort to support this view was made by showing that the new scholar-officials emerged from *hyangni* backgrounds and hence from the medium- to small-landlord class of Koryŏ during the age of military rule (1170–1259). Using their literary and administrative skills, the new scholar-officials entered officialdom through the much-respected literary examination and eventually established themselves as a powerful social group in the waning years of the Koryŏ dynasty.[2]

It has also been argued that King Ch'ungsŏn's attempt at comprehensive reform in 1298 contributed significantly to the formation of a "*sadaebu* society." As soon as he assumed the throne, Ch'ungsŏn entrusted the task of drafting policies for reducing or eliminating the harmful effects of decisions made by the previous king, Ch'ungnyŏl, to new scholar-officials in the Hallim Academy. This entailed the removal of Ch'ungnyŏl's network of nontraditional supporters—the so-called powerful hereditary elites or powerful forces (*kwŏnse chi ka*), who had abused their relationship with

Ch'ungnyŏl, his Mongol consort, and the Mongol court to rise to ministerial ranks, illegally amass great fortunes, and build large landed estates during a major financial crisis.[3] Although Ch'ungsŏn's ambitious attempt at reform lasted only a few months and was forcibly brought to halt by the Mongols, the effort was ostensibly successful to some extent in that Ch'ungsŏn's brief empowerment of the Hallim Academy made it possible for a "*sadaebu* society" to eventually emerge in Koryŏ.

More recent studies challenge this tendency to reduce the political history of late Koryŏ to the conflict between the *kwŏnmun sejok* and the new scholar-officials.[4] The terms *kwŏnmun* (gates of power) and *sejok* (hereditary elites) have been shown to denote different things, which implies that they were not meant to be used together as a compound. The term *sejok* was used to speak of elite families with long histories of service in the central bureaucracy.[5] Unlike the term *kwŏnmun*, which was often used in a critical way to refer to people who abused their power and authority, *sejok* did not necessarily carry a negative connotation. It has also been shown that the term *sadaebu* was not used in historical sources to identify the new social elements that made their appearance during the age of military rule. Rather, the term was used all throughout the Koryŏ period to refer to all officials in the central bureaucracy, that is, the regular bureaucracy.[6] *Sejok* and *sadaebu* are therefore not mutually exclusive terms. Among the *sadaebu* who participated in the reform efforts of the late fourteenth century, there were men who belonged to *sejok* families, among them Kwŏn Kŭn of the Andong Kwŏn and Cho Chun of the P'yŏngyang Cho.

The term *sadaebu*, as one widely cited study similarly points out, was used to refer not to new social elements but to officials who served and came from families that *had the right to serve* in either the civil or the military branch of the central government. The terms *sadaebu*, *sajok* (family of officials), and *sarim* (the forest of officials) were used more frequently after men from nontraditional backgrounds rose to prominence under King Ch'ungnyŏl.[7] Members of the regular bureaucracy and their families used these terms as a way of distinguishing themselves from the eunuchs, slaves, butchers, special district (e.g., *pugok*) residents, falconers, interpreters, and foreign retainers who formed Ch'ungnyŏl's inner circle (*ch'ŭkkŭn*). With these terms, in other words, the regular bureaucracy sought to exert its distinct identity as a self-conscious social group.

What distinguished the regular bureaucracy from Ch'ungnyŏl's nontraditional supporters? Some scholars argue that the regular bureaucracy's efforts to distinguish itself as a social group was informed by its Confucian or Neo-Confucian learning.[8] Late Koryŏ references to *sadaebu*, *sajok*, and *sarim* do tend to emphasize morality and especially the notion of remaining honest and upright (*ch'ŏngnyŏm*). But the frequent appeals to the ideal of *ch'ŏngnyŏm* in late Koryŏ sources need not necessarily be understood as a reflection of the growing influence of Confucian or Neo-Confucian learning among the regular bureaucracy. To appreciate the novelty and historical (as opposed to ideological) nature of these appeals, a detailed examination of the conflict between the regular bureaucracy and Ch'ungnyŏl's nontraditional network of supporters is necessary. The following examination thus begins with the origins of this conflict, which can be found in Koryŏ's decision to surrender to the Mongols in 1259.

MONGOLS AND MONARCHY

Resistance to the Mongols, which began on Kanghwa Island in 1232, effectively came to an end when Prince Chŏn, who posthumously received the temple name Wŏnjong, complied with the demands of the Mongols and left for the Mongol court on May 21, 1259.[9] On July 28, King Kojong passed away while his son was en route to see the Mongol khan Möngke (r. 1251–59), who also suddenly perished two days later while personally leading an attack against the Chinese Song forces in the south. Prince Chŏn therefore did not realize that he was headed right toward a messy succession struggle between the khan's younger brothers, Qubilai (r. 1260–94) and Ariq Böke (d. 1266). Amid this chaos, Prince Chŏn ended up having an audience with Qubilai late that year near the old Song capital of Kaifeng.[10]

Hoping to gain an advantage over his brother, Qubilai wanted the Koryŏ court to quickly recognize him as sovereign and eventually as Great Khan (Qagan). The Koryŏ court, however, was under the control of a new military leader, General Kim Chun, and the throne therefore remained relatively weak. Continuing earlier policies, Kim refused to recognize the Mongols as suzerain and tried to maintain the political structure of military rule established by Ch'oe Ch'unghŏn, but continued resistance on Kanghwa Island had become all but impossible because of constant food shortages.[11]

Shortly upon returning to Koryŏ, Prince Chŏn succeeded his father as king despite the efforts of Kim Chun's military government to seat another prince on the throne.[12] As Qubilai hoped, the new Koryŏ king sent an emissary and formally announced himself to be the great khan's loyal subject. In 1260, the *chaech'u* (officials in the chancellery and security council) also decided to offer prayers for the long life of the great khan at nine different Buddhist monasteries in order to demonstrate their loyalty.[13] In return, Qubilai allowed Koryŏ to maintain certain local customs such as officials' robes and caps—important symbols of Koryŏ's sovereignty—and determine its own reasonable time line for moving the court back to the old capital Kaegyŏng or Songdo.[14] Qubilai also ordered the withdrawal of the *darughachi* and troops stationed in Koryŏ.[15] Koryŏ then complied with the demands of the Mongol court and began to submit annual tribute items (e.g., copper, falcons, otter fur, silk, fine ramie, horses, wood, paper, tribute women, and so on). The Koryŏ king also made another formal trip to Dadu in 1264 as a sign of deference to the great khan, who had recently forced his brother Ariq Böke into submission.[16] All this, however, was only the beginning of a gradual process of negotiation through which the great khan and the Koryŏ king forged a strategic relationship that benefited both men.

Among the many reasons for further strengthening this relationship, none, perhaps, weighed as heavily on Qubilai's mind as geopolitical instability. Although the succession struggle came to an end, problems continued for Qubilai. Chief among his problems was the ongoing war with the Song. Equally troubling, however, was the rise of Qaidu (d. 1301), khan of the Ögödei *ulus* (appanage or community), who refused to formally recognize Qubilai's authority as great khan. The sphere of Qubilai's political influence shrank drastically as Qaidu asserted the autonomy of his *ulus* in Central Asia and consolidated his power in the region after removing the threat posed by Baraq (r. 1266–71), khan of the rival Chaghatai *ulus*.[17] As the fragmentation of the Great Yuan *ulus* (i.e., the Mongol empire in its entirety) progressed in this manner, the need to put a swift end to the war with the Song became even more apparent. Given his aim of securing his eastern flank and facilitating the planned conquest of the Japanese islands, Qubilai naturally saw the necessity of exerting even greater control over Koryŏ.[18]

But the Koryŏ court, still under the control of the military leader Kim Chun, had little interest in complying with Qubilai's demands. As pressure from the great khan mounted, tensions within the political leadership in Koryŏ grew. On January 31, 1269, these tensions erupted and eventually resulted in Kim Chun's death. State councilors and military leaders who wished to preserve the status quo by maintaining diplomatic relations with the Mongols seem to have found the staunchly anti-Mongol attitude of Kim Chun no longer acceptable.[19]

Taking advantage of these tensions at court, the king orchestrated the removal of Kim Chun with the assistance of slave-eunuchs including Kang

Yunso and Kim Chajŏng and military men such as Im Yŏn.²⁰ While the heir apparent Prince Sim (Ch'ungnyŏl) was away visiting the great khan, however, Im Yŏn plotted and executed his plans to remove the king and install the king's younger brother Ch'ang, the Duke of An'gyŏng, on the throne.²¹ On his way back to Koryŏ, Prince Sim caught wind of what had happened to his father, Wŏnjong. A public slave named Chŏng Obu had furtively crossed the Amnok River to inform the prince of what had happened.²² Much to the consternation of some members of his attending retinue, the prince, with encouragement from his Mongolian interpreter, Chŏng In'gyŏng, decided to turn back and seek help from the great khan.²³

Qubilai decided to come to Wŏnjong's aid. Mongol troops entered the newly acquired territories north of the Chabi Pass in Koryŏ, which was placed under the direct control of the new Tongnyŏng Directorate General on March 7, 1270. Im Yŏn realized the gravity of the situation and quickly restored Wŏnjong to the throne. Immediately afterward, in compliance with the great khan's order, Wŏnjong left for the Mongol capital. For obvious reasons, perhaps, Im became extremely anxious when the restored king left for the Mongol capital.²⁴ Anxiety eventually got the best of him, and he is said to have died from anxiety on March 30, 1270. Control over the directorate general of policy formulation (*kyojŏng togam*) was handed over to his son Im Yumu, but the younger Im was assassinated later that same year.²⁵

The age of military rule thus came to an end, but Wŏnjong still had to tackle some serious fiscal problems that threatened his ability to rule. First, he had to find a way to fund the restoration of the old capital Kaegyŏng, which lay in ruins.²⁶ This proved to be no easy task, as the taxable population had shrunk drastically and the state treasury had been drained by continued war with the Mongols.²⁷ The state was in dire financial circumstances for other reasons as well. In 1270, the Sambyŏlch'o (Three Elite Patrols) appropriated the grains stored in an auxiliary state granary and left Kanghwa Island to stage a rebellion against the newly restored monarchy and Mongol overlordship.²⁸ To make matters worse, that same year on July 27, the Mongol prince Qurumshi, who had escorted Wŏnjong back to Koryŏ with armed forces, entered the island and distributed the grains in the Kanghwa granary to officials and commoners. On September 4, lest anyone refuse to move to the old capital, Qurumshi also set homes on the island ablaze. What remained on the island was thus lost in the conflagration.²⁹ Under these dismal circumstances, the king also had to secure funds for the royal tours to the Mongol capital. With the treasury empty, the king therefore resorted to collecting silver and cloth from officials, monasteries, and eventually peasant households.[30]

The king also had to reward those who had played a key role in the assassination of Kim Chun and Im Yumu, again relying on a nontraditional expedient: he rewarded "palace favorites" (*ch'ongsin*, also *p'yehaeng*) with grant land (*susajŏn*) from the landed estates (*chŏnwŏn*) once owned by Kim Chun and Im Yŏn. This decision met with harsh opposition from the *chaech'u*, who urged the king to place these landed estates in the care of the granary for entertaining foreign visitors (*yŏngsonggo*) in 1271.[31] According to a memorial submitted to the Mongol court in 1272, since 1270, the Koryŏ court had expended 17,151 *sŏk* of grains for the purpose of entertaining foreign envoys in the old capital Kaegyŏng and was struggling to produce more to support the suppression of the Sambyŏlch'o rebellion and the planned invasion of Japan.[32] The concerns of the *chaech'u* were thus well founded, but Wŏnjong clearly had other priorities. He had to sustain the loyalty of palace favorites. Under normal circumstances, it could be done by relying on the royal treasury (*t'angjang*), but this was no longer possible for Wŏnjong. Indeed, by the time his son Prince Sim assumed the throne, the royal treasury was completely depleted.[33]

Lastly, and perhaps most importantly, the king had to secure salaries for officials. Relying once again on an expedient that was first used to address the shortage of officials' salaries in 1257, the privy council (*tobyŏngmasa*) recommended that the state set aside land in the capital district as salary rank land (*nokkwajŏn*).[34] The privy council's plan was deceptively simple. In lieu of grains, which the state did not have, officials would be paid with prebend revenues from "reclaimable land" (*kanji*), that is, land originally assigned to nonofficials (e.g., soldiers) that had been abandoned during the war with the Mongols.[35] Palace favorites and royal clan members who had already appropriated abandoned land to create large landed estates in the capital district naturally voiced strong objections, but Hŏ Kong—who had been placed in charge of the personnel authority (*chŏngbang*) in 1269—succeeded in persuading the king to approve the privy council's plan.[36]

For Wŏnjong, the Mongols were thus a mixed blessing. They thwarted Im Yŏn's efforts to maintain military rule in Koryŏ and helped Wŏnjong reclaim the throne, but the Mongol court's constant demands for grains, soldiers, horses, warships, and other tribute items during an unprecedented fiscal crisis threatened Wŏnjong's ability to rule effectively. The fact that

Wŏnjong lacked a strong network of supporters at home in Koryŏ only made his attempt to fully restore monarchical power that much more difficult.

THE KHAN'S SON-IN-LAW

King Wŏnjong did in fact make every effort to build a network of supporters. He tried to buy the loyalty of palace favorites with handsome rewards and appease the rest of the officialdom by approving emergency measures such as the distribution of salary rank land. But Wŏnjong, who had been betrayed by his officials before, wanted insurance against another coup d'état. To this end, he sought to establish a stronger bond between his own royal Wang lineage and the great khan. During his trip to the Mongol capital in 1270, Wŏnjong therefore asked Qubilai to grant his son Prince Sim the honor of taking one of the imperial princesses as his bride.[37] Early next year, in 1271, the king sent an envoy with another formal request for a marriage alliance between the two ruling families, and later that same year, the envoy returned with the much-anticipated news: Qubilai had approved the request.[38]

His approval reflects Qubilai's concerns about unrest in Koryŏ (i.e., the Im Yŏn incident and the Sambyŏlch'o rebellion), the planned campaigns against the Southern Song and the Japanese islands, and the armed conflict between the Ögödei and Chaghatai khanates in Central Asia.[39] These were concerns that Qubilai harbored not necessarily as the great khan of the Great Yuan *ulus* but as the khan of a smaller *ulus* whose sphere of influence was limited to Northeast Asia. The special attention that Koryŏ received from Qubilai was, in other words, the consequence of his decision to focus on the affairs of the smaller *ulus* that was under his direct control.

For these reasons, on June 23, 1274, a year after the suppression of the Sambyŏlch'o rebellion and on the eve of the first Mongol invasion of Japan, Prince Sim was finally allowed to take the great khan's daughter Qutlugh Kelmish as his bride while serving as the great khan's "hostage" (*turqāq*) in Dadu.[40] Fellow hostages—most notably, Kim Pyŏn and the Mongolian interpreter Cho In'gyu—are said to have also played a critical role in the process.[41] This marriage alliance fundamentally redefined Koryŏ-Yuan relations. It resulted in the dual status of the ruler of Koryŏ as both king of a tributary state and son-in-law (*küregen*) of the great khan.

Combining the two separate seals for the imperial son-in-law and Koryŏ king, Qubilai had a new seal forged for the Koryŏ ruler named the Seal of the Branch Secretariat for the Eastern Campaigns, Son-in-Law, and King by Imperial Command in 1281.[42] This status as king and imperial son-in-law proved to be important for Sim, that is, King Ch'ungnyŏl. It allowed him to build a network of supporters, or what some Korean historians call his "inner circle" without abandoning the regular bureaucracy.[43]

ALL THE KING'S MEN

The bifurcated structure of Koryŏ as both tributary state and princely appanage (C. *touxia*) provided Ch'ungnyŏl with a unique opportunity to build a network of supporters and reestablish monarchical authority. This was an opportunity that he was willing to exploit. As a tributary state, Koryŏ was allowed by the great khan to maintain its royal ancestral shrine (*chongmyo*) and altars for soil and grain spirits (*sajik*)—classicist (*yu*) symbols of Koryŏ's sovereignty and, hence, its bureaucracy.[44] But as a princely appanage, Koryŏ could also function largely as an extension of the Great Yuan *ulus* and utilize a means of recruitment unique to the Mongols.[45] Ch'ungnyŏl could, for instance, recruit men loyal to him through such Mongol institutions as the *keshig*, falconry offices (*ŭngbang*), and *bichēchi*. That, in fact, is precisely what he did.

For Ch'ungnyŏl, the *keshig*, or *kŏpsŏl* in Korean, was a particularly useful institution. In addition to its function as bodyguards, the *keshig* could carry out discomfiting tasks. The *keshig* in Koryŏ was entrusted, for instance, with the task of procuring young virgins from reputable families to be sent to Dadu as tribute women.[46] The *keshig*'s deep sense of loyalty to the sovereign had something to do with its unique method of recruitment. Traditionally, the *keshig* was composed of "hostages" or retainers recruited from prominent families who could potentially threaten the khan's authority.[47] While serving in the *keshig*, however, these men were expected to develop a strong personal relationship with the khan and eventually become his most trusted officials.

On July 22, 1271, Ch'ungnyŏl himself went to Dadu as a hostage while he was still Koryŏ's heir apparent and served in the great khan's *keshig*. At the time, he was accompanied by the aide to the department of state affairs on the right Song Pun, the director of armaments Sŏl Konggŏm (exam passed in 1258), the director of the board of revenue Kim Sŏ, the director of the board of rites Kim Pyŏn, and sixteen other "sons of officials" (*ŭigwan yunju*).[48] Ch'ungnyŏl and the other hostages returned after four years of service in Dadu on October 3, 1274. Just days after his return, the new king Ch'ungnyŏl had the sons of officials who had accompanied him to Dadu serve in rotation as palace guards.[49] He referred to them as the *holchŏk*, or *qorchi* in Mongolian (quiver bearers).[50] This was clear indication of his wish, as Chinggisid son-in-law, to have his own *keshig* in Koryŏ.[51]

Ch'ungnyŏl's attempt to build a network of supporters at home in Koryŏ was not limited to the formation of his own *keshig*. The king also permitted the establishment of falconry offices in Koryŏ for supplying the Yuan court with well-trained birds of prey. As Ch'ungnyŏl knew all too well, falconry was a noble pastime among the Yuan elites, who were expected to own a large number of hunting birds. Princes, as a matter of pomp and pageantry, were expected to have more than their retainers, and retainers to have more than commoners.[52] It was beneath the dignity of a prince to fly the same bird twice. Naturally, raptors were in high demand. The falconry offices in Koryŏ were a response to this insatiable appetite for trained raptors. Ch'ungnyŏl enthusiastically supported the establishment of these offices for other reasons as well. The falconry offices supplied him with "archers" (i.e., a private military force) who were put in rotation with the *qorchi* as members of the palace guard.[53] Like the *qorchi*, falconry officials and their falconers often accompanied the king on hunting expeditions and provided both entertainment and security.[54] But that is not all. Falconry offices also provided Ch'ungnyŏl with a means of extracting and exporting silver, the preferred currency of international trade.[55] The regular bureaucracy's repeated criticism of the falconry offices and their exploitation of the Koryŏ populace notwithstanding, Ch'ungnyŏl therefore lavished enthusiastic support and great privileges on this institution. Falconry officials—such as Yun Su, Wŏn Kyŏng, Yi Chŏng, and Pak Ŭi—were allowed to amass great wealth, and their falconers were exempt from corvée duties.[56]

Ch'ungnyŏl's network of supporters in Koryŏ also included those who served as his attending retinue (*sujong*) in Dadu, composed not only of men from nontraditional backgrounds but members of the regular bureaucracy as well. On October 27, 1274, just three weeks after his return to Koryŏ, Ch'ungnyŏl gave handsome rewards to these men. A typical reward was a grant ordinance that gave its owner permanent rights over a piece of private tax-exempt land.[57] According to the *History of Koryŏ*, Song Pun received grant ordinances to acquire precious land in the capital district. He is said to have possessed more land in the capital district than anyone else at the time.[58] The vast majority of land acquired with grant ordinances, however, seems to have belonged to men from nontraditional backgrounds, that is, falconry officials, inner palace retainers, and eunuchs. Some of these "men of low birth" (*ch'ŏnja*)—among them, Yŏm Sŭngik, Pak Ŭi, Chŏng Sŭngo, and Yi Chijŏ—used their grant ordinances to acquire several hundred *kyŏl* of land. These men lured peasant commoners to their large landed estates and made them into tenant farmers.[59]

Rewards for being loyal to the king were not limited to grant ordinances. The king also made it possible for men from nontraditional backgrounds to be granted official titles that they were customarily barred from receiving because of their humble social backgrounds. Recipients of these rewards included former slaves, eunuchs, and palace attendants who could rise only as high as rank 7, like Kang Yunso (slave-eunuch, appointed minister of war; rank 3a), Kim Chajŏng (slave, appointed great general; rank 3b), Ch'a Tŭkkyu (palace aide, appointed general; rank 4a), and Chŏng Obu (slave, appointed general; rank 4a).[60] There were also men from humble backgrounds, for example, Cho In'gyu, who was appointed senior colonel (rank 5a).[61]

THE REGULAR BUREAUCRACY STRIKES BACK

The response of the regular bureaucracy to the steps the king had taken to build a new network of supporters was largely negative. The censorate (*ŏsadae*), remonstrance officials (*nangsa*), circuit commissioners (*anch'alsa*), and royal transmitters (*sŭngsŏn*) soon voiced criticisms. In 1275, the first full year of King Ch'ungnyŏl's reign, the commissioner of the Chŏlla circuit An Chŏn, for instance, was stripped of office for refusing to comply with the demands of a local falconer named O Sukpu.[62] In reprisal, O told the king that An was interfering with the training of gyrfalcons (*haedongch'ŏng*). The furious king tried to exile An to an island, but fellow members of the regular bureaucracy came to his aid. The royal transmitters Pak Hang (exam passed in 1248) and Yi Punsŏng defended An's actions and implored the king to reconsider.[63] Yi argued that An was just doing his duty and refusing to support the falconry official's illegal actions. Unable to ignore Pak's and Yi's pleas, the king lessened An's punishment to dismissal from office.

Yi Punsŏng's efforts to strengthen the regular bureaucracy did not stop there. He also reminded the king that the regular bureaucracy's show of disobedience (as in the case of An Chŏn) was not a show of defiance but a reaction to the breakdown of the regular chain of command. Monks and slaves, Yi explained, used their connections in the palace to get their hands on royal edicts (*sŏnji*), which they put to improper use in acquiring whatever they desired.⁶⁴ Members of the regular bureaucracy disobeyed the king because they had no other means of stopping these unscrupulous men from nontraditional backgrounds. But Yi did more than offer a justification of the disobedient behavior of fellow officials. He also offered a solution that would allow the regular bureaucracy to regain control of the countryside. For "trivial" matters like the training of falcons, Yi persuaded the king to use something he called the "royal message" (sŏnjŏn sosik)—a document drafted by royal transmitters like himself and authorized with just a signature from the king—in place of the royal edict. Yi argued that this new medium of communication would make the process of conveying royal orders less cumbersome, since the royal message did not require the ritual formalities of a royal edict. The king approved Yi's recommendation on July 15, 1275.⁶⁵

But Yi's idea failed to deny men from nontraditional backgrounds undue access to the king. The falconer O Sukpu drafted his own royal message and had the palace favorite Yi Chŏng obtain the king's signature for him. The royal message made it possible for O to turn a large number of commoner households in the southwest region into dependents of his falconry office.⁶⁶ The royal message also granted falconers exemption from corvée duties. The regular bureaucracy quickly responded to this abuse of the royal message medium. The royal transmitter Ch'oe Munbon remonstrated against the king's decision to approve O's royal message. Ch'oe assured the king that he could draft a royal message to circuit commissioners and make sure they procured the necessary number of gyrfalcons. The king ignored Ch'oe's plea.⁶⁷

As demonstrated by his dismissal of Ch'oe's advice, Ch'ungnyŏl had little interest in allowing the regular bureaucracy to limit his authority and the political reach of his palace favorites. This, however, did not stop the regular bureaucracy from trying. On November 21, 1275, the king complied with the request of the Mongol court and changed officials' titles and court language to reflect Koryŏ's lesser status.⁶⁸ The censorate and the remonstrance officials used this as an opportunity to scrutinize appointments. Unlike other officials whose positions were simply renamed, the censorate impeached Supreme General Kang Yunso and had the king strip him of his office on January 3, 1276.⁶⁹ The inspector general's office claimed that Kang could not hold such a high-ranking post, given his slave origins, despite his first-grade merit subject status.

The move against Kang was quickly followed by more attempts to rid the court of all men from nontraditional backgrounds. In the spring of 1276, the exhorter on the right (*u chŏng'ŏn*) Yi Injŏng, Yi Chehyŏn's uncle, led fellow remonstrance officials in the chancellery and protested the king's promotion of palace aides (*naeryo*) and men of humble origins (*mich'ŏn*) who served him during his visits to Dadu to high-ranking posts in the central government.[70] The furious king pushed through the promotions and suspended Yi Injŏng. This punishment, however, was apparently not enough to satisfy the palace favorites, who naturally came to hold a deep grudge against Yi for trying to deny them their promotions. Not long after this incident, the new Koryŏ *darughachi* Sŏngmalch'ŏn'gu (C. Shimotianqu) received an anonymous letter. The letter, no doubt the product of the irritated palace favorites, accused Yi of trying to assassinate the *darughachi*. Sŏngmalch'ŏn'gu had Yi placed in a cangue and his feet shackled.[71]

These scare tactics did not, however, deter the regular bureaucracy from trying to limit the power of the palace and inner palace favorites, those whom late Koryŏ sources tend to call "the wealthy and powerful" (*kwŏn'gwi, kwŏnse chi ka, hose ka,* or *hogang*).[72] Later that year, Chancellery Scholar Kim Ku asked the king to establish an interpreters bureau (*t'ongmun'gwan*) to provide language instruction for scholar-officials under the age of forty with low-ranking central posts (rank 7 or lower). This measure was initiated by the *chaech'u* in order to end its reliance on translators who tended to come from humble backgrounds (*mich'ŏn*). It was not uncommon for these unscrupulous men to alter the message of the king and the court for their own personal gain.[73]

Members of the *chaech'u* continued their attack. They had to. They needed a way to fill the empty state treasury. In the second lunar month of that same year (1277), the privy council asked the king's permission to sell official titles for payments in silver.[74] The privy council had used this expedient before.[75] The king approved the plan, but the *chaech'u* wanted to explore a more fundamental solution to the state's fiscal problems. On March 22, 1277, the *chaech'u* therefore recommended that the king rescind the grant ordinances given to palace aides and "sons of the yurt" (*kŏmnyŏnggu*, C. qieliankou, ger-in k'e'ü), that is, the foreign retainers who served the imperial princess.[76] The *chaech'u* claimed that these men used the grant ordinances to seize fertile fields that "arbitrarily set the mountains and rivers as their boundaries." To make matters worse, these grant ordinances, the *chaech'u* reminded the king, exempted these large landed estates from taxation, which led to state revenue shortfalls. The king, however, did not accept the *chaech'u*'s recommendation.

KORYŎ AS PRINCELY APPANAGE

This political tug of war between the king and the regular bureaucracy entered a new phase the following year. The Yuan official Hong Tagu, King Ch'ungnyŏl's rival, attempted to seize control of the Koryŏ court. On January 14, 1278, subordinate officers who held private grudges against Chancellor Kim Panggyŏng accused him of trying to stage a rebellion on Kanghwa Island.[77] Kim was arrested, interrogated, and tortured by Hong. It was, in fact, Hong who orchestrated these actions against Kim from behind the scenes.[78] Hong's plan was to use Kim's removal as an opportunity to convince the Yuan court to grant him more control over the Koryŏ population and its armed forces. This was not an unlikely scenario given Hong's recent promotion to commander in chief of an eastern expedition field command. After Kim was exiled to an island, Hong tried to exert direct control over Koryŏ: he recommended the promotion of the military men who had helped him remove Kim to key posts in the central government.[79]

King Ch'ungnyŏl immediately sent General In Hu—a Mongolian who first came to Koryŏ with the Mongol imperial princess Qutlugh Kelmish as her retainer—to Dadu and notified Qubilai of what happened. Qubilai questioned Im about Kim Panggyŏng's arrest and concluded that the accusations against Kim were unfounded. Lest Koryŏ fall into a state of unrest, Quibilai summoned both Hong Tagu and Ch'ungnyŏl to Dadu. During his audience with the great khan, Ch'ungnyŏl first demonstrated his worth and then made some requests. Keenly aware of Koryŏ's coming role in the second invasion of Japan, Ch'ungnyŏl informed the great khan of his commitment to the cause. Ch'ungnyŏl promised the great khan that Koryŏ would build warships and prepare provisions for the invading forces. Having demonstrated his worth, Ch'ungnyŏl then asked the great khan to prevent Hong from meddling further in the affairs of the Koryŏ government.[80] Qubilai approved the request. The great khan also allowed Koryŏ to manage its own census records and promised to withdraw all *darughachi* from Koryŏ.[81] This was a major political victory for Ch'ungnyŏl that allowed him to further consolidate power at home.

This consolidation of power was necessary. The king still had to share the power of recruitment and promotions with the regular bureaucracy. This made it difficult at times to reward palace favorites and especially men from nontraditional backgrounds. Indeed, as the king struggled to remove the threat from his political rival Hong from Koryŏ, the regular bureaucracy continued its attack against these men from nontraditional backgrounds. On May 6, 1278, remonstrance officials led by Master of Remonstrance (Saŭi Taebu; rank 3b) Paek Munjŏl refused to ratify appointment letters sent to them, no doubt by the personnel authority, on the grounds that many of the officials who were being granted new appointments "did not have merit or had blemishes in their ancestry."[82] The king was furious and had Paek Munjŏl, Yi Ikpae (exam passed in 1244; grandson of Yi Kyubo), Yi Injŏng, and others arrested by the *qorchi*. The king, however, changed his mind after Yi Chijŏ—a palace favorite—reminded him how inappropriate it was for the *qorchi* to arrest members of the chancellery. Paek and the other remonstrance officials were therefore released.[83]

But Ch'ungnyŏl's successful negotiations with Qubilai that year made it possible for him to take more aggressive political action at home in Koryŏ. On October 28, Ch'ungnyŏl exiled and killed the brothers Yi Punhŭi and Yi Punsŏng. Their deaths were a consequence of their purported alliance with Hong Tagu.[84] A few days later, November 2, the king removed other Koryŏ officials loyal to Hong from power and sent them into exile.[85] The very next day, the king promoted Kim Panggyŏng to chief grand councilor, Pak Hang to chancellery scholar, Sŏl Konggŏm to assistant royal secretary (*ch'umirwŏn pusa*; rank 3a), Song Pun to director of memorials (*chijusa*; rank 3a), and Kim Chujŏng to assistant transmitter on the right. The most important posts in the central bureaucracy had thus been granted to men who served the king as attending officials in Dadu.

After the removal of Hong and others who posed a threat to his authority in Koryŏ, Ch'ungnyŏl was ready to take even more daring steps to further strengthen the throne. On November 14, 1278, Kim Chujŏng, with the help of royal favorites Yi Chijŏ and Yŏm Sŭngik, urged the king to announce the establishment of the *bichēchi* and *sinmunsaek*.[86] Kim argued that the *bichēchi* could serve as a remedy for the bloated *chaech'u*. He also argued that the *sinmunsaek*—a small number of trusted palace aides—could convey the *bichēchi*'s decisions to the king in place of the royal transmitters.[87] The king approved this radical plan to place vital bureaucratic functions that belonged to the *chaech'u* under his control and establish what would eventually be known as the "special office *chaech'u*" (*pyŏlch'ŏng chaech'u*).[88] Kim Chujŏng, Pak Hang, Sŏl Konggŏm, Yi Chonbi, Yŏm Sŭngik, Cho In'gyu, Yi Chijŏ, Kwak Ye (exam passed in 1255), An Chŏn, Yi Hon (exam passed in 1268), and others were appointed to the *bichēchi*.[89] Kim Ŭigwang, Chŏng Sŭngo—a man from humble origins who earned the king's favor by accompanying him twice to Dadu—and other palace aides were appointed to the *sinmunsaek*. The special office *chaech'u* thus consisted mainly of palace favorites who earned the king's trust by serving him at critical moments during his visits to the Yuan capital Dadu.

Despite their weakened authority, the *chaech'u* continued to attempt to curb the king's efforts to work outside regular bureaucratic institutions. The *chaech'u* took advantage of an opportunity that came just two months after the establishment of the *bichēchi* and *sinmunsaek*. The shortage of grains made it necessary to distribute salary rank land to keep the central bureaucracy running. Using this as an opportunity, the privy council once again tried to extend this emergency measure to the land in the capital district that palace favorites had acquired with their grant ordinances, but the king prohibited the conversion of this grant land into rank land for current officials.[90] Palace favorite Song Pun, who is said to have owned more grant land in the capital district than anyone else, persuaded the king to announce this prohibition.[91]

In 1280, the *chaech'u* also attempted to place limits on the activities of the falconry offices, but the king foiled this, too.[92] In the spring of that same year, the censorate submitted memorials that criticized the king's hunting excursions and lavish banquets prepared by the *qorchi* and the falconry offices. The censorate also asked the king to reduce expenditures from the storehouse of the right (*uch'ang*), halt the construction of the palace until the agricultural off-season, and punish the circuit commissioners who used tribute items (silk, ramie, paper, dried meat, fruit, etc.) as bribes. The furious king had the attendant censor (*sisa*, also *siŏsa*) Sim Yang interrogated to find out who was responsible for the report. Head Attendant Censor (Chaptan) Chin Ch'ŏk and Attendant Censor Mun Ŭng were exiled after the interrogation. Palace Censor Yi Sŭnghyu was also removed from office.[93] Fellow censorate official Paek Munjŏl was able to convince the king to release Sim, Chin, and Mun from custody later that month, but the dynastic histories state that "the path of words [i.e., honest and critical advice] was blocked as a consequence."[94] This incident was indeed followed by a noticeable decline in the activity of censorial officials.[95]

As noted earlier, the king's authority reached new heights when Qubilai granted him the Seal of the Branch Secretariat for the Eastern Campaigns, Son-in-Law, and King by Imperial Command in 1281. This allowed him to stand firmly above his rival Hong Tagu, who, along with Hindu (C. Xindu), returned to Koryŏ to lead the eastern expedition force that year.[96] The king's heightened status, assured by the new seal, also allowed him to ignore the legal limitations on promotions determined by birth and grant merit subject status to men from nontraditional backgrounds who demonstrated their loyalty during his frequent visits to Dadu.⁹⁷ The highest honor was granted to those who had helped Ch'ungnyŏl prevent the dethronement of his father, Wŏnjong, in 1269. Chŏng Obu, Chŏng In'gyŏng, Ch'a Tŭkkyu, Yi Chijŏ, and others were named first-grade merit subjects. Na Yu and others were named second-grade merit subjects.⁹⁸ Eunuchs, traditionally limited to rank 7, and the son of Chŏng Sŭngo were also given permission to receive a post that was rank 5 or lower. Later, in 1287, attending retinue merit subjects (*sujong kongsin*) were additionally granted two slaves and one hundred *kyŏl* of land. The king also used this opportunity to indiscriminately reward palace aides regardless of whether they served him as attending officials.⁹⁹

1298

Although Ch'ungnyŏl tried to maintain the bifurcated structure of Koryŏ as both tributary state and princely appanage, the controversial appointments and rewards he authorized as he built a network of supporters in Koryŏ threatened to destabilize this political structure. Ignoring the Koryŏ court convention of barring eunuchs, slaves, *pugok* men, and palace aides from rising to high office, Ch'ungnyŏl continued to flood the upper echelons of the bureaucracy with men from nontraditional backgrounds. Palace aides, falconers, and the *qorchi* helped him enjoy a lifestyle befitting a prince of the Great Yuan *ulus* that he could not enjoy as liberally as the king of Koryŏ. With their assistance, Ch'ungnyŏl could indulge in hunting, flying falcons, and holding lavish banquets.¹⁰⁰

Mongolian interpreters (e.g., Cho In'gyu and Yu Ch'ŏngsin) and the retainers of the imperial princess (In Hu and Ch'a Sin) also helped Ch'ungnyŏl maintain Koryŏ's privileged status within the Great Yuan *ulus* as a princely appanage. They frequently traveled to Dadu as envoys to deliver gifts, celebrate imperial birthdays, and negotiate important matters such as a marriage alliance with the imperial family. Their ability to serve as skillful intermediaries between Koryŏ and Yuan made them valuable political assets to Ch'ungnyŏl. Their political worth therefore depended less on the needs of an independent Koryŏ bureaucracy than on Koryŏ's continued submission to Mongol rule.

It is precisely for these reasons that Cho In'gyu was appointed chancellor. For the same reasons, the palace aide Kim Chajŏng rose to the rank of supreme general (rank 3a) despite his slave background. In 1285, he was also appointed vice commissioner (*pusa*) of the eastern capital, the birthplace of the king's mother.¹⁰¹ The palace aide Yi Chijŏ rose to the rank of finance commissioner on the left (*samsa chwasa*; rank 3a) in 1297.¹⁰² That same year, In Hu was granted concurrent appointments as assistant chancellor (rank 2a) and superintendent of the board of war, Ch'a Sin was promoted to assistant chancellor and junior preceptor of the heir apparent (rank 2b), Pak Ŭi was promoted to royal undersecretary (rank 2b) and adviser to the heir apparent (rank 3a), and Yu Ch'ŏngsin was appointed censor-in-chief (rank 3a) and associate royal secretary (rank 2b).¹⁰³ Despite their nontraditional backgrounds, these men were all allowed to serve as *chaech'u*. The falconry official Yi Chŏng was also granted the *chaech'u* post of assistant royal secretary (rank 2b).¹⁰⁴ Granting *chaech'u* membership to men from such backgrounds was highly unusual. Indeed, the *History of Koryŏ* (Koryŏsa) duly notes that the bestowal of a *chaech'u* post on Yi, a former slave and dog butcher, was unprecedented and improper.

In 1294, an opportunity to dismantle the king's network of supporters finally presented itself to the regular bureaucracy. In late February, Ch'ungnyŏl's greatest patron, Qubilai, passed away. After the great khan's passing, the Yuan court was left with two potential candidates for the throne. Qubilai had already granted the seal of the heir apparent to his grandson Temür (temple name Chengzong), but Temür's older brother Gammala (1263–1302) had supporters who wished to place him on the throne instead.¹⁰⁵ At the council of princes and nobles (*quriltai*) convened in April at the summer palace in Shangdu, Temür's powerful supporters at court, Üs Temür (1242–1295) and Bayan (1237–1295), made sure Temür was selected to succeed his grandfather Qubilai. As the great khan's son-in-law, Ch'ungnyŏl was also there at the council of princes and nobles to participate in the selection process.¹⁰⁶

Using his status as an imperial son-in-law, Ch'ungnyŏl asked the new khan Temür for permission to arrange a marriage between his son Ch'ungsŏn and an imperial princess. Temür denied the request.¹⁰⁷ This no doubt came as a disappointment to Ch'ungnyŏl, who wanted Koryŏ to maintain its privileged status as a son-in-law state in a post-Qubilai world. Temür's reason for not granting Ch'ungnyŏl's request to forge another marriage alliance is unclear, but the marriage would eventually take place in 1296.¹⁰⁸ With the Yuan court's approval, Ch'ungsŏn made a brief trip to Koryŏ to be officially recognized as the head of Koryŏ's central bureaucracy on October 3, 1295.¹⁰⁹ This was the signal that Ch'ungnyŏl was waiting for. A few weeks later, the Koryŏ official and Mongolian interpreter Yu Ch'ŏngsin was sent to formally broach the subject of a marriage alliance between Koryŏ and Yuan.¹¹⁰ Later that year, Ch'ungnyŏl received news that the date was set for his son to marry Buddhaśrī, the daughter of the Prince of Jin, Gammala. Ch'ungnyŏl and Qutlugh Kelmish left for Dadu on October 26 with the bride-price needed to finalize the marriage. They were accompanied by an impressive retinue consisting of 243 officials and 590 servants. They also brought with them 990 horses and various local tribute items.¹¹¹ Eighty-one white stallions were presented as bride-price to the khan. The same number of white stallions was presented to the khan's mother, Kökejin (Bairam-Egechi) (d. 1300), and the Prince of Jin.¹¹²

Everything went as Ch'ungnyŏl planned, but shortly after their return to Koryŏ, the imperial princess Qutlugh Kelmish suddenly became ill. She passed away two weeks later at the monastery Hyŏnsŏng-sa on the twenty-first day of the fifth lunar month of 1297.¹¹³ Learning of his mother's unexpected death, Ch'ungsŏn hurried back to Koryŏ.¹¹⁴ A month after his return to Koryŏ, Ch'ungsŏn made it publicly known that he suspected foul play. He brashly accused his father's favorite palace lady Mubi of hiring shamans and sorcerer monks to curse the late imperial princess. Acting on his suspicions, Ch'ungsŏn asked his father to take everyone associated with the palace lady Mubi into custody for questioning.¹¹⁵ The king asked his son to wait until the completion of the mourning period (i.e., three years) to begin the investigation, but Ch'ungsŏn ignored his father's request and had Mubi and her associates interrogated. During the interrogation, Mubi's conspirators confessed to the crime. Mubi, her elder sister, and their alleged co-conspirators—the eunuchs Ch'oe Seyŏn, To Sŏnggi, Yun Kilson (the son of falconry official Yun Su), and others—were quickly sentenced to death, and forty others involved in the crime received the lesser sentence of exile.¹¹⁶

Korean scholars are in general agreement that the Mubi incident, like the earlier Kim Panggyŏng incident, was a politically motivated purge. The ultimate aim of the purge, they claim, was the removal of Ch'ungnyŏl's network of supporters and, more specifically, the eunuchs who formed the king's inner circle.¹¹⁷ There is ample evidence to support this claim. Many years before the Mubi incident, Ch'ungsŏn is said to have already played a key role in sending the eunuchs Ch'oe Seyŏn and To Sŏnggi into exile.¹¹⁸ But their exile did not last long. King Ch'ungnyŏl soon summoned the eunuchs back to the palace. He even entrusted Ch'oe, who held the title Supreme General despite his status as a eunuch, with the important task of submitting hunting birds to the Yuan court.¹¹⁹ The threat that Ch'oe posed was clear to everyone around him. He used his close relationship with the king to exercise control over promotions, demotions, and court affairs. Remonstrance officials, royal clan members, and even the *chaech'u* therefore feared him.

Ch'ungnyŏl's reaction to the Mubi incident also lends further support to the reading of his son Ch'ungsŏn's actions in political terms. Less than three months after the purge, Ch'ungnyŏl, who had previously not shown any interest in stepping down from the throne, suddenly informed the Yuan court of his wish to have his son replace him as Koryŏ king. The transition of power took place soon thereafter. On March 6, 1298, Ch'ungnyŏl announced his retirement, and three days later, Ch'ungsŏn assumed the throne.[120]

Ch'ungsŏn's actions after the transition of power also supports the political reading of the Mubi incident. Shortly after his enthronement, he introduced sweeping reforms and tried to further restrict the political and economic reach of the palace favorites who had risen to prominence under his father's rule.[121] In a set of enthronement edicts (*chŭgwi kyosŏ*), for instance, Ch'ungsŏn publicly declared his desire to use a narrower definition of merit subject status. He declared that only those equal in merit to Ch'oe Ŭng, Sŏ Hŭi, Yang Kyu, Kang Kamch'an, Ch'oe Sajŏn, Cho Ch'ung, and Kim Panggyŏng—men with unequivocal records of defending the state from domestic or foreign threats—deserved this respected status. This narrower definition was meant to delegitimize those who had been granted the status simply for serving the former king, Ch'ungnyŏl, as his attending retinue during his visits to Dadu.[122] Ch'ungsŏn was particularly critical of the men with flawed backgrounds (*hŭn'gu chi in*) who, as attending-retinue merit subjects of his father's, had been rewarded with inappropriate promotions and upgraded ancestral seats. He therefore strictly forbade the continuation of this practice.[123]

Ch'ungsŏn attempted to address the financial problems associated with palace favorites as well. For instance, he instructed circuit commissioners to investigate "deceitful bullies" (*hohwal chi to*) who used grant ordinances to illegally appropriate land in the countryside. According to Ch'ungsŏn's enthronement edicts, these "bullies" claimed that the land they appropriated was originally unplowed (i.e., ownerless) land, which was in fact nothing more than a convenient excuse for arbitrarily setting mountains and rivers as the borders of their large, tax-exempt, landed estates.[124] Similar abuses also threatened the rank land system. Grant ordinances were being used to lay claim not only to abandoned or unused land but also to land in the capital district that already had rightful owners. The king therefore ordered the investigation of landownership in the capital district to make sure that "those who placed their own gain as top priority" (*chari wi sŏn cha*) were not illegally appropriating land designated as rank land.¹²⁵

As part of his plan to weaken and perhaps even dismantle large landed estates owned by his father's network of supporters, Ch'ungsŏn also tried to deprive them of manpower. With the intention of preventing "those with influence and power" (*yu seryŏk*), such as Yŏm Sŭngik, from collecting wandering peasants and putting them to work on their large landed estates, Ch'ungsŏn ordered the circuit commissioners to return these peasants to their original places of registration and restore their original status, namely taxpaying commoner households.¹²⁶ Similarly, he had circuit commissioners return the local henchmen of the "powerful" (*kwŏnse*) to their original social stations and ranks.¹²⁷ In addition, Ch'ungsŏn had those who forced commoners to become slaves punished and strictly prohibited the cultivation of private grant land (*sap'aejŏn*) by out-resident slaves.¹²⁸ To prevent a shortage of corvée laborers, the king also banned *yangban* officials from converting peasants into slaves.

It is difficult, however, to see how these reform measures could have been effectively carried out since the circuit commissioners and local officials were also targets of Ch'ungsŏn's reforms. In the enthronement edicts, which were based in part on an eighteen-point memorial submitted by Hong Chabŏn two years earlier, in 1296, the circuit commissioners were accused of exploiting commoners so as to secure private gifts to present to the king and "appointment bribes" (*pongsong*) to present to newly appointed local *qorchi* and falconry officials.¹²⁹ Moreover, key members of Ch'ungnyŏl's inner circle (e.g., Cho In'gyu, Yu Ch'ŏngsin, In Hu, Ch'a Sin, Yi Chijŏ, Wŏn Kyŏng, and Pak Ŭi) remained in power after Ch'ungsŏn assumed the throne.¹³⁰ This, too, would have made effective reform difficult if not impossible.

Ch'ungsŏn's effort to dismantle his father's network of supporters was made even more difficult because he lacked supporters of his own.¹³¹ Naturally, he devised a solution to this problem in 1298. Hoping to establish a counterbalance to his father's palace favorites, Ch'ungsŏn attempted to revitalize the regular bureaucracy. He took a two-pronged approach.

First, he tried to maintain the throne's control over recruitment and promotions. The palace-based personnel authority thus became a target of reform. In 1298, he abolished the personnel authority and handed its functions over to the scholars in the Hallim Academy, which he later renamed the Sarimwŏn (Sarim Academy).¹³² This left recruitment and promotions in the hands of the academicians Pak Chŏnji (exam passed in 1268), Ch'oe

Ch'am, O Han'gyŏng (exam passed in 1260), and Yi Chin, Yi Chehyŏn's father (exam passed in 1279). These scholars oversaw more than just personnel administration. Along with other respected scholars such as Yi Sŭnghyu and Kwŏn Tan (exam passed in 1254), they formed Ch'ungsŏn's brain trust. They were responsible, for instance, for preparing Ch'ungsŏn's enthronement edicts. Ch'ungsŏn's plan was to empower those bureaucratic institutions that would be most effective at keeping the unscrupulous actions of Ch'ungnyŏl's palace favorites in check.[133]

Second, Ch'ungsŏn tried to elevate the status of Koryŏ's regular bureaucracy. On June 22, he announced his plan to correct his father's expansion of the *chaech'u* ranks and the confusion that had resulted from the injudicious renaming of government offices and titles in 1275.[134] In compliance with the demands of the Yuan court, his father Ch'ungnyŏl had abolished the honorary senior first-grade preceptors and dukes (*samsa samgong*) and the executive department (*sangsŏsŏng*). The *chungsŏ munhasŏng* (secretariat-chancellery) was renamed the *ch'ŏmŭibu*, the *ch'umirwŏn* (security council) was renamed the *milchiksa*, the *ŏsadae* (censorate) was renamed the *kamch'alsa*, and the Hallim Academy was renamed the Munhansŏ. The six ministries were also either abolished or demoted to the level of a division (*sa*). This resulted in confusion, as government institutions of different ranks were all identified as divisions.[135] To correct this problem, Ch'ungsŏn followed the example of the Yuan bureaucracy and elevated the division to a department (*wŏn*), agency (*pu*), or board (*cho*).[136] The *milchiksa* was thus renamed *kwangjŏngwŏn*, the *kamch'alsa* was renamed *sahŏnbu*, and the Munhansŏ was renamed Sarimwŏn.

Ch'ungsŏn's attempt at comprehensive reform was short-lived, however. His wife, the imperial princess Buddhaśrī, forced him to abdicate after only eight months on the throne. Buddhaśrī took action against her husband for several reasons: the two had a nonexistent relationship as a couple;[137] the king tended to favor another consort, the daughter of Cho In'gyu; and political machinations orchestrated by the retired king Ch'ungnyŏl and his network of supporters influenced Buddhaśrī's decision to rein in Ch'ungsŏn and his attempts at reform.[138]

According to the *History of Koryŏ*, Buddhaśrī was first motivated by her wet nurse and a group of unnamed "bullies" to send a letter to the empress dowager Kökejin. Not coincidentally, the letter was sent not long after Ch'ungsŏn abolished the Personnel Authority. Five days after the letter was sent, Ch'ungsŏn announced his plan to change the names of government offices and officials' titles.[139] As part of the renaming process, Cho In'gyu was promoted to minister of education (*sado*; rank 1a), chancellor (rank 1b), and superintendent of the security council (*ch'am chi kwangjŏngwŏn sa*; rank 2b).¹⁴⁰ After the renaming of offices and titles was announced, Ch'ungsŏn did away with the institution of royal transmitters and had its duties transferred to the Sarimwŏn.¹⁴¹ The power once enjoyed by officials in the Personnel Authority was thus transferred to Ch'ungsŏn's Sarimwŏn favorites.

Retaliation soon followed. An anonymous letter was placed on the palace gate.¹⁴² The letter accused Cho In'gyu's wife of using a shaman to bewitch the king and claimed that a spell made the king love only Cho's daughter and not the imperial princess. Cho In'gyu's entire family, including his sons-in-law, were arrested, interrogated, and tortured. At the imperial princess's request, the Yuan court stepped in. But instead of focusing on Cho and his family, the Yuan court turned its attention to Ch'ungsŏn's reform. A few things caught the Yuan court's attention: Ch'ungsŏn's use of the prohibited senior first-grade duke title Minister of Education and the junior first-grade title Chancellor to honor his father-in-law, Cho In'gyu; the establishment of the department of good governance (*chajŏngwŏn*); and the refusal to unite the king and the imperial princess's *keshig*.¹⁴³ The Yuan court had the Koryŏ court reverse all the changes introduced by Ch'ungsŏn. Honorary first-grade titles were abolished, royal transmitters (i.e., the Personnel Authority) were reinstated, and government office names and officials' titles were renamed again to reflect Koryŏ's lesser status. But the Yuan court did not stop there. Ch'ungsŏn was forced to abdicate.¹⁴⁴ He left for Dadu on September 30. The very next day, the Yuan envoys handed the royal seal back to his father, the retired king Ch'ungnyŏl. Ch'ungsŏn's supporters were purged from court shortly thereafter.¹⁴⁵

The reform efforts led by scholars in the Hallim Academy (or Sarimwŏn) in 1298 thus came to an abrupt end. The Koryŏ court remained strongly divided between the regular bureaucracy and its enemies. The nature of this division was not, as some scholars assume, ideology, class, or nationalism (i.e., pro-Yuan vs. anti-Yuan). Rather, it was the question of who deserved access to alienable and taxable resources (e.g., land, labor, and so on) in the capital and the countryside. The regular bureaucracy continued to argue that access to these resources should remain under the control of traditional bureaucratic institutions. King Ch'ungnyŏl thought otherwise. As part of his effort to build a network of supporters, the king preferred to rely on new institutions borrowed from Yuan China such as the *bichēchi*, *keshig*, and falconry offices.

Wealth naturally tended to flow in the direction of these new institutions and the men who staffed them, many of whom were from nontraditional backgrounds and had acquired wealth and power in unconventional ways. The *sejok* elite regarded them as men who had little or no sense of commitment to the ideals of bureaucratic service, or what Martina Deuchler calls the regular bureaucracy's "professional ethos as *sadaebu*."[146] Hoping to curb the rapid diversification of the elite stratum and redefine the stratum in more exclusivist terms, the late Koryŏ *sejok* began to emphasize its commitment to the ideals of bureaucratic service. They claimed that wealth, if separated from these ideals, could no longer provide the *sejok* or, in this case, the *sajok* with an air of nobility and exclusivity.

But the argument worked both ways. If newcomers could demonstrate that they could adhere to these ideals and withstand the temptations of wealth, then they, too, could claim *sejok* and eventually *sajok* status. It was, in fact, the sincere attempt made by men from nontraditional backgrounds, among them, Cho In'gyu and his children, to behave like legitimate members of the elite stratum, rather than their simple rise to economic and political prominence, that led to the late Koryŏ crisis of identity. As the crisis deepened, it became necessary for elite families, *regardless of background*, to emphasize their ability to remain honest and upright. This was true even for well-established ministerial families such as the Kongam Hŏ and Tangsŏng Hong.

5   BUDDHAS AND ANCESTORS

UNDER MONGOL RULE, THE BUDDHIST ESTABLISHMENT IN KORYŎ Korea slowly began to embark on the long path toward becoming an otherworldly religion that could no longer expect its ritual practices to translate seamlessly into salvation in this world or the next. Scholar-officials like Yi Chehyŏn, Yi Kok, and Yi Saek cautiously advanced the argument that if ritual practices such as holding vegetarian feasts for the dead or building memorial monasteries were to work as they had in the past, these practices needed not only the right outward appearance but, more important, the right moral principles. The focus of giving to a field of merit, they argued, should not be the opulence and splendor of the gift but its conformity with the Way. These scholar-officials made the arguments about the material form and moral substance of giving to a field of merit as divisions within the Koryŏ court were growing deeper and wider during and after King Ch'ungnyŏl's reign. Parvenu families like the P'yŏngyang Cho and Kohŭng Yu tried to overcome these divisions by observing the cherished traditions of establishing great-family credentials such as the construction or restoration of Buddhist monasteries. The commemorative stele inscriptions written for these families and their monasteries tried to demonstrate that they possessed more than just wealth. They also possessed moral principles and, therefore, virtue.

Elite families in this period similarly used death as an occasion to think about greatness and virtue, and they did so in a way that deviated from traditional ways of managing death. They either combined Buddhist methods with alternative practices or abandoned Buddhism altogether. These were not decisions made on a whim. How families managed death had a direct effect on the way they were perceived by their peers, and families that decided to deviate from ritual norms were well aware of this fact. They did, however, share something with the late Koryŏ *sejok*, or hereditary elites, who preferred to rely mainly on Buddhism. Despite their different attitudes toward the management of death, late Koryŏ families all had in common the conscious and at times clearly contrived effort to paint a stylized image of themselves as members of an "officials class," or *sa* families (*sajok*) with family legacies rooted in moral principles rather than simply wealth or high office. Tomb epitaphs left behind by these families reveal that they tried to reinvent themselves by taking a moral stance on wealth. It was the novel compulsion to take such a stand that led some families to abandon Buddhism.

LADY HŎ

On the second day of the fourth lunar month of 1301, state councilor Kim Pyŏn (exam passed in 1268) passed away after a monthlong battle with a fatal illness.[1] Following ritual protocol, the king had the office of state sacrifices honor the state councilor with a dirge (*noesŏ*) that contained his posthumous name Munsin and a formal record of his accomplishments.[2] The office of state sacrifices was also ordered to offer the grieving family financial assistance and funerary provisions, but the state councilor's wife, Lady Hŏ, politely declined the state's customary offer and insisted on preparing everything necessary for the funeral herself.[3] As soon as the funeral was over, she also procured a gravesite for her late husband on the southern slopes of Mount Taedŏk, located just a few miles west of the capital. The state councilor was buried there two months later on the twenty-second day of the fifth lunar month.

This was just the beginning of Lady Hŏ's efforts to fulfill her duties as the spouse of a high-ranking scholar-official. According to the preface to her funerary inscription, Lady Hŏ built a place to live—a mourning shed or the symbolic equivalent thereof—right next to her husband's grave. She lived there for three years so that she could personally attend all the regular graveside sacrifices (*cherye*) for her late husband.[4] These sacrifices were performed twice a month (each new and full moon day) and once annually on the anniversary of Lord Munsin's death. Lady Hŏ also commissioned the construction of a memorial monastery named Kamŭng-sa less than a mile away from the grave, to make sure that prayers for her late husband would continue in perpetuity. The grounds of this monastery would eventually serve as the final resting place for not only Kim Pyŏn but also his son Kim Ryun, Ryun's wife Lady Ch'oe, and Ryun's son-in-law Min Sap'yŏng.[5] The conversion of Lady Hŏ's private wealth, presumably her dowry, into merit for her late husband and family did not end there. Her tomb epitaph claims that she exhausted her wealth funding Buddhist rituals and copying Buddhist scriptures in gold and silver ink.

Even after the completion of the three-year mourning period, Lady Hŏ made a point of visiting her husband's grave on all the important days of the ritual calendar (e.g., the lunar new year, the first full moon of the first month, the fifth day of the fifth lunar month, the fifteenth day of the seventh lunar month, and so on). She stopped going to his grave only after she became a Buddhist nun in 1315. Her decision to receive ordination and live under the Dharma name Sŏnghyo, however, did not mean she would finally let go of the memory of her late husband. On the contrary, living as a nun was Lady Hŏ's way of letting everyone know that she was going to maintain her chastity and remain faithful to her late husband. But her ordination did not result in a life of seclusion. Rather, as pious ladies of her high social standing and elite background in Koryŏ were inclined to do, Lady Hŏ devoted her spare time to a variety of spiritual pursuits. For instance, she sought spiritual guidance from eminent Chinese Buddhist monks who visited Korea and went on pilgrimages to Buddhist monasteries spread across the Korean peninsula. After her husband's death, Lady Hŏ continued to live this life of leisure and privilege for twenty-one years.

On the fourth day of the third lunar month in 1324, Lady Hŏ passed away in a thatched-roof cottage located near her eldest son Kim Ryun's residence in the capital.[6] Her tomb epitaph claims that she moved closer to her son's residence to adhere to the classical ideal of a widow following her son.[7] News of her death soon reached the ears of the king, Ch'ungsuk, no doubt because Kim Ryun was the state councilor. Moved, we are told, by her chastity and righteousness (chŏrŭi), the king granted her the posthumous titles Great Lady of Pyŏnhan and Great Maser Chinhye. A month after her funeral, Lady Hŏ was buried a few paces away from the ancestral gravesite (sŏnyŏng) on Mount Taedŏk where her husband's grave was located. Lady Hŏ herself made the decision to be buried there. According to her tomb epitaph, the burial site was meant to reflect her "wish to remain obedient to her husband."[8]

Lady Hŏ's tomb epitaph contains some novel elements that one would not expect to see for widows from earlier periods. At critical moments after her husband's death, she repeatedly made conscious choices to set herself apart from her peers. She mourned her late husband in a graveside shed for three years, for instance, and in a cultural environment that considered remarriage for widows permissible, she publicly demonstrated her willingness to remain chaste for the rest of her life.[9] As advised in *The Book of Rites* (Li ji), as a widow, she also followed or showed obedience to (*chong*) her son.

Lady Hŏ is the earliest known Korean example of a widow who observed three full years of mourning in a mourning shed, but her actions were not remarkable only because she was a widow. The carefully choreographed ritual steps that she took to honor the dead would have been considered deviations from the usual conduct of mourning even for a male mourner.[10] In Koryŏ, the three-year mourning period was quite rare, because the state required officials to wear mourning for a much shorter period, one hundred days, so that government would operate smoothly.[11] If an official tried to extend the period of mourning beyond one hundred days without resigning first, he was banished from office.[12] The practice of wearing mourning for three years in a graveside mourning shed was deemed extraordinary and exemplary enough to be officially recorded and rewarded with a commemorative arch.[13]

But even as she deviated from the usual conduct of mourning, Lady Hŏ was apparently not willing to completely part ways with old customs of managing death in Koryŏ. As *sejok* families in Koryŏ were inclined to do, she commissioned the construction of a Buddhist monastery and relied on the professional services offered by the Buddhist clergy to seek postmortem salvation for her late husband and, eventually, herself and her children. Lady Hŏ did not insist on following the ritual guidelines of the Confucian classics because she "came under the spell of this canonical literature and interpreted it in the most literal sense."[14] Her motivations for deviating from established norms and customs originated elsewhere.

PEDIGREE

At the end of the preface to Lady Hŏ's funerary inscription, its author, Kim Kaemul, cites a passage from *The Book of Rites* stating that if descendants who maintain their ancestral temples and the altars to the spirits of the land and grain "praised their ancestors for good qualities which they did not possess, that was falsehood; if they did not take knowledge of the good qualities which they did possess, that showed their want of intelligence; if they knew them and did not transmit them (by their inscriptions), that showed a want of virtue:—these are three things of which a superior man should have been ashamed."[15] Kim cites this passage to make the point that the great lady's sons have no reason to be ashamed. They demonstrated their intelligence and virtue by asking Kim to transmit their mother's good qualities, which she did in fact possess, in a funerary inscription and its preface.[16]

What Kim Kaemul offers here is more than just customary praise for the great lady and her sons. Using the passage from *The Book of Rites*, he explicitly and purposefully couches the great lady's actions in classicist (*yu*), or Confucian, terms. This was meant to lend further credence to the funerary inscription's overall argument that Lady Hŏ was a paragon of classicist or Confucian virtue.

Kim strengthens his argument by using formulaic words of praise borrowed from Song dynasty eulogies. In his explanation of the great lady's virtues as a wife, for instance, he states that she capably served her husband, devoted herself to the management of food and weaving (i.e., household finances), and used what she knew of the ritual regulations (*chŏnjang*) to assist in the family rituals. After she became a mother, she instructed her children well before they had an understanding of their respective callings (*ŏp*)—some became monks and others high-ranking scholar-officials, as did Kim Ryun.[17] This emphasis on the lady's ability to manage the household and educate her children—that is, her ability to carry out "the Way of the wife" (*pudo*), to use Kim's own words—was a rhetorical strategy developed in eulogies and tomb epitaphs from the Song. As Beverly Bossler points out, unlike Tang eulogies, in which women are praised for their own literary talents, for Song eulogists, "the primary value of female intelligence and education rests in the education of their sons."[18]

A few twelfth-century Koryŏ tomb epitaphs display a similar emphasis on the Way of the wife, but none go to the extent of trying to demonstrate the wife's strict adherence to classical ideals as does that of Lady Hŏ.[19] What Lady Hŏ's epitaph does share with these earlier epitaphs is the tendency to associate the virtues of the wife with her pedigree. Women were praised, for instance, for their exquisite beauty, inherent disposition toward female propriety, and natural intelligence. This emphasis on pedigree was not, however, in keeping with the rhetorical trends in Song eulogies. In earlier Tang eulogies, filial piety, purity, and chastity were virtues associated with prestigious ancestry, but Song eulogies argue the exact opposite. There was, as Bossler claims, a "transition from the idea that status determines morality to the idea that morality determines status" in Song eulogies.[20] This transition was also accompanied by a change in the attitude toward wealth. Poverty and humble origins were no longer regarded simply as a source of embarrassment. Instead, it became possible to praise families who overcame these limitations as virtuous families.[21]

Lady Hŏ's tomb epitaph makes similar rhetorical moves, but this is not because she lacked wealth or pedigree. She was the daughter of Chancellor Hŏ Kong, a merit subject who posthumously received the great honor of being co-enshrined (*paehyang*) in the royal ancestral shrine with King Ch'ungnyŏl. The chancellor's father was the assistant royal secretary and Hallim academician transmitter Hŏ Su (passed literary examination in 1219), and Su's father was the vice minister of the office of guest affairs Hŏ Kyŏng (exam passed in 1176).[22] As Lady Hŏ's epitaph duly notes, they are all agnatic descendants of the assistant chancellor Hŏ Chae (1062–1144).[23] As for her maternal lineage, Lady Hŏ's epitaph notes that her maternal grandfather is the chancellery scholar Yun Kŭngmin (exam passed in 1248), a descendant of the renowned chancellor Yun Kwan (1040–1111) of the P'ap'yŏng Yun descent group. This list of successful exam takers and high-ranking officials on both sides of her family was probably enough to convince anyone of Lady Hŏ's pedigree, but her epitaph also makes note of the fact that King Ch'ungsŏn took her younger sister as his consort and her nephew as his son-in-law. For precisely this reason, Lady Hŏ's family, the Kong'am Hŏ, was included in King Ch'ungsŏn's 1308 list of "ministerial families" (*chaesang chi chong*), that is, families who could exchange brides with the royal family.[24]

Given her pedigree, Lady Hŏ and the author of her funerary inscription Kim Kaemul had little reason to worry about her great-family credentials. According to the tomb epitaph of another one of Lady Hŏ's younger sisters, written by Yi Chehyŏn, the Kongam Hŏ was, indeed, a "great family" (*taejok*).[25] This is so evident that Yi Chehyŏn does not bother to offer any further evidence or explanation. But in the same inscription, Yi does go to the trouble of explaining that the Kong'am Hŏ, despite being an extremely affluent family, knows how to avoid criticism by maintaining high moral standards. Lady Hŏ's funerary inscription similarly notes that her father, Hŏ Kong, "remained frugal of his own accord, and his virtuous reputation was thus utmost in the world."[26] Neither Kim Kaemul nor Yi Chehyŏn was particularly concerned about the great-family credentials of Lady Hŏ and her sister. There was no apparent need for them to emphasize the conformity of Lady Hŏ and her sister to classicist ideals as a way of compensating for their lack of pedigree, as did, for instance, the P'yŏngyang Cho. Kim and Yi emphasized the virtuous behavior of the two ladies and their father, Hŏ Kong, it would seem, for other reasons.

SAJOK

These reasons played a part in the meteoric rise to power of new social elements during the reign of King Ch'ungnyŏl and his son Ch'ungsŏn. With the support of King Ch'ungnyŏl and the Mongol imperial princess Qutlugh Kelmish, large numbers of men from nontraditional backgrounds began enjoying privileges once enjoyed almost exclusively by members of the regular bureaucracy. One important consequence of this division and the resulting tension, which eventually led to open conflict, was the transformation of the regular bureaucracy into a more self-conscious social group. In order to distinguish themselves more clearly from men of humble origin at court, members of the regular bureaucracy began to identify themselves with greater frequency as *sadaebu, sajok*, and *sarim* during this period.

This interest in the question of identity was a reaction to the separation of wealth from the ideals of bureaucratic service (*sa*). Little changed in this regard after the demise of King Ch'ungnyŏl. Wealth continued to be separated from these ideals, and concerns about the identity of the regular bureaucracy therefore deepened under the reign of his successor, King Ch'ungsŏn, and Ch'ungsŏn's successor, Ch'ungsuk. It was in this context that Kim Kaemul tellingly chose to write about the virtues of Lady Hŏ and her family.

It must be noted here that Kim Kaemul did not write about virtue and moral substance as an indifferent biographer. He was himself personally embroiled in the conflict between the men of humble origin at court and the regular bureaucracy. In 1309, a year after Ch'ungsŏn reassumed the throne, Kim was beaten with wooden staves and exiled to an island for refusing to grant a private request made by the director of the palace treasury (*naeburyŏng*; rank 3a) Kang Yung, a palace favorite.[27] Kang seems to have approached Kim because the latter served as an aide in the office of the royal seal (*chŏnbusi sŭng*). This important position gave Kim control over recruitment and promotions.[28] Kang's request, which existing sources do not specify, was therefore most likely an attempt to inappropriately secure a post or a promotion in the central government for a friend or a client. Kim denied Kang's request, however, and Kang, out of frustration, struck him. In response, Kim attacked Kang with some harsh words: "You were originally a slave. How dare you insult a *sajok*?"[29] Kang was, in fact, a eunuch and the grandson of a slave. Kim, in contrast, was the son of a chancellery scholar and grandson of a scholar-official. Although Kang outranked him, Kim was unwilling to show him any preferential treatment or respect. Kang retaliated by using his influence to have Kim punished and exiled to a remote island.

What made Kim Kaemul a *sajok*? The most obvious difference between Kim and Kang was their family backgrounds. Unlike Kang, who was the descendant of a slave, Kim was from a family that had provided officials to the central government for multiple generations. This, some Korean historians argue, was what made Kim Kaemul a *sajok*.[30] Although Kim had failed to pass the literary examination, his grandfather Kim Koeng had succeeded in 1213.[31] Little else is known about Kim Koeng, but he seems to have ended his career in the central government as a gentleman of the royal library (*pisŏrang*; rank 6b), a low-ranking but honorable post.[32] Kim Kaemul's father, Kim Hwŏn, also passed the literary examination and enjoyed the privilege of having his name recorded in the registry of officials (*sap'an*) in 1260.[33] Eight years later, Kim Hwŏn was appointed to the prestigious Hallim Academy. In 1271, he was promoted to director of the board of rites (*yebu nangjung*; rank 5a) for his role in suppressing the Sambyŏlch'o rebellion. Afterward, he received other reputable and prestigious posts (*ch'ŏngyojik*) such as attendant censor (*siŏsa*), grand master of remonstrance on the right, academician of the security council (*milchik haksa*), and chancellery scholar.[34]

There is, however, another important difference between the slave-eunuch Kang Yung and the *sajok* Kim Kaemul. Unlike Kang, Kim was not willing to use his power and authority to grant promotions for personal gain. Kim thus possessed something that Kang did not—moral integrity and hence virtue. In the preface to the funerary inscription for Kim, Yi Chehyŏn cites Kim's clash with Kang and showers him with these words of praise:

> By nature, the people of Koryŏ [*tongbang*] are very arrogant and do not try to nourish their life force [*ki*] through diligent learning. They therefore aim for opportunistic success to feed and clothe their wives and children. The mediocre person considers this proper, but this does not accord with the morality of the gentleman [*kunja*]. Even if they understand the benefit of righteousness and examine its source, those who do not take the right and wrong of others as their own honor and shame do not possess it [i.e., the morality of the gentleman]. Moreover, in this degenerate age, when officials [*sa*] who lack conviction seek good fortune and avoid misfortune, act like the master inside and act like a slave outside, if one can "move right in the center and yet return alone (to the

proper path)"³⁵ and remain unshakable, how could we not call this an honest official? Ugye Kim [Kaemul] comes close to this.³⁶

In support of this claim, that Kim was an honest official, Yi Chehyŏn cites a few more examples of his moral behavior. In exile, Kim experienced much difficulty but, Yi claims, casually accepted his fate. After he was released from exile, Kim continued to show no interest in pursuing fame and fortune. Instead, he spent the next fifteen years entertaining guests with wine and music and amusing himself with poetry. When King Ch'ungsuk forced Kim to return to work in 1325, "the forest of officials [sarim] hoped for a purge [of men from nontraditional backgrounds]," but Kim and the censorate were demeaned by a foreigner and palace favorite named Wang Samsŏk.³⁷ In desperate need of funds to support himself in Dadu, the king, under house arrest (1321–24), had begun to rely on the assistance of men from mercantile backgrounds, such as Son Ki and Wang Samsŏk.³⁸ They were granted access to high office as a reward for their vital services. Once again, Kim refused to return to work. He became ill and passed away shortly thereafter.

Kim Kaemul was respected by his peers, the sarim, because of his uncompromising and steadfast attitude toward corruption and official misconduct. Kim's father, Kim Hwŏn, was no different. According to his tomb epitaph, written by the retired royal secretary Yi Chin, Yi Chehyŏn's father (exam passed in 1279), Kim Hwŏn "was by nature morally strict [kyŏnggye] and honest and upright [ch'ŏngnyŏm]—if there was someone avaricious, mean, sycophantic, and dishonest in public office, he made strenuous efforts to remove this person from office."³⁹ Claims like this were made frequently during the fourteenth century. Was this, as scholars argue, a reflection of the growing influence of Neo-Confucian or nature-and-principle learning (sŏngnihak) in Korea? Was it their ideological conversion to this form of learning that made Kim and his father sajok, or new scholar-officials?⁴⁰

Evidence suggests otherwise. As Yi Chin notes in his funerary inscription, Kim Hwŏn, who styled himself "Layman Tunch'on" and "Layman Chokhŏn," was a devout Buddhist. The layman often recited Buddhist scriptures and sometimes even experienced the taste of meditation (sŏnmi).⁴¹ Yi Chin, also a sajok, considered this ideal. As Yi himself puts it, "It can be said that he left nothing to be desired." Yi did not make this bold declaration because Kim lived up to the expectations of a new social group. Kim's and Yi's respect for Buddhism and a family's ability to serve in reputable and prestigious posts (*ch'ŏngyojik*) for successive generations shows that they aspired to the old aristocratic ideals of the *sejok*.⁴²

If so, then their emphasis on being honest and upright was clearly not meant to be a rejection of old *sejok* ideals and customs. It was meant to be a rejection of people like Kang Yung and, more importantly, their lack of commitment to the ideals of bureaucratic service. For members of Koryŏ's regular bureaucracy under Mongol rule, this rejection took the form of a conscientious choice. This choice is articulated eloquently in Yi Chehyŏn's funerary inscription for Kim Kaemul:

> What can [be obtained through effort] is learning and [moral] behavior.
> What cannot [be obtained through effort] is status and old age.
> Only after you become a gentleman, then obtain what can [be obtained through effort] and work hard at it.
> Abandon that which cannot [be obtained through effort] and leave it up to Heaven.
> Ah—how could Ugye not feel content?⁴³

For affluent *sejok* families like the Kongam Hŏ, the need to choose either what can be obtained through effort or what cannot be obtained through effort was even more urgent, for this choice would place them on the side of either the regular bureaucracy or its enemies.

MINISTERIAL FAMILIES

In theory, Lady Hŏ's family was in a unique position to represent the regular bureaucracy, for the Kongam Hŏ had been officially named a ministerial family, allowed to exchange brides with the royal Wang clan, by King Ch'ungsŏn in 1308. But the reality of the family's status was more complicated. The inclusion of the Kongam Hŏ in Ch'ungsŏn's list was not simply recognition of its indisputably exalted status. It is also possible that the announcement of the list of ministerial families was made for exactly the opposite reason: to put to rest any doubts—and doubts there were—about their status as the most respected members of the regular bureaucracy.⁴⁴ Simply put, the list was an attempt to address doubts raised by the possibility that Ch'ungsŏn's in-laws were enemies of the regular bureaucracy.

This possibility, however, is precisely what Ch'ungsŏn's list of ministerial families reveals when the families included in the list are examined closely. The list contains not only well-known *sejok* families with a long history of producing ministers and queen consorts such as the Kyŏngwŏn Yi, Ansan Kim, and Chŏngan Im but also parvenu families like the P'yŏngyang Cho and relatively new arrivals to the ministerial class such as the Kongam Hŏ and P'yŏnggang Ch'ae. Although the Kongam Hŏ had produced officials for several generations, few had risen to ministerial status. According to scholarly consensus, it was Lady Hŏ's father, Hŏ Kong, who made it possible for the Kongam Hŏ to be regarded an equal to the Kyŏngwŏn Yi, a family that had produced no less than ten queen consorts and five kings.[45] The P'yŏnggang Ch'ae similarly rose to prominence at a relatively late date, making its entry into the ministerial class when Ch'ae Songnyŏn earned the trust of the military leader Ch'oe Ch'unghŏn and rose to the rank of assistant chancellor.[46]

By putting these families on the same list and naming them ministerial families, Ch'ungsŏn could *raise* the status of the new arrivals to the ministerial class and make them equals of prominent *sejok* families like the Kyŏngwŏn Yi. But why was this necessary? The answer can be found in the political ordeals of Ch'ungsŏn and his return to the Koryŏ throne in 1308. To counterbalance the power of the men who formed his father's inner circle at the turn of the century—most notably, O Cham (exam passed in 1279), Song Pun, his son Song Lin, Lin's cousin Song Pangyŏng, Pangyŏng's brother-in-law Wang Yuso, Wang's follower Sŏk Chu (a man of unknown origin), and Sŏk's sons—Ch'ungsŏn needed his own network of supporters.[47] He initially sought supporters among the regular bureaucracy, but the effort soon expanded to include affluent and powerful officials. In building his own network of supporters, Ch'ungsŏn relied on an old strategy—forging alliances through marriage.

Before his marriage to the imperial princess Buddhaśrī in 1296, Ch'ungsŏn had already taken three Koryŏ consorts for precisely this purpose. First, in 1289, shortly after his capping ceremony, he took the daughter of a royal clansman as his consort.[48] This was far from extraordinary. Consanguineous marriage was a common tradition among royal clan members in Koryŏ.[49] For instance, Ch'ungsŏn's father and grandfather had also taken consorts of royal blood. This was a matter of, among other things, prestige.

The following year (1290), Ch'ungsŏn took the daughter of Hong Mun'gye as his second consort.[50] Although Hong was the scion of a preeminent family of officials (*ŭigwan kapchok*), the choice of his daughter was not without potential problems.[51] Hong had been promoted to assistant transmitter on the right (*chwabu sŭngsŏn*) after playing a key role in the murder of his brother-in-law Im Yumu in 1270, but he retired from politics at the young age of twenty-nine in 1271. According to his biography in the *History of Koryŏ*, Hong decided to retire because he was disillusioned with the broken politics of the time. He was promoted to assistant royal secretary—a *chaech'u* post—the very next year but declined the promotion. Despite this conscious effort to distance himself from court politics, Hong later found himself in serious trouble. In the winter of 1288, he was tortured and exiled by the Mongol imperial princess Qutlugh Kelmish (Ch'ungnyŏl's principal consort) for refusing to send his daughter to Dadu as tribute.[52] Hong was released from exile a few months later. The efforts of his cousin, the assistant chancellor Hong Chabŏn, who had replaced Hong Mun'gye as assistant transmitter on the right in 1271, were critical to securing his release. A year after this unfortunate incident, one of his younger daughters was chosen as Ch'ungsŏn's second consort. Existing sources do not specify the reasons for this choice, but the exalted status of Hong's family, the Tangsŏng Hong, no doubt was an important factor. It was, in fact, for precisely this reason that Im Yŏn (Im Yumu's father), who "rose from humble origins" (*p'yŏngmi i ki*), implored Hong to become his son-in-law.[53]

The respect that Hong received from his peers was not, however, simply a product of his family's reputation. It was something Hong himself had to earn. There is evidence to suggest that his decision to withdraw from the realm of court politics was an extension of his effort to restore his and his family's reputation. When Hong politely declined the promotion to assistant royal secretary in 1272, King Ch'ungnyŏl issued a royal order to convince him to reconsider. In the order, Ch'ungnyŏl tellingly reassured Hong that his marriage to Im's daughter was not a character flaw: "You came from a scholarly family [*haksaga*] and joined the ranks of generals. You formed marital ties with a 'gate of power' [*kwŏnmun*], but how could this be your true intent? You destroyed your own kin in the name of a higher purpose—this is the perfection of loyalty and high moral principles. You completely put people's doubts to rest with a single stoke of your sword."[54] In other words, Hong, the scion of a scholarly family, had married into a "gate of power," and people apparently suspected that he did so with the intention of seeking fame and fortune. Hong allayed these suspicions by not only killing his own kin but also declining the opportunity to join the *chaech'u*. It was this gesture of trying to preserve his and his family's honor that made Hong's daughter an ideal bride for the heir apparent Ch'ungsŏn.

In 1292, Ch'ungsŏn took yet another consort.[55] Despite Cho In'gyu's humble origins as a Mongolian interpreter, his daughter was chosen as the heir apparent's third consort because Cho In'gyu offered something other than family prestige. What was most attractive about Cho was the fact that he was favored by the imperial princess Qutlugh Kelmish, her father, Qubilai, and the Mongol court. Cho's close relationship with the Mongols facilitated his promotion from great general (1278) to assistant chancellor (1288) in the short span of ten years. Just two years before his daughter was chosen as Ch'ungsŏn's third bride, Cho In'gyu was also appointed *darughachi* of the princely appanage of Koryŏ by the Mongol Yuan court.

In 1296, Ch'ungsŏn wed Buddhaśrī and became an imperial son-in-law. Three years later, he ascended the throne but was forced to abdicate that very same year (discussed in chapter 4). While he was away in China serving in the great khan's *keshig*, Ch'ungnyŏl and his favorites made repeated attempts to marry Buddhaśrī off to someone else.[56] The imperial princess's remarriage would make it difficult, if not impossible, for Ch'ungsŏn to legitimately claim the Koryŏ throne. But the plan was foiled once (in 1303) by the great khan Temür and again (in 1306) by the grand councilor on the right Harghasun and the assistant chancellor Ch'oe Yuŏm, Ch'ungsŏn's supporter from Koryŏ. A radical restructuring of power relations within the Mongol court, accomplished after a bloody succession struggle, had worked in Ch'ungsŏn's favor.[57] In 1307, with the support of the new khan and his heir apparent, Ch'ungsŏn carried out a purge of his father's favorites. King Ch'ungnyŏl became ill shortly thereafter and passed away in 1308. Ch'ungsŏn succeeded him as the king of Koryŏ.

Two months after his enthronement, the triumphant Ch'ungsŏn took the daughter of the late chancellor Hŏ Kong as his consort. She was the widow of a royal clansman named Wang Hyŏn.[58] A few weeks later, on December 7, the new king announced that, in keeping with the divine edict of Qubilai, the royal family would no longer practice consanguineous marriage. Instead, he encouraged the royal Wang clan to exchange brides with families with a history of producing successive generations of ministers. The king specifically named fifteen ministerial families as ideal partners: the family of Kim Hon and Wŏnjong's queen consort Chŏngsun, the Ŏnyang Kim (Kim Pyŏn's family), Chŏngan Im, Kyŏngwŏn Yi, Ansan Kim, Ch'ŏrwŏn Ch'oe, Haeju Ch'oe, Kongam Hŏ (Lady Hŏ's family), P'yŏnggang Ch'ae, Ch'ŏngju Yi, Tangsŏng Hong, Hwangnyŏ Min (Min Sap'yŏng's family), Hwangch'ŏn Cho, P'ap'yŏng Yun, and P'yŏngyang Cho. Four of these families—the Ŏnyang Kim, Tangsŏng Hong, P'yŏngyang Cho, and Kongam Hŏ—had affinal ties with Ch'ungsŏn himself.

In addition to being the king's in-laws, these four families also had a few other important things in common. First, they were all relatively recent additions to the ministerial class. They were also extremely affluent with affinal relations to less respectable families. Hong Mun'gye married Im Yŏn's daughter, Hŏ Kong's son Hŏ Kwan married the daughter of the corrupt official and palace favorite Song Pun, and Cho In'gyu's daughter married the former slave Pak Kyŏngnyang.[59] The heads of these families—Hŏ Kong and Cho In'gyu—also amassed large fortunes as palace and inner-palace favorites. Ch'ungsŏn's in-laws thus had blemished credentials as members of the regular bureaucracy. In fact, the regular bureaucracy treated men like Cho In'gyu and Hŏ Kong as corrupt officials and therefore enemies.[60] The inclusion of their families on Ch'ungsŏn's list of ministerial families was meant in part to shield them from further criticism.

Hong Mun'gye and Hŏ Kong and their families were aware, however, that their inclusion on King Ch'ungsŏn's list did not necessarily shield them from criticism and suspicions of corruption. It did not guarantee their status as the most respected members of the regular bureaucracy. This is one reason Hong Mun'gye deemed it necessary to continue to demonstrate his commitment to the ideals of bureaucratic service rather than enjoy fame and fortune. Furthermore, Hong's commitment was not an attempt to establish his family, the Tangsŏng Hong, as a member of a new, ideologically driven social group—the so-called new scholar-officials. Hong Mun'gye's tomb epitaph makes it clear that he respected old *sejok* ideals. Like Kim Hwŏn and Hŏ Kong, Hong Mun'gye consciously distanced himself from fame and fortune, but he still faithfully "lit incense" before the Buddha, enjoyed fine music and food in retirement, and relied on divination to find a geomantically ideal spot near the capital for his final resting place.[61] These were costly practices reserved for *sejok* families. Apparently, in the opinion of a *sajok* or *sadaebu* like Yi Chin, it was still considered appropriate for someone as honest and upright as Hong to be remembered this way in death.

A BREAK WITH TRADITION

Hong was not alone in this regard. Assistant Chancellor Ch'ae Mo similarly devoted the last thirteen years of his life to Buddhist practices, but Min Chi, the author of his tomb epitaph, claims: "What man born in this world does not desire [to enjoy] wealth before his demise? But among those who end their lives in prosperity, rare are those who are without flaws. In [Ch'ae,] this is what I see."[62] Min Chi was right. It was only natural for high-ranking officials like Ch'ae Mo to want to enjoy costly *sejok* customs, such as preparing for death with the help of Buddhism. However, like the tomb epitaphs for Lady Hŏ and Hong Mun'gye, Ch'ae's tomb epitaph reveals that wealth had become an issue that central officials and their families had to reckon with in the early half of the fourteenth century.

The problematization of wealth can also be witnessed in the tomb epitaph for Kim Ryun's father-in-law Ch'oe Sŏ. Ch'oe devoted the last decade of his life to Buddhist practices and chanting the Diamond Sutra, but he had taken "being upright and just as his duty since he first entered service."[63] The tomb epitaph that Yi Chehyŏn prepared for Ch'oe's daughter, that is, Kim Ryun's wife, paints a similar image. Although her husband joined the ministerial ranks, the lady never asked for personal favors for her relatives. How, Yi thus claims, could Kim Ryun have maintained his honest virtue (ch'ŏngdŏk) and the respect he received from his peers without the assistance (naejo) of his wife at home?[64] Her commitment to helping her husband live up to the ideals of bureaucratic service did not, however, prevent Lady Ch'oe from enjoying *sejok* privileges in her afterlife. She was honored with a funerary inscription written by a renowned scholar-official and granted a posthumous title, Great Lady of Pyŏnhan, which had belonged to her mother-in-law, Lady Hŏ. Lady Ch'oe was also able to enjoy the greatest *sejok* privilege of all: she was buried next to her in-laws and her husband at their private memorial monastery Kamŭng-sa. But by the mid-fourteenth century, it had become necessary to take a clear stance on wealth before someone could enjoy these *sejok* privileges.

The tomb epitaphs of high-ranking officials from the early fourteenth century thus bear witness to an emerging trend. Affluent families such as the Haeju Ch'oe (Ch'oe Sŏ's family) and Kongam Hŏ began to ironically emphasize their ability to withstand the temptations of wealth. This was often done by emphasizing one's moral character and, more specifically, the virtues of being honest and upright in tomb epitaphs. As long as this specific kind of integrity—a moral indifference to wealth—was maintained, the affluent Koryŏ elite could still enjoy costly *sejok* customs.

Some central officials, however, chose to follow a different path. Although they similarly tried to show their commitment to the ideals of bureaucratic service and the virtues of being honest and upright, a small but growing number of central officials began to abandon cherished *sejok* customs of managing death. That is to say, they abandoned Buddhism. A good example of someone who took this radical approach is State Councilor Ch'oe Mundo.

To appreciate the radical and perhaps even inapposite nature of Ch'oe Mundo's decision to abandon Buddhism, one must take into account the ways in which his father, Ch'oe Sŏngji, chose to manage death. Assistant Chancellor Ch'oe Sŏngji relied heavily on Buddhist methods. He gave a handsome endowment to the grand Sŏn monastery Sŏnwŏn-sa on Kanghwa Island and had the renowned scholar-official Ch'oe Hae commemorate the occasion with a stele inscription. With the interest generated from the endowment, Sŏnwŏn-sa was expected to hold vegetarian feasts every year on the anniversary of his wife Lady Kim's death. As the daughter of Layman Tunch'on (i.e., Kim Hwŏn), Lady Kim undoubtedly expected her death to be managed this way. Her husband's reliance on Buddhist methods did not stop there. For his parents, the assistant chancellor went so far as to finance the construction of a memorial monastery named Ch'ŏnhwa-sŏnsa.

Ch'oe Mundo, also known by his style name Ch'unhŏn, responded to the deaths of his devout Buddhist parents in a remarkably different way. According to his tomb epitaph, prepared by Yi Chehyŏn, Ch'unhŏn built not a memorial monastery but a family shrine (*kamyo*) and personally observed three years of mourning for both parents.[65]

The preface to his funerary inscription contains some clues as to why Ch'unhŏn chose to deviate from *sejok* customs, customs that his parents had been inclined to trust. After a brief introduction to the circumstances that led to the writing of the funerary inscription, the preface makes the unusual rhetorical move of directing the reader's attention to the title of the inscription, "Funerary Inscription for Senior Scholar Ch'unhŏn" (Ch'unhŏn sŏnsaeng myomyŏng). The preface then introduces an exchange between its author, Yi Chehyŏn, and an unnamed interlocutor who asks Yi, "In his youth, Ch'unhŏn was a military official, and he is six years younger than you, but you still refer to him as 'senior scholar' [*sŏnsaeng*]—how can you explain this?" The rest of the preface is a response to this question.

Yi Chehyŏn begins his response with Ch'unhŏn's illustrious genealogy and duly notes that Ch'unhŏn's father, Ch'oe Sŏngji, was the recipient of the noble title Lord of Kwangyang. He also carefully observes that the lord's father, Piil, retired as assistant chancellor and academician (of the security council?),[66] Piil's father, U, retired as vice minister of the board of personnel and drafter of proclamations (Hallim Academy scholar),[67] and Ch'unhŏn's maternal grandfather, Kim Hwŏn, retired as assistant chancellor and headmaster of the Royal Confucian Academy. Yi underscores these titles in order to advance a simple but important claim. Ch'unhŏn, he writes, "is the descendant of cultured officials [*yua chinsin*]." King Ch'ungsŏn was willing to entrust the Lord of Kwangyang with the important task of managing the secrets of the state and the power of recruitment and promotions for twenty years precisely because he was a cultured official and the descendant of a long line of cultured officials.

It is, of course, not uncommon for tomb epitaphs to list ancestors and their titles as a way of emphasizing the *sejok* credentials of the deceased, but the inclusion of this information in Ch'unhŏn's tomb epitaph also serves a different purpose: Ch'unhŏn needed to distinguish himself from the enemies of the regular bureaucracy who showed no commitment to bureaucratic ideals. Although Ch'unhŏn held high-ranking posts in the central government and gained control over recruitment and promotions, he did so without having first passed the literary examination and serving in provincial posts, as his father had.[68] This was a source of shame and concern for his illustrious *sejok* and *sajok* family, for Ch'unhŏn had failed to live up to bureaucratic ideals.[69]

Yi Chehyŏn, a family friend, similarly showed concern about Ch'unhŏn's *sajok* credentials. After listing Ch'unhŏn's ancestors and their titles, Yi mentions that Ch'unhŏn had served as a member of the khan's *keshig* in Dadu.[70] There, he learned Mongolian and fraternized with those who wore exquisite silk and hats made of bird feathers and carried arrow sheaths made of leather. Naturally, Ch'unhŏn "should have been rich and arrogant," to use Yi's words. But, Yi claims, Ch'unhŏn defied these expectations. He would leave for work with bow and sword in hand, but back at home, he would devote his spare time to reading the writings of Zhou Dunyi, Cheng Yi, Cheng Hao, and Zhu Xi late into the night. Moreover, as the superintendent of the board of punishment, Ch'unhŏn protected the interests of the regular bureaucracy by keeping palace favorites (*p'yehaeng*) in check.[71] According to Yi, all the officials in the regular bureaucracy therefore rejoiced when he was promoted to state councilor.[72]

For these and other reasons, Yi tells his unnamed interlocutor that he cannot but refer to the younger Ch'unhŏn as "senior scholar" (*sŏnsaeng*). Yi's short but revealing funerary inscription for Ch'unhŏn belies his true feelings about the late state councilor:

There are many in the world
who are *yu* but not really a *yu*.
The only person who is not a *yu* but is really a *yu*
is our Ch'unhŏn.

Yi wants to convince the readers of this inscription that the deceased is an *exceptional* figure who truly stood for the interests of the regular bureaucracy. Although he never passed the literary examination and began his career as a military official, Ch'unhŏn still deserved to be called a *yu* ("classicist" or "Confucian scholar") and hence a *sajok* because he showed fondness for Cheng-Zhu learning and defended the integrity of the regular bureaucracy against the interests of palace favorites. But Yi's argument is clearly contrived. Had Ch'unhŏn followed the conventional career path for *sajok*, Yi would not have had to go to the trouble of repeatedly defending him against potential criticism in the first place. For instance, this would have been unnecessary for someone such as Yi, who passed the literary examination in 1301.

Ch'unhŏn's decision to mourn his parents for three years and build a family shrine instead of a Buddhist memorial monastery should be understood as an extension of these concerns about his *sajok* credentials. Ch'unhŏn did not, in other words, deviate from Buddhist customs because of his ideological conversion to Cheng-Zhu learning.[73] He did so because both he and his father needed to demonstrate their commitment to *sajok* ideals. Ch'unhŏn, in fact, was not the only one in his family with blemished *sajok* credentials. His father, Ch'oe Sŏngji, was also regarded by his peers as someone who had failed not only to withstand the temptations of wealth but also to demonstrate his commitment to bureaucratic ideals such as loyalty.

After Ch'ungsŏn purged Wang Yuso and the other Koryŏ officials who opposed him in 1307, Ch'oe Sŏngji and a fellow Koryŏ official named Kwŏn Han'gong were granted control over recruitment and promotions. Both Kwŏn and Ch'oe were granted this privilege, which had belonged to the Personnel Authority, because they had continued to faithfully serve Ch'ungsŏn in Dadu.[74] They were part of Ch'ungsŏn's Dadu-based inner circle who demonstrated their political worth by helping the deposed king seat the Mongol prince Qaishan on the imperial throne.[75]

To the great dismay of the other officials who served Ch'ungsŏn in Dadu, Kwŏn and Ch'oe showed little interest in returning to Koryŏ. Kwŏn and Ch'oe feared, and rightly so, that their return to Koryŏ would entail the loss of control over recruitment and promotions and hence their ability to collect bribes—bribes that surely allowed Ch'oe to afford the generous endowments he made to Sŏnwŏn-sa and the construction of Ch'ŏnhwa-sŏnsa.[76] Officials in Koryŏ, far removed from the center of real power, were not pleased with this arrangement. The royal secretaries Kim Sim and Yi Saon were the first to take action against Kwŏn, Ch'oe, and the palace favorite Pak

Kyŏngnyang. With the help of a eunuch in the household administration of the empress dowager (C. *huizhengyuan*), Kim and Yi were able to convince the director of the household administration to imprison Kwŏn, Ch'oe, and Pak.⁷⁷ Ch'ungsŏn immediately notified the empress dowager, Targi (d. 1322), of what had happened. She released the prisoners and also ordered punishment and exile for Kim and Yi.⁷⁸

Lest Ch'ungsŏn and other imperial clansmen form political cliques in Dadu, the great khan Ayurbarwada, who ascended the throne in 1311, continued to pressure Ch'ungsŏn to return to Koryŏ.⁷⁹ But, rather than return, Ch'ungsŏn chose to nominally seat his son To (temple name Ch'ungsuk) on the Koryŏ throne and retire in 1313.⁸⁰ To prevent the new king To from consolidating his position in Koryŏ, Ch'ungsŏn also named his nephew Wang Ko the heir apparent.⁸¹ Through this unconventional arrangement, Ch'ungsŏn and his Dadu-based network of supporters—Ch'oe Sŏngji included—were able to exert influence on Koryŏ from afar until the death of Ayurbarwada in the spring of 1320.⁸² The great khan's death was followed by political turmoil at court in Dadu. With the support of the empress dowager, the grand councilor on the right Temüder (d. 1322) carried out a purge of his enemies. Supporters of the new khan Shidebala also removed their enemies from court.⁸³ Seemingly as part of this purge, Ch'ungsŏn was exiled to Turfan (Xigaze in present-day Tibet) on January 10, 1321.⁸⁴ The personnel authority was restored in Koryŏ soon thereafter.⁸⁵

No doubt aware of this shift in the political winds, Ch'oe Sŏngji chose not to follow the retired king into exile. He consequently became an object of ridicule.⁸⁶ In the eyes of his peers in the regular bureaucracy, Ch'oe was not only corrupt but also disloyal. He therefore looked for opportunities to redeem himself. Not long after Ch'ungsŏn was exiled, on May 29, 1321, the new Koryŏ king To was also summoned to Dadu and placed under house arrest.⁸⁷ Taking advantage of the king's precarious status, Kwŏn Han'gong, Cho Chŏk, Ch'ae Hongch'ŏl, Ch'ae Hajung (Ch'ae Hongch'ŏl's son), and others attempted to seat his rival the Sim Prince Wang Ko on the throne in 1322.⁸⁸ Their plan was to submit a petition ratified by the Koryŏ bureaucracy to the Yuan court, but surveillance officials led by the vice censor-in-chief (*kamch'al chibŭi*) Yun Sŏnjwa and other prominent officials, such as Kim Ryun—that is to say, the regular bureaucracy—refused to sign the petition.⁸⁹ As Yi Chehyŏn made sure to note in his preface to Ch'oe Sŏngji's funerary inscription, Ch'oe decided to side with the regular bureaucracy on this issue and refused to sign another petition prepared by the supporters of the Sim Prince Wang Ko.⁹⁰

This second petition was related to an attempt to deprive Koryŏ of its sovereignty. In the first lunar month of 1323, Yu Ch'ŏngsin and O Cham approached the Yuan court about the possibility of turning Koryŏ into a branch secretariat.[91] Ch'oe Sŏngji helped Yi Chehyŏn put an end to this discussion in Koryŏ.[92] Ch'oe and Yi also sent a letter to the grand councilor on the left Baizhu and requested that the Yuan court allow Ch'ungsŏn to be released from exile.[93] Although the exile continued, Baizhu gave the order to move Ch'ungsŏn from the more remote Xigaze (C. Sasijie) to the closer Amdo (C. Duosima).[94]

A few months later, in September, Baizhu and the great khan Shidebala were assassinated, and Yesün Temür—the son of Prince Gammala and hence Ch'ungsŏn's brother-in-law—was enthroned as the new great khan. This drastically altered Koryŏ-Yuan relations. Ch'ungsuk was allowed to return to Koryŏ. The retired king Ch'ungsŏn was also released from exile. But father and son soon found themselves in conflict once again. Ch'ungsuk tried to punish the supporters of Wang Ko for trying to undercut his authority, but Ch'ungsŏn prevented him from doing so.[95] Perhaps because he had made the fateful choice to reject Wang Ko, Ch'oe Sŏngji immediately decided to retire. But this may have been unnecessary, for Ch'ungsŏn passed away the very next year in 1325.

For Ch'oe Sŏngji, retirement was not a time for atonement, regret, or critical self-reflection. It was a time to indulge in the pleasures of the *sejok* elite. He spent this time endowing Buddhist monasteries and preparing for death. Yi Chehyŏn writes in his preface to Ch'oe's funerary inscription that the last six years of the Lord of Kwangyang's life also consisted of entertaining guests with lofty conversations and delightful songs sung by a talented female entertainer. This, however, was not time idled away. Ch'oe, Yi Chehyŏn claims, indulged in *sejok* pleasures in order to avoid politics. As with Hong Mun'gye, this was proof of the lord's virtue. Indeed, as Yi writes in his inscription: "In office, he followed the rites; in retirement, he was righteous."[96]

Despite Yi's efforts to paint a positive image of the lord and his son, there was no way to hide their blemished credentials as *sajok*. In 1325, the need to demonstrate these credentials became evident. That year, five months after Ch'ungsŏn's death, King Ch'ungsuk announced an edict.[97] It tried to address many familiar issues such as the illegal appropriation of land and labor by powerful families (*kwŏnse chi ka*), the corruption of the recruitment and promotion system, and the need to properly reward merit subjects. What the edict addressed, then, were the concerns of the regular bureaucracy.

Having spent the last few years struggling to defend himself against attempts to replace him with Wang Ko, Ch'ungsuk wanted, above all else, a healthy bureaucracy that upheld *sajok* ideals such as loyalty and filial piety. For precisely this reason, as part of the edict, Ch'ungsuk announced his intention to reward filial sons and chaste wives with commemorative arches.[98] He also announced his intention to reward those who followed his father to Turfan (Xigaze in present-day Tibet).[99] Ch'ungsuk's edict thus made it abundantly clear that opportunistic officials like Ch'oe Sŏngji had committed a grave political mistake. It was under these conditions that Ch'oe Mundo, certainly with his father's approval, made the novel choice to deviate from *sejok* and hence Buddhist customs.

THE MUSONG YUN

Few, however, followed Ch'oe Mundo's example. But the regular bureaucracy showed growing interest in taking "alternative" classicist methods of managing death as an exceptionally important way of demonstrating filial piety. Evidence of this can be found at the end of Ch'ungsuk's reign. Two months after the king's death on the 24th day of the third lunar month (May 3rd) in 1339, the royal inspector's office publicly announced a set of prohibition orders (*kŭmnyŏng*) that gave voice to the concerns of the regular bureaucracy.[100] Koryŏ was without a sovereign, as Ch'ungsuk had passed away and his son Ch'unghye's efforts to succeed his father were hampered by the all-powerful chancellor on the right Bayan of the Merkid (d. 1340) and the Sim Prince Wang Ko.[101] The Koryŏ court was also thrown into disarray as Ch'unghye carried out a purge of officials close to Wang Ko and the former king Ch'ungsuk (e.g., the former station clerk Sin Ch'ŏng).[102]

At this moment of political crisis, the royal inspector's office led the effort to restore public morality. Using King Ch'ungsuk's funeral and the issue of proper ritual decorum as an excuse, the royal inspector's office announced measures that addressed a broad spectrum of issues related to improper or immoral behavior. Among the many groups targeted for reform were corrupt Buddhist abbots, shamans who performed sacrifices for *sadaebu* families, monks who collected alms in exchange for prayers for the dead, housewives who formed pallbearers societies (*hyangdo*), and *sadaebu* who mourned their parents for just three days or had their slaves wear mourning for three years in a graveside shed in their stead.

Although there is no evidence that these orders were enforced, they do reveal the regular bureaucracy's concerns about its identity, which is couched primarily in ritual and moral terms. As Koryŏ entered the second half of the fourteenth century, a small number of officials began to show their commitment to the *sajok* ideals articulated in the orders. In 1355, a young scholar named Chŏng Mongju, for instance, built a graveside shed and began the formal mourning process for his late father, which he personally observed for three full years. King Kongmin rewarded Chŏng's exemplary display of filial piety with a commemorative arch.[103] In 1356, the master of remonstrance and auxiliary academician of the security council (*chik chehak*) Chŏng Sado similarly began the ritual process of mourning his late mother for three years in a graveside shed.[104] He was rewarded with a noble title.

The timing of these exemplary acts of filial piety was critical. On January 22, 1356, the king abolished the custom of three-year graveside mourning.[105] He made this decision in response to a dispute between Assistant State Councilor Kim Yong and Assistant Chancellor Kim Po. Kim Po was a palace favorite who earned the king's trust by attending the king during his stay in Dadu before his enthronement.[106] Kim Yong tried to keep Kim Po, who just lost his mother, away from court by submitting a false edict to the privy council mandating that officials mourn their parents for three years. King Kongmin discovered Kim Yong's subterfuge and had him exiled to Cheju Island.[107] The king also abolished the custom of three-year graveside mourning because of this incident. However, two years later, in 1357, the remonstrance official Yi Saek recommended that the custom be revived. The king followed Yi's recommendation, hence the rewards granted to Chŏng Mongju and Chŏng Sado.[108]

Chŏng Mongju was exemplary in other ways as well. He is known to have promoted the use of Zhu Xi's ritual manual *Family Rituals* and the construction of family shrines in place of memorial monasteries.[109] Although few in number, there were others willing to follow Chŏng's example. Assistant Chancellor Yun T'aek and his family, the Musong Yun, are known to have built a family shrine. The decision to deviate from older and much-respected Buddhist methods of managing death was, according to his funerary inscription and preface, prepared by Yi Saek, made by the assistant chancellor himself. For his mother, Lady Kim of Chillyegun, Yun built an "offering hut" (*cheryŏ*) just south of her grave for performing seasonal sacrifices and, presumably, before that, the three-year mourning ritual.[110] Because he became ill and passed away on his way to the offering hut, the family decided to bury him next to the offering hut south of his mother's grave. Lest his children and grandchildren deviate from his example, Yun is said to have offered the following final words to his family on his deathbed:

> Our Chŏnghŏn [i.e., my grandfather] had risen from humble origins, but he had acquired a reputation for being honest and loyal. My father unfortunately passed at a young age, and, day and night, I feared I would make a mistake and not be able to continue [Chŏnghŏn's] will. I received undeserved support and salary from the king. I am also more than eighty years old. All of this is [the product] of the hidden virtue of my ancestors and the legacy of Chŏnghŏn. All of you should guard this [legacy] and not let it decline. When I die, do not have scruples about not using Buddhist customs. Do not be wasteful.[111]

Yun's eldest son, Kusaeng, honored this final wish. Instead of endowing or building a memorial monastery, he converted the graveside hut built by his father into a family shrine, and there, in keeping with the instructions found in Zhu Xi's *Family Rituals*, he performed seasonal and annual sacrifices for his father and ancestors.[112]

Why did the Musong Yun abandon Buddhism? Yun T'aek is known to have reminded King Kongmin of the need to abandon his pursuit of the immoral teachings of Buddhism and to respect, instead, the Way of Confucius.[113] In 1390, when King Kongyang attempted to grant the monk Ch'anyŏng the title Royal Preceptor, Yun T'aek's grandson Yun Sojong similarly composed a vehement critique of Buddhism and argued against this appointment in a memorial to the throne.[114] This seems to imply that the Musong Yun were opposed to Buddhism on ideological grounds.

There is, however, good reason to question this hasty conclusion. As policy adviser on the left (*chwa sangsi*), Yun Sojong's primary duty was to remonstrate with the king for misconduct or wrongdoing. Yun T'aek, as academician of the security council, also saw himself as serving a similar duty.[115] Both T'aek and his grandson were responsible for keeping the king's power in check and looking out for the interests of the regular bureaucracy. Yun T'aek's criticism of Buddhism was not so much the expression of his anti-Buddhist sentiment as his attempt to prevent the king from straying from the ambitious reforms he had launched at the beginning of his reign. Led by the newly appointed acting prime minister (*sŏp-chŏngsŭng*) Yi Chehyŏn, these reforms were primarily meant to restore power to the regular bureaucracy, but the king began to devote much of his attention to the royal preceptor T'aego Pou, whose suggestion to move the capital to the southern capital (present-day Seoul) posed a serious threat to the capital-based bureaucratic elite.[116] According to his funerary inscription, Yun T'aek's memorials to the throne specifically targeted these political gestures made by Pou and the king's preference for the Buddhist notion of emptiness over lessons from *The Extended Meaning of the Great Learning* (Daxue yanyi), a text that emphasizes the need for rulers to cultivate themselves before they attempt to rule over their subjects.[117]

Similarly, Yun Sojong's critical attitude toward Buddhism stems largely from his concerns about the king's attempt to appoint Pou's disciple Ch'anyŏng as royal preceptor. Although little is known about the monk Ch'anyŏng, his stupa inscription lists, among others, Prime Minister Hong Yŏngt'ong, Chancellor Yi Saek, and Supervisor of Kaesŏng U Inyŏl as his devoted lay followers.[118] As supporters of King U and officials in charge of the personnel authority, these men also happened to form the most formidable opposition to what was perhaps the inevitable rise of the reformist branch of government led by Yi Sŏnggye. Yun Sojong was a prominent member of this reformist branch. In 1388, shortly after Yi Sŏnggye's infamous return from Wihwa Island, Yun Sojong, who was named a merit subject after the founding of the Chosŏn dynasty, submitted a memorial to the throne asking for the execution of the above figures on the grounds of treason against the throne.[119]

It should also be noted here that the same Yun Sojong had a brother in the *saṅgha* named Sŏnch'ang and an agnatic relative by the name of Namjŏn Pumok who once served as abbot of the influential temple Susŏn-sa, the monastery founded by Chinul. Little is known about him, but Pumok, like the leading *sajok* officials of his time, is said to have voiced his concerns about the regent Sin Ton.

Furthermore, although Yun Kusaeng is said to have followed the ritual instructions of Zhu Xi, he made some significant deviations from the instructions in Zhu's *Family Rituals*. The family shrine was built not inside the home of the eldest son, that is, the ritual heir, but near the grave. The location of the family shrine reflects the desire not only to honor Yun T'aek's offering hut but also to conform to the popular Koryŏ custom of performing sacrifices at the graves of one's ancestors. The Yun family shrine also housed a funerary portrait instead of a spirit tablet. The record that Paek Munbo wrote to commemorate the family shrine claims that this deviation from Zhu's instructions was permissible because the funerary portrait, which was usually housed in a Buddhist memorial monastery, was a gift from the king.[120]

Ideological conversion, then, cannot serve as an adequate explanation for the Musong Yun's decision to abandon Buddhism. Something else compelled Yun T'aek and his family to break with old customs.

Like Ch'oe Mundo, Yun Kusaeng—Yun T'aek's eldest son—needed to strengthen his father's *sajok* credentials, for his father's career was far from ideal in the eyes of the regular bureaucracy. Yun T'aek's career began in an ideal way. He passed the literary examination in 1280 and was initially appointed to the low-ranking clerical post of office manager (*noksa*), but he failed to advance his career significantly for the next few decades. In 1332, for reasons that remain unclear, Yun T'aek was able to travel to Dadu and meet King Ch'ungsuk, who was under house arrest. The king had few supporters at the time.[121] Yun used this opportunity to earn his trust. In fact, Ch'ungsuk trusted him enough to place the future of his son Wang Ki, the future King Kongmin, in his care. Yun thus became a palace favorite, and promotions quickly followed. From the lowest rank in the central bureaucracy, Yun was quickly promoted to administrative assistant (*p'an'gwan*; rank 5a) of the western capital. Not long after, in 1338, King Ch'ungsuk promoted him again to assistant transmitter on the right (*u pu taeŏn*; rank 3a), which meant that Yun was entrusted with the power of recruitment and promotions as a senior official in the personnel authority.[122] The following year, he was promoted to transmitter on the right.

Yun's meteoric rise to this position of immense authority and power, however, was short-lived. Ch'ungsuk passed away that year and was succeeded by his son Ch'unghye. As a member of the former king's inner circle and protector of the rival for the Koryŏ throne (i.e., Kongmin), Yun knew that he had to withdraw from politics, and that is precisely what he did.[123] But retirement did not last long. Yun was promoted to academician of the security council after Wang Ki ascended the throne in 1351, but he chose retirement again the following year when the new king ignored his proposals for reform.[124]

The arc drawn by Yun T'aek's career deviated from the ideal career pattern for members of the regular bureaucracy. He found success only as a palace favorite, and his credentials were thus blemished. The effort to restore his reputation began as soon as he passed away. Three months after the funeral, Yun T'aek's grandson Yun Sojong visited his teacher Yi Saek with the family record (*kajang*) that he himself had just compiled and requested a funerary inscription for his late grandfather.[125] Yun Sojong seems to have had to produce his own family record because his family's entry into the central bureaucracy was relatively new. It began with his great-grandfather Yun Hae—Great Master Ch'ŏnghŏn—who retired as headmaster of the Confucian academy. Virtually nothing, however, is known about Hae's father, Yun Yangbi, who was the township headman (*hojang*) of Musong County, in North Chŏlla.

Although Yun Hae had thus opened the doors for his children to follow in his footsteps and enter the central bureaucracy, the untimely death of his son Sup'yŏng jeopardized plans for becoming a great family in the capital. Sup'yŏng's son T'aek, however, was able to receive an education from his paternal aunt's husband Yun Sŏnjwa of the illustrious P'ap'yŏng Yun descent group and passed the literary examination. T'aek's sons Kusaeng, Pongsaeng, and Tongmyŏng and their sons Hyojong, Sojong, Hoejong, and Hŭngjong were also able to become central officials. Even after the founding of the Chosŏn dynasty, Sojong's descendants continued to receive high posts in the central bureaucracy. Most notable among them is his great-grandson, Chief State Councilor (Yŏngŭijŏng) Yun Chaun (1416–1478). By the late fifteenth century, there could be no doubt that the Musong Yun had become a great *sejok* family.

The situation was quite different when Yun Sojong visited his teacher Yi Saek to ask for a funerary inscription for his grandfather. Although his father Kusaeng had passed the literary examination, he had never acquired high office. The family's reputation thus depended largely on the reputation of his grandfather T'aek and great-grandfather Hae. Naturally, the project of transforming the Musong Yun into a *sajok* family began with Hae.

The preface portrays Hae as a man of moral integrity. While serving as record keeper (*sarok*) in Sangju, North Kyŏngsang, Hae is said to have gotten into a dispute with the local magistrate over the punishment of a man who had violated his sister. Hae killed the man. Rain then fell and ended the severe drought that was affecting Sangju. This, of course, was meant to prove that what Hae did was righteous.[126] As an official in the board of punishment and the office of the inspector general, Hae is also said to have "maintained propriety of his own accord." After serving as circuit commissioner in Kyŏngsang, Chŏlla, Yanggwang, and Hoeyang (present-day Kang'wŏn), he was promoted to vice censor-in-chief, but he was so poor that he ostensibly "could not continue to eat even gruel and had to fill his empty stomach with boiled beans." Hae, the preface goes on to tell, was therefore known as an honest official (*ch'ŏngbaengni*). On his deathbed, Hae's grandson T'aek therefore tried to establish honesty as the family's legacy; or this, at least, is what his tomb epitaph wants its readers to believe.

This is also the message that the Musong Yun's conspicuous decision to abandon Buddhist customs in favor of the family shrine was meant to convey to its peers, the *sajok*.

The plan worked. Legislation mandating the use of family shrines for officials and their families was not enacted until 1390.[127] Few took the new law seriously. In 1391, the civil governor (*kwanch'alsa*) of the Chŏlla circuit No Sung, citing Yun Kusaeng's willingness to adopt this new custom long before it was legally mandated by the state, honored his family with a commemorative arch and a special decree exempting his descendants from corvée duty.[128] Once the exception, the Musong Yun were thus touted as the new norm. There could therefore be no doubt that the Musong Yun was an exemplary *sajok* family.

The fourteenth century thus bore witness to subtle but important changes to customs concerning death in Koryŏ. For centuries, the *sejok* expected to be able to enjoy the privilege of receiving unending prayers after death. This was possible because of the miraculous power of Buddhist monks to transform wealth into postmortem salvation. Under Mongol rule, this power could no longer be taken for granted. Wealth and salvation had become incommensurables.

For the officials and their families who sought to distinguish themselves from perceived enemies of the regular bureaucracy, it had also become necessary to take a firm stand on wealth. As a consequence of the rapid flow of wealth in the direction of the enemies of the regular bureaucracy, wealth had become problematized. Wealth, simply put, had to be dissociated from the ideals of bureaucratic service. It is for this reason that we begin to see more frequent references to officials who are "honest and upright" during this period.

The need to distance oneself from wealth meant that the *sajok* had to seek alternatives to Buddhist methods of managing death, for these methods assumed wealth. The costly and elaborate methods of Buddhism infused the path toward postmortem salvation with a sense of individual drama. The size of the donations made to finance prayers for the dead directly shaped the trajectory of the dead person's spirit.[129] But a flattening of this postmortem space began to occur in the fourteenth century as aspiring *sajok* families sought a less costly method of honoring their dead in Zhu Xi's *Family Rituals*. Strict adherence to the guidelines in this manual ensured that the ancestors of families of equal social standing would occupy the same, indistinguishable postmortem space. This space was no longer accessible through solemn Buddhist chants and the visual presence of the dead in their funerary portraits. By the time the Musong Yun had become exemplars of filial piety, this process of flattening the postmortem space occupied by the *sajok* dead was irreversible.

CONCLUSION

THE ASSUMPTIONS ABOUT WEALTH AND RELIGION THAT GUIDED the early Koryŏ elite were no longer current by the end of the dynasty. Wealth was just wealth, and religion was something else. The architects of the new Chosŏn state wanted to keep it that way. Based on the futile dream of establishing stronger state control over alienable and taxable resources like land and labor, reformists within the late Koryŏ officialdom who would go on to hold high posts in the new Chosŏn government drafted legislation that would allow the state to keep wealth and religion (or, more specifically, Buddhism) apart. In 1390, new legislation was enacted to require the office-holding class to rebuild its identity around the practice of Confucian-style ancestor worship at the ancestral hall or family shrine. More legislation supporting this effort passed in the early fifteenth century. The state had two expectations after this legislation was enacted. First, it expected to be able to claim authority and control over moral values. Second, it also expected to be able to keep inheritance, that is, alienable and taxable resources, away from an unregulated spiritual marketplace (i.e., Buddhism). As part of this effort to build a wall between religion and wealth, the Chosŏn kings issued royal orders to try to regulate the number of monasteries in well-populated areas. The less contact the better.

These measures did not amount to a suppression of Buddhism as some claim, but it did allow the state to push Buddhism into the margins of public authority in Korea. Buddhism and especially the monasteries that had once been officially recognized as "places of aid and remedy" (*pibo chi so*) could, in other words, no longer make the state's presence known to the public through their power to convert wealth into salvation, protection, and aid. This prerogative was to belong only to the state and its central bureaucracy. These efforts began to accelerate and become visibly more intense during the reign of Wang Yo, or King Kongyang, the last monarch to sit on the Koryŏ throne.[1] These efforts took the form of a heated debate. At its heart was the issue of the value of restoring Yŏnbok-sa, a Buddhist monastery in the capital.

On February 14, 1390, a monk by the name of Pŏbye from the grand Sŏn monastery Yŏnbok-sa had an audience with King Kongyang. During his audience with the king, Pŏbye made a point of mentioning that Yŏnbok-sa's five-story wooden stupa had fallen into disrepair.[2] He then encouraged the king to restore the stupa as well as the monastery's three ponds and nine wells, which had also been left in ruins for quite some time. The restorations, Pŏbye promised the king, would "bring peace and prosperity to the kingdom and its people." The king was delighted. He wished to seize the opportunity to prove himself a worthy monarch, so he named two trusted senior officers in the five military commands, Sim Inbong and Kwŏn Wan, assistant directors of the directorate for construction (*chosŏng togam*), to oversee the restoration of Yŏnbok-sa and its dilapidated stupa.

A few months later, the restoration project hit its first snag. Squatters had settled in an area that had once belonged to the monastery. On September 6 of the same year, King Kongyang decided to have thirty homes in this area removed to make room for the restoration of Yŏnbok-sa's famed three ponds and nine wells.[3] This, however, could not have been an easy decision to make, for criticism was sure to follow. All the more so because it came on the heels of another controversial decision the king had made four days earlier. Citing a claim made in Tosŏn's *Record of Secrets* (Milgi), the office of astronomy and geomancy (*sŏun'gwan*) had advised the king to relocate the capital to Hanyang (present-day Seoul).[4] The purpose of this move, as the office explained, was to give the "terrestrial force" (*chidŏk*) of the Koryŏ capital Songdo a chance to replenish itself. The king chose to follow the office's advice.

Not long after this decision was made, the vice director of the board of punishment (*hyŏngjo ch'ongnang*; rank 4a) and third censor on the left (*chwa hŏnnap*; rank 5a) Yun Hoejong, the grandson of Yun T'aek, submitted a memorial to the throne.[5] In his memorial, Yun clearly articulated his objections to the king's wish to restore Yŏnbok-sa and his plans to move the capital. The king, Yun claimed, was being beguiled by specialists of apocryphal weft-texts (*ch'amwi*)—that is, Tosŏn's *Record of Secrets*—and the monk Pŏbye.[6] Citing a passage from the Neo-Confucian classic *Mencius*, the superintendent of the security council, merit subject, and royal-in-law Kang Hoebaek (exam passed in 1376) similarly argued against the king's ambitious plan.[7] Kang cited *Mencius* in order to set the king's priorities straight: it is human accord, and not the earth's advantages, that determines the fate of the kingdom.⁸ Calamities, Kang also points out, are actually Heaven's way of showing its love for the sovereign. According to Kang, the best way to repay this love would be for the king to reflect fearfully on his daily behavior and be frugal.

King Kongyang, however, chose to disregard Yun's and Kang's advice. Shortly after his return from a royal tour of Hanyang in March 1391, the king issued an order to have the residents of the capital district and Yanggwang circuit (present-day Kyŏnggi and Ch'ungch'ŏng) supply five thousand logs for the restoration of the Yŏnbok-sa stupa.⁹ This proved to be an overwhelming burden for the residents. Many cattle died in the process of transporting the harvested logs, and the residents naturally came to resent the king's commitment to restoring the stupa. Criticism of the project soon followed. Chancellery Scholar Chŏng Tojŏn, a politically active figure who wielded much influence at court at the time, made the king painfully aware of the trouble that he was causing for the people.¹⁰ Chŏng's criticism notwithstanding, on April 27, 1391, the king had the directorate of expanding merit (hongbok togam) grant Yŏnbok-sa two thousand bolts of cloth, to cover the growing cost of repairing its grand stupa.¹¹ A month later, on May 20, the transmitter on the right Yu Chŏnghyŏn also implored the king to cease the restoration of the monastery, but his plea, like Chŏng's, fell on deaf ears.¹²

King Kongyang remained firm in spite of continued opposition from his officials, but his stubborn insistence on restoring Yŏnbok-sa was not another instance of royal hubris or the unrestrained expression of fervent piety. Kongyang's commitment to the restoration project had something to do with the serious problems he faced as the new sovereign of Koryŏ. Among other things, Kongyang had seen drought, famine, and astrological and environmental anomalies—calamities (chae)—chip away at royal virtue (tŏk) and hence his mandate to rule. Like many Koryŏ kings before him, Kongyang believed that the relocation of the capital to Hanyang and the restoration of Buddhist monasteries such as Yŏnbok-sa, renowned for their power to control rain and protect the state, could serve as a legitimate means of reinvigorating damaged virtue, both royal and terrestrial. But a number of his key senior officials did not agree with his response to the recurring calamities. On June 7, 1391, Kongyang therefore resorted to another well-known ritual response to calamities: he issued a royal order and asked his officials for frank advice.

Not long after he issued the royal order, Kongyang received a lengthy memorial from the headmaster of the Royal Confucian Academy Kim

Chasu (exam passed in 1374).[13] The headmaster asked the king to halt the restoration of the monastery. He offered three reasons: the construction causes people unnecessary suffering; there are more urgent matters that required the king's attention, such as repairing the royal ancestral shrine; and Heaven is moved not by the building of monasteries but by the cultivation of royal virtue.[14] The headmaster's memorial was followed by the submission of another lengthy memorial by the erudite of the academy Kim Ch'o (exam passed in 1388). His memorial was, in essence, a harshly worded rebuke of Buddhism. The point of the memorial was to paint Buddhism as an "abnormality" (koe). Buddhism is abnormal in the sense that it encourages the severing of human relationships (innyun), parasitizes the productive labor of others, and makes absurd claims about its ability to prolong life and secure a better rebirth for the faithful. The erudite even called for disbanding the Buddhist establishment, turning monks into soldiers, and executing anyone who tried to become a monk. He also recommended the use of family shrines so as "to block unnecessary expenditure" in the name of endowing or constructing Buddhist monasteries.[15] Kongyang was understandably displeased with the erudite's memorial.

But more memorials made their way to the king. Policy Adviser on the Left Hŏ Ŭng, Superintendent of the Board of Personnel Chŏng Ch'ong, and Assistant Royal Secretary Nam Ŭn submitted lengthy memorials criticizing the Yŏnbok-sa project.[16] Much to his displeasure, Chancellery Scholar Chŏng Tojŏn, who held concurrent appointments as headmaster of the royal academy and commissioner of the right army (ugun ch'ongjesa), also submitted a memorial reminding the king of the limits and problems inherent in supporting Yŏnbok-sa's restoration. Facing such unrelenting opposition, the king seems to have had no choice but to abandon the cause, which he reluctantly did on July 9.

The very next day, however, Kongyang received encouraging memorials from the former vice supervisor of the directorate of medicine (chŏnŭi pujŏng) Kim Chŏn and former superintendent of the ministry of taxation Chŏng Sach'ŏk. In his memorial, Kim encouraged the king to follow the example of the dynastic founder, who had used Buddhism to manage "the ebb and flow of the mountains and rivers and the continuity and discontinuity of the channels of terrestrial force [chimaek]."[17] Kongyang gladly accepted their advice. But opposition soon followed. On July 19, the office of royal decrees and state records (yemun ch'unch'ugwan) asked for the impeachment of Kim Chŏn on the grounds that he had tried to flatter the king.[18] The call for Kim's impeachment was ignored. In response, Pak Ch'o and other students in the Royal Confucian Academy submitted a vitriolic memorial similar in tone and content to the memorial submitted earlier by their teacher Kim Ch'o.[19] The king, again, was immensely displeased.

The king had good reason to show his deep irritation. The headmaster of the Royal Confucian Academy was in a position to offer the king advice; students in the academy were not. Teachers and students in the academy were well aware of this fact. Realizing what Pak and the other students were attempting to do, the second assistant master of the academy (*saye*) Yu Paeksun tried to dissuade them from submitting the memorial. Pak Ch'o, Yun Hyang, Han Ko, and twelve other students ignored Yu's advice and submitted the memorial that bore their signatures. Other students, such as Sŏ Pongnye, however, refused to sign the memorial.[20] Erudites, most notably Kim Ch'o and Hwang Hŭi (exam passed in 1385), decided to use Sŏ as an example and had him kicked out of the academy. The headmaster Kim Chasu was furious at the erudites for dismissing Sŏ without first seeking his approval. As punishment, he imprisoned the erudites' private slaves and had Sŏ return to the academy. In retaliation, Kim Ch'o and the other erudites refused to offer the headmaster a formal greeting in the morning. Kim Chasu, deeply insulted, informed the king of his decision to withdraw from his post. The king did not allow the headmaster to step down from his post, however, and had Kim Ch'o and the others taken briefly into custody. This punishment did not satisfy the king, who wanted to have Kim Ch'o executed, but Chancellor Chŏng Mongju came to the defense of Kim and the students at the academy.[21] Unable to ignore the chancellor's plea, the king limited their punishment to forty blows of the stick.

Despite the impassioned opposition mounted by the teachers and students at the Royal Confucian Academy, King Kongyang proceeded as planned. On August 3, the restoration of Yŏnbok-sa resumed. Kongyang, it seemed, had won the hard-fought political battle. As he had hoped, the project was completed on May 9, 1393. But Kongyang himself was not able to celebrate the occasion. By the time the restoration of the monastery was complete, he had passed away after ceding the throne to the military strongman Yi Sŏnggye, who founded the Chosŏn dynasty in 1392.

Why did the restoration of Yŏnbok-sa incite such controversy? Rejecting earlier interpretations that attributed the critical attitude toward the Yŏnbok-sa project to the growing prominence and politicization of Neo-Confucianism, influential studies of this period argue that the memorials submitted by Chŏng Tojŏn, Kim Chasu, Kim Ch'o, and Pak Ch'o had less to do with ideological differences than with the pressing economic concerns of the state and a bloated, corrupt Buddhist establishment. More recently, it has been suggested that the memorials were, in fact, all products of shrewd political calculations aimed at overthrowing Wang clan rule and installing General Yi Sŏnggye as king.[22] The arguments presented in this book, however, point to a different reading of the Yŏnbok-sa debate: the restoration project stood at the center of this impassioned controversy because it became a convenient way for reformists at court to channel their concerns about wealth and, more specifically, its privatization. There is no denying that the regular bureaucracy was concerned about the corruption and decay of Buddhism. But modern scholarship on the so-called anti-Buddhist movement of the late Koryŏ and early Chosŏn period has tended to jump to the conclusion that this corruption and decay were a consequence of the mixture of wealth and religion. On the contrary, the separation of wealth and religion is what made it possible to speak of corruption and decay.

The reformists of the late Koryŏ period spoke of the corruption of Buddhism because they wanted to keep wealth and religion separate, and because the late Koryŏ state was in the middle of a dire fiscal crisis precipitated largely by the withdrawal of Mongol support, repeated invasions by the Red Turbans and Japanese pirates, and the increase in large landed estates and hence the privatization of land and labor.[23] In response to this crisis, the reformists wanted to keep taxable and inalienable resources under the firm control of the state and its central bureaucracy. This, they believed, could be done by preventing the resources from becoming privatized, or, to use the reformists' words, wasted on social parasites and abnormalities.

Also at stake in the Yŏnbok-sa controversy is the definition of virtue (*tŏk*). King Kongyang wanted to preserve the old definition, which assumed the existence of a seamless connection between wealth and virtue (i.e., the power over the material and immaterial worlds). This model of virtue is what sustained the mythology of the sage-ruler, who, for Koryŏ, was the dynastic founder. The reformists wanted to advance a different definition of virtue, which kept wealth and virtue conceptually apart. From the reformists' perspective, virtue was less power and the ability to provide the state with aid and remedy than moral integrity and ethical conduct. Wealth had no role to play in the cultivation of virtue. By keeping wealth and virtue apart in this way, the reformists attempted to take legitimacy away from the state's customary support of Buddhism. The separation of wealth and virtue, the reformists believed, would allow the state to maintain better control over wealth and prevent it from falling into the hands of private corporations like the Buddhist establishment.

The Yŏnbok-sa controversy was the culmination of changes that began under Mongol rule. The influx of nontraditional social elements in the elite stratum precipitated a crisis of identity, which in turn led the most highly regarded intellectuals of fourteenth-century Koryŏ to separate wealth from salvation and bureaucratic ideals. Without these changes, it would have been difficult, if not impossible, to push Buddhism into the margins of public authority. This process of transforming Buddhism into an otherworldly religion that no longer had any influence over the public domain, however, was a slow one.

In celebration of the completion of the Yŏnbok-sa stupa restoration, the dynastic founder of Chosŏn, Yi Sŏnggye, ordered the renowned scholar-official Kwŏn Kŭn to pen a stupa restoration record. Like his predecessor, King Kongyang, Yi was not inclined to simply let go of the old definition of virtue. But the damage, so to speak, was already done. Kwŏn Kŭn had thus been entrusted with an impossible task. As a member of the reformist camp, Kwŏn had to defend the definition of virtue as moral integrity and ethical conduct, but as a loyal subject of the king, he had to respect the old definition of virtue as well.

Kwŏn begins his celebratory account of the restoration with a brief description of the monastery. According to Kwŏn, Yŏnbok-sa is the largest monastery in the capital, ostensibly consisting of more than a thousand structures.[24] Making good use of his knowledge of the religious and historical significance of Yŏnbok-sa, Kwŏn notes that the monastery features three ponds, nine wells, and, of course, a five-story stupa, which was designed according to geomantic theories (p'ungsu). After noting these critical features of the monastery, Kwŏn goes on to explain that it is not clear when exactly the stupa fell into disrepair because the monastery had suffered the consequences of many invasions and bloody internal conflicts under Wang clan rule. Using the seemingly innocuous fact of his ignorance, Kwŏn, a literatus skilled in the use of rhetoric, surreptitiously binds the fate of the monastery to the competence of the ruler, which allows him to criticize the fallen Koryŏ dynasty ruled by the Wang clan on moral and religious grounds and to shower praise on the new ruler, Yi Sŏnggye, or T'aejo. As evidence of the Wang clan's moral failures, Kwŏn points specifically to recent attempts to restore the stupa. King Kongmin, Kwŏn reminds his readers, had tried, but to no avail. A mad monk by the name of Changwŏnsim used his connections with the wealthy and powerful to achieve the same goal, but he, too, failed.[25] And after his coronation, King Kongyang similarly "exerted much effort in worshipping the Buddha and, as part of this effort, ordered the monk Ch'ŏn'gyu and others to hire craftsmen to begin construction" of Yŏnbok-sa, but Kongyang proved no more successful than his predecessors.[26]

Restoration, Kwŏn admits in his account, did begin under Kongyang's rule. A new foundation was laid for a large stupa five bays wide and five bays deep in the second lunar month of 1391. The plan was to build five stories above this large foundation and then place a flat piece of stone on the top, presumably to support a finial, but opposition from officials brought construction to a halt. The restoration project resumed only because Yi Sŏnggye encouraged it, Kwŏn claims and offers the following explanation of Yi's intentions:

> Our Highness gained the minds and hearts of Heaven and men with his divine martial prowess and suddenly received the title of lord sovereign. He established his rule over the people and the altars of Earth and Grain. With utmost benevolence and great virtue, he cared for living things. Many wise men did their best to assist him. The Way of his rule was splendid and grand. The hundred evils were all removed, and the ten thousand moral transformations were all rendered anew. If it was governance that could strengthen the kingdom and comfort the people, there was nothing he did not try. He thought the Buddha's Way, compassion, and love for living things could benefit our kingdom, so he guarded the methods for worshipping [the Buddha] and did not abolish them. . . . The Buddha's relics [lit., śarīra] were interred on top [inside the finial], the canon was placed in the middle,[27] and a statue of Vairocana was installed at the bottom [of the stupa] so as to seek merit for the kingdom and forever benefit it for ten thousand years.[28]

With Yi's enthusiastic support, construction was quickly completed under *his* reign as the first monarch of the newly established Chosŏn dynasty in the twelfth lunar month of 1392. A few months later, the stupa was fully adorned with new paintings and decorative patterns.[29] The following month, a Mañjuśrī assembly was held at the monastery, and it is at this point in the restoration process that the new king Yi Sŏnggye ordered Kwŏn to compose a record of its restoration.[30]

Kwŏn's record neatly captures the fault line that divided the late Koryŏ and early Chosŏn courts, eloquently articulated in the contrast drawn between Kongyang and T'aejo Yi Sŏnggye. Both men were similarly engaged in the restoration of Yŏnbok-sa, but, according to Kwŏn, their intentions were drastically different. Whereas Kongyang supported the restoration for personal religious reasons, Yi did so not for his own sake but for the sake of his kingdom and his people. This morally upright intention, Kwŏn argues, is what allowed Yi to complete the restoration of Yŏnbok-sa. The conceptual changes that occurred to the notion of wealth, salvation, and virtue during the fourteenth century made it possible to speak of the transformation of wealth into salvation or virtue in either private or public terms. Few Chosŏn officials, however, were willing to follow Kwŏn's example. As concerns about the privatization of wealth increased under the new dynasty, Buddhism came to be associated less with public authority than with private interests. Pushed out of one domain (the public) and into the other (the private), Buddhism in Korea thus became not a religion in decline but a religion that assumed an increasingly otherworldly and private character.

NOTES

Introduction

1. Kwŏn's grave was discovered in 1989 in what is now Sŏgongni, P'aju, about thirty kilometers east of Kaesŏng, when the National Museum of Korea received a tip about a desecrated grave that contained murals. Although a stele naming another person was placed in front of the grave, a nearby slab of stone bearing the tomb epitaph (i.e., a funerary inscription and its preface) for Kwŏn Chun and a fragment from the same stone slab inside the grave made it possible to identify the grave as Kwŏn Chun's (see Munhwajae Kwalliguk Munhwajae Yŏn'guso, *P'aju Sŏgongni Koryŏ pyŏkhwamyo*; Kwŏn Hyosuk, "Chuin pakkwin myo"; and *KMC*: 613).
2. This account is based on Kwŏn's tomb epitaph in *KMC*: 632–35.
3. While in retirement, Yun T'aek was granted the honorary title Assistant Chancellor in 1363 (*KS* 106: 35a). Earlier in 1352, Yun T'aek had been allowed to retire with the junior second-grade title Mayor of Kaesŏng.
4. *KMC*: 578.
5. For the Buddhist practices used by the Koryŏ elite to manage death, see Hŏ, *Koryŏ pulgyosa yŏn'gu*, 2–102. For related Chinese Buddhist practices, see Teiser, *The Ghost Festival*, and Teiser, *The Scripture*.
6. The above account of Yun T'aek's death and funeral is based on the preface to his funerary inscription (see *KMC*: 576–79).
7. See the *Yunssi punmyogi* (Record of the Yun family's graveside shrine) in *TMS* 69: 19a–23a; cf. *KS* 121: 21b. For an annotated English-language translation of Zhu's *Family Rituals*, see Ebrey, *Chu Hsi's "Family Rituals."*
8. Kim Yongsŏn identifies the site as a clan gravesite (*Koryŏ kŭmsŏngmun yŏn'gu*, 195). Yun T'aek chose to be buried in Kŭmju, South Ch'ungch'ŏng, rather than his own ancestral seat, Musong County, North Chŏlla. This may be because his father, Sup'yong, had left Musong County to join his wife's household. Uxorilocal residence was not uncommon during the Koryŏ (Deuchler, *Confucian Transformation of Korea*, 66). As Yun T'aek's mother's surname was Kim, she likely was a member of the Kŭmsan Kim descent group whose ancestral seat was Kŭmju.
9. On the ministerial class, see Pyŏn T'aesŏp, "Koryŏ chaesang ko."
10. According to the preface to the funerary inscription for Wŏn Sŏnji written by the famed scholar-official Ch'oe Hae, there was an old custom (*kosa*) in Korea of honoring officials in the chancellery and security council with funerary

inscriptions and prefaces that detailed the ancestry, family, and accomplishments of the deceased (*KMC*: 469). The practice of using funerary inscriptions as markers of distinction was borrowed from China. For an explanation of the Chinese practice during the Tang (618–907) and Song (960–1279) periods, see Tackett, *Destruction*, esp. the introduction, and Bossler, *Powerful Relations*, esp. chap. 1.

11. For a comprehensive overview of Koryŏ's government examination system and a convenient list of examination passers, see Hŏ, *Koryŏ ŭi kwagŏ chedo*. Using Kwŏn's descent group as a representative example, Yi Sugŏn has shown that local elites were transformed into more complex agnatic and affinal networks during the late Koryŏ (see "Yŏmal Sŏnch'o t'osŏng ijok ŭi sŏngjang kwa punhwa").

12. On the relationship between mortuary customs and elite identity in Koryŏ, see Hŏ, *Koryŏ pulgyosa yŏn'gu*, 2–102.

13. See, e.g., Deuchler, "Neo-Confucianism"; Deuchler, *Under the Ancestors' Eyes*, esp. 49; and To Hyŏnch'ŏl, *Koryŏmal sadaebu*. To argues that the late Koryŏ court was divided between two political cliques who embodied different impulses for social action: the "old customs party" (*kubŏpp'a*) and the "new customs party" (*sinbŏpp'a*). For a critique of To, see Yi Ponggyu, "Koryŏmal sadaebu," cited in Yi Ikchu, *Yi Saek*, 27. In her book *Koryŏ hugi sadaebu wa sŏngnihak suyong*, Ko Hyeryŏng similarly refers to conservative (*on'gŏn*) and radical (*kŭpchin*) cliques in late Koryŏ Neo-Confucianism but argues that both emerged from the same group of scholar-officials in the "acceptance [of Neo-Confucianism] period" (*suyonggi*). Kwŏn and Yun belong to this period.

14. On Yi Chehyŏn's attitude toward Buddhism, see Pyŏn Tongmyŏng, "Sŏngnihak." On Yi Saek's life and writings, see Yi Ikchu, *Yi Saek ŭi salm kwa saenggak*. On Yi Saek's view of governance and policy, see To Hyŏnch'ŏl, *Mogŭn Yi Saek ŭi chŏngch'i sasang yŏn'gu*. For a study in German of Yi Saek's work and life, see Hans-Jürgen Zaborowski, *Der Gelehrte*.

15. On the-Koryŏ and early Chosŏn reforms, see Duncan, *Origins*, chap. 5; Kwŏn Yŏngguk, "14-segi chŏnban kaehyŏk chŏngch'i ŭi naeyong"; and Kim Kidŏk, "14-segi huban kaehyŏk chŏngch'i ŭi naeyong."

16. A classic source for this account of the anti-Buddhist movement is Ki-baik Lee, *New History of Korea*, 166. See also Pak Yongun, *Koryŏ sidaesa*, 643–47. For a convenient summary of relevant literature in Korean, see Ch'ae Sangsik, "Koryŏ-Chosŏn sigi pulgyosa," 79–90.

17. *KS* 107: 15a. Kwŏn Pu's father, Kwŏn Tan, who is said to have originally aspired to become a celibate monk before he entered the officialdom, devoted his twilight years to the pursuit of enlightenment and eventually became a monk in 1304 (*KMC*: 427–28). The commitment of Kwŏn Pu's descendants to both Buddhism and Neo-Confucianism is evident in the writings of Pu's great-grandson Kwŏn Kŭn (see Kalton, "Writings of Kwŏn Kŭn"). On the contributions of the Kwŏn family to the growth of Neo-Confucianism—both ancient learning (C. *guwen*) and Cheng-Zhu learning—in Korea and the affinal network they formed with other prominent families in the capital, see Cha, "The Civilizing Project," 217–42, 265–86.

18. Yi Chehyŏn claims that Tohak was introduced to Korea by two specific figures: his son's father-in-law Paek Ijŏng, who returned from China with "books about

nature-and-principle" (sŏngni chi sŏ) authored by Cheng Yi and Zhu Xi, and his own father-in-law Kwŏn Pu, who introduced Tohak through the publication of Zhu Xi's commentaries on the Four Books (YP 2: 10a).

19. The five blessings are longevity, wealth, health, love of virtue, and a natural death (see Legge, Chinese Classics, Vol III, Part II, 343).
20. KMC: 635.
21. Evidence of Kwŏn's wealth is found in his biography in the History of Koryŏ (Koryŏsa). During a visit to Kwŏn's house, King Ch'ungsuk, for instance, is said to have exclaimed that the house was far beyond what he could afford (KS 107: 16). King Ch'ungsŏn had paid fifty catties (C. jin) of silver and purchased a house that once belonged to the chancellor An Hyang as a gift for his favorite, Kwŏn.
22. KMC: 634.
23. There are exceptions, but they are few in number. I have identified two tomb epitaphs from the twelfth century that explicitly mention the virtue of being frugal: the epitaphs for Pak Hwang and King Sukchong's fifth son, Wang Hyo (see KMC: 129–31, 185–88 respectively). It is worth noting that both were written during the reign of King Ŭijong, which was characterized by "a prevailing climate of mismanagement and debauchery" and "a dramatic shift in the social status of the palace attendants" (Shultz, Generals and Scholars, 17–18).
24. See Hŏ, Koryŏ pulgyosa yŏn'gu, 2–102 (for a partial English-language translation, see Hŏ, "Buddhism and Koryŏ Society"), and Han Kimun, Koryŏ sawŏn ŭi kujo wa kinŭng, 217–351.
25. Although scholars typically regard the Andong Kwŏn as a sejok family, this family's rise to prominence was quite late (see Kim Kwangch'ŏl, Koryŏ hugi sejokch'ŭng yŏn'gu, 73–74). Their status as sejok was far from certain, hence, I argue, Kwŏn Chun's rather blatant attempt to liken his family to the Kyŏngwŏn Yi.
26. Three of his daughters married King Munjong. They are the queen mother Inye Sundŏk, In'gyŏng hyŏnbi, and Injŏl hyŏnbi (see KS 88: 18a–19b and KMC: 23). The queen mother gave birth to three kings: Sunjong, Sŏnjong, and Sukchong. For a detailed study of Yi Chayŏn and his extended family, see Fujita, "Ri Shien to sono kakei."
27. Kwŏn Chun's brother Kwŏn Chae was adopted by King Ch'ungsŏn. The king granted his adopted son the name Wang Hu (KMC: 545–47). One granddaughter (the daughter of Kwŏn Chun's eldest son) was King Ch'ungsuk's consort Subi (KS 89: 24a–b). The other granddaughter (his daughter's daughter) was King Ch'unghye's consort Hwabi (KS 89: 25b).
28. KMC: 542.
29. Deuchler, Confucian Transformation of Korea, 27. Deuchler has recently raised questions about her own thesis (see "Is 'Confucianization of Korea' a Valid Concept of Analysis?"). In response, Boudewijn Walraven countered that the Confucianization of Korea did occur (see "Beyond 'Confucianization'"). Like Deuchler, Walraven, however, has recently come to question this notion of Confucianization (see "Buddhist Accommodation and Appropriation"). In her new study, Under the Ancestors' Eyes, Deuchler argues for a focus on the tension between the "social" (e.g., kinship) and the "political" (e.g., individual

achievement) rather than on ideology. Confucianism, she claims, was used to buttress the social and counter the threat of the political. This argument has its own problems, as discussed below.

30. For a critique of the problem of confusing agent with subject, see Asad, *Genealogies of Religion*, 16. See also his critique of secular definitions of agency in his *Formations of the Secular*. As he points out, the study of agency should focus not on the subjective content of ideology but on "specific political economic conditions which make certain rhetorical forms [i.e., ideology] objectively possible, and *authoritative*" ("Anthropology," 616).

31. Earlier studies tend to understand the anti-Buddhist movement in socioeconomic terms as a product, that is, of the conflict between the *kwŏnmun sejok* and the so-called new scholar-officials (*sinhŭng sadaebu*), a new class of officials who emerged from modest economic backgrounds (see, e.g., Kim Yun'gon, "Sinhŭng sadaebu ŭi taedu," 148–49, and Pak Yongun, *Koryŏ sidaesa*, 644). In keeping with more recent studies that critique this "new scholar-officials" thesis, Deuchler argues that the negative attitude toward Buddhism in the late Koryŏ period was a product of the conflict not between the *kwŏnmun sejok* and new scholar-officials but between the *kwŏnmun* and the *sejok* (see *Under the Ancestors' Eyes*, esp. part 1).

32. Deuchler, *Under the Ancestors' Eyes*, 49.

33. For Deuchler's use of the notion of "strategy of distinction," see ibid., 3. Deuchler borrows this notion from Pierre Bourdieu's *Distinction*.

34. The growing tendency among *sejok* families to regard themselves as *sadaebu* families or families with a tradition of supplying the regular bureaucracy with officials was key to this process. John Duncan makes a similar observation, but he leaves the question of how exactly this awareness came into being unanswered (see *Origins*, 89, 97). Deuchler claims that this awareness was the consequence of the conflict between the *sejok* and *kwŏnmun* (see *Under the Ancestors' Eyes*, 46, 54–55).

35. See, e.g., Takahashi, *Richō bukkyō*, 37–43; Yi Sangbaek, "Yubul yanggyo kyodae ŭi kiyŏn e taehan il yŏn'gu"; and Han Ugŭn, *Yugyo chŏngch'i wa pulgyo*. Recently, historians have attempted to find evidence of corruption in Buddhist writings (see, e.g., Vermeersch, "Views on Buddhist Precepts"). Vermeersch's study provides, however, not so much evidence of actual corruption but evidence of the Buddhist establishment's interest in experimenting with new teachings (about precepts and morality) imported from China.

36. For Gernet's own summary of his view of the "interpenetration of commerce and religion," see his *Buddhism in Chinese Society*, 227–28, 231–47. Gustavo Benavides similarly argues for the close relationship between Buddhism and economics, but he seems more inclined to see the two as forming a mutually beneficial relationship rather than a conceptually inseparable or interpenetrating one (see "Economy"). Benavides's article advances a view that resonates strongly with the well-known views of Max Weber and his work on the relationship between Christianity and capitalism. Benavides argues that Buddhism was not just a beneficiary but rather a constitutive element of a monetized economy. Similar efforts to demonstrate Buddhism's role as an important constitutive element in the

development of "capitalist" activities in China are also found in Adamek, "Impossibility of the Given," and Walsh, *Sacred Economies*.
37. Gernet, *Buddhism in Chinese Society*, 310.
38. In an elegant summary of Pierre Bourdieu's reflections on the arbitrariness of "cultural tastes" and "distinction," Alain Bresson similarly writes: "A dominant social stratum abandons one element of distinction in favor of another as soon as it is widely disseminated. What counts is not the signified of the elements of distinction, but rather its signifier as a social marker" (*Making of the Ancient Greek Economy*, 18).
39. For a convenient overview of the state's efforts to redefine its relation to the Buddhist establishment, see U-gŭn Han, "Policies toward Buddhism."
40. For the state's efforts to control land and labor during this period, see the classic studies by Sudō, "Kōrai makki yori Chōsen shoki" and "Kōraichō yori Chōsen shoki"; and Yi Sangbaek, *Yijo kŏn'guk ŭi yŏn'gu*.
41. On the Red Turban incursion and its impact, see Robinson, *Empire's Twilight*, 130–219.
42. For a study of the destruction of monasteries and the efforts to restore them during the late Koryŏ period, see Yi Pyŏnghŭi, *Koryŏ hugi sawŏn kyŏngje yŏn'gu*, 173–334.
43. For the collapse of the Yuan paper currency bloc and limited state-level trade with China, see Yi Kanghan, *Koryŏ wa Wŏn cheguk ŭi kyoyŏk ŭi yŏksa*, esp. chap. 8. The importance of the Yuan paper currency bloc for the Koryŏ economy is noted in Robinson, *Empire's Twilight*, 49. On the negative economic impact of the Japanese pirate raids, see Yi Hyŏnjong, "Waegu," 229–34; Pak Chonggi, "Koryŏmal waegu"; and Hazard, "Japanese Marauding."
44. I borrow this idea of pushing Buddhism into the margins of public authority from Timothy Brook, who distinguishes public authority from the narrower terms of state control. Public authority, as Brook explains, expresses the reception of the state's authority in the local arena; in other words, it "exists to the extent that people are aware of and respond to the presence of the state" ("At the Margins," 162). For an argument against the claim that Buddhism was simply suppressed or persecuted by the Chosŏn state, see also Baker, "Privatization of Buddhism."

1. Sowing the Seeds of Salvation with Wealth

1. In 1017, the practice of converting one's home into a Buddhist monastery and wives (presumably after their husband's death) becoming nuns was banned (*KS* 85: 8b–9a). This ban, however, seems to have been largely ignored. In 1101, for instance, the ban had to be proclaimed once again (*KS* 85: 10a–b). This second ban appears to have been ignored as well (see chap. 5). Another relevant ban was announced in 1275: Koryŏ subjects were banned from going to monasteries except for the purpose of performing vegetarian feasts for the anniversary of their parents' deaths (*KS* 85: 13b). These bans had less to do with doubts about giving to the Buddhist establishment than with the Koryŏ throne's efforts to maintain control over valuable material and symbolic resources. Indeed, until Buddhism was

pushed into the margins of public authority during the Chosŏn dynasty, the faithful, the throne included, continued to give generously to the Buddhist establishment.

2. The stele is currently housed in the Kaesŏng History Museum in North Korea. It is 238 centimeters tall and 130.3 centimeters wide.
3. In his study of the Hyŏnhwa-sa stele, Sem Vermeersch, for instance, claims that "the whole project was intended to obliterate claims of illegitimacy through a show of filial piety" ("Royal Ancestor Worship," 116). The real driving force behind the production of the stele and the construction of the monastery were "practical concerns for legitimation and political authority" (132). These claims were made earlier by Kim Ch'anghyŏn in his article "Koryŏ Hyŏnhwa-sa pi punsŏk" as well. Focusing on the political function of the monastery, Han Kimun argues that Hyŏnhwa-sa was used as "a center to gather supporters from his inner political circle and Buddhist forces" (*Koryŏ sawŏn ŭi kujo wa kinŭng*, 253). In his study of late Koryŏ memorial monasteries, Chin Sŏnggyu argues that the aristocracy was involved in the construction of these monasteries during a period when Buddhism had grown corrupt simply for personal gain (see "Koryŏ hugi wŏnch'al e taehayŏ").
4. See, e.g., Ch'ae Sangsik, *Koryŏ hugi pulgyo-sa yŏn'gu*, 11–53.
5. See Chŏng Yongsuk, *Koryŏ wangsil chongnaehon yŏn'gu*, 80–99. The use of marriage alliances, however, is a strategy that goes back to the dynastic founder T'aejo (Deuchler, *Confucian Transformation of Korea*, 57–58). As Deuchler points out, the use of consanguineous marriage was not limited to the royal family (ibid., 60).
6. *KS* 88: 10a.
7. *KS* 4: 1b, *KS* 88: 10.
8. Hyŏnjong fled the capital on February 9, 1011, and was able to return to the palace, which was left in ruins, on April 5, 1011 (*KS* 4: 6b, 7b).
9. This took place on May 12, 1009 (*KS* 4: 2b).
10. This visit took place on June 16 (*KS* 4: 12a). For the location of the tomb, see *CKS*: 244.
11. During the Khitan invasions, T'aejo's remains were moved to prevent the invaders from doing them harm. In 1016, Hyŏnjong had the remains relocated to a site on Mount Songak (*KS* 4: 20a). For more on the burial, relocation, and reburial of T'aejo's remains, see Horlyck, "Ways of Burial," 90–91.
12. *KS* 90: 3b. A year earlier, in 1016, Hyŏnjong also ordered the construction of a monastery named Pongsŏn Honggyŏng-sa near present-day Ch'ŏnan in South Ch'ungch'ŏng. The monastery was constructed to honor Wang Uk's wish to create a place where weary travelers could rest and, perhaps more importantly, to secure an important way station between the capital and the southwestern region of the peninsula, where the central government's presence was still relatively weak. For this point, see Kang Hyŏnja, "Koryŏ Hyŏnjongdae Pongsŏn Honggyŏng-sa ŭi kinŭng"; and Kang, "Koryŏ Hyŏnjongdae Pongsŏn Honggyŏng-sa ŭi ch'anggŏn paegyong." This is also noted in Ch'oe Pyŏnghŏn, "Koryŏ chunggi Hyŏnhwa-sa," 116.
13. This was September 8, 1017 (*KS* 4: 24b).
14. For the conventions of royal ancestor worship in Koryŏ, see Hŏ, *Koryŏ pulgyosa yŏn'gu*, 47–102.

15. Koryŏ kings frequently built monasteries with a separate portrait hall (chinjŏn) in which to house the funerary portraits of their parents, siblings, and themselves. These monasteries were often simply called "memorial monasteries" (wŏndang or wŏnch'al). Hŏ Hŭngsik has shown that these memorial monasteries and portrait halls enjoyed special privileges as official structures associated with the royal cult (Koryŏ pulgyosa yŏn'gu, 47–102). This seems to have been especially true for the monasteries that housed memorial portraits of King Injong's agnatic ancestors. For these monasteries, the state appointed portrait hall attendants (chinjŏnjik), officials of moderate rank, and guards (wisukkun) with honorary military rank to look after the portrait halls.
16. KS 4: 27a, 36a–b.
17. Ch'ae's inscription for the reverse side of the stele was completed a year after Chu's in the tenth lunar month of 1022 (HKC: 453).
18. Ibid., 442.
19. Ibid., 446.
20. Ibid., 446.
21. Mount Yŏngch'wi was chosen as the site of construction for two reasons. First, as noted in the stele preface, it was located near the burial grounds of Hyŏnjong's parents. Second, the mountain provided an ideal landscape in which to build a monastery. In his monastery record, Ch'ae Ch'ungsun describes the king's response to the natural environs of the monastery this way: "face it up close, and it is lovable; gaze at it from afar, and it is like a painting" (HKC: 448).
22. The king also furnished the new monastery with a Perfection of Wisdom Sutra fund (Panyagyŏng po) that would help cover the costs of printing the texts on these woodblocks. Ch'oe Pyŏnghŏn argues that the fund probably was not simply for printing the Perfection of Wisdom Sutra but for printing the entire canon ("Koryŏ chunggi Hyŏnhwa-sa," 107). For a counterargument, see Vermeersch, Power of the Buddhas, 351–52. As an offering to honor Chŏngjong, King Munjong made a set of Buddhist scriptures with the gold and silver utensils in Chŏngjong's spirit hall (hondang) and the silk that the Khitan Liao had sent as a condolence offering (KS 8: 11b–12a). Clearly, making an offering of a set of Buddhist scriptures was a fine example of showing respect for one's ancestors and deceased monarchs (Vermeersch, Power of the Buddhas, 355).
23. On the Fan's charitable estate, see Twitchett, "Fan Clan's Charitable Estate." The earliest known family-based charitable fund (ŭijae) in Koryŏ was established by Yi Yangjik (fl. late 13th–early 14th century). A record for the charitable fund can be found in KJJ 2: 1a–2b. The author of the record, Yi Kok, and Yi Yangjik were close friends (see KJJ 7: 3a).
24. For the history of the use of monastic endowments for moneylending in Buddhism and Chinese Buddhism in particular, see Gernet, Buddhism in Chinese Society, esp. 167–86. Gernet also explains the introduction of the Buddhist concept of consecrated ("permanent") property to China (chap. 3). For a study of monastic endowments (po) in Koryŏ, see Han Kimun, "Koryŏsidae sawŏnbo." For an example of a donor making a specific request that his donations be used as capital for generating interest, see Ch'oe Hae, Sŏnwŏn-sa chesŭng ki (Record of offering

vegetarian feasts to the *saṅgha* at Sŏnwŏn-sa), in *CGCB* 1: 20b–21b. Ch'oe Hae's record and the size and function of endowments are discussed in more detail in chapter 2.

25. Giving to a field of merit was not, in other words, an instance of what Thorstein Veblen famously called "conspicuous consumption" (a conscious strategy of distinction) but an instance of cultural competency (a structuring structure) at work; for structuring structure or habitus and the formation of taste, see Bourdieu, *Distinction*. Impressive forms of giving, such as Hyŏnhwa-sa, articulated *the ability to give, appropriate, and consume as if wealth were seed and salvation its fruit*. As long as this ability and its value could be taken for granted, the ritual custom of giving to a field of merit remained effective and popular regardless of the private motives or fervor of the people who practiced it. On the limits of using (ulterior) motives to explain the efficacy and appeal of ritual, see Sharf, "Ritual." For a cogent critique of the instrumentalist view of ritual, see also Bell, *Ritual Theory, Ritual Practice*, esp. chap. 8. For a demonstration of how metaphors influence behavior and structure experience, see Fernandez, "Persuasions and Performances;" and Lakoff and Johnson, *Metaphors We Live By*.

26. I borrow this expression from Peter Brown, who argues that Christian metaphors for giving infused the act of generosity with a sense of drama (*Through the Eye*, 86).

27. According to one rough estimate, a *kyŏl* was equivalent to 10,000 square meters, or 2.5 acres (Vermeersch, *Power of the Buddhas*, 273–74). However, *kyŏl* would later refer not to *size* or surface area but to *quality* of crop yield (Palais, "Land Tenure in Korea," 197).

28. There is some disagreement as to whether these donations were actually made. The relevant entry in the *History of Koryŏ* (Koryŏsa) (September 3, 1020) ends with the phrase "did not *nap*" (*punap*). Here, *punap* could be read either as "did not make the donation" or as "did not accept it [i.e., the arguments against the donation]." Sem Vermeersch claims that the entry should be read as "no donations were made" (*Power of the Buddhas*, 292–93). The size of the donation is quite astonishing considering the fact that the total area of arable land during the late Koryŏ is said to have been about 620,000 *kyŏl* (Kang Chinch'ŏl, *Kaejŏng Koryŏ t'oji chedosa*, 142). But in the *History of Koryŏ*, the phrase "did not *nap*" usually refers to the king's refusal to accept the recommendation of his officials. In fact, since the commemorative stele for Hyŏnhwa-sa mentions a sizable donation of land (discussed below), there is good reason to believe that the donation was indeed made.

29. For information on Pŏpkyŏng and his relationship with Hyŏnjong, see Ch'oe Pyŏnghŏn, "Koryŏ chunggi Hyŏnhwa-sa," 113, and Vermeersch, "Buddhist Temples," 199–200.

30. As Yi Pyŏnghŭi points out, there are a few different transcriptions of the Hyŏnhwa-sa stele, and they all read the two characters before the character *kyŏng* differently (*Koryŏ sigi sawŏn kyongje yŏn'gu*, 12). The *Haidong jinshi yuan* (compiled in 1832) transcription reads "two thousand" (Liu, *Haidong jinshi yuan, fulu shang*, 9a); Hŏ Hŭngsik's transcription in the *Han'guk kŭmsŏk chŏnmun* reads "one hundred" (*HKC*: 445); and the *Chōsen kinseki sōran* (published in 1919) transcription leaves the two characters blank (*CKS*: 245). According to Kim

Yongsŏp and Kang Chinch'ŏl, *kyŏl* and *kyŏng* were used interchangeably during the Koryŏ (see Kim, "Koryŏ sigi ŭi yangjŏnje"; and Kang, *Kaejŏng Koryŏ t'oji chedosa yŏn'gu*, 364–65). Yi Pyŏnghŭi (*Koryŏ sigi sawŏn kyongje yŏn'gu*) thus surmises that the 2,000 *kyŏng* refers to the total amount of land donated by *yangban* officials and royal clan members (mentioned in the stele) as well as the 1,240 *kyŏl* of military support land (mentioned in the *History of Koryŏ*). If *kyŏl* and *kyŏng* do refer to the same unit of measurement, then an endowment of 100 *kyŏng* seems disproportionately small for a monastery of Hyŏnhwa-sa's size. This low estimate also appears unlikely considering the number of slaves donated to the monastery. Consider also the fact that 100 *kyŏl* was equal to the salary of one high-ranking official, according to the "field and woodland rank system" (*chŏnsi kwa*) (Kang Chinch'ŏl, *Kaejŏng Koryŏ t'oji chedosa*, 39). Ch'oe Pyŏnghŏn also follows the *Haidong jinshi yuan* transcription and reads the donation as 2,000 *kyŏng* of land ("Koryŏ chunggi Hyŏnhwa-sa," 105). Unfortunately, the size of one *sŏk* is also unclear, but 1 *kyŏl* of land was expected to produce anywhere from two to six *sŏk* of grains in prebend rent.

31. The Koryŏ elite shared this attitude with their Chinese peers (see Chikusa, *Chūgoku bukkyō shakaishi kenkyū*, 133–34; Halperin, *Out of the Cloister*, 184; and Gernet, *Buddhism in Chinese Society*, 206–7). Chikusa argues persuasively that the transition from the aristocratic society of the Tang to a scholar-official society, or *shidaifu*, during the Song presented officials with the problem of the uncertain fate of their descendants and hence the ancestral rites for their descent groups. He attributes the popularity of graveside monasteries (C. *fensi*) during the Song to this uncertainty (see also Chikusa, *Sō Gen Bukkyō bunkashi kenkyū*, 454).
32. On sympathetic response or resonance in Buddhism, see Sharf, *Coming to Terms*, 77–133.
33. For an English-language study of this genre, see Wu, "On Chinese Sacrificial Orations."
34. See Ch'oe Ch'iwŏn, *Kyewŏn p'ilgyŏngjip*, vol. 16; and *TMS* 109: 1a–5a. For two Buddhist elegies that he composed in 882 for a Chinese official named Gao Zhaoyi, see ibid., vol. 15, and *TMS* 114: 25a–26a. For a list of all the sacrificial orations in *Tongmunsŏn* and a formal analysis of their content, see Cho Sŏnok, "'Tongmunsŏn' sojae chemun yŏn'gu." For a critical study of the historical conditions that made the selection of Buddhist texts in the *Tongmunsŏn* possible, see Hŏ Hŭngsik, *Koryŏ pulgyosa yŏn'gu*, 768–87.
35. On the use of tea as an offering, see *TMS* 109: 19a.
36. *HPC* 6: 360b22–c3. For alternative English-language translations, see Peter H. Lee, *Columbia Anthology*, 17, and McCann, *Early Korean Literature*, vii. My translation differs slightly from theirs. For an insightful analysis of the elegy in its proper ritual context, see Yang, "'Che mangmae ka.'" I follow Yang's analysis in my translation.
37. For the use of paper or spirit money in the economy of the afterlife, see Teiser, "The Growth of Purgatory," 133–35.
38. For research on the symbolism of Wŏlmyŏng's song, see the references in Yang, "'Che mangmae ka.'"

39. *TMS* 111: 16a–b. The three evil destinies are the three undesirable realms of rebirth within the six realms, namely, hell beings, hungry ghosts, and animals. The other three are humans, demigods, and gods. The highest stage (*sangp'um*) seems to refer to the highest stage in the nine stages of rebirth in Amitābha's Pure Land.
40. See Teiser, *Scripture on the Ten Kings*, esp. 1, 25–26.
41. For a detailed study of the development of this notion of purgatory and its relation to faith in the ten kings in Chinese Buddhism, see Teiser, *Scripture on the Ten Kings*. For notions of the afterlife and the cult of the ten kings in Koryŏ, see Kim Youngmi, "Buddhist Faith," and Cheeyon Kwŏn, "Scripture of the Ten Kings."
42. See *TMS* 111: 24b–25a.
43. Ch'ungji seems to have also prepared a separate sacrificial oration (*chemun*) for the event (*HPC* 6: 396a1–b4). But this is not clear. The sacrificial oration mentions the "completion of seven" (*tanch'il*), which may refer either to the end of the first week or to the end of the seventh week.
44. *HPC* 6: 405a3–4, *TMS* 112: 21b3–4.
45. For the eulogy, see *HPC* 6: 405a8–17, and *TMS* 112: 21b–22a.
46. Teiser, *The Ghost Festival*, 4, 31–35.
47. *HKC*: 450.
48. Chan master Dahui Zonggao (1089–1163) frequently used the general sermon (C. *pushuo*) for the purpose of praying for the dead (see Levering, "Ta-hui and Lay Buddhists").
49. *HPC* 6: 714b24–c2.
50. Ibid., 715a4–8.
51. Koryŏ Buddhists were no doubt indebted to the extensive treatment that the concept of the field of merit received in China. For the treatment of this concept in China, see Tokiwa Daijō, *Shina bukkyō no kenkyū*, 471–98; cited in Teiser, *The Ghost Festival*, 210.
52. *Taedo namsŏng Hŭngbok-sa kal* (Tablet for Hŭngbok-sa in Nancheng of Dadu), in *ICJ* 7: 5b.
53. *Yŏju Sillŭk-sa taejanggakki* (Record of Tripiṭaka Hall at Sillŭk-sa in Yŏju), in *HKC*: 1217; cf. *CKS*: 509.
54. According to Yi's record, the construction of the library began in 1380. It was completed in 1382.
55. *T* 12.374.375b10–12.
56. *T* 12.374.371c13–375b20.
57. *T* 25.1509.84c2–3.
58. The commentary also explains that those worthy of receiving offerings—members of the *saṅgha*—are like the wealthy and influential people of the world who garner respect from other people. They, too, earn respect with the "wealth" of their moral purity, meditative concentration, and wisdom and the influence of liberation and liberating insight (*T* 25.1509.223c15–18).
59. *T* 25.1509.223c18–224a7. For other scriptural references to Bakkula, see Lamotte, *Le Traité*, 1387.
60. *T* 25.1509.123b9–10, 130c3–4, and esp. 282b8–10.

61. *T* 25.1509.115a14–b23. A slightly different version of this story can be found in the *Divyāvadāna*. For an English-language translation of this story ("Brāhmaṇḍārikā-avadāna") from the *Divyāvadāna*, see Rotman, *Divine Stories*, 139–43.
62. Teiser attributes this power to the "dialectic of asceticism"—renouncing family allows one to enrich the family—practiced by the monastic community (see *The Ghost Festival*, 203–8). For a similar reading of this dialectic, see Benavides, "Economy," 88.
63. Teiser, *The Ghost Festival*, 210–11; see *T* 39.1792.506a5–14. The last sentence is not included in Teiser's English-language translation of the passage.
64. See Gregory, *Inquiry*, 93.
65. *T* 12.374.391a14–16.
66. *T* 12.374.418a4–5.
67. The *icchantika* problem has been the subject of much debate in Buddhism. For these debates and their relation to the perfection of giving (S. *dāna*), see Buswell, "The Path to Perdition."
68. The buddha nature of the insentient was the subject of heated debate in Chinese Buddhism (see Sharf, "How to Think").
69. *T* 30.1564.22a6–7.
70. *T* 30.1564.22a11–14.
71. In his rich and informative study on the sudden and gradual debate, Luis O. Gómez offers an elegant summary of this issue (see his "Purifying Gold," esp. 134).
72. These verses (with some variations in some cases) were also reproduced in the influential Chan genealogy *Jingde chuandeng lu* (Jingde era record of the transmission of the lamp); *T* 51.2076.219c17–18, 220c28–29, 221c24–25, 222b18–19, 223a17–18, 236b14–15).
73. Yampolsky, *The Platform Sūtra*, 176.
74. Ibid.
75. Later Chan authors therefore felt it necessary to slightly alter the verse (Sharf, "How to Think," 219). As Sharf points out, this verse also seems to be engaging in an altogether different doctrinal controversy about the buddha nature of insentient things.
76. Yampolsky, *The Platform Sūtra*, 177.
77. Ibid. As Yampolsky admits, the third line of the verse is unclear, but it does clearly refer to self-realization or awakening (C. *ziwu*).
78. For South and Southeast Asian examples of the use of this metaphor to engage with the problem of identity and difference and also causality, see Collins, *Selfless Persons*, 185–88, 218–24. For the use of this metaphor in Yogācāra, see Lusthaus, *Buddhist Phenomenology*, 193–94.
79. The Sautrāntikas used the seed (S. *bīja*) metaphor precisely to overcome this conceptual problem of the same source producing two different states of mind, namely, the wholesome (S. *kuśala*) and the unwholesome (S. *anuśaya*). As Padmanabh S. Jaini succinctly explains in his article on their use of this metaphor, the seed metaphor was used in this context to avoid the problem of mistakenly

granting ontological status to the two different states of mind before their operation or "fruition." As seeds, they are but potentialities (see Jaini, "Sautrāntika Theory of Bīja").

80. Brown, *Through the Eye*, 84.

2. Dark and Mysterious Ways

1. For Ch'oe Hae's *Sŏnwŏn-sa chesŭnggi* (Record of offering vegetarian feasts to the *saṅgha* at Sŏnwŏn-sa) can be found in *CGCB* 1: 20b–21b.
2. Ch'oe Sŏngji retired in 1324 (*KS* 108: 11a).
3. The size of a bushel in Koryŏ remains unclear.
4. Lady Kim was the daughter of Assistant Chancellor Kim Hwŏn. According to Ch'oe Sŏngji's funerary inscription, she passed away three years before her husband (*KMC*: 468). Curiously, no mention is made of Munjin in Ch'oe Sŏngji's funerary inscription.
5. *CGCB* 1: 21a.
6. *CGCB* 1: 20b.
7. "Yuandao" in Ma, *Han changli wenji jiaozhu*, 7–11. For an English-language translation of this essay, see de Bary and Bloom, *Sources of Chinese Tradition*, 569–73.
8. *CGCB* 1: 20b.
9. Ibid., 20b.
10. Ibid., 21a.
11. Ch'oe's *Song sŭng Sŏnji yu Kŭmgangsan sŏ* (Preface to bidding farewell to the monk Sŏnji who is traveling to Mount Kŭmgang) can be found in *CGCB* 1: 21b–23b.
12. Ibid., 21b.
13. According to the sutra, the bodhisattva Dharmodgata resides on this mountain in the middle of the sea. For a discussion of the cult of Dharmodgata in Korea, see McBride, *Domesticating the Dharma*, 132–33. For a more detailed account of sources that mention this bodhisattva, see Stiller, "Kŭmgangsan," 24–32.
14. For the account of the arrival of these icons, see Stiller, "Kŭmgangsan," 35–36.
15. The term "evil destinies" refers to the three undesirable realms of rebirth within the six realms of rebirth, namely, hell beings, hungry ghosts, and animals.
16. *CGCB* 1: 22b–23b.
17. See *Tut'asan Kanjang-am chungyŏnggi* (Restoration record of Kanjang-am on Mount Tut'a) in *CGCB* 1: 5a–7b. Ch'oe Hae and Yi Yŏnjong's friendship most likely dates back to 1303 when the two men passed the civil service examination (see Hŏ, *Koryŏ ŭi kwagŏ chedo*, 513). The two scholar-officials also traveled together to China in 1320 to take the civil service examination for foreigners (see *KRS* 35: 3a–b, *KRS* 74: 8a).
18. According to the *History of Koryŏ* (Koryŏsa), Yi Sŭnghyu was *relieved* of his post (*KS* 29: 11a). This, however, was not the end of his career in the central government. In 1298, King Ch'ungsŏn invited Yi Sŭnghyu to serve once again (*KSC* 22: 3b–4a).
19. For a study of Yi Sunghyu's views about Buddhism; see Chin, "Yi Sŭnghyu ŭi pulgyogwan."

20. *CGCB* 1: 6a.
21. Ibid., 6b.
22. Ibid., 7b.
23. Ch'oe Hae's contempt for the wealthy is also visible in his poem "Lotus in the Rain" (Uha) (see *TMS* 19: 7a).
24. Martina Deuchler also uses the notion of a "crisis of identity" to underscore the late Koryŏ elite's concerns about the exposure of "the *social* to the threat of being rendered obsolete by the *political*" (*Under the Ancestors' Eyes*, 38). Unlike Deuchler, I use the notion to explain how the "social" and the "political" became incommensurate.
25. For the former interpretation, see Pak Yongun, *Koryŏ sidaesa*, 644; Kim Ch'ungnyŏl, *Koryŏ yuhaksa*; Ko Hyeryŏng, *Koryŏ hugi sadaebu*, 147–49; Pyŏn Tongmyŏng, *Koryŏ hugi sŏngnihak*, 115; Ko Hyeryŏng, "Ch'oe Hae (1287–1340) ŭi saengae wa sasang"; and Kim Inho, *Koryŏ hugi sadaebu*, 124–25, 164–70. For the latter interpretation, see Han Ugŭn, *Yugyo chŏngch'i wa pulgyo*, 7; Ch'ae Sangsik, "Ch'oe Hae"; Ku Sanu, "14-segi," 76–79; Song Ch'anghan, "Ch'oe Hae ŭi ch'ŏkpullon e taehayŏ"; and Pak Yongun, *Koryŏ sidaesa*, 643. See also Takahashi Tōru, *Richō bukkyō*, 37. Some scholars, for example, Pak Yongun, Yun Kiyŏp, and Pyŏn Tongmyŏng, support both interpretations; see Yun, *Koryŏ hugi ŭi pulgyo*, 125–26, and Pyŏn, "Sŏngnihak."
26. *KS* 63:18–20; cited in Deuchler, *Confucian Transformation of Korea*, 135.
27. These memorials are examined more closely in the conclusion.
28. Studies that advance this view are too numerous to cite here. For a few representative examples, see Yun Yonggyun, *Shushigaku*; Yi Sangbaek, "Yubul yanggyo kyodae"; Yi Kibaek, *Han'guksa sillon*, 187–207; Kim Yun'gon, "Sinhŭng sadaebu ŭi taedu"; Yi Kinam, "Ch'ungsŏn wang"; Yi T'aejin, *Han'guk sahoesa*, 111–48; To Hyŏnch'ŏl, *Koryŏmal sadaebu*; Deuchler, *Confucian Transformation of Korea*; and Ko Hyeryŏng, *Koryŏ hugi sadaebu*.
29. The term *yangban*, or "two branches," refers to the civil and military branches of the central bureaucracy.
30. See Duncan, *Origins*, 97, 233.
31. Ibid., 237. For the argument in favor of Neo-Confucianism as a new ideology, see Deuchler, *Confucian Transformation of Korea*.
32. For ancient-style learning and the interests of the *yangban*, see Duncan, *Origins*, 265. For the *yangban*'s desire to perpetuate the Koryŏ system, see ibid., 203. The *yangban*, as Duncan again points out, found the idea of an activist government attractive because they began to see the offices that they and their forebears held in the dynastic government as the primary source of status and prestige.
33. Ibid., chap. 4.
34. See Yi Sangbaek's influential essay "Yubul yanggyo kyodae," which was originally published in Japanese in the second (1938) and third (1939) issues of *Tōyō shisō kenkyū*. The Japanese scholar Takahashi Tōru was, however, the first to suggest that the corruption of Buddhism was the cause behind the late Koryŏ anti-Buddhist movement (*Richō bukkyō*, 37–43).
35. According to the biography, Unam-sa was granted thirty *sŏk* of rice each month, and all other necessities were provided for (*KS* 114: 3a). The monastery housed the

funerary portrait of King Kongmin's Mongolian consort Huiyi Luguo Imperial Princess. For the large endowments made to the monastery, see *KS* 89: 30a.
36. *KS* 114: 3a–b.
37. The military was placed under the control of a new governing body known as the Consolidated Army Command (Samgunbu) in 1391. Men loyal to Yi (Cho Chun, Chŏng Tojŏn, and Pae Kŭngnyŏm) were appointed its commissioners (*KRS* 46: 1a, *KRSC* 35: 1a).
38. Rank land is land that the state set aside in the capital district (Kyŏnggi) to pay officials their salaries in the form of prebends; see Duncan, *Origins*, 206–11.
39. The "fiscal crisis" thesis was developed further in Han Ugŭn's influential study of the anti-Buddhist policies of the late Koryŏ and early Chosŏn dynasty (see Han, *Yugyo chŏngch'i wa pulgyo*). For an English-language translation of part of this study, see Han, "Policies toward Buddhism."
40. *KS* 78: 38b. For Cho Chun and the rank land law, see Duncan, *Origins*, 206–11.
41. *KS* 78: 41a–b.
42. *KS* 108: 12a–b. Ch'ae's biography in the *History of Koryŏ* states that the new land registers compiled by Ch'ae were so inconsistent with past registers that peasants found it difficult to make a living. Ch'ae is even said to have used the cadastral survey as an opportunity to steal land from peasants and privately acquire immense wealth. His continuous pursuit of wealth and power would eventually result in his exile in 1321 (*KS* 35: 5b). There is a reference to official land registers used in 1285, which seems to imply that not all registers were lost during the Mongol invasions (*KS* 78: 4b–5a). This reference also indicates that monasteries had already developed large landed estates with grant ordinances (*sap'ae*), which were not recorded in official land registers. Whether the new registers compiled by Ch'ae reflect land acquired through these grant ordinances is unclear.
43. See Duncan, *Origins*, 211.
44. *T'aejo sillok* 7: 12b; noted in Han, *Yugyo chŏngch'i wa pulgyo*, 17.
45. The king is known to have made lavish donations to Hŭngch'ŏn-sa, the memorial monastery for his late queen consort Sindŏk (see *T'aejo sillok* 11: 4a). Han Ugŭn mistakenly assumes that the rank land law provisions concerning monastic property and the remonstrance official Han Sanghwan's advice were effectively carried out.
46. *T'aejo sillok* 12: 1a; noted in Han Ugŭn, *Yugyo chŏngch'i wa pulgyo*, 17. Han mistakenly identifies the source of this reference in the *T'aejo sillok* as *kwŏn* 13. The correct reference is *kwŏn* 12. Han also notes a reference to an emergency measure that was taken on November 10. Taxes were collected from all *kongjŏn* and *sajŏn* (land assigned to individuals) with a few exceptions—which means monasteries were taxed—to compensate for the loss of revenue that resulted from floods in the southern regions of Korea. But this was an emergency measure limited to the year of the flooding (1397).
47. *T'aejong sillok* 7: 7b; noted in Han Ugŭn, *Yugyo chŏngch'i wa pulgyo*, 19. The total amount of arable land in the capital district reported by the Censor General was roughly 149,300 *kyŏl* (and roughly 800,000 *kyŏl* for the entire kingdom). That means merit subject land, tax-exempt land, constituted more than one-fifth of the

total arable land available in the capital district. Rank land is said to have been roughly 84,100 *kyŏl*. The recommendation was made to collect 2 *tu* of rice per 1 *kyŏl*.
48. In total, seventy monasteries were officially recognized in Tosŏn's record. For a general overview of Tosŏn's geomantic theories and relevant sources, see Byŏnghŏn Ch'oe, "Tosŏn's Geomantic Theories." For the translation of *Milgi* as "Secret Record," see Vermeersch, *Power of the Buddhas*, 297.
49. *T'aejong sillok* 3: 23a; noted in Han Ugŭn, *Yugyo chŏngch'i wa pulgyo*, 19. The aforementioned monastery, Unam-sa, is said to have had a permanent assembly of one hundred monks; see *T'aejong sillok* 10: 25b.
50. *T'aejong sillok* 4: 7a; noted in Han Ugŭn, *Yugyo chŏngch'i wa pulgyo*, 20.
51. *T'aejong sillok* 10: 25b.
52. Each of the five Kyo and two Sŏn schools were allowed one monastery in the old and new capitals. Every prefecture was allowed one monastery from Kyo and Sŏn. Every district was allowed one monastery from either Kyo or Sŏn.
53. Monasteries with 100 permanent resident monks were allowed 20 male slaves, 50 monks were allowed 10 male slaves, and 10 monks with 2 male slaves.
54. *T'aejong sillok* 10: 28b.
55. *T'aejong sillok* 11: 13a.
56. Han Kimun has demonstrated that these monasteries also existed in the Koryŏ period (see Han, "Koryŏ sidae Chabok-sa"). For a closer look at Chabok-sa monasteries from the early Chosŏn period, see Yun Kiyŏp, "Chosŏnch'o kunso chongp'a."
57. On January 8, 1408, the state council also received approval from the king to add 88 Chabok-sa monasteries to the list of 242. It seems these new Chabok-sa monasteries were granted to monks whose monasteries had become unsustainable or less desirable as a result of the 1406 reform (see Kim Kapchu, *Chosŏn sidae sawŏn kyŏngjesa yŏn'gu*, 19–23).
58. See also the similar argument made by Kim Kapchu in ibid., 15–25.
59. Kim Kapchu assumes that these monasteries were thus allowed only one or two *kyŏl* of woodlands (making it virtually impossible for them to sustain themselves), but the king seems to have actually granted an *additional* one or two *kyŏl* of woodlands on top of what the monasteries already possessed (ibid., 20).
60. Ibid., 19. Kim also demonstrates that in later periods, the Buddhist establishment was able to develop large landed estates as it once did during the Koryŏ.
61. This is shown in ibid., esp. chap. 2.
62. When speaking of the relation between Buddhism (or religion) and the state in premodern Korea, the role of Buddhism is all too often reduced to provider of protection or legitimation (see, e.g., Hatada, "Kōraichō ni okeru jiin keizai," 561–67, and Vermeersch, *Power of the Buddhas*). This instrumentalist and reductionist reading of Buddhism rightfully demonstrates that Buddhism played a vital sociopolitical role in premodern Korea, but it may leave one with the misleading impression that religion is merely a "cultural" reflection of or reaction to deeper problems or concerns. One could cite the famous ten injunctions and especially the second injunction attributed to the dynastic founder, T'aejo, in

support of the claim that the Koryŏ elite distinguished between religion, wealth, and power; see Breuker, *Establishing a Pluralist Society*, 356–69 (my thanks to the anonymous reviewer for pointing this out). But the second injunction against the excessive construction of memorial monasteries does not necessarily support this claim when understood in context. The injunction appeared early in the dynasty's history when the young throne needed to establish firm control over this valuable symbolic resource (i.e., Buddhism) and some radical changes took place within the elite stratum. The injunction, in other words, was not necessarily made to counter waste and conspicuous consumption.

63. The reference to T'aejo's donation of land to Haein-sa can be found in the *Kayasan Haein-sa kojŏk* (Old record of Haein-sa on Mount Kaya) in *CKS* 1: 495–96; cited in Yi Pyŏnghŭi, *Koryŏ sigi sawŏn kŏongje yŏn'gu*, 8, 143 n. 7, and Vermeersch, *Power of the Buddhas*, 281. The donation made to Unmun-sŏnsa is noted in *Samguk yusa* (*HPC* 6: 343b23); cited in Yi Pyŏnghŭi, *Koryŏ sigi sawŏn kyŏngje yŏn'gu*, and Vermeersch, *Power of the Buddhas*, 287. The donation to Chikchi-sa is mentioned in *Chikchi-saji* (Chikchi-sa gazetteer), published in 1776; cited in in Yi Pyŏnghŭi, *Koryŏ sigi sawŏn kyongje yŏn'gu*, 8, and Vermeersch, *Power of the Buddhas*, 288–89.

64. See *Kayasan Powŏn-sa ko kuksa chejŭngsi Pŏbin samjung taesa chi pi* (Stele for the late state preceptor and triple-exalted great master posthumously named Pŏbin of Powŏn-sa on Mount Kaya), dated 978, in *HKC*: 1: 417 (cf. Han'guksa yŏksa yŏn'guhoe, *Yŏkchu Namal Yŏch'o kŭmsŏngmun* 1: 312); cited in Vermeersch, *Power of the Buddhas*, 291, and Yi Pyŏnghŭi, *Koryŏ sigi sawŏn kyŏngje yŏn'gu*, 120. For the role of the royal preceptor as the king's spiritual counterpart, see Vermeersch, *Power of the Buddhas*, 145. Powŏn-sa had an ordination platform and was recognized by the state as a place where monks could receive official certification (*KS* 6: 8a–b).

65. This information is provided in the *Changan-sa chunghŭngbi* (Changan-sa restoration stele), dated 1345, in *CKS*: 640; cited in Yi Pyŏnghŭi, *Koryŏ sigi sawŏn kyŏngje yŏn'gu*, 24. This endowment consisted of parcels of land from the Chŏlla, Yanggwang, and Sŏhae circuits.

66. It is worth noting here that Hyŏnhwa-sa and Powŏn-sa each received 50 slaves for every 1,000 *kyŏng* of land.

67. See Han Kimun, *Koryŏ sawŏn ŭi kujo wa kinŭng*, 57, 233, and Yi Pyŏnghŭi, *Koryŏ sigi sawŏn kyŏngje yŏn'gu*, 13. Like Hyŏnhwa-sa, Hŭngwang-sa is said to have had 1,000 monks in residence. Yi demonstrates that the minimum amount of grains needed to sustain a monastic population of 1,000 monks was about 1,200 *sŏk* during the Koryŏ. There is also evidence that the monastery's wealth increased even during the reign of King Munjong. In 1058, for instance, the king gave Hŭngwang-sa all the land grants, fisheries, boats, and slaves that belonged to Kyŏngch'ang Palace (*KS* 8: 10a).

68. Kukch'ŏng-sa housed the portrait of the queen mother Inye Sundŏk, Yi Chayŏn's daughter and Munjong's queen consort (*KS* 11: 9b). Ch'ŏnsu-sa was Sukchong's memorial monastery (*KS* 14: 9a). Another monastery that may have possessed a large land endowment is Anhwa-sa. The monastery was originally built by T'aejo in 930, but it came to house the funerary portraits of King Yejong and his queen

consort, Sundŏk (d. 1118), who was the daughter of the powerful minister Yi Chagyŏm (*KS* 14: 33b, *KS* 15: 4a). See the discussion of these memorial monasteries in Hŏ, *Koryŏ pulgyosa yŏn'gu*, 68–84.

69. For the total amount of arable land, see *KS* 78: 38a–b. According to a memorial submitted by Cho Chun in 1389, arable land on record had shrunk to 500,000 *kyŏl* or less, and this, as Cho explains, meant that there was only 170,000 *kyŏl* of land grants left to pay post stations, ferry stations, public hostels, *hyangni*, Buddhist monasteries, and so on (*KS* 78: 36b–37a).
70. See *KS* 78: 27a; noted in Hatada, "Kōraichō ni okeru jiin keizai," 563, and Kamata, *Chōsen bukkyōshi*, 154. See also the discussion of this memorial in Vermeersch, *Power of the Buddhas*, 297–98.
71. For the "public" nature of *kongjŏn*, see Hatada, "Kōrai no kōden."
72. For the use of monasteries as alternative palaces, see *KSC* 9: 14b, *KS* 30: 24a, and *KS* 40: 14b. For the use of monasteries as diplomatic-ritual spaces, see the discussion of Taeun-sa below. In 1181, the highest-ranking officials in the central bureaucracy gathered at the monastery Pongŭn-sa to carry out an official inspection of the weights and measures used in the central market of the capital (*KS* 85: 12a).
73. *KS* 7: 36a–b.
74. Ibid., 40a–b.
75. According to the "treatise on law" (*KS* 85) in the *History of Koryŏ*, monks were barred from seeking lodging among commoners (6a), fighting over slaves (8b), making wine (8b, 9a), wearing overly luxurious clothes (8b), playing secular music (9a), and using post-station horses to transport their wealth (9b). Tellingly, many of these legal measures were recommended and put into effect during King Hyŏnjong's reign. For a discussion of Koryŏ period regulations concerning monks and nuns, see Kim Yŏngmi, "Koryŏ sidae pulgyogye."
76. The difference in size of donations should not be used to hastily argue that larger donations were made for political ("ideological") purposes whereas smaller donations were made primarily for private ("religious") ones. There is no evidence to substantiate this argument, at least not in the context of Koryŏ Buddhism.
77. See *KS* 8: 21b.
78. See *KS* 9: 18a. Taeun-sa also housed a royal funerary portrait, but it is unclear whose portrait was hung in the monastery's portrait hall (*KS* 83: 6b).
79. In 918, T'aejo declared that the practice of extracting 6 *sŏk* per 1 *kyŏng* of land was excessive, so he limited it to 3 *sŭng* per *pu* (*KS* 78: 21a). If the *History of Koryŏ* followed traditional Chinese measurements, then 1 *sŏk* should be the equivalent of 10 *tu*, 10 *tu* the equivalent of 100 *sŭng*, and 1 *kyŏl* the equivalent of 100 *pu*. For the units of measurement, see Wilkinson, *Chinese History*, 237. For *kyŏl* and *pu*, see Kang Chinch'ŏl, *Kaejŏng Koryŏ t'oji chedosa*, 364. There is general agreement among historians of Koryŏ, however, that 1 *sŏk* was the equivalent of 15 *tu* (Yi Chongbong, "Koryŏ sidae ŭi yangje," esp. 205–6). Either way, it seems that T'aejo had limited the prebends from *kongjŏn* to 2 or 3 *sŏk* per *kyŏl*, that is, half or less than half of what it used to be. In 992, the prebends collected from *kongjŏn* were similarly set at an average of about 2 to 3 *sŏk* per 1 *kyŏl* or *kyŏng* of fertile paddy field, which is

25 percent of total yield (*KS* 78: 44a). All in all, this seems to suggest that a land grant of 100 *kyŏng*, if it composed of *kongjŏn*, was expected to produce 200 to 300 *sŏk* of grains as income for the monastery. If the land grant was of *sajŏn* (which was said to have been taxed at the rate of 50 percent of total yield), then the income presumably would have been higher—about 400 to 600 *sŏk* of grains (*KS* 78: 44a). James Palais cautiously suggests that the 50 percent rent on *sajŏn* may have been a legal limit on sharecropping on privately owned land ("Land Tenure in Korea," 143). In his famous land reform memorial, Cho Chun recommended the rate of taxation for both *kongjŏn* and *sajŏn* be fixed at 20 *tu*, that is, 3 *sŏk* per *kyŏl* (*KS* 78: 27b). Palais argues, however, that the 10 percent *cho* (prebend) rate for *kongjŏn*, which was set at 2 or 3 *sŏk*, was probably idealistic Confucian propaganda and that the real rate was closer to 7 *sŏk* per *kyŏl* (just under 30 percent) (133–34). This would mean that 100 *kyŏng* of land was expected to produce 700 *sŏk* of prebend rent.

80. This is noted in the *Chogyesan Susŏn-sa chungch'anggi* (Restoration record of Susŏn-sa on Mount Chogye), dated 1207 (see No Myŏngho et al., *Han'guk kodae chungse*, 387–89. For a textual critical analysis of this source, see Hŏ Hŭngsik, *Han'guk chungse pulgyosa yŏn'gu*, 284–302. Yi Pyŏnghŭi speculates that, since Hŭngwang-sa (2,800 units) could accommodate 1,000 monks in residence, the size of Yongsu-sa (90 units) must have accommodated no more than 31 or 32 monks (*Koryŏ hugi sawŏn kyŏngje yŏn'gu*, 352 n. 63). Indeed, Kilsang-sa, similar in size (100 units), is said to have accommodated 30 to 40 monks (see No et al., *Han'guk kodae chungse*, 387; Buswell, *Tracing Back the Radiance*, 27; and Yi Pyŏnghŭi, *Koryŏ hugi sawŏn kyŏngje yŏn'gu*, 373). One unit (*kan* or *k'an*) is approximately six square feet.

81. No et al., *Han'guk kodae chungse*, 389. Yi Pyŏnghŭi understood this passage to mean that poor commoners were mobilized and made to suffer in support of the restoration effort, but the evidence Yi marshals in support of this reading is anecdotal, impressionistic, and ideologically driven and therefore unreliable.

82. Structures that measured 80 units in total size were added to the monastery (see No et al., *Han'guk kodae chungse*, 388, and Buswell, *Tracing Back the Radiance*, 30).

83. This is noted in the *Chogye-san che ise ko Tansok-sa chuji Susŏn-sa chu chŭngsi Chin'gak kuksa pimyŏng* (Stele inscription for the former abbot of Tansok-sa, second-generation abbot of Susŏn-sa on Mount Chogye, posthumously titled State Preceptor Chin'gak), in *TYSC* 35: 8a. For a textual critical analysis of this source, see Hŏ, *Han'guk chungse pulgyosa yŏn'gu*, 329–46. There is no way to know for sure whether or not the community at Susŏn-sa actually grew in number, but one source indicates that the full assembly at the monastery consisted of ninety-six individuals (No et al., *Han'guk kodae chungse*, 389).

84. The size of Susŏn-sa's permanent property implies that the monastery was entitled to prebend rent from at least 5,000 *kyŏl* of land (if one assumes that only 2 *sŏk* of rice was collected per *kyŏl*). There are three documents that detail the permanent property of Susŏn-sa from the early thirteenth century. They are *Chogyesan Susŏn-sa chungch'anggi* Hyesim's *Sangjubogi* (Record of [Susŏn-sa's] permanent treasury), and a government survey of Susŏn-sa's property compiled sometime between 1221 and 1226. For the *Sangjubogi*, see *HPC* 6: 65b–66a. For the government survey, see No et al., *Han'guk kodae chungse*, 373–403. The government

survey also includes a copy of the restoration record. For an English-language summary of the survey, see Buswell, *Tracing Back the Radiance*, 90 n. 166. A detailed study of the economic activities of Susŏn-sa can be found in Yi Pyŏnghŭi, *Koryŏ hugi sawŏn kyŏngje yŏn'gu*, 371–410.

85. See No et al., *Han'guk kodae chungse*, 389–391. The contents of these donations have been studied by Pak Chonggi (see *Chibae wa chayul ŭi konggan*, 345–62). Monastic endowments, as Han Kimun has shown, were not limited to the funding of memorial rites. Similar endowments were made for printing Buddhist texts, maintaining important monastic property (e.g., the monastery's bell), and praying for the long life of the king and the well-being of the state (*ch'uksŏng yuhyangbo*) (see Han, *Koryŏ sawŏn*, 278–81, and Han, "Koryŏsidae sawŏnbo").

86. Pak Chonggi points out that the land or, more precisely, prebend rents donated to prayers for the king and state came not from land owned privately by individuals but from land owned by the state (*Chibae wa chayul ŭi konggan*, 354–55). In contrast, land donated for the purpose of praying for deceased family members was privately owned land. Pak also took the presence of land privately owned by Ch'oe and his military supporters in the southwestern region of Korea as evidence of the extensive privatization of land in this area during the age of military rule.

87. This argument can be found in Ch'ae Sangsik, *Koryŏ hugi pulgyosa yŏn'gu*, 11–67; Min Hyŏn'gu, "Wŏlnam-sa chi," 42–55; and Buswell, *Tracing Back the Radiance*, esp. 17–20. Studies that cite Ch'ae Sangsik's work are too numerous to cite here, but some notable examples are Shultz's *Generals and Scholars* and Pak Yongun's *Koryŏ sidaesa*. For the connection between powerful aristocratic families and the Buddhist establishment, see Han Kimun, *Koryŏ sawŏn ŭi kujo wa kinŭng*, 61–75; Pak Yujin, "Koryŏ sidae sŭngnyŏ"; and Vermeersch, "Buddhist Temples or Political Battlegrounds?"

88. Ch'ae Sangsik's (*Koryŏ hugi pulgyosa yŏn'gu*) focus on the Buddhist establishment's "social function" is meant to serve as a critique of earlier scholarship, which tends to focus on either the support that Susŏn-sa received from military officials (political context) or the doctrinal innovations of its founding abbot (philosophical context).

89. For the resistance staged by the conservative Buddhist establishment, see the classic study by Kim Chongguk, "Kōrai bushin seiken"; Shultz, *Generals and Scholars*, 136–38; Min, "Wŏlnam-sa chi"; and Kim Tangt'aek, *Koryŏ ŭi muin chŏnggwŏn*, 323–37. On the tendency to attribute the popularity of Sŏn Buddhism among military men to its simplicity and iconoclasm, see Min, "Wŏlnam-sa chi," 56, and Shultz, *Generals and Scholars*, 139. On the patronage of Sŏn monasteries by officials who supported the military government, see Shultz, "Twelfth-Century Koryŏ Politics." On the popularity or "revival" (*puhŭng*) of Sŏn Buddhism in the twelfth century, see Ch'oe Pyŏnghŏn, "Koryŏ chunggi Yi Chahyŏn," and Hŏ Hŭngsik, *Koryŏ pulgyosa yŏn'gu*, 463–97.

90. For the contradictions, see Kim Yun'gon, "Koryŏ kwijok sahoe ŭi che mosun"; cited in Ch'ae Sangsik, *Koryŏ hugi pulgyosa yŏn'gu*, 31. For the purges, see Shultz, "Twelfth-Century Koryŏ Politics," and Shultz, "Han Aninp'a ŭi tŭngjang kwa kŭ yŏkhal."

91. Ch'ae Sangsik, *Koryŏ hugi pulgyosa yŏn'gu*, 28–29. Ch'ae also suggests that scholars may have begun to see themselves as a social group distinct from the *hyangni* base from which they arose during this period (ibid., 43). There is little evidence, however, to substantiate this view.
92. Ibid., esp. 8–9, 233. A similar argument was made earlier by Ch'oe Pyŏnghŏn, "Susŏn kyŏlsa ŭi sasangsajŏk ŭiŭi," 22.
93. This is also noted in Hatada, "Kōraichō ni okeru jiin keizai," 585–93. The peasant population—arguably the most important source of state revenue—responded to this problem in various ways. Some chose to become wandering peasants, and others rose up in revolt (see Ch'ae Ungsŏk, *Koryŏ sidae ŭi kukka wa chibang sahoe*, 222–32, and Pak Chonggi, *Chibae wa chayul ŭi konggan*, 407–15).
94. Ch'ae Sangsik rightly points out that commoners participated in the restoration of Kilsang-sa, but this does not necessarily imply that they did so because they were drawn to Chinul's and Hyesim's reformist cause. Also, it should be noted here that the full assembly at the monastery consisted of only ninety-six individuals (see No et al., *Han'guk kodae chungse*, 389, and Buswell, *Tracing Back the Radiance*, 90 n. 166).
95. A cursory glance at the social background of early Koryŏ monks for whom some information is available reveals that from the very beginning of the dynasty, they continued to emerge from various backgrounds, including the capital-based aristocracy, educated families, and local aristocracy (see Vermeersch, *Power of the Buddhas*, 379–416).
96. For the same reasons that made the famed Koryŏ monk Ŭich'ŏn influential, Ch'ae Sangsik argues that the Sŏn learning imported by Tamjin from China became influential because it never went beyond the tastes of the capital-based aristocracy. But there is little evidence to suggest that Tamjin, Chinul, and Hyesim taught fundamentally different forms of Sŏn learning. All three monks showed deep interest in promoting the style of Chan, or Sŏn, learning that flourished in Song dynasty China. On Tamjin's pilgrimage to China, see Chŏng Sua, "Hyejo kuksa Tamjin kwa 'Chŏnginsu,'" 618–19. Citing the lack of any reference to Tamjin in Chinul's and Hyesim's writings, Han Kimun claims that Tamjin was forsaken by the monks at Susŏn-sa because of his ties to King Myŏngjong (see "Yech'ŏn 'Chungsu Yongmun-sagi'"). I find this particular argument from Han's otherwise excellent article unconvincing.
97. The celebration of the completion of Sŏnwŏn-sa in 1245 was overseen by Sŏn master Honwŏn, who had once studied under Hyesim. In 1252, Honwŏn followed in his former teacher's footsteps and served as the fourth-generation abbot of Susŏn-sa (*TMS* 117: 10a–b). Iryŏn, the author of *Samguk yusa*, also served as the abbot of Sŏnwŏn-sa and taught the kind of Sŏn learning explored by Hyesim (Ch'ae Sangsik, *Koryŏ hugi pulgyosa yŏn'gu*, 122, 137–142).
98. See *KS* 129: 44b–45a. As seen earlier in the case of the Lord of Kwangyang, Sŏnwŏn-sa continued to grow economically after the age of military rule. The monastery seems to have thrived economically even in the second half of the fourteenth century. In 1360, Japanese pirates raided Kanghwa Island and attacked two monasteries, Sŏnwŏn-sa and Yongjang-sa. There, they killed 300 people (monks?) and stole more than 40,000 *sŏk* of rice (*KSC* 27: 10b).

99. The same assumption informs Kim Hodong's study of Chinul, Hyesim, and Susŏn-sa (see Kim, "Koryŏ musin chŏnggwŏn").
100. For this claim, see Ch'ae Sangsik, *Koryŏ hugi pulgyosa yŏn'gu*.
101. *Chungsu Kŏndong-sŏnsagi* (Kŏndong-sŏnsa restoration record), dated 1327, in *ICJ* 6: 19b–21b.
102. During King Kongmin's reign, generals (*changgun*) in the palace guard were renamed *hogun* (*KS* 77: 30a). The *Sinjŭng Tongguk yŏji sŭngnam* (Geographic survey of Korea, enlarged edition) lists the Ha descent group as a Kyŏngwŏn *t'osŏng* (local surname) (*TYS* 9: 20b).
103. *ICJ* 6: 21a.
104. Curiously, there is no mention of Ha Wŏnsŏ in any other existing historical record. There is also no record of notable high-ranking officials from the Kyŏngwŏn Ha descent group during the Koryŏ. Given Ha Wŏnsŏ's position in the royal guard, it seems likely that he had gained King Ch'ungnyŏl's favor while serving as a member of his *keshig* (household guards). A more detailed explanation of the *keshig* is provided in chapter 4.

3. This Way of Ours

1. Min, "Cho In'gyu wa kŭ ŭi kamun (sang)" and "Cho In'gyu wa kŭ ŭi kamun (chung)."
2. Duncan, *Origins*, 129–30.
3. These accusations were leveled against Cho In'gyu's sons (*KS* 105: 43b), one of whom was accused of stealing from funds collected to pay for the king's visit to the Mongol capital. Cho In'gyu himself was similarly accused of tricking people into becoming hunters and trappers and using them to enrich himself (*KS* 105: 35).
4. Yŏm Sŭngik's engagement in unscrupulous activities such as capturing wandering peasants and forcing them to work as laborers on his large landed estates is recorded in his biography in the *History of Koryŏ* (see *KS* 123: 8a–11a, 24a). For a study of Yŏm in English, see Puggioni, "Life and Times of Yŏm Sŭng-ik."
5. For this anecdote, see *KS* 123: 10a–b, and *YP* 2: 6b–7a.
6. Yŏm retired in 1288 (*KSC* 21: 7b). He would eventually give up all official titles and become a monk on April 22, 1302 (*KS* 32: 10a).
7. *KS* 105: 16b. For a comparison of Hong and Cho, see also No Yongp'il, "Hong Chabŏn," 50–56.
8. *KS* 105: 39b. Min Hyŏn'gu thinks Cho In'gyu's grandfather may have belonged to the class of wandering peasants who were uprooted during the period of military rule ("Cho In'gyu wa kŭ ŭi kamun [sang]," 19). Yi Sugŏn, however, argues that Cho's ancestors on both his father's and mother's side were *hyangni* (*Han'guk chungse sahoesa yŏn'gu*, 329–31; cited in Duncan, *Origins*, 306 n. 110). As Yi points out, Cho's father is said to have been a low-ranking (rank 7a) military official in the capital police, and his maternal grandfather was also a low-ranking (8b) official who tended gardens. This is mentioned in Cho In'gyu's funerary inscription (*KMC*: 629). But neither post, it seems, necessarily required one to have a *hyangni* background. Moreover, Yi does not offer a good explanation as to why Cho's

funerary inscription makes no mention of his background, which was de rigueur in Koryŏ funerary inscriptions. Also, as Kim Tangt'aek points out, all the translators seem to have been recruited from men of humble birth ("Ch'ungnyŏl wang ŭi pogwi," 201–2).

9. Sangwŏn was the hometown of Cho's grandmother, which seems to imply that his grandfather had moved there (Min, "Cho In'gyu wa kŭ ŭi kamun [sang], 19; *KS* 105: 36b.). Sangwŏn was a subordinate county in the Hwangju District, but the district came under the direct control of the Mongols in 1269 as part of the Yuan dynasty's Tongnyŏng Directorate General. On its return to Koryŏ in 1290, Sangwŏn became a subordinate county of P'yŏngyang.

10. For his relationship with the princess, see Min, "Cho In'gyu wa kŭ ŭi kamun (sang)," 21–22. Cho seems to have earned the imperial princess's trust and favor by supplying her with otter fur acquired by illegal means; see note 3 above.

11. On the Mongolian term *bichēchi*, see de Rachewiltz, "Personnel and Personalities," 100–102, 137 n. 2, and Kim Hodong, "Mong-Wŏn chegukki han saengmongin kwalli ŭi ch'osang," 85 n. 43. For a convenient summary of the Korean scholarship on Koryŏ's *bichēchi*, see Pak Yongun, "Koryŏ hugi *bishechi* (p'iljajŏk pich'ikch'i) e taehan yŏn'gu." For a list of officials appointed to the *bichēchi*, see Kim Kwangch'ŏl, *Koryŏ hugi sejokch'ŭng yŏn'gu*, 139, and Yi Kinam, "Ch'ungsŏn wang ŭi kaehyŏk," 81. As Kim Kwangch'ŏl points out, almost all the officials known to have worked as *bichēchi* in Koryŏ were from relatively obscure descent groups or families from nontraditional backgrounds, like the P'yŏngyang Cho. Many of them had passed exams and had special skills such as knowledge of the Mongolian language. As explained in chapter 4, the *bichēchi* was established to strengthen the throne's control over alienable and taxable resources, which included not only land, labor, and local goods but also official titles and ranks.

12. For Royal Undersecretary Cho's appointment as censor-in-chief, see *KS* 30: 6b; for finance commissioner, see *KS* 30: 7b; and for assistant chancellor, see *KS* 30: 12a. A list of his appointments and dates can also be found in Cho's funerary inscription (see *KMC*: 629–30).

13. In 1290, the Yuan court appointed Cho *darughachi* (judge) of the princely appanage of Koryŏ and granted him the Mongol symbol of authority, the gold tiger plaque (C. *jinhufu*) (*KS* 30: 23b); for Mongolian seals of authority, see Pelliot, "Notes sur le 'Turkestan'," 35–58. In 1293, Cho was additionally appointed grand master of excellent counsel (*KS* 30: 37b). In 1307, he was granted the noble title Lord of P'yŏngyang (*KS* 32: 29a). As Morihira Masahiko points out, Cho's appointment as *darughachi* seems to be the earliest evidence of the Mongols' treatment of Koryŏ as a princely establishment or appanage, which implies that the Mongols saw Koryŏ as a territory of the Yuan dynasty rather than an independent state (*Mongoru hakenka no Kōrai*, 62–66). Morihira first presented this argument in 1998, but he revised his view slightly in a more recent publication after it was met with harsh criticism from Kim Hodong and Yi Kaesŏk (see Kim, *Mongol cheguk kwa Koryŏ*, 112–13, and Yi, "Tae Monggoguk-Koryŏ kwan'gye yŏn'gu ŭi chaegŏmt'o," 58). In response, Morihira claims that his point was to describe Koryŏ as a *potential* appanage of the Prince of Koryŏ (*Mongoru hakenka no Kōrai*, 99 n. 33).

14. For this monopoly, see Duncan, *Origins*, esp. chap. 2.
15. *KS* 33, 24a–b.
16. In 1309, Cho Sŏ was granted the post of state councilor (*p'yŏngni*, also *ch'ŏmŭi chamni*; rank 2b) and inspector-general (*taesahŏn*; rank 2a) (see *KS* 33: 26a and 27b respectively). The Mongol emperor, who took his daughter as a consort, appointed Sŏ assistant field commander (C. *fu yuanshuai*) of Koryŏ. As Min Hyŏn'gu points out, this appointment, which was made because of the marriage of his eldest daughter to the Mongol aristocrat the Prince of Anji, granted him a status almost equal to that of the Koryŏ king ("Cho In'gyu wa kŭ ŭi kamun [chung]," 5–6). Sŏ's younger brother Ryŏn held the post of assistant royal secretary (*milchik pusa*; rank 2b) before Cho In'gyu's death. In 1310, their younger brother Yŏnsu was granted the post of finance commissioner (rank 3a) (*KS* 33: 38a). Wi does not seem to have passed the civil service examination, but he would eventually receive the post of superintendent of the security council (*p'an milchiksa sa*; rank 2b) and assistant chancellor (*KS* 105: 44a). He would also inherit his father's noble title.
17. According to the Gregorian calendar, this would be July 13, 1308.
18. *Cho In'gyu myojimyŏng* (Funerary inscription for Cho In'gyu), in *KMC*: 629–32.
19. For more on deathbed practices and conceptions of the afterlife during the Koryŏ, see Kim Youngmi, "Buddhist Faith."
20. *KMC*: 631. Drafter of proclamations was a post in the Hallim Academy held concurrently by officials who also served in a different capacity; see Sudō, *Kōraichō kanryōsei no kenkyū*, 267–313, and Pak Yongun, "*Koryŏsa*" *paekkwanji yŏkchu*, 210–11. In 1307, as a Hallim Academy scholar, Pang accompanied Cho to Yuan China in honor of the emperor's birthday (*KMC*: 632).
21. This inscription, *Cho Chŏngsuk kong sadanggi* (Record for Lord Cho Chŏngsuk's offering hall), can be found in *KJJ* 3: 7b–11b. Yi Kok was appointed vice director of the left and right offices of the secretariat at the Eastern Expedition Field Headquarters in Dadu in 1335. He returned to Koryŏ in 1344 and the very next year was given the rank of assistant chancellor and received the noble title Lord of Hansan. Cho Ch'ungsin is the son of Cho Yŏnsu. The *History of Koryŏ* proves two noble titles for Cho Ch'ungsin: Lord of Sangwŏn (granted in 1354) and Lord of P'yŏngyang (see *KS* 38: 24a and *KS* 105: 42b respectively).
22. Ŭisŏn and Yi Kok seem to have developed a close friendship as neighbors in the Mongol capital. According to a poem that Yi wrote to bid Ŭisŏn farewell, the two frequently went sightseeing together and enjoyed each other's company (*KJJ* 18: 5b). Another poem that Yi Kok gave to Ŭisŏn as a gift makes it clear that Ŭisŏn resided in Qinglian Monastery and Yi Kok lived in a nearby house in the Mongol capital (*KJJ* 16: 9a). The same poem also makes it clear that poetry served as an important medium of friendship. More poems exchanged by the two are in Yi Kok's collection of writings (see, e.g., *KJJ* 16: 6a, 8a–b, 11a, 11b, and *KJJ* 18: 8a–b).
23. Mount Ch'ŏnggye is located in present-day Ŭiwang, Kyŏnggi.
24. It was standard procedure to dedicate all new and restored monasteries to the king. This was done to circumvent the ban on constructing private memorial monasteries (Vermeersch, *Power of the Buddhas*, 306).

25. *Ch'ŏnggye-sa sajŏggi pi* (Stele record of the historical traces of Ch'ŏnggye-sa), in *Kyŏnggi kŭmsŏk taegwan*, vol. 5, 15–22. This stele inscription was prepared in 1689 by Cho In'gyu's eleventh-generation descendant and recent literary licentiate (*chinsa*) Cho Un in commemoration of the monastery's restoration after a devastating fire that had consumed it earlier that year.
26. Manŭi-sa was located in present-day Hwasŏng, Kyŏnggi.
27. Most of what we know about Manŭi-sa is derived from information provided in Kwŏn Kŭn's *Suwŏn Manŭi-sa ch'uksang Hwaŏm pŏphoe chungmokki* (Record of the details of the Hwaŏm dharma assembly organized to honor the king at Manŭi-sa in Suwŏn), in *TMS* 78: 9a–11a. Kwŏn's record was completed sometime in the second lunar month of 1392. For more information on Manŭi-sa, see Hwang, *Koryŏ hugi Chosŏn ch'o pulgyosa yŏn'gu*, 237–49. As for Hon'gi's identity, in a colophon for the *Pŏphwa yŏnghŏmjŏn* (Miracle tales about the Lotus Sutra), he is recorded as Cho In'gyu's elder brother (*HPC* 6: 570b; noted in Hŏ Hŭngsik, *Koryŏ pulgyosa yŏn'gu*, 823, and Ch'ae Sangsik, *Koryŏ hugi pulgyosa yŏn'gu*, 193–94). As Hŏ and Ch'ae point out, given the fact that the colophon was prepared by Cho In'gyu's great-grandson, there seems little reason to doubt the relationship between Hon'gi and Cho.
28. *TMS* 78: 9a.
29. *HPC* 6: 570b.
30. It was not uncommon for the abbacies of important monasteries to be taken by multiple generations of the same aristocratic family in Koryŏ (see Han Kimun, *Koryŏ sawŏn ŭi kujo wa kinŭng*, 61–75; Pak Yujin, "Koryŏ sidae sŭngnyŏ"; and Vermeersch, "Buddhist Temples or Political Battlegrounds?").
31. Ch'ae Sangsik, *Koryŏ hugi pulgyosa yŏn'gu*, 194; see also Han Kimun, *Koryŏ sawŏn ŭi kujo wa kinŭng*, 329–30. For the prayers offered to Cho Tŏgyu, see *HPC* 6: 570b.
32. *TMS* 78: 9a–9b.
33. The monastery was also granted an additional 70 *kyŏl* of land by Chancellor Yi Sŏnggye (*TMS* 78: 9b).
34. When Pak Hŏjung voiced his concerns about Ŭisŏn at the privy council, Ŭisŏn's brother State Councilor Cho Yŏnsu, not surprisingly, defended Ŭisŏn (*KS* 105: 43b).
35. See, e.g., Ch'ae Sangsik, *Koryŏ hugi pulgyosa yŏn'gu*, 196.
36. *KJJ* 3: 10b; noted in Min, "Cho In'gyu wa kŭ ŭi kamun (chung)," 9–10. Tianyuan Yansheng Monastery was state-sponsored and therefore one of the largest monasteries in Yuan China (see Ōyabu, *Gendai no hōsei to shūkyō*, 127–42). The portrait hall (C. *shenyudian*) for the Mongol Prince Gammala (1263–1302) was built at Lushi Monastery, which was granted an official plaque bearing the name Tianyuan Yansheng (*YS*: 668 [*juan* 30, Taidingdi third year, second lunar month]; cited in Ōyabu, *Gendai no hōsei to shūkyō*, 135). But as Ōyabu Masaya also points out, there may have been more than one temple with the name Tianyuan Yansheng.
37. Construction was completed three years later in 1319 (see Yi Kok's *Kyŏngsa Poŭn kwanggyo-sagi*, dated 1336, in *KJJ* 2: 5a–b).
38. Ch'ungsuk and Wang Ko used to be political rivals who fought to claim the Koryŏ throne. The P'yŏngyang Cho were actively involved in the formation of this political rivalry. I shall have more to say about this rivalry later (see esp. chap. 5).

39. *KJJ* 2: 5b–6a. According to Yi Kok, the monastery, covering an area of 50 *mu* (approximately 30 acres) in the capital, had an endowment that consisted of 3,170 *mu* of land spread across three different territories. For the size of 1 *mu* of land, see Wilkinson, *Chinese History*, 243. More than 500,000 *min* in paper currency notes were used to build the monastery.
40. *KJJ* 2: 6a.
41. Yi Chehyŏn's *Myoryŏn-sa sŏkchijogi* (Record of the stone tea cauldron at Myoryŏn-sa), in *ICJ* 6: 24b; noted in Ch'ae, *Koryŏ hugi pulgyosa yŏn'gu*, 195 n. 50.
42. Kyŏngi was appointed state preceptor in 1295 (*KS* 31: 8b). The title in use at the time was Kukchon (State Honored One) and Kukt'ong (State Controller). The original title for state preceptor, Kuksa, had to be avoided because it was also used by the Mongol court (Vermeersch, *Power of the Buddhas*, 261 n. 85). There is little reason to doubt that Kyŏngi was from Paengnyŏn-sa; see his sacrificial oration in *TMS* 109: 25a; cited in Ch'ae Sangsik, *Koryŏ hugi pulgyosa yŏn'gu*, 189. See also Hŏ, *Koryŏ pulgyosa yŏn'gu*, 821.
43. This is noted in Yi Chehyŏn's *Myoryŏn-sa chunghŭngbi* (Commemorative stele for the restoration of Myoryŏn-sa), in *ICJ* 6: 26b.
44. In a sacrificial oration that Chŏngo wrote for Kyŏngi, the latter is clearly called "older brother in the Dharma" (*pŏphyŏng*) and "older brother in our lineage" (*munhyŏng*) (*TMS* 111: 12a–b).
45. For a study of Chŏngo's career, see Kang Hosŏn, "Muoe kukt'ong Chŏngo." Kang's study, however, claims that Chŏngo had little relation to the P'yŏngyang Cho and Myoryŏn-sa. The evidence for this claim is unconvincing.
46. See *Yŏngbongsan Yongam-sa chungch'anggi* (Yŏngbongsa Yongam-sa restoration record), in *TMS* 68: 13b, and Vermeersch, *Power of the Buddhas*, 235.
47. Chŏngo did not accept the five cloisters (*TMS* 68: 14a).
48. This monastery frequently served as a location for holding royal banquets, greeting foreign emissaries and royalty, and royal outings under Mongol rule (see, e.g., *KS* 89: 1b, 40: 36a, 28: 5a, 35: 32b).
49. See the account in *TMS* 68: 14a. A more detailed account can be found in Min Chi's *Kukch'ŏng-sa kŭmdang chubul Sŏkka yŏrae sari yŏngigi* (Record of the miracle concerning the relics inside the main icon, the *tathāgata* Śākyamuni, of Kukch'ŏng-sa's golden hall), in *TMS* 68: 7b–12b. Min's record notes that others also contributed to the reconstruction of the golden hall. The three main icons inside the golden hall were the Buddha Śākyamuni, Samantabhadra, and Mañjuśrī.
50. For Chŏngo's appointment as state preceptor, see *TMS* 68: 14a; cited in Ch'ae, *Koryŏ hugi pulgyosa yŏn'gu*, 185. Chŏngo served as abbot of Tong paengnyŏn-sa in Sangju, North Kyŏngsang, from 1280 to 1290 (Ch'ae Sangsik, *Koryŏ hugi pulgyosa yŏn'gu*, 190).
51. The Ch'ŏnt'ae monk Sinjo also served as abbot of this monastery (Ch'ae Sangsik, *Koryŏ hugi pulgyosa yŏn'gu*, 193).
52. As Ch'ae Sangsik points out, the royal preceptor Hon'gu, who belonged to the Mount Kaji branch of the Sŏn sect, assumed the abbacy of Yŏngwŏn-sa sometime between 1314 and 1322 (*Koryŏ hugi pulgyosa yŏn'gu*, 192).
53. *Koryŏguk Ch'ŏnt'ae Purŭn-sa chunghŭnggi* (Restoration record of Ch'ŏnt'ae Purŭn-sa in Koryŏ), in *KJJ* 3: 1a–2b.

54. Although this is certainly meant to be taken as hyperbole, there is some truth to Yi Kok's exaggerated claim. The Koryŏ capital, Songdo, boasted well over thirty grand monasteries (one hundred by some accounts), each housing several hundred monks and nuns. Sŏng Hyŏn similarly made the following observation: "In the old Silla capital there were more monasteries than homes, and the same is true for Songdo; the royal palace and grand homes were all connected to monasteries, and not a single month went by without the king and his consorts lighting incense at the monasteries" (*Yongjae ch'onghwa* 8, 634 [cf. 190]). For a study of the archaeological remains of Buddhist monasteries in and around the Koryŏ capital, see Ko Yusŏp, *Songdo ŭi kojŏk*. For a more recent study, see Chabanol, "Study."
55. *KJJ* 3: 1b–2a.
56. *KS* 31: 22b. Chang was famous for having one of the most lavish homes in the capital. Its outer walls were decorated with mosaic tiles arranged in the form of flowers. The outer walls were so famous that they acquired the name "the Chang house wall" (Chang-ga chang) (*KS* 123: 34b).
57. *KS* 33: 6b.
58. *KS* 31: 23b.
59. *KJJ* 3: 1a.
60. See *ICJ* 6: 26b. According to the stele inscription, construction of the monastery, which began in the fall of 1283, was completed the very next year. However, the *History of Koryŏ* states that the king and the imperial princess visited the monastery on the *ŭlmyo* day of the sixth (?) lunar month of 1283 (*KS* 29: 44b; cf. *KSC* 20: 40a). No such day exists, so this could be a clerical error or a reference to a visit made on August 4 (i.e., the *ŭlmyo* day of the seventh lunar month). As Ch'ae Sangsik points out, the king seems to have visited the monastery at least once every year (*Koryŏ hugi pulgyosa yŏn'gu*, 182). Following a Yuan dynasty custom, the king and his officials also made sure to visit the monastery on the fifteenth day of the first lunar month and pray for the long life of the current Yuan emperor (*KS* 32: 1a).
61. *KS* 32: 12b. On November 6, 1308, the year he ascended the throne, King Ch'ungsŏn (son of the Qiguo Imperial Princess) went to Myoryŏn-sa to pay his mother's portrait a visit (*KS* 33: 20b). The very next year, on November 5, Ch'ungsŏn converted Sunyŏng Palace into a memorial monastery for his late mother (*KS* 33: 30a–b). The monastery was granted a plaque bearing the name Minch'ŏn-sa. The attempt to use a palace to establish Minch'ŏn-sa was first made in 1277 by King Ch'ungnyŏl (*KS* 28: 27b).
62. *ICJ* 6: 27a.
63. For the removal of the portrait from Ch'ŏngun-sa in 1321, see *KS* 35: 6a. For the location of Ch'ŏngun-sa, see *TYS* 5: 16a. In 1368, King Kongmin lit incense on the anniversary of the death of his father, Ch'ungsuk, the twenty-fourth day of the third lunar month, at Myoryŏn-sa (*KS* 41: 18a). Kongmin made a trip to the monastery on the same day in 1354, presumably to light incense for his late father (*KS* 38: 21a). But, curiously, two years earlier in 1352, the first year of his reign, Kongmin lit incense on the anniversary of his father's death at Minch'ŏn-sa (*KS* 38: 8a). The following year, he lit incense for his father at another monastery, Kwangmyŏng-sa (*KS* 38: 16a).

64. *ICJ* 6: 27a.
65. *KS* 89: 14a. The letters were placed on the palace door by the controller of the directorate of fisheries and natural resources Yun Ŏnju. Unfortunately, nothing else is known about this figure. For the Mongol rulers' use of their princesses to interfere in Koryŏ politics, see Kim Sŏngjun, "Yŏdae Wŏn kongju ch'ulsin wangbi."
66. For instance, see Kim Sŏngjun, "Yŏdae Wŏn kongju ch'ulsin wangbi"; noted in Duncan, *Origins*, 174. For King Ch'ungsŏn's attempt at reform, see chapter 4.
67. *KS* 32: 29a; see also Min, "Cho In'gyu wa kŭ ŭi kamun (sang)," 26–27.
68. *KSC* 24: 20–21. For the involvement of the P'yŏngyang Cho, see Min, "Cho In'gyu wa kŭ ŭi kamun (chung)," 8. King Ch'ungnyŏl was the first Koryŏ king to be invested as Simyang (C. Shenyang) Prince by the Mongols. His son Ch'ungsŏn inherited this title of nobility, which was later changed to the Sim Prince in 1310 (Robinson, *Empire's Twilight*, 33). Wang Ko is the grandchild of Ch'ungnyŏl and his first consort, Court Lady Chŏnghwa (d. 1319), who was Korean. For a study of the historical circumstances that led to the attempt to place Wang Ko on the throne, see Kim Tangt'aek, *Wŏn kansŏpha*, 72–100; Kim Hyewŏn, "Koryŏ hugi Sim(yang) wang ŭi chŏngch'i kyŏngjejŏk kiban"; and Yi Sŭnghan, "Koryŏ Ch'ungsŏn wang ŭi Simyang wang p'ibong."
69. *KS* 35: 13b. The Yuan emperor Yesün Temür had the king grant Cho Yŏnsu clemency.
70. This is a reference to the poem "Splendid Are the Flowers" (C. Changchang zhe hua), in the *Decade of Beishan* chapter of the *Shijing* (Legge, *Chinese Classics Vol. IV, Part II*, 385).
71. *ICJ* 6: 27b.
72. *Cho Chŏngsuk kong sadanggi*, in *KJJ* 3: 11b.
73. For a similar claim, see Chu Ungyŏng. "Kamyo ŭi sŏllip paegyŏng kwa kŭ kinŭng," 61–63.
74. Kim Yongsŏn argues that such records appeared sometime between the founding of the Koryŏ and the earliest reference to a *po* in the early twelfth century (*Koryŏ kŭmsŏngmun yŏn'gu*, 47–73).
75. This is noted in Yi Kok's *Kyŏngsa Kŭmson mit'a-sagi* (Record of Kŭmson mit'a-sa in the capital), in *KJJ* 2: 6a–7a; cited in Han Kimun, *Koryŏ sawŏn ŭi kujo wa kinŭng*, 308 n. 326. Criticism of this practice can also be found in the funerary epitaph for Kim Kwangjae (*KMC*: 563). This practice continued well into the fifteenth century (see Sŏng Hyŏn, *Yongjae ch'onghwa* 2, 15a–b).
76. On Yŏmyang-sŏnsa's restoration, see Yi Kok's *Koryŏguk Kangnŭngbu Yŏmyang sŏnsa chunghŭnggi* (Restoration record of Yŏmyang-sŏnsa in Kangnŭngbu of Koryŏ), in *KJJ* 2: 11a–12a.
77. Yi Kok prepared the restoration record for Pogwang-sa, *Chunghŭng Tae Hwaŏm Pogwang-sagi* (Restoration record of the great Hwaŏm Pogwang-sa), in *KJJ* 3: 4a–5b. Restoration began in 1337 and ended in 1343. In 1345, Yi Chehyŏn was asked to write a commemorative stele inscription for the offering hall at Pang's memorial monastery Sŏnhŭng-sa; see *Kwangnok taebu p'yŏngjang chŏngsa sangnak puwŏn'gun Pang kong sadangbi* (Stele for the grand master for splendid happiness,

assistant chancellor, great lord of Sangnak, Lord Pang's offering hall), in *ICJ* 7: 2b–5b. Although Pang was a eunuch, Yi noted that he came from a *sajok* (family of officials) in Osŏng County, Kyŏngsang. Pang's biography in the *History of Koryŏ*, however, states that he is from Chungmo County in Sangju (*KS* 122: 21a). Pang's influence made it possible for his father, a county clerk (*hyŏlli*), to be promoted to county magistrate (*hyŏllyŏng*) and, later, district shepherd (*moksa*) of Sangju.

78. Restoration began in 1314 and ended in 1323.
79. *Taewŏn Koryŏguk Kwangju Sinbok-sŏnsa chunghŭnggi* (Restoration record of Sinbok-sŏnsa of the Koryŏ kingdom of the great Yuan), in *KJJ* 3: 12b.
80. The Kwangju Pak, a *hyangni* descent group, seems to have entered the central bureaucracy under Mongol rule (see Yi Sugŏn, *Han'guk chungse sahoesa yŏn'gu*, 266–67).
81. For the limits placed on men from *pugok*, see the discussion in Duncan, *Origins*, 33–34. In his study of Koryŏ period government exams, Hŏ Hŭngsik offers some interesting reflections on how men like Yu Ch'ŏngsin were able to rise above the limits placed on them by the state (*Koryŏ ŭi kwagŏ chedo*, 202–3).
82. *Chinjong-sagi* (Chinjong-sa record), in *MMG* 1: 8b.
83. Ibid., 9a.
84. This is a quote from Yongjia Xuanjue's (675–713) "Song of Realizing the Way" (Zhengdao ge) (T51.2076.460a15).
85. Here, "red hat" may refer to the hat or crown worn by the Sa-skya lamas who maintained close ties with the Mongol rulers. For the influence of the Sa-skya sect during this period, see Franke, "Tibetans in Yüan China," and Petech, "Tibetan Relations."
86. *Sunam chin ch'an* (Encomium for Sunam's portrait), in *KJJ* 7: 12b–13a.
87. Vermeersch, *Power of the Buddhas*, 286–95.
88. See Im Ch'un's *Sorim-sa chungsugi* (Sorim-sa restoration record), in *TMS* 65: 4b. See also the discussion of this temple in Vermeersch, *Power of the Buddhas*, 308. Kongsŏng County was located in Sangju, North Kyŏngsang.
89. *Chungsu Kaegug-nyulsa ki* (Kaegug-yulsa restoration record), in *ICJ* 6: 18b.
90. See Yi Pyŏnghŭi, "Koryŏ hugi sawŏn," 223.

4. All the King's Men

1. Yi Kibaek, *Han'guksa sillon*, 189–91. As Pak Yongun points out, Yi changed the third character to *se* (strong) in the revised edition of his influential history textbook published in 1976 (*Koryŏ sahoe wa munbŏl kwijok kamun*, 73).
2. See, e.g., Yi Usŏng, "Koryŏjo ŭi 'i' e taehayŏ" and "Koryŏ ŭi yŏngŏpchŏn."
3. Because they are not descendants of the old aristocratic descent groups, Yi Kinam, who made this argument, refers to these powerful forces as the "new aristocracy" (*sinhŭng kwijok*) ("Ch'ungsŏn wang ŭi kaehyŏk," 65). He also refers to them as the "new power stratum" (*sinhŭng kwŏllyŏkch'ŭng*). In contrast to this new power stratum, Yi refers to Hallim Academy officials as the "new [political] force" (*sinjin seryŏk*). He also argues that Ch'ungsŏn's reform efforts were anti-Yuan in character (ibid., 70). Yi Ikchu rightly rejects this reading of the reform efforts and argues

instead that Ch'ungsŏn's aim was simply to remove his father's inner circle, the so-called new power stratum ("Koryŏ Ch'ungnyŏl wangdae ŭi chŏngch'i sanghwang").

4. See Kim Tangt'aek, "Ch'ungnyŏl wang ŭi pogwi" (reprinted in Kim, *Wŏn kansŏpha*, 5–42), and Kim Kwangch'ŏl, *Koryŏ hugi sejokch'ŭng yŏn'gu*. This is also pointed out in Pak Yongun, *Koryŏ sahoe wa munbŏl kwijok kamun*, 128–43, and Deuchler, *Under the Ancestors' Eyes*, chap. 2.

5. Kim Kwangch'ŏl (*Koryŏ hugi sejokch'ŭng yŏn'gu*) claims that families with histories of producing officials of rank 5 and above and with at least one *chaech'u* member count as *sejok*. He identifies forty-six families as possible *sejok*.

6. Kim Kwangch'ŏl, *Koryŏ hugi sejokch'ŭng yŏn'gu*, 169–78.

7. Kim Tangt'aek, *Wŏn kansŏpha*, 28.

8. Yi Sŏngmu, *Chosŏn ch'ogi yangban yŏn'gu*, 19–31; Ko Hyeryŏng, *Koryŏ hugi sadaebu*, 26–45; Pak Yongun, *Koryŏ sahoe wa munbŏl kwijok kamun*, 157–62; Deuchler, *Confucian Transformation of Korea*, 89–128; and Deuchler, *Under the Ancestors' Eyes*, 45–51.

9. For a detailed study of Prince Chŏn's journey, see Kim Hodong, *Mongol cheguk kwa Koryŏ*, 83–92. Kim states that the prince left for the Mongol court on May 14, but this seems to be a mistake.

10. Kim Hodong surmises that their meeting took place in late December (ibid., 85).

11. See ibid., 88.

12. Kim Chun tried to place Prince Chŏn's younger brother on the throne while the prince was away visiting the Mongol court, but the *chaech'u* succeeded in thwarting Kim's plan, and Prince Chŏn was able to succeed his father (*KS* 24: 44a–b). As John Duncan points out, this seems to imply that the *chaech'u* resumed a leading role in political affairs (*Origins*, 156).

13. *KS* 25: 18a. The Yuan court provided a positive response to this gesture in an edict (*KS* 25: 19a–b).

14. See *KS* 25: 19a, and Kim Hodong, *Mongol cheguk kwa Koryŏ*, 96–97. Yi Ikchu argues that a more traditional relationship developed between Korea and the Mongols in 1278, namely "serving the great" (*sadae*). According to Yi, what made this possible were the "old rulings of Qubilai" (*Sejo kuje*) or "the divine edict of Qubilai" (*Sejo sŏngji*), which allowed Koryŏ to maintain local customs (see his "Koryŏ-Wŏn kwan'gye ŭi kujo wa Koryŏ hugi chŏngch'i ch'eje" and his "Koryŏ-Wŏn kwan'gye ŭi kujo e taehan yŏn'gu"). Morihira Masahiko and Kim Hodong rightly reject Yi's thesis (see Morihira, *Mongoru hakenka no Kōrai*, 426, and Kim, *Mongol cheguk kwa Koryŏ*, 119).

15. *KS* 25: 19a and *KSC* 18: 9b.

16. *KS* 26: 5a–b.

17. On Qaidu, see Biran, *Qaidu*.

18. Kim Hodong argues that the Great Mongol State was called "Da Yuan" or the "Great Yuan" in areas that used the Chinese script (see his "Monggol cheguk kwa Tae Wŏn"). For the strategic importance of securing Qubilai's eastern flank, that is, Koryŏ, see Robinson, *Empire's Twilight*, 36.

19. Kim Tangt'aek, *Koryŏ ŭi muin chŏnggwŏn*, 404.

20. *KSC* 18: 32a–34a. For Kang Yunso, who received the title Great General and the elevated status of first-grade merit subject for his role in the assassination of Kim Chun, see also *KS* 123: 7a. For Kim Chajŏng, see also *KS* 130: 18b.
21. See *KS* 26: 21a. Kim Tangt'aek suggests that the brief success of Im Yŏn's coup, which state councilors silently condoned, may have something to do with the influence that eunuchs exerted after the removal of Kim Chun and state councilors' fear of the growing influence of the Mongols (*Koryŏ ŭi muin chŏnggwŏn*, 398–406). Prince Sim left for Dadu on May 29 (*KS* 26: 20b).
22. *KS* 26: 23a, *KSC* 18: 37b.
23. For Chŏng's role, see *KS* 107: 12a. For the consternation of the prince's accompanying retinue (most notably, Im Yŏn's son Im Yugan), see *KSC* 18: 37b–38a and *KS* 130: 24a–b.
24. *KS* 26: 32b.
25. *KS* 26: 33b, *KS* 106: 41a–b, *KSC* 18: 49a–b.
26. When the king moved back to Kaegyŏng in 1270, he and his officials were forced to hold court in makeshift tents (*KS* 26: 35a–b). Carpenters from Yuan China were hired to assist in the restoration of the palace. In 1281, a fire consumed the directorate of construction (*chosŏng togam*) in charge of the restoration. Laborers rejoiced and called the fire a warning from Heaven (*KS* 29: 32a–b).
27. Consider, for instance, the fact that more than 200,000 people from Koryŏ were taken captive by the Mongols in 1254 (*KSC* 17: 18b). In a memorial submitted to the great khan, the Koryŏ court explained that the taxable population had shrunk to two or three out of every one hundred (*KS* 25: 30b). Although the explanation is certainly an exaggeration that was meant to serve primarily as an excuse for not supplying the Mongols with troops and provisions, the explanation assumes that both courts were aware of the reduced tax base in Koryŏ. In another memorial submitted in 1272, the Koryŏ court also asked for further reductions in the Mongol court's demand for soldiers and provisions. According to the memorial, since 1270, the Koryŏ court had supplied more than 109,199 *sŏk* of grains. Feed for cows and horses amounted to a whopping 432,005 *sŏk* (*KS* 27: 28b).
28. *KS* 26: 34b. The Sambyŏlch'o units fled to the island of Chindo. Their rebellion was suppressed four years later in 1273.
29. *KS* 26: 36b. The *History of Koryŏ* (Koryŏsa) refers to Qurumshi as "Turyŏn'ga." As Kim Hodong points out, the two names refer to the same person (*Mongol cheguk kwa Koryŏ*, 100). Qurumshi is the great-grandson of the renowned Mongol commander Muqali (1170–1223).
30. This measure was used in 1259, 1261, 1264, 1266, 1271, 1274, and 1279 (*KS* 24: 41b–42a, KS 27: 7b, KS 79: 23a–25a; noted in Yi Kanghan, *Koryŏ wa Wŏn cheguk ŭi kyoyŏk ŭi yŏksa*, 41–42). In 1273, gold was collected from grand Buddhist monasteries (150 catties from Hŭngwang-sa, 100 catties from Anhwa-sa, and 70 catties from Poje-sa) and high-ranking officials (*chaech'u*, royal transmitters, and all higher-ranking officials) for the same purpose. In 1276, a traveling expenses bureau (*panjŏnsaek*) was established to collect silver and cloth from officials of all ranks, households in the capital, and even the countryside.
31. *KS* 27: 6a.

32. *KS* 27: 28b–29a.
33. Because the royal treasury (*t'angjang*) was completely depleted by 1275, silver was collected from the various royal clansmen, *chaech'u*, royal transmitters, supreme generals, and even retired officials. This silver was used to satisfy the demands of Yuan envoys (*KS* 79: 24b).
34. *KS* 78: 18b. The office for the distribution of (salary) land (*kŭpchŏn togam*) was first established in 1257 for this purpose. The land distributed in place of salaries in 1257 was on Kanghwa Island.
35. The 1271 rank land law utilized only *panjŏng*, half an allotment for an adult male (soldier), and excluded land privately owned by *yangban* families (*yangban choŏp chŏn*) in the capital district. This limitation may have been a compromise. The *panjŏng* appropriated for the purpose of supporting the central officials was originally intended to serve as a means of support for men who provided specific services to the state, such as soldiers. *Panjŏng* was a land/prebendal grant smaller in size than the *chokchŏng*, or full allotment (the size of one *chokchŏng* was set at 17 *kyŏl* for soldiers in 1356) (see *KS* 81: 18b). In 1344, Yi Chehyŏn stated that everything except the land granted to *yangban* officials' families (*kubunjŏn*) in the capital district had been converted to rank land fifty years earlier (*KSC* 25: 37a). This implies that even full allotments were eventually (?) converted to rank land. The 1271 reference to *panjŏng* may have been intended to be nothing more than a convenient myth. As O Ilsun points out, the system of using land allotments to pay soldiers may have already fallen apart by then ("Koryŏ hugi t'oji pun'gŭpche," 279–82). This may be why the land converted to rank land was referred to as "reclaimable land" as early as 1298 (*KS* 78: 5b). The term "reclaimable land," as Yi Kyŏngsik argues, refers to land that had once been tilled but was deemed to have lost its rightful prebend recipient during the land survey conducted in 1269 (Yi, *Chosŏn chŏn'gi t'oji chedo yŏn'gu*, 58–59; see also Pak Kyŏngan, *Koryŏ hugi t'oji chedo yŏn'gu*, 114–23). Yi's study and Min Hyŏn'gu's influential work on this subject correct some mistaken views found in Fukaya Toshigane's earlier study "Kōraichō rokkadenkō" (see Min, "Koryŏ ŭi nokkwajŏn"). A useful summary and update of this research can also be found in O Ilsun's "Koryŏ hugi t'oji pun'gŭpche." See also the discussion in Duncan, *Origins*, 94, 182–84.
36. *KS* 78: 18b–19a, *KSC* 19: 4a. The personnel authority was an institution that was first used under Ch'oe House rule to handle all matters related to recruitment and promotions instead of the board of personnel and the board of war. Hŏ was recommended to the personnel authority by Yu Kyŏng, who moved this institution to a location next to the king's private quarters in the palace after the assassination of Ch'oe Ŭi, the last of the Ch'oe House rulers (*KSC* 17: 39a).
37. Mongol officials seem to have already known by 1269—when Prince Sim visited Dadu—that Qubilai had promised one of his daughters to the prince (*KS* 26: 26b). Corroborative evidence can be found in the funerary inscription for Chŏng In'gyŏng (*KMC*: 424). Kim Hodong acknowledges this evidence but argues that it is highly unlikely that members of the prince's retinue could have broached this sensitive subject on their own (*Mongol cheguk kwa Koryŏ*, 102–3). For a comprehensive study of the use of marriage alliances as a political strategy within the

Great Yuan *ulus*, see Zhao, *Marriage as Political Strategy*. For the use of this strategy by the Koryŏ royal family and the Mongols, see Zhao, "Control through Conciliation." For more sources in Chinese and Japanese, see Robinson, *Empire's Twilight*, 332 n. 11.

38. *KS* 27: 24a.
39. See Kim Hodong, *Mongol cheguk kwa Koryŏ*, 107–9, 116–17. For Qubilai's concerns about Song China, and the Ögödei and Chaghatai khanates in Central Asia, see also Robinson, *Empire's Twilight*, 100–102.
40. It was customary for the Mongols to demand that conquered territories send hostages from prominent families.
41. For serving Prince Sim during his time as hostage and arranging the marriage between the prince and the khan's daughter, Kim was honored as a second-grade merit subject, presumably in 1282 (*KMC*: 412). On Cho's role, see *KMC*: 629.
42. The seal arrived on April 16 (*KS* 29: 23a; see also Yŏ-Wŏn kwan'gyesa yŏn'gut'im, *Yŏkchu Wŏn Koryŏ kisa*, 240). The importance of the seal in bringing the debate about Ch'ungnyŏl's status to a close was pointed out by Morihira Masahiko (*Mongoru hakenka no Kōrai*, chaps. 1 and 3).
43. For "inner-circle politics" (*ch'ŭkkŭn chŏngch'i*) during King Ch'ungnyŏl's reign, see Yi Ikchu, "Koryŏ Ch'ungnyŏl wangdae ŭi chŏngch'i sanghwang." For a convenient summary of other studies that refer to inner-circle politics, see Pak Yongun, *Koryŏ sahoe wa munbŏl kwijok kamun*, 71–84, 105.
44. This was noted by Yao Sui (1238–1313) in his *Gaoli Shenwang shi xu* (Preface to the poems of Prince Sim of Koryŏ), which can be found in Yao's collection of writings *Muan ji* (see Chang Tongik, *Wondae Yŏsa charyo chimnok*, 128; see also Morihira, *Mongoru hakenka no Kōrai*, 70–71).
45. As Morihira Masahiko points out, the Yuan seems to have officially recognized Koryŏ as a princely appanage sometime after 1281 (*Mongoru hakenka no Kōrai*, 63).
46. See *KS* 123: 10a, *KS* 89: 8b. Hŏ Kong had been entrusted with this task (*KS* 30: 11b) and was appointed chancellor shortly thereafter. For more information on Koryŏ tribute women, see Ryu Hongnyŏl's classic study "Koryŏ ŭi Wŏn e taehan kongnyŏ." Although it is frequently cited in Korean scholarship on late Koryŏ, Ryu's work should be used with caution. Its arguments are heavily inflected by the author's nationalistic views.
47. Not all *keshig*, however, were hostages (Morihira, *Mongoru hakenka no Kōrai*, 149).
48. *KS* 27: 16b. On Kim Pyŏn, who served the heir apparent Prince Sim for four years in Dadu, see *KMC*: 412. Although many of the hostages, like Im Yugan, wanted to return home quickly to Koryŏ, Kim Sŏ, Sŏl In'gŏm, and others are known to have argued against this, citing the importance of a tighter bond between Prince Sim and the Yuan court to Koryŏ's future (*KS* 27: 27a).
49. *KS* 82: 2a–b.
50. Only a few of the "sons of officials" (*ŭigwan chaje*) who served in Ch'ungnyŏl's *qorchi*, also known as the "quiver bearers unit" (*kungjŏnbae*), are identified by name in the *History of Koryŏ* (see *KS* 125: 9b, 106: 1b, 104: 35a–b, and 28: 5b). Since he was not the son of an official, Great General Kang Yunso was not chosen to

accompany the crown prince to Dadu, but he went anyway without the king's approval (*KS* 123: 7b).

51. Kim Pogwang made a similar argument ("Koryŏ Ch'ungnyŏl wang," 153–54). In the first lunar month of the following year, Ch'ungnyŏl had the number of shifts reduced from four to three (*KS* 82: 2b). The Mongol practice traditionally consisted of four three-day shifts, so the total cycle of shifts thus consisted of twelve days (see Atwood, "*Ulus* Emirs," 143; Morihira, *Mongoru hakenka no Kōrai*, 66, 157–61; and Pak Yongun, "Koryŏ hugi *bishechi*," 251). During a shift, a *keshig* leader was put in charge of the imperial guards. For an explanation of the Mongolian terms used to refer to the palace guards, see Pelliot, "Les Mots Mongols," 261–62. For the relevant terminology in Koryŏ sources, see the discussion in Morihira, *Mongoru hakenka no Kōrai*, 151–61. For more information on the *keshig*, see also Allsen, "Guard and Government." Katayama Tomoo has also published extensively on the subject (see, e.g., Katayama, "Kōsetsu to Genchō kanryōsei"). For a comprehensive list of Katayama's publications on the subject, see the bibliography in Morihira, *Mongoru hakenka no Kōrai*, 490. See also Xiao, *Yuandaishi xintan*, 59–111.
52. Allsen, *The Royal Hunt*, 69.
53. *KS* 82: 2b. Like the *keshig*, falconry officers were used as the king's personal bodyguards in 1287; see *KS* 82: 2b. For a classic study of falconry offices in Koryŏ, see Naitō, "Kōrai jidai no takabō ni tsuite."
54. See, e.g., *KS* 28: 17a.
55. See Yi Kanghan, "1270–80 nyŏndae," and the extended discussion in his *Koryŏ wa Wŏn cheguk ŭi kyoyŏk ŭi yŏksa*. The Mongols began collecting household taxes in silver as early as 1251. This was known as the *baoyin* levy. Some of the silver thus collected was entrusted to *ortoq* merchants to generate more income through moneylending and trade with western Asia. For a few representative studies of the silver levy, the *ortoq* merchants, and the use of silver as the currency of international trade, see Abe, *Gendaishi no kenkyū*, 75–232; Moriyasu, "Shiruku rōdo tōbu ni okeru senka"; Shurmann, *Economic Structure*, 88–107; Allsen, "Mongol Princes"; Endicott-West, "Merchant Associations"; and von Glahn, "Monies of Account."
56. Falconry offices were installed all over the peninsula. In 1279, Yun Su was named falconry commissioner (*ŭngbangsa*) of the Chŏlla circuit. The others mentioned above were named special directors entrusted with royal edicts (*wangji sayong pyŏlgam*) and appointed to other circuits (*KS* 29: 3a). For a more comprehensive list of men who operated falconry offices during King Ch'ungnyŏl's reign, see Yi Ikchu, "Koryŏ Ch'ungnyŏl wangdae ŭi chŏngch'i sanghwang," 193. In 1308, King Ch'ungsŏn officially granted two falconry commissioners the rank of 3b and two vice commissioners (*pusa*) the rank of 4b (*KS* 77: 27b). On the exemption of falconers from corvée duty, see *KS* 99: 8b. Evidence of the stupendous wealth owned by the falconry offices can be readily found. The landed wealth of the falconry offices is said to have been so immense, for instance, that it could generate 200,000 *sŏk* of grains, enough to feed the entire eastern expedition force (*KS* 104: 28b). Falconry officials also became independently wealthy. It was not uncommon for the king and his Mongol consort to spend the night at the falconry official Yi

Chŏng's private residence (see *KS* 28: 28b). The extravagance and waste that these officials displayed in front of the king was a constant source of concern for the regular bureaucracy. The fact that Yi was a former slave and Pak Ŭi a man of *pugok* origin also contributed to these concerns (*KS* 124: 6b).

57. *KS* 28: 3a. For a detailed study of the abuse of grant ordinances during this period, see Pak Kyŏngan, *Koryŏ hugi t'oji chedo yŏn'gu*, 129–60, and Yi Sukkyŏng, *Koryŏmal Chosŏnch'o sap'aejŏn yŏn'gu*.
58. *KS* 125: 7b. Song Pun first made a name for himself by assisting his father, Song Songnye, with removing Im Yumu in 1270. Song Pun would later receive the title Chancellor held by his father.
59. *KS* 123: 9b. For the generous private land grants offered to Yi Chijŏ, see *KS* 123: 25b. Tenant farmers were known as *ch'ŏgan* (Duncan, *Origins*, 185).
60. *KS* 123: 7b–8a. For a comprehensive overview of men from nontraditional backgrounds who rose to prominence under Mongol rule, see Hong Sŭnggi, *Koryŏ kwijok sahoe wa nobi*, 341–404.
61. For Cho's appointment to senior colonel in 1274, see *KMC*: 629.
62. *KSC* 19: 29b–30a. O would later be exiled and his wealth confiscated for speaking ill of Yŏm Sŭngik (*KS* 123: 9b).
63. *KS* 106: 38b, 123: 14a–b, and *KSC*: 19: 30a–b. Both Yi and Pak were concerned about the regular bureaucracy's control over provincial appointments. These appointments were coveted because they gave central officials direct access to free-floating resources in the countryside. Yi explained to King Ch'ungnyŏl that it was reasonable for men (like himself) who possessed talent in both military and civil affairs to be granted appointments as circuit commissioners. The king accepted his recommendation (*KSC* 19: 31a–b). But Yi's recommendation to grant such appointments to military officials stood in stark contrast to the opinion of Pak Hang, who argued the exact opposite. As Pak reminded the king, civil officials had always been required to demonstrate their worth in a provincial post before being promoted to a key post in the capital. This, he pointed out to the king, was the customary "path of employment" (*saro*) for civil officials (*tongban*) (*KSC* 19: 31b). All in all, it seems safe to say that although both Yi and Pak defended the circuit commissioner An Chŏn and stood for the interests of the regular bureaucracy, they did not necessarily form a united front.
64. *KS* 123: 13b and *KSC* 19: 30a–b. The practice of relying on special directors entrusted with royal edicts to collect items from the various circuits was carried out earlier during Ch'oe House rule (*KS* 129: 44a).
65. *KS* 123: 15a, *KSC* 19: 30b, and *KS* 28: 9a. Yi Punsŏng and his older brother Yi Punhŭi wielded much political power because of their role in the restoration of monarchical power after many decades of military rule. Yi Punsŏng's spouse was the daughter of King Kojong and an unnamed concubine. The older brother continued to rise through the ranks. He was promoted to royal undersecretary in 1276 and then royal secretary two years later, which made him a member of the esteemed *chaech'u* elite (see *KS* 28: 16a and 30a respectively). For an example of a "royal message," see the message drafted by Cho In'gyu for Susŏn-sa (dated 1281) in No et al., *Han'guk kodae chungse*, 18–21.

66. O placed the commoner households (*minho*) on the islands included in the Naju and Changhŭng administrative districts, South Chŏlla, as well as the households in Hongju's Kogyangch'on, South Ch'ungch'ŏng.
67. *KSC* 19: 30b–31a.
68. *KS* 28: 11a.
69. Ibid., 12a. See also *KS* 123: 7b.
70. *KS* 106: 29b, 75: 24b–25a; and *KSC* 19: 35b–36a. Palace aides, who were both eunuchs and non-eunuchs, could not receive a rank above the relatively low rank of 7 (see *KS* 75: 24b–25a). However, the *History of Koryŏ* records that this rule came to be regularly ignored during King Ch'ungnyŏl's reign. Palace aides belonged to a branch of the central government known as the southern branch (*namban*). As Cho Chwaho demonstrates in his study of the southern branch, palace aides were usually men of humble origin ("Yŏdae namban ko," 11–17). Palace aides should not be confused with palace attendants (*naesi*), who were usually recruited from among the sons of prominent *yangban* families. For the history of the use of palace attendant appointment as a fast track to gaining high office, see Sudō, *Kōraichō kanryōsei no kenkyū*, 465–94, and Kim Pogwang, "Koryŏ sidae naesi." Hong Sŭnggi cautiously suggests that many of the slaves who rose to prominence under Mongol rule probably entered officialdom as palace aides. Hong also surmises that there were probably more public slaves than private slaves who entered officialdom this way (*Koryŏ kwijok sahoe wa nobi*, 367).
71. *KSC* 19: 36a. After his innocence was revealed, Yi was released.
72. This label has been the source of much scholarly debate. For a convenient summary, see Pak Yongun, *Koryŏ sahoe wa munbŏl kwijok kamun*, 73–84. For a case-by-case analysis of these terms and their frequent use under Mongol rule to refer to palace and inner-palace favorites, see Kim Kwangch'ŏl, *Koryŏ hugi sejokch'ŭng yŏn'gu*, 26–34.
73. See *KSC* 19: 37a; noted in Kim Tangt'aek, *Wŏn kansŏpha*, 28.
74. *KSC* 19: 42a–b.
75. Ibid., 34b–35a.
76. *KS* 28: 22a and *KSC* 19: 42b. The term "sons of the yurt" refers to the artisans, craftsman, and skilled workers who attended imperial clansmen and clanswomen of the Great Yuan *ulus*. In the case of Koryŏ, it refers to the inner-palace favorites attached to the Mongol consorts. For the translation "sons of the yurt," see Cleaves, "Sino-Mongolian Inscription," 51 n. 170. For a preliminary examination of these foreign retainers in Koryŏ, see Peter Yun, "Mongols and Western Asians."
77. These accusations were made by Wi Tŭgyu and No Chinŭi, who would later be promoted to supreme general and general respectively on the recommendation of Hong Tagu (*KS* 28: 30a). Hong, Wi, and No were trying to exploit similar concerns about Kim that were raised in 1277 (*KSC* 19: 40a, *KS* 28: 19b; cf. *YS* 15: 4620 [*juan* 208, Waiyi 1, Gaoli]). Details of the events that led to Kim's fall are recorded in his biography in the *History of Koryŏ* (*KS* 104: 13b–22a). In recognition of his role in suppressing the Sambyŏlch'o rebellion, Kim Panggyŏng was promoted to chancellor in 1273 (see *KS* 27: 41a). See also the discussion in Kwŏn Sŏnu, "Koryŏ Ch'ungnyŏl wangdae Kim Panggyŏng mugo sagŏn."

78. Hong Tagu, a man of Korean descent, was the son of Hong Pogwŏn, who was appointed Senior Official of Koryŏ Military and Commoner Populations (C. Gaoli Junmin Zhangguan) by the Mongols. Hong Pogwŏn's role, which his sons inherited, was to expedite the Mongol conquest of Koryŏ. His sons served in the great khan's *keshig* and enjoyed great privileges as high-ranking Mongol officials. As David M. Robinson points out, the Hong family continued to compete with the Koryŏ royal family over control of the Korean populations in Liaodong and the Korean peninsula. The investiture of King Ch'ungnyŏl as the Simyang (C. Shenyang) Prince in the early fourteenth century only exacerbated the situation (Robinson, *Empire's Twilight*, 28–34).
79. *KS* 28: 30a and *KSC* 20: 2a.
80. *KS* 28: 34a–b and *KSC* 20: 6b–7b.
81. Ikeuchi, "Kōrai ni chūzai shita Gen no tatsurokaseki ni tsuite," 279. A *darughachi*, however, was still appointed to oversee affairs in Tamna, Cheju Island.
82. *KS* 28: 31b. Paek was opposed to the employment of men from nontraditional backgrounds, but he apparently did not have reservations about their line of work. His son Paek Hyoju was a falconer (*KS* 31: 27a).
83. *KS* 106: 1a–b and *KSC* 20: 3b–4a.
84. Yi Punhŭi's biography in the *History of Koryŏ* cautiously notes that a late night visit that Yi made to see Hong about Kim Panggyŏng's arrest caused people to suspect a possible alliance between the two (*KS* 123:1 11b). The fact that Yi and his brother did not show support for Kim Panggyŏng only made it easier for others to suspect an alliance between them and Hong. But some scholars claim that there was indeed an alliance. The historian Yi Ikchu, for instance, claims that the brothers' decision to side with Hong Tagu was a strategic move intended to compensate for the loss of their greatest patron, King Wŏnjong. Their position, as Yi points out, became precarious as Ch'ungnyŏl attempted to build his own inner circle ("Koryŏ Ch'ungnyŏl wangdae ŭi chŏngch'i sanghwang," 173–74).
85. *KS* 28: 45a–b.
86. See *KS* 28: 45b and 104: 45a. Kim Chujŏng was the father-in-law of the son of the falconry official Yun Su. In 1283, Kim was placed in charge of the falconry offices (*KS* 29: 44b–45a).
87. Kim Tangt'aek, *Wŏn kansŏpha*, 18–19. The purpose of the royal transmitters was to maintain proper distance between the king and the bureaucracy so that individual and political cliques could not exert undue influence on the king (noted in Duncan, *Origins*, 159).
88. The relationship between the *bichēchi* and the personnel authority (*chŏngbang*) is not clear. Yi Kinam argues that the *bichēchi* constitute a special *chaech'u* within the existing personnel authority ("Ch'ungsŏn wang ŭi kaehyŏk," 78–83). Kim Ch'anghyŏn similarly argues for the functional inseparability of the *bichēchi* and the personnel authority (*Koryŏ hugi chŏngbang yŏn'gu*, 78–81, 131–42). Kim Kwangch'ŏl, however, thinks the *bichēchi* constituted a separate government office staffed exclusively by officials loyal to King Ch'ungnyŏl (see "Koryŏ Ch'ungnyŏl wangdae"). Pak Yongun similarly presents evidence that supports the claim that

the two were separate institutions, but he also admits that there was considerable overlap between the two institutions ("Koryŏ hugi *bishechi*," 261–62). That there was some overlap seems undeniable. Whatever their relation may have been, it is clear that the establishment of the *bichēchi* made it possible for the king to exert even more control over the personnel authority and hence recruitment and promotions.

89. For this list of officials in the *bichēchi*, see Kim Chujŏng's biography in the *History of Koryŏ* (*KS* 104: 45a–b). For a more convenient list that includes name, title, rank, and office, see also Yi Kinam, "Ch'ungsŏn wang ŭi kaehyŏk," 80. Yi Kinam also provides a table that conveniently identifies a *bichēchi* official's place of origin and indicates whether or not that official passed the government examination (ibid., 81). As Kim Tangt'aek points out, there are three *bichēchi* officials who were students (*munsaeng*) of Chancellor Yu Kyŏng and argues that their appointment to the *bichēchi* had something to do with Yu Kyŏng's close relationship with the king (*Wŏn kansŏpha*, 20). Although this is not implausible, Yu Kyŏng's influence was apparently not responsible for the appointment of students like An Chŏn to the *bichēchi*. According to An's biography in the *History of Koryŏ*, he entered the *bichēchi* with the help of the palace aide Yi Chijŏ, not Yu Kyŏng (*KS* 106: 38b). This also explains why An Chŏn, who previously clashed with the king over the issue of falconry officials, could enter the *bichēchi*.

90. See *KS* 78: 19a.
91. *KS* 125: 7b.
92. *KS* 29: 9b.
93. *KSC* 20: 23a, *KS* 29: 11a, and *KS* 106: 27b.
94. *KS* 106: 29a and *KSC* 20: 24a; cited in Yi Ikchu, "Koryŏ Ch'ungnyŏl wangdae," 178–79. On Paek Munjŏl's role in the release of Sim, Chin, and Mun, see also *KS* 29: 11a. Yi Sŭnghyu, as noted in chapter 2, chose to retire from politics.
95. Yi Ikchu, "Koryŏ Ch'ungnyŏl wangdae," 179. Im Chŏnggi's biography in the *History of Koryŏ* uses him as an example of the collapse of the regular process of recruitment and promotion. Despite the censorate's effort to prevent his appointment, Im became a special director entrusted with a royal edict for the Chŏlla circuit and was later promoted to Chŏlla circuit commissioner. Im and other pacification commissioners at the time were regarded by their peers as unworthy of their official positions (*KS* 123: 19b–20a).
96. This second expedition was impressive in scale. It consisted of one hundred thousand troops, fifteen thousand Korean sailors, and nine hundred boats. Various factors led to the failure of this expedition, but the most famous is perhaps the typhoon that struck the coast of Kyushu and destroyed half the expedition force. This led to serious problems for Qubilai: he not only lost the "mantle of invincibility" that drove the Mongol empire but also had to face serious revenue shortages resulting from the costly invasion of Japan (Rossabi, "Reign of Khubilai Khan," 484).
97. The issue of granting these officials merit subject status was discussed on February 5 and carried out four months later on June 15 (see *KS* 29: 36a–b and 38b respectively). Yi Ikchu also makes this point ("Koryŏ Ch'ungnyŏl wangdae ŭi chŏngch'i sanghwang," 178).

98. Kim Pyŏn seems to have also received his second-grade merit subject status at this time (*KMC*: 412).
99. *KS* 30: 8a.
100. See, e.g., *KS* 123: 15b. 124: 3b–5a, 30: 12a, and 31: 11a.
101. Even the imperial princess Qutlugh Kelmish found the appointment of a former slave as vice commissioner of the king's mother's birthplace to be inappropriate (*KSC* 20: 43b). This was not the first time Kim was asked to represent the central government. In 1277, he had served as the king's envoy to Tamna. Before Kim, palace aide eunuchs had never been granted such appointments. He was entrusted with the important task of bringing Koryŏ's defense forces back to the peninsula (*KS* 28: 22b). The reason Ch'ungnyŏl relied so heavily on Kim is unclear. It may have been his Mongolian-language skills. In 1282, Kim was sent as an official envoy to Dadu to celebrate the arrival of the new year (*KS* 29: 36a). This was a highly prestigious appointment usually reserved for men with refined Mongolian skills such as Cho In'gyu or the imperial princess's foreign retainers, for example, In Hu.
102. *KS* 31: 18b. Yi would later become assistant chancellor (rank 2a), making him a member of the esteemed *chaech'u*. Like Cho In'gyu, he received the noble title Lord (Kun).
103. *KS* 31: 18b.
104. *KS* 124: 4a–b.
105. See Hsiao, "Mid-Yüan Politics," 495–96.
106. For the history and function of the council of princes and nobles as an institution, see Endicott-West, "Imperial Governance." For a partial list of the people present at the council, see Rashīd al-Dīn Ṭabīb, *Successors of Genghis Khan*, 320–21.
107. *KS* 31: 8b.
108. It is possible that Temür's hesitation had something to do with his reservations about Ch'ungsŏn's bloodline. When he received the completed veritable record for his grandfather, he noticed that Ch'ungsŏn's mother, Qutlugh Kelmish, was recorded as a princess (C. *gongzhu*). Temür questioned this, noting the fact that she was not the daughter of Qubilai's first wife, Chabui (d. 1281) (*YS*: 407 [*juan* 19, Chengzong second year, eleventh month]). Yi Ikchu claims that this negative attitude toward Qutlugh Kelmish was a consequence of Ch'ungnyŏl's refusal to show support for Temür at the council of princes and nobles ("Ch'ungsŏn wang chŭgwinyŏn," 117). As Yi himself is willing to admit, however, there is little evidence to support this claim. Temür's comment about Qutlugh Kelmish probably had more to do with his particularly deep respect for his grandmother. For Temür's respect for his grandmother, whom he honored with the posthumous title Empress Zhaorui shunsheng and a eulogy, see *YS*: 2872 (*juan* 114, *houfei* 1). On Chabui and the way she shaped Qubilai's rule, see Rossabi, "Khubilai Khan," 167–72.
109. In 1295, the Yuan court transferred Ch'ungnyŏl's noble titles to Ch'ungsŏn (*KSC* 21: 37a). The *History of Yuan* (Yuan shi) has "king of Koryŏ" in place of "the crown prince of Koryŏ," but this seems to be a mistake (*YS* 2: 414 [*juan* 19, Chengzong first year, eleventh month]). During his short stay in Koryŏ, Ch'ungsŏn was granted the title Chief Grand Councilor and placed in charge of the chancellery,

security council, and censorate as well as given control over Koryŏ's central forces (see *KSC* 21: 37b–38a and *KS* 31: 9a–b). Ch'ungsŏn arrived in Koryŏ on the October 3, 1295, and returned to Dadu on January 16, 1296. He seems to have gone to Dadu three years earlier in the summer of 1292 (*KS* 30: 31a).

110. *KS* 31: 10b. Yu left on February 14.
111. *KS* 31: 13b. The officials who accompanied the king and the imperial princess to Dadu to celebrate the heir apparent Ch'ungsŏn's marriage were all granted highly irregular promotions. Their new posts were four ranks higher than their old posts (*KS* 31: 17b).
112. *KS* 31: 14b, *KS* 33: 3b, and *KSC* 21: 41b.
113. *KS* 31: 17a. This is June 18 according to the Gregorian calendar.
114. *KS* 31: 17b. Ch'ungsŏn arrived on July 12.
115. According to the *History of Koryŏ*, the king frequently went "hunting" to escape the jealousy of the imperial princess and see Mubi (*KS* 31: 11b).
116. *KS* 31: 17b–18a and *KSC* 21: 43a–b. For a brief, English-language discussion of Ch'oe Seyŏn, see Duncan, *Origins*, 165.
117. See Yi Kinam, "Ch'ungsŏn wang ŭi kaehyŏk," 74–78; Yi Ikchu, "Koryŏ Ch'ungnyŏl wangdae ŭi chŏngch'i sanghwang," 187–89; and Kim Kwangch'ŏl, "Koryŏ Ch'ungsŏn wang ŭi hyŏnsil insik," 53. There is some disagreement, however, about who orchestrated this purge. Kim Sŏngjun argues that it was Ch'ungsŏn. According to Kim, Ch'ungsŏn's marriage to Buddhaśrī and the strong support he therefore received from the Yuan court made such a bold political move possible ("Yŏdae Wŏn kongju ch'ulsin wangbi," 159–61). Yi Ikchu reads the incident as the outcome of Ch'ungnyŏl's costly political mistake. Yi claims that Ch'ungnyŏl made himself the new khan's enemy when he supported Gammala at the council of princes and nobles ("Ch'ungsŏn wang chŭgwinyŏn," 117–18). This argument, however, is speculative at best.
118. The circumstances that led to the exile are detailed in Ch'oe's biography in the *History of Koryŏ* (*KS* 122: 15a–18b; see also *KSC* 21: 10a and *KS* 30: 15a). Although Ch'ungsŏn was only thirteen years of age at the time (in 1288), he had ostensibly accomplished what the *chaech'u* had repeatedly failed to do: remove Ch'oe. According to existing sources, the cause of Ch'oe's downfall was his arrogance and abuse of power. Although he eventually returned to court, Ch'ungsŏn's mother, Qutlugh Kelmish, later punished Ch'oe for similar reasons. The queen had him slapped, placed in a cangue, and detained for disobeying her order. The queen had prohibited him from expanding his home near the palace, but Ch'oe ignored the order and enlarged the house once owned by Cho In'gyu (*KS* 122: 15a–b).
119. *KS* 31: 13a. Ch'oe had accompanied the falconry official Wŏn Kyŏng to Dadu earlier in 1285 (*KS* 30: 3a).
120. See *KS* 122: 15a–18b.
121. Yi Ikchu also makes this observation ("Ch'ungsŏn wang chŭgwinyŏn," 115).
122. *KS* 75: 3b; also noted in Kim Tant'aek, *Wŏn kansŏpha*, 38–39.
123. *KS* 84: 23b. During Ch'ungnyŏl's reign, many tried to take advantage of the his trip to Dadu. In 1289, for instance, so many applied to go that it was not easy for the king to decide the size of his attending retinue. Breaking with earlier court

custom, he even decided to leave the royal historians behind in Koryŏ so as to accommodate the large number of people willing to accompany him to Dadu (*KS* 30: 20a). Ch'ungsŏn's attempt to limit the influence of men from nontraditional backgrounds was short-lived. He himself ended up relying on eunuchs such as Pang Sinu and former farmers, including Pak Ryŏ and Yi Kongbo, to forge important political ties to key members of the imperial family and regain control of the Koryŏ court (*KSC* 23: 13b).

124. *KS* 78: 5a, 84: 22b–23a. The "deceitful bullies" mentioned here are clearly palace aides and "sons of the yurt" who came to Koryŏ with the imperial princess. These men acquired large landed estates using the grant ordinances that they received from the king. It should also be noted here that Ch'ungnyŏl had granted land in the capital district to members of the *qorchi* in 1283 (*KSC* 29: 42a–b). This land was called "grazing land" (*pangmokso*). The bullies here could therefore also refer to the *qorchi*.

125. *KS* 78: 5b.

126. *KS* 84: 23a–b. Efforts to address the problem of wandering peasants had been made earlier, in 1285, but apparently to no avail (*KS* 30: 2a). Although Ch'ungsŏn does not name Yŏm in his royal edict, the latter's biography in the *History of Koryŏ* mentions his reliance on this unscrupulous practice (*KS* 123: 8a–11a, 123: 24a). According to one of Ch'ungsŏn's royal edicts, it was not uncommon for men like Yŏm to force commoners to become slaves (*KS* 85: 43a–b).

127. *KS* 84: 22b–23a. According to Ch'ungsŏn's edict, the powerful tended to arbitrarily promote their henchmen to the rank of senior eighth-grade captain (*sanwŏn*). Using their elevated status, these henchmen terrorized local officials and commoner peasants.

128. *KS* 85: 43b.

129. See *KS* 84: 23b–24b. In his memorial, Hong Chabŏn also criticized "appointment bribes" and recommended that they be prohibited. For his explanation and critique of appointment bribes, see *KS* 84: 21a. For a detailed study of Hong's memorial submitted in 1296, see No Yongp'il, "Hong Chabŏn." The influence of Hong's memorial is also noted in Duncan, *Origins*, 174.

130. Yi Ikchu, "Ch'ungsŏn wang chŭgwinyŏn," 120–21. In Hu and Ch'a Sin probably supported Ch'ungsŏn because they had recently lost their most important patron, Qutlugh Kelmish. Cho In'gyu was Ch'ungsŏn's father-in-law, and Pak Ŭi was Cho In'gyu's son-in-law.

131. Kim Ch'anghyŏn rightly rejects Yi Ikchu's claim that Ch'ungsŏn's reform was intended to put an end to inner-circle politics. As Kim points out, Ch'ungsŏn was even more dependent on inner-circle politics ("Ch'ungsŏn wang ŭi t'ansaeng," 126 n. 66).

132. *KS* 109: 1b and *KSC* 22: 4b; also noted in Kim Tangt'aek, *Wŏn kansŏpha*, 36, and Kim Kwangch'ŏl, "Koryŏ Ch'ungsŏn wang ŭi hyŏnsil insik," 15–16.

133. Yi Kanghan, "Koryŏ Ch'ungsŏn wang ŭi chŏngch'i kaehyŏk," 274–76. Yi Kanghan, like Yi Ikchu, attributes similar reforms carried out in Yuan China as a key reason behind Ch'ungsŏn's reform effort.

134. As Yi Ikchu points out, during Ch'ungnyŏl's reign, the *chaech'u* still referred to the five chancellery and seven security council officials (*ojae ch'ilch'u*), but the position of chancellor was split into left and right chancellors and new positions such as the associate superintendent of the security council (*tong p'an milchiksa sa*) were created. A greater number of officials also came to share key posts in the security council. Naturally, the *chaech'u* increased in size ("Ch'ungsŏn wang chŭgwinyŏn," 131–32; see also Pyŏn T'aesŏp, *Koryŏ chŏngch'i chedosa yŏn'gu*, 99–104). Ch'ungsŏn reduced the number of *chaech'u* to a more manageable seven officials. He continued this policy after he ascended the throne again in 1308 (Yi Kanghan, "Koryŏ Ch'ungsŏn wang ŭi chŏngch'i kaehyŏk," 273).
135. Yi Ikchu, "Ch'ungsŏn wang chŭgwinyŏn," 126.
136. Ibid., 131.
137. See her biography in the *History of Koryŏ* (*KS* 89: 13a–16a).
138. Yi Ikchu has interpreted Buddhaśrī's involvement in the removal of Ch'ungsŏn differently. In contrast to Yi Kinam, who proposed that Ch'ungsŏn tried to reject Yuan overlordship in 1298, Yi Ikchu argues that there was nothing anti-Yuan about the content of Ch'ungsŏn's reform measures. According to Yi Ikchu, Ch'ungsŏn complied with the demands of the Yuan court and tried to address the problems introduced by his father's inner circle. The renaming of offices and titles were also in keeping with the Yuan court's demands. Why, then, would the Yuan court force Ch'ungsŏn to abdicate? Yi Ikchu claims that this had something to do with Ch'ungsŏn taking bold political action without seeking the court's approval first (see Yi Kinam, "Ch'ungsŏn wang ŭi kaehyŏk," 89, and Yi Ikchu, "Ch'ungsŏn wang chŭgwinyŏn," 134). I agree with Yi Ikchu that the reforms have little, if anything, to do with Ch'ungsŏn's supposed anti-Yuan attitude but find his argument about the forced abdication of Ch'ungsŏn unconvincing. It fails to adequately explain why the Yuan court restored the names of offices and titles used during Ch'ungnyŏl's reign.
139. The letter was sent on June 17, and the king announced his edict on June 22.
140. *KS* 33: 10b.
141. *KS* 77: 23b–24a and *KSC* 22: 6b. This included both royal transmitters and the transmitter in charge of the personnel authority (*chŏngsaek sŭngsŏn*). As the title implies, this transmitter was qualitatively different from the other transmitters in that he was less the king's spokesperson than the personnel authority. For the transmitter in charge of the personnel authority, see *KS* 75: 3a. For an English-language translation of the relevant passage, see Shultz, *Generals and Scholars*, 76–77.
142. The letter was later revealed to have been written by the recorder in the office of fisheries Yun Ŏnju. Unfortunately, nothing else is known about Yun.
143. *YS* 15: 4622 (*juan* 208, Waiyi 1, Gaoli).
144. *KS* 31: 22b–23a and *YS* 2: 420 (*juan* 19, Chengzong second year, seventh month). As Kim Ch'anghyŏn rightly claims, the Yuan court did not summon Ch'ungsŏn to Dadu in order to put an end to his "anti-Yuan" efforts. Rather, the Yuan court was reining in an overconfident and overambitious imperial clan member ("Ch'ungsŏn wang ŭi t'ansaeng," 125–26).

145. See Yi Ikchu, "Ch'ungsŏn wang chŭgwinyŏn," 138.
146. Deuchler, *Under the Ancestors' Eyes*, 46.

5. Buddhas and Ancestors

1. This would be May 18 on the Gregorian calendar.
2. Kim Pyŏn's tomb epitaph is in *KMC*: 412. The posthumous name is not mentioned directly in the epitaph, but it was customary for the king to grant posthumous names in dirges (see, e.g., *KMC*: 52, 188, 285, 396). The dirge also customarily contained a record of the accomplishments of the dead (see *KMC*: 330). Kim's epitaph also does not mention the office of state sacrifices by name, but this office handled state support for the funerals of chancellery officials and the granting of official dirges (see, e.g., *KMC*: 152, 566, 578, 588). For a thorough analysis of Kim Pyŏn's tomb epitaph, see Yi Ikchu, "Myojimyŏng charyo."
3. *KMC*: 446. As her tomb epitaph points out, Lady Hŏ, following local Koryŏ custom (*kuksok*), did not have a personal name (*KMC*: 445). The office of state sacrifices offered *chaech'u* officials state funerals (*yejang*)—posthumous names, financial support, and funerary provisions (*KS* 64: 20a–22b; noted in Deuchler, *Confucian Transformation of Korea*, 77).
4. It is unclear whether or not she is the one performing the sacrifices.
5. See *KMC*: 412 (Kim Pyŏn), 447 (Lady Hŏ), 532 (Kim Ryun's wife), 535 (Kim Ryun), and 562 (Min Sap'yŏng). Min's wife, Kim Ryun's eldest daughter (1302–1374), was not buried on the grounds of Kamŭng-sa because the capital lay in ruins after the Red Turban incursion in 1361. She therefore moved to her late husband's hometown Yŏhŭng (present-day Yŏju, Kyŏnggi) and was buried there after her death in 1374 (*KMC*: 582).
6. This corresponds to April 6, 1324, in the Gregorian calendar.
7. This is one of the so-called three obediences mentioned in the "Single Victim at the Border Sacrifices" (Jiaotesheng) chapter of the *The Book of Rites* (Li ji): "The woman follows (and obeys) the man:—in her youth, she follows her father and elder brother; when married, she follows her husband; when her husband is dead, she follows her son" (Legge, *Li Chi*, 1:441).
8. *KMC*: 447. It is unclear why the great lady's tomb epitaph refers to her husband's gravesite as the "ancestral gravesite" (*sŏnyŏng*). It may be possible that Kim Pyŏn's father and his spouse were buried there.
9. This should not be hastily taken as evidence of the growing influence of Neo-Confucianism. Bettine Birge has convincingly shown that similar concerns about chastity came to be voiced more frequently during the Yuan for reasons that have little to do with Confucianism or Neo-Confucianism ("Levirate Marriage"). As Birge demonstrates elsewhere, legislative changes that encouraged female chastity in Yuan China were part of an effort, not to promote Confucian values, but to preserve taxable households that could support fighting men ("Women and Confucianism," 225-29). It also seems worth pointing out here that although the dynastic history of Koryŏ condemns kings for taking their father's concubines as

their own (e.g., Ch'ungsŏn and Ch'unghye), this practice was perfectly acceptable from the perspective of Mongol custom and law.
10. The expression "deviation from the usual conduct of mourning" is borrowed from Deuchler, *Confucian Transformation of Korea*, 76.
11. This also coincides with the hundredth-day vegetarian feast performed for the dead at Buddhist monasteries (*KS* 33: 4b).
12. In 1046, the board of personnel asked the king to banish the professor of astronomy Sŏ Ung from office for not returning to work after one hundred days of mourning. The king, citing Sŏ's talents as an astronomer, specially granted the professor an extra one hundred days of mourning (*KS* 6: 35b–36a). When the assistant director of sacrifice (*chaeje pusa*) at the western capital Chang Ch'ungŭi passed away, his eldest son, the vice director of the central service office (*chungsangsŏ sŭng*) Chang Kwangbu, resigned from his office to mourn his father in a mourning shed for three years (*KMC*: 233). This, however, did not mean that Kwangbu rejected Buddhism and adopted (Neo-)Confucianism. Before the mourning period, Kwangbu, in keeping with custom, collected his father's remains from the western capital and kept it at a monastery named Kwangdŏk-sa until the funeral.
13. A good example is Ha Yunwŏn who was told by King U that national exigencies warranted shortening the three-year mourning period to one hundred days (*KS* 112: 32a–b; cited in Deuchler, *Confucian Transformation of Korea*, 76). The record of Kwŏn Kŏŭi (an official during at the time of King U) and No Chun'gong, who observed the full three-year mourning period, in the *History of Koryŏ* (Koryŏsa) states that "the mourning customs at the time were in disorder and everyone wore mourning for one hundred days" (*KS* 121: 20b). Officials were granted leave for one hundred days (see *KS* 64: 20a–22b passim). In 1122, King Yejong issued an order that asked officials to shorten the mourning period even further to three days, treating one day as the equivalent of one full month of mourning (*KS* 14: 42a).
14. Deuchler, *Confucian Transformation of Korea*, 26.
15. Legge, *Li Chi*, 2:253. This is a quote from the "Summary Account of Sacrifices" (Jitong) chapter of the *The Book of Rites*.
16. *KMC*: 447.
17. *KMC*: 446.
18. Bossler, *Powerful Relations*, 19.
19. Most notable in this regard are the funerary inscriptions for the Hallim academician Ch'oe Nubaek's wife Yŏm Kyŏngae and Yŏm's mother, Sim Chiŭi (see *KMC*: 93-95, 200–201 respectively). See also the funerary inscription for the director of the finance commission on the left Yu Yŏngjae's (d. 1170) wife Lady Cho (*KMC*: 320-21). Lady Cho was the granddaughter of Assistant Chancellor Mun Kongwŏn of the powerful Namp'yŏng Mun descent group and the older sister of Chancellor Cho Yŏngin.
20. Bossler, *Powerful Relations*, 22.
21. Ibid., 23.

22. For the dates on which Hŏ Su and Hŏ Kyŏng passed the literary examination, see Hŏ, *Koryŏ ŭi kwagŏ chedo*, 497 and 502 respectively. Min Hyŏn'gu claims that Hŏ Kong's descent group was not a traditionally prominent one. The Kongam Hŏ was not, in other words, a proper member of the capital-based aristocracy. Citing Yi Usŏng's influential article on the so-called new scholar-officials, Min claims that it was the clerically talented Hŏ Kong who made his family and descent group prominent (Min, "Koryŏ hugi kwŏnmun sejok ŭi sŏngnip," 28–29, and Yi Usŏng, "Koryŏjo ŭi 'i' e taehayŏ"). Regardless of whether or not Lady Hŏ's family was in fact a family with a pedigree, the point is that this family was *understood* by its contemporaries to be a family with a pedigree.
23. For Hŏ Chae's funerary inscription, see *KMC*: 78–83. For more detailed information on the history of Lady Hŏ's descent group, see Pak Yongun, *Koryŏ sahoe wa munbŏl kwijok kamun*, 252–67.
24. *KS* 33: 24a–b.
25. *KMC*: 481. Lady Hŏ's younger sister was the spouse of the superintendent of the finance commission Kim Sun, who was the son of Chancellor Kim Panggyŏng of the Andong Kim descent group.
26. *KMC*: 445. Hŏ's biography in the *History of Koryŏ* also emphasizes his frugality. According to the biography, Hŏ did not engage in commercial activities (*sanŏp*) (*KS* 105: 13a). This, however, is a misleading portrayal. He actively exploited his position as head of the personnel authority to acquire immense wealth. While serving as royal transmitter in charge of the personnel authority, Hŏ received bribes from many circuit commissioners. Hŏ even bore a grudge against the attendant censor Kim Sŭngmu for impeaching the circuit commissioners who submitted bribes (*KS* 102: 9a).
27. *KSC* 23: 19a, *KS* 106: 20b–21a, and *KMC*: 461. For more information about Kang, see Hong Sŭnggi, *Koryŏ kwijok sahoe wa nobi*, 382–84.
28. Kim Ch'anghyŏn, *Koryŏ hugi chŏngbang yŏn'gu*, 109–10. As Kim points out, King Ch'ungsŏn maintained direct control over recruitment and promotions through the office of the royal seal (*chŏnbusi*) (ibid., 108–11).
29. *KS* 106: 20b–21a.
30. See, e.g., Kim Tangt'aek, *Wŏn kansŏpha*, 23, and Ko Hyeryŏng, *Koryŏ hugi sadaebu wa sŏngnihak suyong*, 29–32.
31. Hŏ, *Koryŏ ŭi kwagŏ chedo*, 501.
32. *KMC*: 418. Kim Kaemul's funerary inscription states that Kim Koeng had held the title Royal Inspector (Kamch'al Ŏsa; rank 6b).
33. Ibid.
34. See Duncan, *Origins*, 84.
35. This is a quote from the *I Ching* (Yi jing) (Legge, *The I Ching*, 108).
36. *KMC*: 461.
37. For Wang's biography, see *KS* 124: 23b–25b.
38. For a study of these men, see Yi Sukkyŏng, "Koryŏ Ch'ungsuk wang Ch'unghye wang," 89–100. For the difficulty that the Koryŏ sovereigns experienced because of their tours to Dadu, see Kim Tangt'aek, *Wŏn kansŏpha*, 167–83.

39. *KMC*: 419. According to Kim's biography in the *History of Koryŏ*, while Kim was serving as the local recruitment commissioner (*pubusa*) of the Chŏlla circuit, he made the dangerous move of seizing the food tribute items being submitted to the king by the circuit commissioner No Kyŏngnyun in 1275. After he realized that half the items being submitted were private tribute items (*sasŏn*), he seized them and placed them in the state treasury (*kukko*). No informed the king of what had happened, and Kim was dismissed from office (*KS* 106: 20a). The biography also observes that he was so morally strict, honest, and upright that people feared him.
40. See Ko Hyeryŏng, *Koryŏ hugi sadaebu*, 7–53.
41. *KMC*: 419.
42. Yi Chin's praise for Kim Hwŏn's honest and upright character does not mean that Yi himself lived up to these expectations. In fact, Yi was known to have exploited the influence of his son Yi Chehyŏn to steal other people's slaves (*KSC* 24: 19b).
43. *KMC*: 462.
44. Kim Tangt'aek, *Wŏn kansŏpha*, 65. Historians offer various interpretations of the ministerial families. Yi Kinam, for instance, argues that ministerial families were the enemies of the regular bureaucracy ("Ch'ungsŏn wang ŭi kaehyŏk," 64). Other than the P'yŏngyang Cho, there is little evidence to support Yi's argument. Martina Deuchler argues that the ministerial families "all enjoyed high social prestige and, for Ch'ungsŏn, who clearly strove to distance himself from his father's poor preferences of people to serve him, what was apparently most important was that they possessed social profiles incontestably untainted by *kwŏnmun* excesses" (*Under the Ancestors' Eyes*, 37). There is good reason to question this understanding of the ministerial families.
45. See Min Hyŏn'gu, "Cho In'gyu wa kŭ ŭi kamun (chung)," 18; Pak Yongun, *Koryŏ sahoe wa munbŏl kwijok kamun*, 256; and Kim Tangt'aek, *Wŏn kansŏpha*, 48–52 passim.
46. Kim Tangt'aek, *Wŏn kansŏpha*, 52.
47. For more about Sŏk Chu and his sons, see *KS* 125: 21b–22a. They were arrested and taken to China in 1303. Sŏk Ch'ŏnbo and Sŏk Ch'ŏn'gyŏng were exiled to Anxi. Sŏk Chu and Sŏk Ch'ŏn'gi were later stripped of their wealth and sent into exile for participating in Wang Yuso's plot against Ch'ungsŏn in 1307.
48. This is the daughter of Wang Yŏng, the Marquis of Sŏwŏn (*KS* 30: 16b). Two years earlier, in 1287, she was selected to be a tribute woman, but Ch'ungsŏn is said to have saved her from this fate by telling his mother the imperial princess that he intended to marry the marquis's daughter. Why Ch'ungsŏn chose her as his consort under these conditions is unclear (see *KSC* 21: 5b–6a and *KS* 89: 8b).
49. Deuchler, *Confucian Transformation of Korea*, 60.
50. *KS* 30: 22b. She passed away in 1306.
51. Yi Chin (Yi Chehyŏn's father) refers to Hong's family with the expression *ŭigwan kapchok* in Hong's funerary inscription (*KMC*: 434).
52. *KS* 106: 41b–42a and *KS* 30: 16a.
53. *KMC*: 434.
54. Ibid.

55. As Kim Ch'anghyŏn points out, Ch'ungsŏn seems to have begun coital relations with a Mongol woman who later received the title Ŭibi sometime before 1292 ("Ch'ungsŏn wang ŭi t'ansaeng," 112–14). Korean sources, however, make no mention of Ch'ungsŏn granting her official status as a consort.
56. See Yi Chŏngnan, "Ch'ungnyŏl wangdae Kyeguk taejang kongju ŭi kaehon undong"; Kim Sŏngjun, "Yŏdae Wŏn kongju"; and Kim Kwangch'ŏl, "Hong Chabŏn yŏn'gu," 14–25.
57. See *KS* 32: 18a and *KSC* 23: 5a–7a respectively. In 1306, when Wang Yuso, Song Lin, and others brought the issue of Buddhaśrī's remarriage to the attention of the grand councilor on the left Aqutai (d. 1307), the Yuan court was in the middle of a crisis that involved the Mongol princes Qaishan (temple name Wuzong) (r. 1307–11) and Ayurbarwada (temple name Renzong) (r. 1311–20). At the time, the Yuan court was split between supporters of the Mongol prince Ānanda (e.g., the empress Bulughan and Aqutai) and supporters of the princes Qaishan and Ayurbarwada (e.g., Harghasun and Ch'ungsŏn). After the loss of his greatest supporter, the empress dowager Kökejin (Bairam-Egechi) (d. 1300), Ch'ungsŏn was left defenseless against Temür's wife, empress Bulughan, who supported his father, Ch'ungnyŏl. Bulughan repeatedly thwarted efforts to restore Ch'ungsŏn to the Koryŏ throne. When the great khan passed away in February 1307, a battle for the throne immediately ensued, and Qaishan and Ayurbarwada emerged victorious. During the succession crisis, Ch'ungsŏn therefore decided to come to the aid of Ayurbarwada and his mother, Targi, which resulted in Bulughan and her political ally Aqutai being removed from power (see *KS* 32: 28a–b; Hsiao, "Mid-Yüan Politics," 504–5; Dardess, *Conquerors and Confucians*, 9–18; Ko Pyŏngik, "Koryŏ Ch'ungsŏn wang ŭi Wŏn Mujong ongnip"; Kim Ch'anghyŏn, "Ch'ungsŏn wang ŭi t'ansaeng," 128–35; and Kim Kwangch'ŏl, "14-segich'o Wŏn ŭi chŏngguk tonghyang," 310–14). For his critical role in the succession struggle, Ch'ungsŏn was rewarded with the noble title Simyang Prince.
58. *KS* 33: 21a.
59. According to the *Record for Lord Cho Chŏngsuk's Offering Hall* (Cho Chŏngsuk kong sadanggi) (*KJJ* 3: 7b–11b) and Cho In'gyu's tomb epitaph (*KMC*: 629–32), Cho had four sons-in-law. Neither source, however, mentions Pak Kyŏngnyang as his son-in-law; see Min Hyŏn'gu, "Cho In'gyu wa kŭ ŭi kamun (chung)," 11–12. However, Pak is mentioned as Cho's son-in-law in the *History of Koryŏ* (*KS* 105: 38b and *KS* 124: 7a–b). Ch'ungsŏn's Mongol consort Buddhaśrī's biography identifies the falconer Pak Ŭi as Cho's son-in-law, but I suspect this is a mistake. The biographer may have had Pak Kyŏngnyang's earlier name Pak Sŏn in mind. Curiously, the biography does mention Pak Kyŏngnyang by this name, but he is not identified as Cho's son-in-law. Min Hyŏn'gu suggests that Pak Kyŏngnyang may have married the daughter of Cho's concubine ("Cho In'gyu wa kŭ ŭi kamun [chung]," 12 n. 150).
60. For instance, see *KS* 102: 9a (for Hŏ Kong) and *KS* 105: 36b–37a (for Cho In'gyu).
61. See *KMC*: 435–36.
62. *KMC*: 415. Ch'ae was once appointed special director entrusted with a royal edict (*wangji sayong pyŏlgam*). As noted in chapter 4, central officials abused this appointment and used it to privately amass great wealth.

63. *KMC*: 422.
64. *KMC*: 532.
65. *KMC*: 528. Ch'oe's mother passed away in 1327 and his father in 1330. Ch'oe therefore wore mourning for a total of six years.
66. The title used here is *taejehak*. After 1302, the academician of the security council was called *chehak*. The title *taejehak* replaced the title *taehaksa* (great academician), of the institute for the advancement of literature, in 1308 (see Pak Yongun, "*Koryŏsa*" *paekkwanji yŏkchu*, 232–40). The great academician in the *pomun'gak* (hall for treasuring culture) also used the title *taejehak*, but not until 1314. The term *taejehak* here could refer to any one of these titles.
67. There are two extant versions of Ch'oe Mundo's funerary inscription. One is the actual tomb epitaph currently housed at the National Museum in Seoul. The other is the draft that was included in Yi Chehyŏn's collection of writings, *Ikche chip*. The *Ikche chip* version reads "Hallim Academy scholar" (*ICJ* 7: 28a). In Koryŏ, the drafter of proclamations (*chijego*) was usually held as a concurrent post by an official in the Hallim Academy (see Sudō Yoshiyuki, *Kōraichō kanryōsei no kenkyū*, 267–313).
68. Ch'oe Sŏngji passed the literary examination in 1284 and served as secretary (*kwan'gi*) of the old Silla capital (*KMC*: 467).
69. Ch'oe Mundo's son Sagŏm passed the literary examination in 1340. According to the preface to a poem that Yi Kok wrote in celebration of the occasion, Ch'oe Sagŏm explained to Yi that he took the literary examination in honor of his grandmother Lady Kim's wish. She regretted the fact that her own son failed to continue the family tradition of producing exam passers, as it had done for five successive generations. Ch'oe Sagŏm explained that his father could not study for the examination because he had to serve in the great khan's *keshig* (*KJJ* 9: 9b). Evidently, Ch'oe Mundo's failure to take and pass the literary examination was a source of shame and concern for his family.
70. Ko Hyeryŏng believes that Ch'unhŏn traveled to Dadu as a "hostage" (*turqāq*) in 1313 ("Wŏn kansŏpki sŏngnihak suyong ŭi il tanmyŏn," 150).
71. In a poem he wrote to celebrate Ch'unhŏn's promotion to superintendent of the board of punishment, Yi Kok wrote: "While leisurely spending twenty years in Nanpu, [the superintendent] did not go near fame and fortune even in his dreams" (*KJJ* 16: 5a). Ko Hyeryŏng reads the twenty years mentioned in this poem as a reference to the time he spent in China ("Wŏn kansŏpki sŏngnihak suyong ŭi il tanmyŏn," 153).
72. *KMC*: 528.
73. For the use of the family shrine and Cheng-Zhu learning, see Deuchler, *Confucian Transformation of Korea*. Kim Yongsŏn argues that the use of the family shrine and clan gravesites (*chokpun*) were due to the influence of Neo-Confucian funerary practices (*Koryŏ kŭmsŏngmun yŏn'gu*, 188–98). Other studies trace the rise and spread of the family shrine and Cheng-Zhu learning to the collapse of Koryŏ's territorial status system (Hŏ Hŭngsik, *Koryŏ pulgyosa yŏn'gu*, 31–44, and Chu Ungyŏng, "Kamyo ŭi sŏllip paegyŏng kwa kŭ kinŭng").
74. Ch'ungsŏn abolished the personnel authority in 1298, but his father restored it soon after Ch'ŭngson was dethroned. As soon as he seized control of the Koryŏ

court in 1307, Ch'ungsŏn once again abolished the personnel authority and transferred its authority to the board of personnel (*chŏllisa*) and the board of war (*kunbusa*). The letters of appointment were submitted to Kwŏn and Ch'oe, who determined which letters would receive Ch'ungsŏn's signature (*KSC* 33: 7a–b and 9a; noted in Kim Ch'anghyŏn, *Koryŏ hugi chŏngbang yŏn'gu*, 103). Later that same year, Ch'ungsŏn handed control over recruitment and promotions to Assistant Chancellor Yi Hon (exam passed in 1268), who was placed in charge of the Hallim Academy and the "board of recruitment" (*sŏnbu*), which was created by combining the board of personnel and the board of war. Kim Ch'anghyŏn suspects that this was Ch'ungsŏn's response to growing complaints about Kwŏn and Ch'oe, who nevertheless continued to exercise control over personnel matters (*Koryŏ hugi chŏngbang yŏn'gu*, 104–8).

75. *KMC*: 467. A large number of the men who belonged to Ch'ungsŏn's network of supporters were Yuan eunuchs of Koryŏ origin, such as Pang Sinu, who served as the interface between Ch'ungsŏn and the Yuan imperial family. Many of them received noble titles in 1309 after Ch'ungsŏn's reenthronement (*KSC* 23: 22a–23a).

76. *KS* 125: 28b and *KSC* 23: 28b. Indeed, shortly after Ch'ungsŏn and Ch'oe returned to Koryŏ in 1313, remonstrance officials refused to ratify appointments made by Ch'ungsŏn. In retaliation, Ch'ungsŏn imprisoned, exiled, and demoted them (*KS* 34: 14b–15b and *KSC* 24: 1a–b).

77. Kim Sim was in a unique position to forge meaningful relationships with people in the empress dowager's household administration. His daughter Dharmaśrī was Ayurbarwada's concubine (*KS* 104: 47b and *YS* 9: 2698 [*juan* 106, *biao* 1, *houfeibiao*]). She was later named second empress. The *History of Koryŏ* refers to the elevation of Dharmaśrī's official status to empress in 1328, but this is clearly a mistake (*KS* 35: 23a–b). For an explanation of the increased authority and power of the empress dowager's household administration and the political tension between the empress dowager and the emperor (Ayurbarwada), see Kim Kwangch'ŏl, "14-segich'o Wŏn ŭi chŏngguk tonghyang," 305–10.

78. This event is detailed in Kim Sim's biography (see *KS* 104: 47b–48b). Kim and Yi remained in exile for five years.

79. With the assistance of the grand councilor on the right Temüder, Ayurbarwada made a few futile attempts to weaken the imperial princes and sons-in-law (Hsiao, "Mid-Yüan Politics," 520–22).

80. The Yuan court allowed Ch'ungsŏn to retire, but the retired king was forced to return to Koryŏ (*KS* 34: 9b–10a). Ch'ungsŏn, however, returned to Dadu the very next year (*KSC* 24: 3a). Kim Kwangch'ŏl argues persuasively that the Yuan court's decision to send Ch'ungsŏn back to Koryŏ was an extension of its efforts to prevent imperial clansmen from forming political cliques in Dadu ("14-segich'o Wŏn ŭi chŏngguk tonghyang," 317).

81. Ko was the son of Ch'ungsŏn's half brother Wang Cha. Cha's mother was Ch'ungnyŏl's first consort, Court Lady Chŏnghwa, who was a member of the royal Wang clan. Ch'ungsŏn had Ko inherit his noble title Sim Prince in 1316 (*KSC* 24: 5b and *YS* 2: 572 [*juan* 25, *benji* 25, Renzong 2]).

82. Ch'ungsŏn maintained control over not only recruitment and promotions but also the state treasury (Kim Tangt'aek, *Wŏn kansŏpha*, 77).
83. Temüder, who had the support of the empress dowager Targi, carried out a purge of his enemies. Despite his young age, Shidebala also carried out his own ambitious purge. In the summer of 1320, he dismantled the empress dowager's household administration and removed her supporters from court (*YS* 3: 603 [*juan* 27, *benji* 27, Yingzong 1]; Hsiao, "Mid-Yüan Politics," 528–30; and Dardess, *Conquerors and Confucians*, 37–38).
84. *KS* 35: 3b–4a. As David M. Robinson points out, the reason behind Ch'ungsŏn's exile is unclear, but Shidebala seems to have made his decision because Ch'ungsŏn had political ties to his grandmother, the empress dowager Targi (*Empire's Twilight*, 106, 335 n. 49). Kim Kwangch'ŏl advances a similar argument ("14-segich'o Wŏn ŭi chŏngguk tonghyang," 315–43). Existing sources identify the eunuch Boyantugusi as the person directly responsible for Ch'ungsŏn's exile (*KS* 122: 19a–b). For Temüder's possible involvement in Ch'ungsŏn's exile, see Kim Ch'anghyŏn, "Ch'ungsŏn wang ŭi t'ansaeng," 145. Kim does not deny the importance of Ch'ungsŏn's relationship with the empress dowager to understanding his exile.
85. *KS* 35: 4a.
86. *KS* 35: 3b, 108: 10b–11a. Ch'oe's tomb epitaph provides an unconvincing excuse (*KMC*: 467–68).
87. Kim Hyŏngsu makes the unpersuasive claim that Ch'ungsuk may have been placed under house arrest for his "anti-Yuan" tendencies ("Koryŏ Ch'ungsuk wang 12-nyŏn (1325) kyosŏ," 5).
88. *KS* 35: 9b; and *KSC* 24: 20b–21a, 23a–b. The officials who signed Kwŏn's petition were dismissed from office in 1324; see *KS* 35: 13b. For a detailed study of the historical circumstances that sustained the conflict between the supporters of Ch'ungsuk and the Sim Prince, see Kim Kwangch'ŏl, "Ch'unghye wang ŭi wangwi kyesŭng."
89. *KSC* 24: 23b–24a.
90. *KMC*: 468; see also *KSC* 24: 46a–b.
91. For a study of the circumstances that led to this incident, see Kim Hyewŏn, "Wŏn kansŏpki ipsŏngnon kwa kŭ sŏnggyŏk."
92. *KMC*: 468.
93. *KMC*: 468.
94. *KSC*: 24: 30b. This order was given in the second lunar month.
95. *KS* 35: 13a–b; noted in Kim Hyŏngsu, "Koryŏ Ch'ungsuk wang 12-nyŏn (1325) kyosŏ," 9, 11–12.
96. *KMC*: 468.
97. For a detailed study of the edict, see Kim Kwangch'ŏl, "Koryŏ Ch'ungsuk wang 12-nyŏn"; and Kim Hyŏngsu, "Koryŏ Ch'ungsuk wang 12-nyŏn (1325) kyosŏ."
98. *KS* 35: 19b.
99. *KS* 35: 19a.
100. For an analysis of the prohibition orders, see Kim Hyŏngsu, "Ch'ungsuk wang hu 8-nyŏn."
101. As Kim Hyŏngsu points out, Bayan maintained hostile relations with Ch'unghye because the latter was close to his political rival El Temür (d. 1333) ("Koryŏ

Ch'ungsuk wang 12-nyŏn [1325] kyosŏ," 101–2). After the death of their khan Tugh Temür in 1332, Bayan split with El Temür. They had been partners in the restoration of 1328 and the removal of Temüder's faction at court (Dardess, *Conquerors and Confucians*, 31–52). For the conflict between Wang Ko and Ch'unghye, see Kim Kwangch'ŏl, "Ch'unghye wang ŭi wangwi kyesŭng," and Paek Inho, *Koryŏ hugi pu-Wŏn seryŏk yŏn'gu*, 108–13. Koryŏ officials frantically formed cliques to side with either Ch'unghye or Wang Ko. On September 27, tension between the two cliques developed into armed conflict. Ch'unghye's faction emerged victorious.

102. *KSC* 25:12b–13a; see also Kim Hyŏngsu, "Koryŏ Ch'ungsuk wang 12-nyŏn (1325) kyosŏ," 103.
103. *KS* 117: 1b.
104. *KMC*: 605.
105. *KS* 64: 28b.
106. *KS* 114: 21a.
107. *KSC* 26: 27a.
108. *KS* 64: 28b.
109. *KS* 117: 19b.
110. *Yunssi punmyo ki*, in *TMS* 69: 19a–23a.
111. *KMC*: 578.
112. Yun Kusaeng's biography in the *History of Koryŏ* mistakenly distinguishes the ancestral hall (*sau*) from the offering hut (*chesil*). It also mistakenly attributes the construction of the offering hut to Yun Kusaeng (*KS* 121: 21a–b).
113. *KMC*: 578.
114. *KS* 120: 13b–15a. See also *KSC* 34, 56b–57b. Other noted scholar-officials such as Chŏng Mongju and Sŏng Sŏngnin voiced similar concerns about the appointment; see the discussion in Goulde, "Anti-Buddhist Polemic," 188–90. Ch'anyŏng was appointed royal preceptor in 1383 and again by King Ch'ang in 1388 (*CKS*: 716 and Vermeersch, *Power of the Buddhas*, 413–14).
115. *KMC*: 577.
116. *KS* 39: 15b–16a. Similar claims about the need to move the capital to the southern capital had been made almost three centuries earlier by Kim Wije (*KS* 122: 1a–3b). Pou had a deep connection with the southern capital. He established his career and reputation with the help of Ch'ae Hongch'ŏl, his son Ch'ae Hajung, and Kim Mun'gwi, who owed their wealth and power, to a great extent, to their ties with the Mongols. In 1341, Ch'ae Hajung and Kim Mun'gwi invited Pou to stay at the monastery Chunghŭng-sa on Mount Samgak (present-day Mount Pukhan in Seoul). In 1348, Pou relocated to Mount Sosŏl, also near the southern capital. For King Kongmin's reforms, see Hong Yŏngŭi, *Koryŏmal chŏngch'isa yŏn'gu*, 55–99, and Kim Kidŏk, "14-segi huban kaehyŏk." For Yi Chehyŏn's role in the late Koryŏ reforms, see Yi Sukkyŏng, "Yi Chehyŏn seryŏk ŭi hyŏngsŏng kwa kŭ yŏkhal."
117. *KMC*: 578. This is usually used by scholars as evidence of the growing influence of Neo-Confucianism; see Pyŏn Tongmyŏng, *Koryŏ hugi sŏngnihak*, chap. 5. For an explanation of the theories of the ideal sovereign in *The Extended Meaning of the*

Great Learning and its place in late Koryŏ intellectual history, see To Hyŏnch'ŏl, *Koryŏmal sadaebu*, 24, 225–38.
118. *CKS*: 718.
119. *KS* 126: 40a–41b.
120. *TMS* 69: 20a.
121. Kim Hyŏngsu, "Koryŏ Ch'ungsuk wang 12-nyŏn (1325) kyosŏ," 26–27.
122. *KMC*: 577; see also Kim Ch'anghyŏn, *Koryŏ hugi chŏngbang yŏn'gu*, 116–17, 121–25.
123. In 1348, Yun T'aek and Yi Sŭngno tried to convince the Yuan court to allow Wang Ki to succeed his half brother Ch'unghye's son Ch'ungmok. Yun and Yi submitted a memorial directly to the Yuan secretariat and argued that Ch'ungmok's half brother Wang Chŏ—Wang Ki's rival—was too young to take the throne. Their efforts were foiled by Wang Chŏ's material kin, the P'ap'yong Yun. Wang Chŏ was also criticized by Kim Ryun's son Kim Kyŏngjik, who consequently was exiled to an island (*KSC* 26: 2a–b, *KS* 37: 18b, and *KS* 110: 12a). After Wang Ki removed Wang Chŏ and took the throne, Yun T'aek and Kim Kyŏngjik were both promoted to key posts in the security council, as academician and assistant royal secretary respectively (*KSC* 26: 7b).
124. *KSC* 26: 13b.
125. *KMC*: 576.
126. *KMC*: 576. This story is also recorded in Hae's biography in the *History of Koryŏ* (*KS* 106: 31b).
127. Deuchler, *Confucian Transformation of Korea*, 134.
128. *KS* 121: 21b.
129. Peter Brown makes a similar observation about early Christian methods of managing death (see *Ransom of the Soul*, esp. 14). In the Christian context, an afterlife infused with a sense of individual drama emerged from an earlier Christianity that honored the notion of the waiting of souls, which left little room for an interest in individual destinies after death. In Koryŏ Buddhism, the opposite is true. A flattened postmortem space associated with Zhu Xi's *Family Rituals* (C. Jiali) displaced Buddhist methods of managing death, which used wealth to write distinctly individualized destinies for the dead.

Conclusion

1. See *KS* 45: 15a. When Wang Yo (1345–1394) was removed from the throne in 1392, he was granted the title Lord Kongyang. Later, King T'aejong of the Chosŏn dynasty restored his status as former king of Koryŏ and posthumously granted him the temple name Kongyang (*KS* 46: 46a).
2. The destruction of the monastery presumably took place during the Red Turban occupation of the capital (November 1361–February 1362).
3. See *KSC* 34: 62b. According to Sin Ton's biography in the *History of Koryŏ* (Koryŏsa), the nine wells had to be dug up again because they were themselves sacred sites associated with the dragon cult and, hence, rain (*KS* 132: 9a–b). The dragon cult had strong associations with the royal cult. According to the *History of*

Koryŏ, the dynastic founder Wang Kŏn's grandfather Chakchegŏn had taken the dragon king's daughter as his bride. She is said to have traveled back and forth between Kaegyŏng and the dragon king's palace in the western sea through a well located just outside the window of their villa in Songak (i.e., Kaegyŏng). This villa later became the natal home of the dynastic founder, Wang Kŏn, who later converted the home into the Sŏn temple Kwangmyŏng-sa. The first well that the dragon king's daughter dug after her marriage to Chakchegŏn became Kaegyŏng's great well (*taejŏng*) (see *KS*, "Koryŏ segye": 6b–7a; for an English-language translation, see Rogers, "*P'yŏnnyŏn t'ongnok*," 8–10).

4. See *KS* 45: 31a and *KSC* 34: 62a. For the significance of Hanyang during the Koryŏ, see Bruneton, "Séoul à l'époque Koryô."
5. See *KS* 120: 21b–23a and *KSC* 34: 62b–63b. Yun was appointed third censor on the left (rank 5a) on February 16, 1390. It is not clear when he was appointed vice director of the board of punishment (rank 4a), but he seems to have held both posts as concurrent appointments until Cho Hyu was appointed third censor on the left in 1391 (*KS* 46: 6b).
6. For the Han apocryphal weft-texts, see Dull, "A Historical Introduction"; for their relation to Daoist notions of kingship, see Seidel, "Imperial Treasures."
7. Kang Hoebaek was the younger brother of Kang Hoegye, King Kongyang's son-in-law.
8. In his memorial, Kang cites the following passage from *Mencius* 2B/1: "Heaven's seasons are less crucial than the earth's advantages, and the earth's advantages are less crucial than human accord" (Bloom, *Mencius*, 38). For the memorial, see *KS* 117: 27b–29a.
9. See *KS* 119: 8a. The exact dates are unclear, but this order was issued after the king visited the monastery Hoeam-sa on March 15. The king returned to the capital Kaegyŏng on March 23. The order was probably issued shortly thereafter.
10. See *KS* 119: 8a.
11. See *KS* 46: 2b. The origins of the directorate of expanding merit are unclear, but this office seems to have been established during the reign of King Kongmin for the purpose of securing funds for the lavish funeral of his Mongolian consort Huiyi Luguo Imperial Princess. In 1391, King Kongyang shut down the directorate and attempted to replace it with the support storehouse for paper currency (*chasŏm chŏhwago*) (*KS* 79: 14a–16a). The effort to introduce paper currency would be short-lived and abandoned a year later, in 1392.
12. *KS* 46: 6b and *KSC* 5: 5b.
13. For Kim Chasu's dates, biography, and writings, see Sin, *Sangch'on sŏnsaeng ŭi saengae wa sasang*. Kim Chasu's death is also recorded in *T'aejong sillok* 26: 41a.
14. Kim makes the case for royal virtue by citing the story of Duke Jing of Song (see He Ning, *Huainanzi jishi*, 866–67). Kim also cites the famous story of the metal-bound coffer (*jinteng*) of the Duke of Zhou in the classic *Documents* (Shangshu). For an English-language translation of the story, see de Bary and Bloom, *Sources of Chinese Tradition*, 32–35.
15. *KSC* 45: 11b.

16. Hŏ Ŭng, Chŏn Oryun, Chŏn Paegyŏng, and others had been appointed to the office of remonstrance a month earlier (see *KS* 46: 6b–7a). For the list of remonstrance officials who may have participated in the drafting of the memorial, see *KS* 117: 15b.
17. *KS* 46: 13b; see also *KSC* 35: 24b.
18. *KS* 46: 15a.
19. *KSC* 45: 25a–28a and *KS* 120: 34b–42a. For a partial English-language translation of Pak Ch'o's memorial, see Peter H. Lee et al., *Sources of Korean Tradition*, 212–13.
20. *KS* 120: 42b.
21. *KSC* 45: 30a.
22. See Yi Chŏngju, "Kongyang wangdae ŭi chŏngguk tonghyang." This essay is included in Yi's *Sŏngnihak suyonggi Pulgyo pip'an*.
23. Problems associated with the privatization of land and labor during the late Koryŏ are well known (see, e.g., Duncan, *Origins*, chap. 4; Song Pyŏnggi, "Nongjang ŭi paltal"; O, "Koryŏ hugi t'oji pun'gŭpche ŭi pyŏndong kwa nokkwajŏn"; Wi Ŭnsuk, "Nongjang ŭi sŏngnip kwa kujo"). Wi Ŭnsuk and An Pyŏngu have shown that the economic problems of the late Koryŏ had less to do with the lack of agricultural productivity than with the privatization of resources (Wi, *Koryŏ hugi nong'ŏp kyŏngje yŏn'gu*, and An, "Koryŏ hugi nongŏp saengsallyŏk ŭi paltal kwa nongjang"). The abuse of grant ordinances by kings desperate to build a network of supporters contributed significantly to the privatization process. For the impact of frequent Japanese pirate raids in the Korean peninsula during this period, see Yi Hyŏnjong, "Waegu." For an interpretation of the rise of the reformists from the perspective of tributary politics, see Clark, "Autonomy, Legitimacy."
24. *CKS*: 725–27.
25. The Chosŏn king T'aejong's veritable record contains a reference to a monk named Changwŏnsim who was famous for his displays of compassion and devotion to public works (*T'aejong sillok* 12: 8a).
26. *CKS*: 726.
27. This was not completed, it seems, until the seventeenth day of the tenth lunar month (November 29), 1393 (Byŏnghyŏn Choi, *Annals of King T'aejo*, 319).
28. *Yŏngbok-sa t'ap chungch'ang chi ki*, in *CKS*: 726.
29. The *Veritable Record of T'aejo* (*T'aejo sillok*) states that the construction was completed on the twenty-eighth day of the third lunar month (May 17), 1393 (Byŏnghyŏn Choi, *Annals of King T'aejo*, 257).
30. Yi Sŏnggye attended the assembly at the monastery (Byŏnghyŏn Choi, *Annals of King T'aejo*, 258).

GLOSSARY OF CHINESE CHARACTERS

Romanization represents Korean pronunciation unless marked as Chinese (C) or Japanese (J).

Place-Names, Descent Groups, and General Terms

anch'alsa 按察使
Andong Kim 安東金
Andong Kwŏn 安東權
Anhwa-sa 安和寺
Ansan Kim 安山金
Anxi (C) 安西

Baoen Guangjiao Monastery (C) 報恩光教寺
baoyin (C) 包銀

Chabi Pass 慈悲嶺
Chabok-sa 資福寺
chae 災 calamities
chae 齋 vegetarian feast
chaech'u 宰樞
chaeje pusa 齋祭副使
chaesang 宰相
chaesang chi chong 宰相之宗
chaesin 宰臣
Chahyo-sa 慈孝寺
chaja 自恣
chajŏngwŏn 資政院
Chakchegŏn 作帝建
ch'am chi kwangjŏngwŏn sa 叅知光政院事
chamdŏk 潛德
ch'amwi 讖緯

Changan-sa 長安寺
Changan-sa chunghŭngbi 長安寺重興碑
changchang zhe hua (C) 裳裳者華
Chang-ga chang 張家墻
changgun 將軍
Changhŭng 長興
Ch'anghwa 昌和
ch'ansŏngsa 贊成事
chaptan 雜端
chari wi sŏn cha 自利為先者
chasŏm chŏhwago 資贍楮貨庫
che 祭
chehak 提學
chemun 祭文
cherye 祭禮
cheryŏ 齋廬
chesil 齋室
chesul kwa 製述科
chi 志 intention
ch'i 侈
chi milchiksa sa 知密直司事
chi munhasŏng sa 知門下省事
chidŏk 地德
chigonggŏ 知貢舉
chijego 知制誥
chijusa 知奏事
chik munha 直門下

197

GLOSSARY OF CHINESE CHARACTERS

chik chehak 直提學
Chikchi-sa 直指寺
Chikchi-saji 直指寺誌
ch'ilch'il 七七
chimaek 地脈
chinjŏn 真殿
Chinjong-sa 眞宗寺
Chinjong-sagi 眞宗寺記
chinjŏnjik 真殿直
chinsa 進士
chinsin 真身
chinyŏng 真影
cho 曹
Cho Chŏngsuk kong sadanggi 趙貞肅公祠堂記
Cho In'gyu myojimyŏng 趙仁規墓誌銘
ch'ŏgan 處干
Chogye 曹溪
Chogyesan che ise ko Tansok-sa chuji Susŏn-sa chu chŭngsi Chin'gak kuksa pimyŏng 曹溪山第二世故斷俗寺住持修禪社主贈諡眞覺國師碑銘
Chogyesan Susŏn-sa chungch'anggi 曹溪修禪社重創記
chokchŏng 足丁
ch'ŏkpul undong 斥佛運動
chokpun 族墳
Cholgo ch'ŏnbaek 拙藁千百
chŏllisa 典理司
ch'ŏmŭi ch'amni 僉議叅理
ch'ŏmŭibu 僉議府
ch'ŏn X so 薦X疏
chŏnbusi 典符寺
chŏnbusi sŭng 典符寺丞
Ch'ŏnch'u Hall 千秋殿
chong 從
Chŏngan Im 定安任
ch'ŏngbaengni 清白吏
chŏngbang 政房
ch'ŏngdŏk 清德
Ch'ŏnggye, Mount 清溪山
Ch'ŏnggye-sa 清溪寺
Ch'ŏnggye-sa sajŏggi pi 清溪寺事蹟記碑
chŏnghye ssangsu 定慧雙修
Ch'ŏngju Yi 清州李

chongmyo 宗廟
ch'ŏngnyŏm 清廉
chŏngsaek sŭngsŏn 政色承宣
ch'ongsin 寵臣
Ch'ŏngun-sa 青雲寺
ch'ŏngyojik 清要職
Ch'ŏnhwa-sŏnsa 天和禪寺
ch'ŏnja 賤者
chŏnjang 典章
chŏnjŏk 田籍
Chŏnju 全州
Chŏnju Ch'oe 全州崔
chŏnsi kwa 田柴科
Ch'ŏnsu-sa 天壽寺
Ch'ŏnt'ae 天台
chŏnŭi pujŏng 典醫副正
chŏnwŏn 田園
choŏp 祖業
chŏrŭi 節義
Ch'ŏrwŏn Ch'oe 鐵原崔
Chōsen kinseki sōran (J) 朝鮮金石総覧
Chosŏn 朝鮮
Chosŏn wangjo sillok 朝鮮王朝實錄
chosŏng togam 造成都監
chŭgwi kyosŏ 即位教書
ch'ŭkkŭn 側近
ch'uksŏng yuhyang po 祝聖油香寶
ch'uksu chae 祝壽齋
ch'umirwŏn 樞密院
ch'umirwŏn pusa 樞密院副使
Chunghŭng Tae Hwaŏm Pogwang-sagi 重興大華嚴普光寺記
Chungmo County 中牟縣
chungnangjang 中郎將
chungsangsŏ sŭng 中尚署丞
chungsŏ munhasŏng 中書門下
Chungsu Kaegug-nyulsagi 重修開國律寺記
Chungsu Kŏndong-sŏnsagi 重修乾洞禪寺記
Chungsu Yongmun-sagi 重修龍門寺記
chungyu 中有
Ch'unhŏn sŏnsaeng myomyŏng 春軒先生墓銘
chwa chungch'an 左中贊

GLOSSARY OF CHINESE CHARACTERS

chwa sangsi 左常侍
chwabu sŭngsŏn 右副承宣
chwahŏnnap 左獻納

Da Yuan (C) 大元
Da zhidu lun (C) 大智度論
Dadu (C) 大都
daxiang (C) 大祥
Daxue (C) 大學
Daxue yanyi (C) 大學衍義
Duosima (C) 朶思麻

fannao (C) 煩惱
fensi (C) 墳寺
fu yuanshuai (C) 副元帥

Gaoli junmin zhangguan (C) 高麗軍民長官
Gaoli Shenwang shi xu 高麗瀋王詩序
gongzhu (C) 公主
guan (C) 貫
guwen (C) 古文

Haedong kŭmsŏgwŏn 海東金石苑
haedongch'ŏng 海東青
Haein-sa 海印寺
Haeju Ch'oe 海州崔
haengjang 行狀
haksaga 學士家
Hallim Academy 翰林院
Han'guk kŭmsŏk chŏnmun 韓國金石全文
Han'guk Pulgyo chŏnsŏ 韓國佛教全書
Hanyang 漢陽
hawŏn 下院
Hoeam-sa 檜巖寺
Hoeyang 淮陽
hogang 豪強
hogŏl 豪傑
hohwal chi to 豪猾之徒
hojang 戶長
holchŏk 忽赤
hongbok togam 弘福都監
Hongfan (C) 洪範
Hongju 洪州

hose ka 豪勢家
houfei (C) 后妃
houfeibiao (C) 后妃表
Hua, Mount (C) 華山
Huangqing (C) 黃慶
Huayan jing (C) 華嚴經
huizhengyuan (C) 徽政院
Hŭngbok-sa 興富寺
Hŭngch'ŏn-sa 興天寺
hŭn'gu chi in 痕咎之人
Hŭngwang-sa 興王寺
hwa 化
Hwabi 和妃
Hwangch'ŏn Cho 橫川趙
Hwangju 黃州
Hwangnyŏ Min 黃驪閔
Hwaŏm 華嚴
hyangdo 香徒
hyangga 鄉歌
hyangni 鄉吏
hyo 孝
Hyohaengnok 孝行錄
hyŏlli 縣吏
hyŏllyŏng 縣令
hyŏn 玄
hyŏngjo ch'ongnang 刑曹摠郎
Hyŏnhwa-sa 玄化寺
Hyŏnsŏng-sa 賢聖寺

Ikchejip 益齊集
imul 異物
in 仁
innyun 人倫

Jiali (C) 家禮
jiao (C) 教
jiayi dafu (C) 嘉議大夫
jin (C) 斤
Jingde chuandeng lu (C) 景德傳燈錄
jinhufu (C) 金虎符
jinteng (C) 金縢

kabo 家譜
kabŏp 家法
kach'ŏp 家牒

Kaegug-nyulsa 開國律寺
Kaegyŏng 開京
kaesan 開山
kajang 家狀
Kaji, Mount 迦智山
kajŏn 家傳
Kajŏngjip 稼亭集
kamch'al chibŭi 監察執義
kamch'al ŏsa 監察御史
kamch'alsa 監察司
kamt'ong 感通
kamŭng 感應
Kamŭng-sa 感應寺
kamyo 家廟
kan or k'an 間
Kanjang-am 看藏庵
kanji 墾地
kaŏp 家業
karok 家錄
Kayasan Haein-sa kojŏk 伽倻山海印寺古籍
Kayasan Powŏn-sa ko kuksa chejŭngsi Pŏbin samjung taesa chi pi 迦耶山普願寺故國師制贈諡法印三重大師之碑
ki 氣 life force
ki 記 record
ki ŏ mich'ŏn 起於微賤
ki to tangyŏn 其道當然
kiilbo 忌日寶
Kilsang-sa 吉祥寺
Kiwŏn 祇園
koe 恎
Kogyangch'on 谷陽村
Kŏjo-sa 居祖寺
kŏmnyŏnggu 怜怜口
Kŏndong-sŏnsa 乾洞禪寺
Kongam Hŏ 孔巖許
kongjŏn 公田
Kongsŏng County 功成縣
kongŭisa 共議事
kŏpsŏl 怯薛
Koryŏ myojimyŏng chipsŏng 高麗墓誌銘集成
Koryŏ myŏnghyŏnjip 高麗名賢集

Koryŏguk Ch'ŏnt'ae Purŭn-sa chunghŭnggi 高麗國天台佛恩寺重興記
Koryŏguk Kangnŭngbu Yŏmyang-sŏnsa chunghŭnggi 高麗國江陵艷陽禪寺重興記
Koryŏsa 高麗史
Koryŏsa chŏryo 高麗史節要
kosa 故事
kubŏpp'a 舊法派
kubunjŏn 口分田
kukchon 國尊
Kukch'ŏng-sa 國清寺
Kukch'ŏng-sa kŭmdang chubul Sŏkka yŏrae sari yŏnggigi 國清寺金堂主佛釋迦如來舍利靈異記
kukko 國庫
kuksa 國師
kuksok 國俗
kukt'ong 國統
Kŭmgang, Mount 金剛山
Kŭmgangsan'gi 金剛山記
Kŭmju 錦州
kŭmnyŏng 禁令
kŭmowi 金吾衛
Kŭmsan Kim 錦山金
Kŭmsin, Mount 金身山
kun 君 lord
kun 郡 prefecture
kunbusa 軍簿司
kungjŏnbae 弓箭陪
kunja 君子
kŭpchŏn togam 給田都監
kwan 館
Kwangdŏk-sa 廣德寺
kwan'gi 管記
kwangjŏngwŏn 光政院
Kwangju 廣州
Kwangju Pak 廣州朴
Kwangmyŏng-sa 廣明寺
Kwangnok taebu p'yŏngjang chŏngsa sangnak puwŏn'gun Pang kong sadangbi 光祿大夫平章政事上洛府院君方公祠堂碑
kwi 貴

kwibuga 貴富家
kwŏn 權 powerful
kwŏn 卷 volume
kwŏndo 權度
kwŏn'gwi 權貴
kwŏnmun 權門
kwŏnmun sejok 權門世族
kwŏnse chi ka 權勢之家
Kyewŏn p'ilgyŏngjip 桂苑筆耕集
Kyo 教
kyojŏng togam 教定都監
kyŏl 結
kyŏmbyŏng 兼併
kyŏng 頃
Kyŏngch'ang Palace 景昌院
kyŏnggye 耿介
Kyŏngju Yi 慶州李
Kyŏngsa Kŭmson mit'a-sagi 京師金孫彌陀寺記
Kyŏngsa Poŭn kwanggyo-sagi 京師報恩光教寺記
Kyŏngwŏn Yi 慶源李

Li ji (C) 禮記
Lunyu (C) 論語
Lushi Monastery (C) 盧師寺

mae 昧
Mandŏk, Mount 萬德山
mangjok 望族
Manŭi-sa 萬義寺
Mengzi (C) 孟子
mich'ŏn 微賤
milchik haksa 密直學士
milchik pusa 密直副使
milchiksa 密直司
Milgi 密記
min (C) 緡
Minch'ŏn-sa 旻天寺
minho 民戶
Mogŭn mun'go 牧隱文藁
Mogŭn sigo 牧隱詩藁
moksa 牧使
mu (C) 畝
Muan ji (C) 牧庵集

mugung 無窮
Munchŏng 文貞
mun'gye 文契
munha sijung 門下侍中
munhansŏ 文翰署
munhyŏng 門兄
munsa 文士
munsaeng 門生
Musong Yun 茂松尹
myŏngmyŏng 冥冥
Myŏngsun Palace 明順宮
Myoryŏn-sa 妙蓮寺
Myoryŏn-sa chunghŭngbi 妙蓮寺重興碑
Myoryŏn-sa sŏkchijogi 妙蓮寺石池竈記

naeburyŏng 內府令
naejo 內助
naeryo 內僚
naesi 內侍
Naju 羅州
namban 南班
Namp'yŏng Mun 南平文
nangsa 郎舍
Nanpu 南浦
nap 納
noesŏ 誄書
noju 老呪
nokkwajŏn 祿科田
noksa 錄事
nongjang 農莊
noyŏk 老譯

obok 五福
ojae ch'ilch'u 五宰七樞
Ŏnyang Kim 彥陽金
ŏp 業
ŏsa taebu 御史大夫
ŏsadae 御史臺
Osŏng County 吳城縣

paehyang 配享
Paengnyŏn-sa 白蓮社
p'an milchiksa sa 判密直司事
pangmokso 放牧所
p'an'gwan 判官

panjŏng 半丁
panjŏnsaek 盤纏色
Panyagyŏng po 般若經寶
p'anye pinsisa 判禮賓寺事
P'ap'yŏng Yun 坡平尹
pi 妃
pibo 裨補
pibo chi so 裨補之所
p'iljajŏk 必闍赤
pimyŏng 碑銘
pisŏrang 秘書郎
po 寶 endowment
po 譜 family record
poch'ŏp 譜牒
Pogwang-sa 普光寺
Poje-sa 普濟寺
pok 福
pokchŏn 福田
pomun'gak 寶文閣
Pomyŏng-sa 普明寺
Pongsŏn Honggyŏng-sa 奉先弘慶寺
pongsong 封送
Pongŭn-sa 奉恩寺
pon'gwan 本貫
pon'gwan che 本貫制
Pŏphwa yŏnghŏmjŏn 法華靈驗傳
pŏphyŏng 法兄
Pŏpsang 法相
posŏl 普說
Powŏn-sa 普願寺
pu 府 military garrison *or* agency
pu 負 unit of measurement
pubusa 部夫使
pudo 婦道
pugok 部曲
puhŭng 復興
pulgasaŭi 不可思議
punap 不納
P'ungak, Mount 楓岳山
Purŭn-sa 佛恩寺
pushu 普說
p'yehaeng 嬖幸
P'yohun-sa 表訓寺
pyŏlch'ŏng chaech'u 別廳宰樞
pyŏlsŏ 別墅

P'yŏnggang Ch'ae 平康蔡
p'yŏngmi i ki 平微而起
p'yŏngni 評理
P'yŏngyang Cho 平壤趙

Qinglian Monastery (C.) 青蓮寺

ri 理

sa 士 bureaucratic service or official(s)
sa 司 division
sadae 事大
sadaebu 士大夫
sadang 祠堂
sado 司徒
Saganwŏn 司諫院
sahŏnbu 司憲府
sajik 社稷
sajok 士族
Saju 泗州
Sambyŏlch'o 三別抄
Samch'ŏk County 三陟縣
Samch'ŏn-sa 三川寺
Samgak, Mount 三角山
Samguk yusa 三國遺事
Samgunbu 三軍部
Samhwa-sa 三和寺
samsa chwasa 三司左使
samsa sa 三司使
samsa samgong 三師三公
sangju 常住
Sangju 尚州
Sangjubogi 常住寶記
sangp'um 上品
sangsŏsŏng 尚書省
Sangwŏn 祥原
sangyang 常養
sanŏp 產業
sanwŏn 散員
sanzang fashi (C) 三藏法師
sap'ae 賜牌
sap'an 士板
sarim 士林
Sarimwŏn 詞林院
saro 仕路

sarok 司祿
sasa 祀事
sase 事勢
Sasijie (C) 撒思結
sasŏn 私膳
Sasu County 泗水縣
sau 祠宇
saŭi taebu 司議大夫
saye 司藝
se 勢
sebo 世譜
sejok 世族
Sejo kuje 世祖舊制
Sejo sŏngji 世祖聖旨
Shangdu (C) 上都
shangen (C) 善根
Shangshu (C) 尚書
shenyudian (C) 神御殿
shidaifu (C) 士大夫
shifangcha (C) 十方剎
Shijing 詩經
Sillŭk-sa 神勒寺
sim 心
Sinbok-sŏnsa 神福禪寺
sinbŏpp'a 新法派
sindo 神道
sinhŭng kwijok 新興貴族
sinhŭng kwŏllyŏkch'ŭng 新興權力層
sinhŭng sadaebu 新興士大夫
Sinjŭng Tongguk yŏji sŭngnam 新增東國輿地勝覽
sinmunsaek 申聞色
siŏsa 侍御史
sisa 侍史
siwi hogun 侍衛護軍
sŏ 序
Sŏhae circuit 西海道
sŏk 石
sŏm 苫
Sŏn 禪
sŏnbu 選部
Song 宋
Song sŭng Sŏnji yu Kŭmgangsan sŏ 送僧禪智遊金剛山序
Songak, Mount 松岳山
Songdo 松都
Sŏnggyun'gwan 成均館
sŏngni chi sŏ 性理之書
sŏngnihak 性理學
sŏngsim 誠心
Sŏnhŭng-sa 禪興寺
sŏnji 宣旨
sŏnjŏn sosik 宣傳消息
sŏnmi 禪味
sŏnsa 禪師
Sŏnwŏn-sa 禪源寺
Sŏnwŏn-sa chesŭnggi 禪源寺齋僧記
sŏnyŏng 先塋
sŏp chŏngsŭng 攝政丞
Sorim-sa 少林寺
Sorim-sa chungsugi 小林寺重修記
Sosŏl, Mount 小雪山
sŏun'gwan 書雲觀
sujong 隨從
sujong kongsin 隨從功臣
Sun'am chin ch'an 順菴真讚
sŭng 升
Sunyŏng Palace 壽寧宮
susajŏn 受賜田
Susŏn-sa 修禪社
Suwŏn Manŭi-sa ch'uksang Hwaŏm pŏphoe chungmokki 水原萬義寺祝上華嚴法會衆目記
suyonggi 受容期

Taedŏk, Mount 大德山
Taedo namsŏng Hŭngbok-sa kal 大都南城興富寺碣
taedoryang 大道場
taehaksa 大學士
taejanggun 大將軍
taejehak 大提學
taejok 大族
taejŏng 大井
T'aejo sillok 太祖實錄
T'aejong sillok 太宗實錄
t'aemyo 太廟
taesahŏn 大司憲
taesang 大常
taesŏnsa 大禪師

Taeun-sa 大雲寺
Taewŏn Koryŏguk Kwangju Sinbok-sŏnsa chunghŭnggi 大元高麗國廣州神福禪寺重興記
Taishō shinshū daizōkyō shinshū daizōkyō (J) 大正新脩大藏經
talch'in 達嚫
t'alchŏm 奪占
T'amna 耽羅
tanch'il 斷七
t'angjang 帑藏
Tangsŏng Hong 唐城洪
Tianshi dao (C) 天師道
Tianyuan Yansheng Monastery (C) 天源延聖寺
tobyŏngmasa 都兵馬使
todang 都堂
togam 都監
Tohak 道學
tohobu 都護府
tŏk 德
Tŏkcha Palace 德慈宮
Tong paengnyŏn-sa 東白蓮社
tongban 東班
tongbang 東方
Tongguk Yi sanggukchip 東國李相國集
Tongmun sŏn 東文選
t'ongmun'gwan 通文館
Tongnyŏng Directorate General 東寧府
tono chŏmsu 頓悟漸修
t'osŏng 土姓
tosŭngt'ong 都僧統
touxia 投下
tu 斗
tunjŏn 屯田
Tut'a, Mount 頭陀山
Tut'asan Kanjang-am chungyŏnggi 頭陀山看藏庵重營記

u pu taeŏn 右副代言
u sŭngji 右承旨
uch'ang 右倉
ugun ch'ongjesa 右軍摠制使
uha 雨荷
ŭigwan kapchok 衣冠甲族
ŭigwan yunju 衣冠胤胄
ŭijae 義財
ŭijŏngbu 議政府
ŭm 蔭
ŭmdŏk 陰德
Unam-sa 雲庵寺
ŭngbang 鷹坊
ŭngbangsa 鷹坊使
Unggok 熊谷
Unmun-sŏnsa 雲門禪寺
Uran Bowl assembly 盂蘭盆會

wangfu duanshiguan (C) 王府斷事官
wangji sayong pyŏlgam 王旨使用別監
wangsa 王師
Wenyuange Siku quanshu (C) 文淵閣四庫全書
Wihwa Island 威化島
wisukkun 圍宿軍
wŏn 院
wŏnch'al 願刹
wŏndang 願堂

xiangyang zhi dao (C) 相養之道
xiaoxiang (C) 小祥
xindi (C) 心地

yangban 兩班
yangban choŏp chŏn 兩班祖業田
yebu nangjung 禮部郎中
yejang 禮葬
yemun ch'unch'ugwan 藝文春秋館
Yi jing (C) 易經
yitian (C) 義田
Yŏg'ong p'aesŏl 櫟翁稗說
Yŏhŭng 驪興
Yŏhŭng Min 驪興閔
Yŏju Sillŭk-sa taejanggakki 驪州神勒寺大藏閣記
Yŏmyang sŏnsa 艷陽禪寺
Yŏnbok-sa 演福寺
Yongam-sa 龍岩寺
Yŏngbongsan Yongam-sa chungch'anggi 靈鳳山龍岩寺重創記
Yongjae ch'onghwa 慵齋叢話

Yŏngch'wisan 靈鷲山
yŏngdang 影堂
Yongjang-sa 龍藏寺
yŏngsonggo 迎送庫
yŏngŭijŏng 領議政
Yŏngwŏn-sa 瑩原寺
yu 儒
yu seryŏk 有勢力
yua chinsin 儒雅縉紳
Yuan shi (C) 元史
Yuandao (C) 原道

Yujŏm-sa 榆岾寺
yujŏn 儒典
Yulan pen jing (C) 盂蘭盆經
Yunssi punmyogi 尹氏墳廟記

Zhangyi Gate (C) 彰義門
Zhengdao ge (C) 證道歌
Zhong lun (C) 中輪
Zhongyong (C) 中庸
ziran cheng (C) 自然成
ziwu (C) 自悟

Personal Names (dates provided when known)

An Chŏn 安戬 (d. 1298)
An Hyang 安珦 (1243–1306)
An'gyŏng, Duke of 安慶公
Anji, Prince of 安吉王
Anping, Princess (C) 安平公主

Baizhu (C) 拜住 (1298–1323)
Boyantugusi (C) 伯顏禿古思 (d. 1323)

Ch'a Sin 車信
Ch'a Tŭkkyu 車得珪
Ch'ae Ch'ungsun 蔡忠順 (d. 1036)
Ch'ae Hajung 蔡河中 (d. 1357)
Ch'ae Hongch'ŏl 蔡洪哲 (1262–1340)
Ch'ae Mo 蔡謨 (1229–1302)
Ch'ae Songnyŏn 蔡松年 (d. 1251)
Chakchegŏn 作帝建
Chang Ch'ungŭi 張忠義 (1109–1180)
Chang Kwangbu 張光富
Chang Sunyong 張舜龍 (1255–1297)
Changwŏnsim 長遠心
Changwŏnsim 長願心 A character in *The Annals of King T'aejong*
Ch'anyŏng 粲英 (1328–1390)
Cheng Hao (C) 程顥 (1035–1085)
Cheng Yi (C) 程頤 (1033–1107)
Chengzong (C) 成宗 (r. 1294–1307)
Chigong 指空 (d. 1361)
Chin Ch'ŏk 陳倜
Chinhye, Great Master 真慧大師
Chinul 知訥 (1158–1210)

Cho, Lady 夫人趙氏 (1128–1218)
Cho, Minister 趙尚書
Cho Chŏk 曹頔 (d. 1339)
Cho Chun 趙浚 (1346–1405)
Cho Ch'ung 趙冲 (1171–1220)
Cho Ch'ungsin 趙忠臣
Cho Hyu 趙休 (d. 1411)
Cho In'gyu 趙仁規 (1237–1308)
Cho Ryŏn 趙璉 (d. 1322)
Cho Sŏ 趙瑞 (d. 1313)
Cho Tŏgyu 趙德裕 (1314–1352)
Cho Un 趙橒
Cho Wi 趙瑋 (1287–1348)
Cho Wich'ong 趙位寵 (d. 1176)
Cho Yŏngin 趙永仁 (1133–1202)
Cho Yŏnsu 趙延壽 (1278–1325)
Ch'oe, Lady 夫人崔氏 (1279–1347)
Ch'oe Ch'am 崔昷
Ch'oe Ch'iwŏn 崔致遠 (b. 857)
Ch'oe Ch'unghŏn 崔忠獻 (1149–1219)
Ch'oe Hae 崔瀣 (1287–1340)
Ch'oe Munbon 崔文本 (1233–1276)
Ch'oe Mundo 崔文度 (1292–1345)
Ch'oe Munjin 崔文進
Ch'oe Nubaek 崔婁伯 (1110–1205)
Ch'oe Piil 崔毗一 (d. 1319)
Ch'oe Sagŏm 崔思儉
Ch'oe Sajŏn 崔思全 (1067–1139)
Ch'oe Sawi 崔士威 (961–1041)
Ch'oe Seyŏn 崔世延 (d. 1297)
Ch'oe Sŏ 崔瑞 (1233–1305)

GLOSSARY OF CHINESE CHARACTERS

Ch'oe Sŏngji 崔誠之 (1265–1330)
Ch'ŏe Sŭngno 崔承老 (927–989)
Ch'oe U 崔佑 Ch'oe Pi-il's father
Ch'oe U 崔瑀 alt. Ch'oe I 崔怡 (d. 1249)
Ch'oe Ŭi 崔竩 (d. 1258)
Ch'oe Ŭng 崔凝 (898–932)
Ch'oe Yuŏm 崔有渰 (1239–1331)
Chokhŏn, Layman 足軒居士
Chŏn, Prince 倎
Chŏn Oryun 全五倫
Chŏn Paegyŏng 全伯英
Chŏng Ch'ong 鄭摠 (1358–1397)
Chŏng In'gyŏng 鄭仁卿 (1237–1305)
Chŏng Kasin 鄭可臣 (1224–1298)
Chŏng Mongju 鄭夢周 (1338–1392)
Chŏng Obu 丁伍孚
Chŏng Sach'ŏk 鄭士偁
Chŏng Sŭngo 鄭承伍
Chŏng Tojŏn 鄭道傳 (1342–1398)
Chŏnghŏn 正獻
Chŏnghwa, Court Lady 貞和宮主 (d. 1319)
Chŏngo 丁午
Chŏngsuk 貞肅
Chŏngsun, Queen 靜順王后 (d. 1236)
Ch'ŏn'gyu 天珪
Chu Chŏ 周佇 (d. 1024)
Ch'unggyŏng 冲鏡 (1191–1271)
Ch'ungji 冲止 (1226–1293)
Ch'unhŏn 春軒

Dahui Zonggao (C) 大慧宗杲 (1089–1163)

Fan Zhongyan (C) 范仲淹 (989–1052)

Gao Zhaoyi (C) 高昭義

Ha Wŏnsŏ 河元瑞
Ha Yunwŏn 河允源 (fl. late fourteenth century)
Han Ko 韓皐 (d. 1407)
Han Sanghwan 韓尙桓
Han Yu (C) 韓愈 (768–824)
Hansan, Lord of 韓山君
Hŏ, Lady 夫人許氏 (1255–1324)

Hŏ Chae 許載 (1062–1144)
Hŏ Kong 許珙 (1233–1291)
Hŏ Kwan 許冠
Hŏ Kyŏng 許京 (fl. late thirteenth to early fourteenth century)
Hŏ Su 許遂 (fl. thirteenth century)
Hŏ Ŭng 許應 (d. 1411)
Hong Chabŏn 洪子藩 (1237–1306)
Hong Mun'gye 洪文系 (1242–1316)
Hong Pogwŏn 洪福源 (1206–1258)
Hong Tagu 洪茶丘 (1244–1291)
Hong Yŏngt'ong 洪永通 (d. 1395)
Hon'gi 混其
Hongsŏ 洪恕
Hon'gu 混丘 (1251–1322)
Honwŏn 混元 (1191–1271)
Huiyi Luguo Imperial Princess (C) 徽懿魯國大長公主 (d. 1365)
Hwang Hŭi 黃喜 (1363–1452)
Hyegŭn 惠勤 (1320–1376)
Hyesim 惠諶 (1178–1234)

Im Chŏnggi 林貞杞 (d. 1288)
Im Yŏn 林衍 (d. 1270)
Im Yumu 林惟茂 (d. 1270)
In Hu 印候 (1250–1311)
In'gyŏng hyŏnbi 仁敬賢妃
Injŏl hyŏnbi 仁節賢妃 (d. 1082)
Inye Sundŏk, Queen Mother 仁睿順德太后 (d. 1092)
Iryŏn 一然 (1206–1289)

Jiguo Imperial Princess (C) 薊國大長公主 (d. 1351)
Jin, Prince (C) 晉王
Jing, Duke of Song (C) 宋景公 (r. 517–452 BCE)

Kang Cho 康兆 (d. 1011)
Kang Hoebaek 姜淮柏 (1357–1402)
Kang Kamch'an 姜邯贊 (948–1031)
Kang Yung 姜融 (d. 1349)
Kang Yunso 康允紹
Kim, Lady of Chillyegun 進禮郡夫人金氏

GLOSSARY OF CHINESE CHARACTERS

Kim Chajŏng 金子廷
Kim Chasu 金子粹 (1351–1413)
Kim Ch'o 金貂
Kim Chŏn 金琠
Kim Chu-jŏng 金周鼎 (d. 1290)
Kim Chun 金俊 (d. 1269)
Kim Chunggu 金仲龜 (1175–1242)
Kim Hon 金琿 (1239–1311)
Kim Hwŏn 金晅 (1258–1305)
Kim Kaemul 金開物 (1272–1327)
Kim Koeng 金閎
Kim Ku 金坵 (1211–1278)
Kim Kwangjae 金光載 (d. 1363)
Kim Kyŏngjik 金敬直
Kim Panggyŏng 金方慶 (1212–1300)
Kim Po 金普
Kim Pyŏn 金賆 (1248–1301)
Kim Ryun 金倫 (1277–1348)
Kim Sim 金深
Kim Sŏ 金惰 (d. 1284)
Kim Sun 金恂 (1258–1321)
Kim Sŭngmu 金承茂
Kim Ŭigwang 金義光 (d. 1296)
Kim Wije 金調硨
Kim Yong 金鏞 (d. 1356)
Kim Yŏngŭi 金令義
Ko Chongsu 高宗秀
Ko Yongbo 高龍普 (d. 1362)
Kwak Ye 郭預 (1232–1286)
Kwangyang, Lord of 光陽君
Kwŏn Chae 權載 (1296–1349)
Kwŏn Chun 權準 (1281–1352)
Kwŏn Han'gong 權漢功 (d. 1349)
Kwŏn Kŏŭi 權居義
Kwŏn Kŭn 權近 (1352–1409)
Kwŏn Pu 權溥 (1262–1346)
Kwŏn Tan 權㫜 (1228–1311)
Kwŏn Wan 權緩 (d. 1417)
Kyŏngi 景宜

Min Chi 閔漬 (1248–1326)
Min Sap'yŏng 閔思平 (1295–1359)
Mubi 無比 (d. 1297)
Mun Kongwŏn 文公元 (1084–1156)
Mun Ŭng 文應

Munjŏng 文貞
Munsin 文慎
Muoe 無畏
Myohye 妙慧

Na Yu 羅裕 (d. 1292)
Nam Ŭn 南誾 (1354–1498)
Namjŏn Pumok 南田夫目 (1320–1398)
No Chinŭi 盧進義 (d. 1278)
No Chun'gong 盧俊恭
No Kyŏngnyun 盧景綸
No Sasin 盧思慎 (1427–1498)
No Sung 盧嵩 (1337–1414)

O Cham 吳潛
O Han'gyŏng 吳漢卿 (1242–1314)
O Sukpu 吳淑福

Pae Kŭngnyŏm 裵克廉 (1352–1392)
Paek Hyoju 白孝珠
Paek Ijŏng 白頤正 (1247–1323)
Paek Munbo 白文寶 (1303–1374)
Paek Munjŏl 白文節 (d. 1282)
Pak Ching 朴澄
Pak Ch'o 朴礎 (1367–1454)
Pak Chŏnji 朴全之 (1250–1325)
Pak Hang 朴恒 (1227–1281)
Pak Hŏjung 朴虛中 (1244–1325)
Pak Hwang 朴瑄 (1103–1152)
Pak Kyŏn 朴堅
Pak Kyŏngnyang 朴景亮 (d. 1320)
Pak Ryŏ 朴侶
Pak Sŏn 朴瑄
Pak Swaenooldae 朴鎖魯兀大
Pak Ŭi 朴義 (d. 1321)
Pang Sinu 方臣祐 (1267–1343)
Pang Usŏn 方于宣
Pŏbye 法猊
Pŏpkyŏng 法鏡
P'yŏngyang, Lord of 平壤君
Pyŏnhan, Great Lady of
　卞韓國大夫人

Qiguo Imperial Princess (C) 齊國大長公
　主 (1259–1297)

Renzong (C) 仁宗 (r. 1311–20)

Shizu (C) 世祖 (r. 1260–71)
Sim, Prince 諶 (Ch'ungnyŏl)
Sim Chiŭi 沈志義 (1083–1162)
Sim Inbong 沈仁鳳
Sim Prince 瀋王 Wang Ko
Sim Yang 沈錫
Simyang (C. Shenyang) Prince 瀋陽王
Sin Ch'ŏng 申青
Sin Ton 辛旽 (d. 1371)
Sindŏk, Queen 神德王后 (1356–1396)
Sinjo 神照
Sŏ Hŭi 徐熙 (942–998)
Sŏ Kŏjŏng 徐居正 (1420–1488)
Sŏ Pongnye 徐復禮
Sŏ Ton'gyŏng 徐敦敬
Sŏ Ung 徐雄
Sŏk Chu 石冑
Sŏl In'gŏm 薛仁儉
Sŏl Konggŏm 薛公儉 (1224–1302)
Son Ki 孫琦
Sŏnch'ang 宣暢
Sŏng Hyŏn 成俔 (1439–1504)
Song Lian (C) 宋濂 (1310–1381)
Song Lin (C) 宋璘 (d. 1307)
Song Pangyŏng 宋邦英 (d. 1307)
Song Pun 宋玢 (d. 1318)
Sŏng Sŏngnin 成石璘 (1338–1423)
Song Songnye 宋松禮 (d. 1289)
Sŏnghyo 性曉
Sŏngmalch'ŏn'gu 石末天衢
Sŏnji 禪智
Sŏwŏn, Marquis of 西原侯
Subi 壽妃 (d. 1340)
Sundŏk, Queen 順德王后 (d. 1118)

T'aego Pou 太古普愚 (1301–1382)
T'aejo 太祖
T'aejong 太宗 (r. 1400–18)
Taidingdi 泰定帝 (r. 1323–28)
Tamjin 曇眞 (fl. late eleventh to early twelfth century)
Tamuk 曇昱
T'anmun 坦文 (900–975)

To 燾 (Ch'ungsuk)
To Sŏng-gi 陶成器 (d. 1297)
Tosŏn 道詵
Tunch'on, Layman 鈍村居士
Turyŏn'ga 頭輦哥

U, Superintendent 禹判事
U Inyŏl 禹仁烈 (1337–1403)
Ugye 愚溪
Ŭibi 懿妃
Ŭich'ŏn 義天 (1055–1101)
Ŭisŏn 義旋 (fl. 1284–1348)

Wang Ch'ang 王淐
Wang Chŏ 王胝 (1338–1351)
Wang Hu 王煦 (1296–1349)
Wang Hyo 王俣 (1093–1161)
Wang Ki 王祺 (Kongmin)
Wang Ko 王暠 (d. 1334)
Wang Kŏn 王建 (r. 918–43)
Wang Sam-sŏk 王三錫
Wang Uk 王郁 (d. 996)
Wang Yo 王瑤 (Kongyang)
Wang Yŏng 王瑛 (d. 1291)
Wang Yuso 王惟紹 (d. 1307)
Wi Tŭgyu 韋得儒 (d. 1278)
Wŏlmyŏng 月明 (fl. 742–65)
Wŏn Kyŏng 元卿 (d. 1302)
Wŏn Sŏnji 元善之 (1281–1330)
Wŏnhye, State Preceptor 圓慧國師
Wu of Liang, Emperor (C) 梁武帝 (r. 502–49)
Wuzong (C) 武宗 (r. 1307–11)

Xindu (C) 忻都

Yang Kyu 楊規 (d. 1011)
Yao Sui (C) 姚燧 (1238–1313)
Yi Chagyŏm 李資謙 (d. 1127)
Yi Chayŏn 李子淵 (1003–1061)
Yi Chehyŏn 李齊賢 (1287–1367)
Yi Chijŏ 李之氐 (d. 1317)
Yi Chin 李瑱 (1244–1321)
Yi Ch'ŏm 李詹 (1345–1405)
Yi Chonbi 李尊庇 (1233–1287)

Yi Chŏng 李貞
Yi Hon 李混 (1312–1372)
Yi Hye 李惠
Yi Ikpae 李益培 (d. 1292)
Yi Imjong 李林宗
Yi Inbok 李仁復 (1308–1374)
Yi Injŏng 李仁挺
Yi Kok 李穀 (1298–1351)
Yi Kongbo 李公甫
Yi Punhŭi 李汾禧 (d. 1278)
Yi Punsŏng 李汾成
Yi Saek 李穡 (1328–1396)
Yi Saon 李思溫
Yi Sŏnggye 李成桂 (1335–1408)
Yi Sŏngsŏ 李成瑞 (1319–1379)
Yi Sŭnghyu 李承休 (1224–1300)
Yi Yangjik 李養直 (fl. late thirteenth to early fourteenth century)
Yi Yŏnjong 李衍宗
Yingzong (C) 英宗 (r. 1320–23)
Yŏm Kyŏngae 廉瓊愛 (1110–1146)
Yŏm Sŭngik 廉承益 (d. 1302)
Yongjia Xuanjue (C) 永嘉玄覺 (675–713)
Yose 了世 (1163–1240)
Yu Chŏnghyŏn 柳廷顯 (1355–1426)
Yu Ch'ŏngsin 柳清臣 (d. 1329)
Yu Kyŏng 柳璥 (1217–1289)
Yu Paek-sun 柳伯淳 (d. 1420)
Yu T'ak 柳濯 (1311–1371)
Yu Yŏngjae 柳英材 (d. 1170)

Yun Chaun 尹子雲 (1416–1478)
Yun Hae 尹諧
Yun Hoejong 尹會宗
Yun Hŭngjong 尹興宗
Yun Hyang 尹向 (1374–1418)
Yun Hyojong 尹孝宗
Yun Kilson 尹吉孫 (d. 1297)
Yun Kŭngmin 尹克敏 (fl. thirteenth century)
Yun Kusaeng 尹龜生
Yun Kwan 尹瓘 (1040–1111)
Yun Ŏnju 尹彥周
Yun Po 尹珤 (d. 1329)
Yun Pongsaeng 尹鳳生
Yun Sojong 尹紹宗 (1345–1393)
Yun Sŏnjwa 尹宣佐 (1265–1343)
Yun Su 尹秀 (d. 1283)
Yun Sup'yong 尹守平
Yun T'aek 尹澤 (1289–1370)
Yun Yangbi 尹良庇

Zhang Daoling (C) 張道陵 (fl. second century)
Zhaorui shunsheng, Empress (C) 昭睿順聖皇后
Zhenzong 眞宗 (r. 997–1022)
Zhou, Duke (C) 周公
Zhou Dunyi (C) 周敦頤 (1017–1073)
Zhu Xi (C) 朱熹 (1130–1200)
Zongmi (C) 宗密 (780–841)

BIBLIOGRAPHY

Abbreviations and Primary Sources

CGCB   Ch'oe Hae. *Cholgo ch'ŏnbaek*. In *Koryŏ myŏnghyŏnjip*, vol. 2, 389–426. Seoul: Sŏnggyun'gwan Taehakkyo Taedong Munhwa Yŏn'guwŏn, 1973.

CKS   Chōsen sōtokufu. *Chōsen kinseki sōran*. Seoul: Chungang Munhwa Ch'ulp'ansa, 1968.

HKC   Hŏ Hŭngsik, ed. *Han'guk kŭmsŏk chŏnmun*. 3 vols. Seoul: Asea Munhwasa, 1984.

HPC   Tongguk taehakkyo Han'guk Pulgyo chŏnsŏ p'yŏnch'an wiwŏnhoe, ed. *Han'guk Pulgyo chŏnsŏ*. 13 vols. Seoul: Tongguk Taehakkyo, 1994.

ICJ   Yi Chehyŏn. *Ikchejip*. In *Koryŏ myŏnghyŏnjip*, vol. 2, 233–343. Seoul: Sŏnggyun'gwan Taehakkyo Taedong Munhwa Yŏn'guwŏn, 1973.

KJJ   Yi Kok. *Kajŏngjip*. In *Koryŏ myŏnghyŏnjip*, vol. 3, 1–147. Seoul: Sŏnggyun'gwan Taehakkyo Taedong Munhwa Yŏn'guwŏn, 1973.

KMC   Kim Yongsŏn. *Koryŏ myojimyŏng chipsŏng*. 4th ed. Ch'unch'ŏn: Hallim Taehakkyo Ch'ulp'anbu, 2006.

KS   Chŏng Inji et al., eds. *Koryŏsa*. 3 vols. Seoul: Asea Munhwasa, 1972.

KSC   Minjok munhwa ch'ujinhoe, trans. *Koryŏsa chŏryo*. Seoul: Sinsŏwŏn, 2004.

MMG   Yi Saek. *Mogŭn mun'go*. In *Koryŏ myŏnghyŏnjip*, vol. 3, 796–973. Seoul: Sŏnggyun'gwan Taehakkyo Taedong Munhwa Yŏn'guwŏn, 1973.

MSG   Yi Saek. *Mogŭn sigo*. In *Koryŏ myŏnghyŏnjip*, vol. 3, 149–795. Seoul: Sŏnggyun'gwan Taehakkyo Taedong Munhwa Yŏn'guwŏn, 1973.

T   Takakusu Junjirō and Watanabe Kaigyoku, eds. *Taishō shinshū daizōkyō shinshū daizōkyō*. 85 vols. Tokyo: Taishō Issaikyō Kankōkai, 1924–32.

TMS   Sŏ Kŏjŏng et al. *Tongmunsŏn*. Seoul: Minjok Munhwasa, 1994.

TYS   No Sasin et al. *Sinjŭng Tongguk yŏji sŭngnam*. Seoul: Sŏgyŏng Munhwasa, 1994.

TYSC   Yi Kyubo. *Tongguk Yi sanggukchip*. Seoul: Myŏngmundang, 1982.

YP   Yi Chehyŏn. *Yŏgong p'aesŏl*. In *Koryŏ myŏnghyŏnjip*, vol. 2, 344–77. Seoul: Sŏnggyun'gwan Taehakkyo Taedong Munhwa Yŏn'guwŏn, 1973.

YS   Song Lian et al., eds. *Yuan shi*. Beijing: Zhonghua Shuju, 1976.

For the sake of convenience, citations from the *Han'guk Pulgyo chŏnsŏ* are indicated by the volume number, followed by the page number, register, and, when appropriate, line numbers (e.g., *HPC* 6: 360b22–c3). Citations from the *Taishō shinshū daizōkyō shinshū daizōkyō* are similarly indicated by the volume number, followed by the text number, page number, register, and, when appropriate, line numbers (e.g., *T* 12.374.375b10–12). Citations from the *Koryŏsa, Koryŏsa chŏryo, Ikchejip, Kajŏngjip, Mog'ŭn mun'go, Mog'ŭn sigo, Tongmunsŏn, Tongguk Yi sanggukchip, Yŏg'ong p'aesŏl,* and *Sinjŭng Tongguk yŏji sŭngnam* are indicated by original volume number and page number with folio (e.g., *KS* 8: 11b–12a). Citations from the veritable records of Chosŏn kings from the *Chosŏn wangjo sillok*—the Kuksa p'yŏnch'an wiwŏnhoe online edition (http://sillok.history.go.kr/)—are also indicated by the name of the veritable record, followed by original volume number and page number with folio (e.g., *T'aejong sillok* 12: 8a). Citations from the *Yuan shi* will be indicated by page number, original volume number, and the year and month of the relevant emperor's reign (temple name followed by year of reign) if available (e.g., *YS*: 2872 [*juan* 114, *houfei* 1], *YS* 2: 414 [*juan* 19, Chengzong first year, eleventh month], *YS* 15: 4622 [*juan* 208, Waiyi 1, Gaoli]).

Secondary Sources

14-segi Koryŏ Sahoe Sŏnggyŏk Yŏn'guban, ed. *14-segi Koryŏ ŭi chŏngch'i wa sahoe.* Seoul: Minŭmsa, 1994.

Abe Takeo. *Gendaishi no kenkyū.* Tokyo: Sōbunsha, 1972.

Adamek, Wendi L. "The Impossibility of the Given: Representations of Merit and Emptiness in Medieval Chinese Buddhism." *History of Religions* 45, no. 2 (2005): 135–80.

Allsen, Thomas T. "Guard and Government in the Reign of the Grand Qan Möngke." *Harvard Journal of Asiatic Studies* 46, no. 2 (1986): 495–521.

———. "Mongol Princes and Their Merchant Partners, 1200–1260." *Asia Major*, 3rd ser., 2, no. 1 (1989): 83–126.

———. *The Royal Hunt in Eurasian History.* Philadelphia: University of Pennsylvania Press, 2006.

An Pyŏngu. "Koryŏ hugi nongŏp saengsallyŏk ŭi paltal kwa nongjang." In 14-segi Koryŏ Sahoe Sŏnggyŏk Yŏn'guban, *14-segi Koryŏ ŭi chŏngch'i wa sahoe*, 293–335.

Asad, Talal. "Anthropology and the Analysis of Ideology." *Man* 14, no. 4 (1979): 607–27.

———. *Formations of the Secular: Christianity, Islam, Modernity.* Palo Alto: Stanford University Press, 2003.

———. *Genealogies of Religion: Discipline and Reasons of Power in Christianity and Islam.* Baltimore: Johns Hopkins University Press, 1993.

Atwood, Christopher P. "*Ulus* Emirs, *Keshig* Elders, Signatures, and Marriage Partners." In *Imperial Statecraft: Political Forms and Techniques of Governance in Inner Asia, Sixth–Twelfth Centuries*, edited by David Sneath, 141–73. Bellingham: Center for East Asian Studies, Western Washington University for Mongolia and Inner Asia Studies Unit, University of Cambridge, 2004.

Baker, Don. "Privatization of Buddhism in the Chosŏn Dynasty." *Sungkyun Journal of East Asian Studies* 14, no. 2 (2014): 153–69.

Bell, Catherine. *Ritual Theory, Ritual Practice.* Oxford: Oxford University Press, 1992.

Benavides, Gustavo. "Economy." In *Critical Terms for the Study of Buddhism*, edited by Donald S. Lopez Jr., 77–102. Chicago: The University of Chicago Press, 2005.

Biran, Michael. *Qaidu and the Rise of the Independent Mongol State in Central Asia.* New York: Routledge, 1997.

Birge, Bettine. "Levirate Marriage and the Revival of Widow Chastity in Yüan China." *Asia Major*, 3rd ser., 8, no. 2 (1995): 107–46.

———. "Women and Confucianism from Song to Ming." In *The Song-Yuan-Ming Transition in Chinese History*, edited by Paul Jakov Smith, Richard von Glahn, Peter K. Bol, and Lucille Chia, 212–40. Cambridge, MA: Harvard University Asia Center, 2003.

Bloom, Irene. *Mencius.* Reprint. New York: Columbia University Press, 2011.

Bossler, Beverley J. *Powerful Relations: Kinship, Status, & the State in Sung China (960–1279).* Cambridge, MA: Council on East Asian Studies, Harvard University, 1998.

Bourdieu, Pierre. *Distinction: A Social Critique of the Judgement of Taste.* Translated by Richard Nice. Cambridge, MA: Harvard University Press, 1984.

Bresson, Alain. *The Making of the Ancient Greek Economy: Institutions, Markets, and Growth in the City-States.* Translated by Steven Rendall. Princeton: Princeton University Press, 2016.

Breuker, Remco E. *Establishing a Pluralist Society in Medieval Korea, 918–1170: History, Ideology, and Identity in the Koryŏ Dynasty.* Leiden: Brill, 2010.

Brook, Timothy. "At the Margins of Public Authority: The Ming State and Buddhism." In *Culture & State in Chinese History: Conventions, Accommodations, and Critiques*, edited by Theodore Huters, R. Bin Wong, and Pauline Yu, 161–81. Stanford: Stanford University Press, 1997.

———. "Funerary Ritual and The Building of Lineages in Late Imperial China." *Harvard Journal of Asiatic Studies* 49, no. 2 (1989): 465–99.

Brown, Peter. *The Ransom of the Soul: Afterlife and Wealth in Early Western Christianity.* Cambridge, MA: Harvard University Press, 2015.

———. *Through the Eye of a Needle: Wealth, the Fall of Rome, and the Making of Christianity in the West, 350–550 AD.* Princeton: Princeton University Press, 2012.

Bruneton, Yannick. "Séoul à l'époque Koryô: La Capitale du Sud sous la dynastie des Wang." *Revue de Corée* 101 (1997): 230–60.

Buswell, Robert E., Jr. "The Path to Perdition: The Wholesome Roots and Their Eradication." In *Paths to Liberation: The Mārga and Its Transformations in Buddhist Thought*, edited by Robert E. Buswell, Jr., and Robert Gimello, 107–34. Honolulu: University of Hawai'i Press, 1992.

———. "Thinking about 'Korean Buddhism': A Continental Perspective." *Journal of Korean Religions* 1, nos. 1–2 (2010): 43–55.

———. *Tracing Back the Radiance: Chinul's Korean Way of Zen.* Honolulu: University of Hawai'i Press, 1991.

Cha, Joohang. "The Civilizing Project in Medieval Korea: Neo-Classicism, Nativism, and Figurations of Power." PhD diss., Harvard University, 2014.

Chabanol, Elizabeth. "Study of the Archaeological and Historic Sites of Kaesŏng." *Transactions of the Royal Asiatic Society, Korea Branch* 80 (2005): 35–58.

Ch'ae Sangsik. "Ch'oe Hae ŭi sasangjŏk kyŏnghyang kwa pulgyo insik." In *Koryŏ sidae yŏn'gu I*, 115–43. Seoul: Han'guk Chŏngsin Munhwa Yŏn'guwŏn, 2000.

———. *Koryŏ hugi pulgyosa yŏn'gu.* Seoul: Ilchogak, 1991.

———. "Koryŏ-Chosŏn sigi pulgyosa yŏn'gu hyŏnhwang kwa kwaje." *Han'guk saron* 28 (1998): 51–107.
Ch'ae Ungsŏk. *Koryŏ sidae ŭi kukka wa chibang sahoe: "Pon'gwanje" ŭi sihaeng kwa chibang chibae chilsŏ*. Seoul: Sŏul Taehakkyo Ch'ulp'anbu, 2000.
Chang Tongik. *Koryŏ hugi oegyosa yŏn'gu*. Seoul: Ilchogak, 1994.
———. *Wŏndae Yŏsa charyo chimnok*. Seoul: Sŏul Taehakkyo Ch'ulp'anbu, 1997.
Chikusa Masaaki. *Chūgoku bukkyō shakaishi kenkyū*. Kyoto: Dōhōsha Shuppan, 1982.
———. *Sō Gen Bukkyō bunkashi kenkyū*. Tokyo: Kyūko Shoin, 2000.
Chin Sŏnggyu. "Koryŏ hugi wŏnch'al e taehayŏ." *Yŏksa kyoyuk* 36 (1984): 91–131.
———. "Yi Sŭnghyu ŭi pulgyogwan." *Chindan hakpo* 99 (2005): 211–31.
Cho Chwaho. "Yŏdae namban ko." *Tongguk sahak* 5 (1957): 1–17.
Cho Sŏnok. "'Tongmunsŏn' sojae chemun yŏn'gu." *Munch'angŏ nonmunjip* 37 (2000): 203–31.
Ch'oe, Byŏng-hŏn. "Tosŏn's Geomantic Theories and the Foundation of the Koryŏ Dynasty." *Seoul Journal of Korean Studies* 2 (1989): 65–92.
Ch'oe Ch'iwŏn. *Kyewŏn p'ilgyŏngjip*. Translated by Yi Sanghyŏn. Seoul: Han'guk kojŏn pŏnyŏgwŏn, 2009.
Ch'oe Pyŏnghŏn. "Koryŏ chunggi Hyŏnhwa-sa ŭi ch'anggŏn kwa Pŏpsangjong yungsŏng." In Pulgyo sahakhoe, *Koryŏ chung-hugi pulgyosaron*, 99–129.
———. "Koryŏ chunggi Yi Chahyŏn ŭi sŏn kwa kŏsa pulgyo ŭi sŏnggyŏk." In Pulgyo sahakhoe, *Koryŏ chung-hugi pulgyosaron*, 189–216.
Choi, Byŏnghyŏn, trans. *The Annals of King T'aejo: Founder of Korea's Chosŏn Dynasty*. Cambridge, MA: Harvard University Press, 2014.
Choi, Mihwa. "State Suppression of Buddhism and Royal Patronage of the Ritual of Water and Land in the Early Chosŏn Dynasty." *Seoul Journal of Korean Studies* 22, no. 2 (2009): 181–214.
Chŏng Sua. "Hyejo kuksa Tamjin kwa 'Chŏnginsu': Puk-Song Sŏnp'ung ŭi suyong kwa Koryŏ chunggi Sŏnjong ŭi puhŭng ŭl chungsimŭro." In Yi Kibaek Sŏnsaeng Kohŭi Kinyŏm Han'guk Sahak Nonch'ong Kanhaeng Wiwŏnhoe, *Han'guk sahak nonch'ong*, vol. 1, 616–39.
Chŏng Yongsuk. *Koryŏ wangsil chongnaehon yŏn'gu*. Seoul: Saemunsa, 1988.
Chu Ch'aehyŏk. "Hong Pogwŏn ilga wa Yŏ-Wŏn kwan'gye (il)." *Sahak yŏn'gu* 24 (1974): 1–53.
Chu Ungyŏng. "Kamyo ŭi sŏllip paegyŏng kwa kŭ kinŭng." *Yŏksa kyoyuk nonjip* 7, no. 1 (1985): 43–78.
Chung, Chaishik. "Chŏng Tojŏn: 'Architect' of Yi Dynasty Government and Ideology." In *The Rise of Neo-Confucianism in Korea*, edited by Wm. Theodore de Bary and JaHyun Kim Haboush, 59–88. New York: Columbia University Press, 1985.
Clark, Donald N. "Autonomy, Legitimacy, and Tributary Politics: Sino-Korean Relations in the Fall of the Koryŏ and the Founding of the Yi." PhD diss., Harvard University, 1978.
Cleaves, Francis W. "Sino-Mongolian Inscription of 1335 in Memory of Chung Ying-jui." *Harvard Journal of Asiatic Studies* 13 (1950): 1–131.
Collins, Steven. *Selfless Persons: Imagery and Thought in Theravāda Buddhism*. Cambridge: Cambridge University Press, 1982.

Dardess, John W. *Conquerors and Confucians: Aspects of Political Change in Late Yüan China*. New York: Columbia University Press, 1973.
de Bary, Wm. Theodore, and Irene Bloom, eds. *Sources of Chinese Tradition*. Vol. 1, *From Earliest Times to 1600*. 2nd ed. New York: Columbia University Press, 1999.
de Rachewiltz, Igor. "Personnel and Personalities in North China in the Early Mongol Period." *Journal of the Economic and Social History of the Orient* 9, no. 1/2 (1966): 88–144.
Deuchler, Martina. *The Confucian Transformation of Korea: A Study of Society and Ideology*. Cambridge, MA: Harvard University Press, 1992.
——. "Is 'Confucianization of Korea' a Valid Concept of Analysis?" *Sungkyun Journal of East Asian Studies* 7, no. 2 (2007): 3–6.
——. "Neo-Confucianism: The Impulse for Social Action in Early Yi Korea." *Journal of Korean Studies* 2 (1980): 71–111.
——. *Under the Ancestors' Eyes: Kinship, Status, and Locality in Premodern Korea*. Cambridge, MA: Harvard University Asia Center, 2015.
Dull, Jack. L. "A Historical Introduction to the Apocrypha (Ch'an-Wei) Texts of the Han Dynasty." PhD diss., University of Washington, 1966.
Duncan, John B. *Origins of the Chosŏn Dynasty*. Seattle: University of Washington Press, 2000.
Ebrey, Patricia Buckley, ed. *Chu Hsi's "Family Rituals": A Twelfth-Century Chinese Manual for the Performance of Cappings, Weddings, Funerals, and Ancestral Rites*. Princeton: Princeton University Press, 1991.
Endicott-West, Elizabeth. "Imperial Governance in Yüan Times." *Harvard Journal of Asiatic Studies* 46, no. 2 (1986): 523–49.
——. "Merchant Associations in Yüan China: The Ortoγ." *Asia Major*, 3rd ser., 2, no. 1 (1989): 127–54.
Fernandez, James W. "Persuasions and Performances: Of the Beast in Every Body . . . and the Metaphors of Everyman." *Daedalus* 101, no. 1 (1972): 39–60.
Franke, Herbert. "Tibetans in Yüan China." In *China under Mongol Rule*, edited by John D. Langlois, Jr., 296–328. Princeton: Princeton University Press, 1981.
Fujita Ryōsaku. "Ri Shien to sono kakei." *Seikyū gakusō* 13 (1933): 1–37; (1934): 109–35.
Fukaya Toshigane. "Kōraichō rokkadenkō." *Chōsen gakuhō* 48 (1968): 259–74.
Gernet, Jacques. *Buddhism in Chinese Society: An Economic History from the Fifth to the Tenth Centuries*. Translated by Franciscus Verellen. New York: Columbia University Press, 1995.
Gómez, Luis O. "Purifying Gold: The Metaphor of Effort and Intuition in Buddhist Thought and Practice." In *Sudden and Gradual: Approaches to Enlightenment in Chinese Thought*, edited by Peter N. Gregory, 67–165. Honolulu: University of Hawai'i Press, 1987.
Goulde, John Isaac. "Anti-Buddhist Polemic in Fourteenth and Fifteenth Century Korea: The Emergence of Confucian Exclusivism," PhD diss., Harvard University, 1985.
Gregory, Peter N. *Inquiry into the Origin of Humanity*. Honolulu: University of Hawai'i Press, 1995.
Halperin, Mark. *Out of the Cloister: Literati Perspectives on Buddhism in Sung China, 960–1279*. Cambridge, MA: Harvard University Press, 2006.
Han Kimun. *Koryŏ sawŏn ŭi kujo wa kinŭng*. Seoul: Minjoksa, 1998.

———. "Koryŏ sidae Chabok-sa ŭi sŏngnip kwa chonjae yangsang." *Minjok munhwa nonch'ong* 49 (2011): 279–328.

———. "Koryŏsidae sawŏnbo ŭi sŏlch'i wa unyŏng." *Yŏksa kyoyuk nonjip* 13/14 (1990): 361–91.

———. "Yech'ŏn 'Chungsu Yongmun-sagi' pimun ŭro pon Koryŏ chunggi sŏnjonggye ŭi tonghyang." *Munhwa sahak* 24 (2005): 73–105.

Han, Ugŭn. "Policies toward Buddhism in the Late Koryŏ and Early Chosŏn." In *Buddhism in the Early Chosŏn: Suppression and Transformation*, edited by Lewis R. Lancaster and Chai-shin Yu, 1–58. Berkeley: Institute of East Asian Studies, University of California, 1996.

Han Ugŭn. *Yugyo chŏngch'i wa pulgyo: Yŏmal Sŏnch'o tae pulgyo chŏngch'aek*. Seoul: Ilchogak, 1993.

Han'guksa yŏksa yŏn'guhoe, ed. *Yŏkchu Namal Yŏch'o kŭmsŏngmun*. 2 vols. Seoul: Hyean, 1996.

Hatada Takashi. "Kōrai no kōden." *Shigakku zasshi* 77, no. 4 (1968): 1–43.

———. "Kōrai no Meisō Shinsō jidai ni okeru nōmin ikki." *Rekishigaku kenkyū* 2, no. 4 (1934).

———. "Kōraichō ni okeru jiin keizai." *Shigaku zasshi* 43, no. 5 (1932): 557–93.

Hazard, Benjamin Harrison, Jr. "Japanese Marauding in Medieval Korea: The Wako Impact on Late Koryŏ." PhD diss., University of California, Berkeley, 1967.

He Ning. *Huainanzi jishi*. Beijing: Zhonghua Shuju, 1998.

Hŏ Hŭng-sik. "Buddhism and Koryŏ Society." In *Buddhism in Koryŏ: A Royal Religion*, edited by Lewis R. Lancaster, Kikun Suh, and Chai-shin Yu, 1–33. Fremont, CA: Asian Humanities Press, 2002.

Hŏ Hŭngsik. *Han'guk chungse pulgyosa yŏn'gu*. Seoul: Ilchogak, 1994.

———. *Koryŏ pulgyosa yŏn'gu*. Seoul: Ilchogak, 1981.

———. *Koryŏ ŭi kwagŏ chedo*. Seoul: Ilchogak, 2005.

Hong Sŭnggi. *Koryŏ kwijok sahoe wa nobi*. Seoul: Ilchogak, 1983.

Hong Yŏngŭi. *Koryŏmal chŏngch'isa yŏn'gu*. Seoul: Hyean, 2005.

Horlyck, Charlotte. "Ways of Burial in Koryŏ Times." In *Death, Mourning, and the Afterlife in Korea: From Ancient to Contemporary Times*, edited by Charlotte Horlyck and Michael J. Pettid, 83–111. Honolulu: University of Hawai'i Press, 2014.

Hsiao Ch'i-ch'ing. "Mid-Yüan Politics." In *The Cambridge History of China*. Vol. 6, *Alien Regimes and Border States, 907–1368*, edited by Herbert Franke and Denis Twitchett, 490–560. New York: Cambridge University Press, 1994.

Hucker, Charles O. *A Dictionary of Official Titles in Imperial China*. Stanford: Stanford University Press, 1985.

Hwang In'gyu. *Koryŏ hugi Chosŏn ch'o pulgyosa yŏn'gu*. Seoul: Hyean, 2003.

Ikeuchi Hiroshi. "Kōrai ni chūzai shita Gen no tatsurokaseki ni tsuite." *Tōhō gakuhō* 18 (1929): 277–83.

Jaini, Padmanabh S. "The Sautrāntika Theory of Bīja." *Bulletin of the School of Oriental and African Studies* 22, no. 1/3 (1959): 236–49.

Jan, Yün-hua. "Chinese Buddhism in Ta-tu: The New Situation and New Problems." In *Yüan Thought: Chinese Thought and Religion under the Mongols*, edited by Hok-lam Chan and Wm. Theodore de Bary, 375–417. New York: Columbia University Press, 1982.

Kalton, Michael. "The Writings of Kwŏn Kŭn: The Context and Shape of Early Yi Dynasty Neo-Confucianism." In *The Rise of Neo-Confucianism in Korea*, edited by Wm. Theodore de Bary and JaHyun Kim Haboush, 89–123. New York: Columbia University Press, 1985.

Kamata Shigeo. *Chōsen bukkyōshi*. Tokyo: Tōkyō Daigaku Shuppankai, 1987.

Kang Chinch'ŏl. *Kaejŏng Koryŏ t'oji chedosa yŏn'gu*. Seoul: Ilchogak, 1997.

Kang Hosŏn. "Muoe kukt'ong Chŏngo wa Wŏn kansŏpki Paengnyŏn kyŏlsa ŭi chŏn'gae." *Chindan hakpo* 120 (2014): 1–29.

Kang Hyŏnja. "Koryŏ Hyŏnjongdae Pongsŏn Honggyŏng-sa ŭi ch'anggŏn paegyong: 'Pongsŏn Honggyŏng-sa kalgi' rŭl chungsimŭro." *Chungang saron* 21 (2005): 82–126.

———. "Koryŏ Hyŏnjongdae Pongsŏn Honggyŏng-sa ŭi kinŭng: 'Pongsŏn Honggyŏng-sa kalgi' rŭl chungsimŭro." *Sahak yŏn'gu* 84 (2006): 35–108.

Katayama Tomoo. "Kōsetsu to Genchō kanryōsei." *Shigaku zasshi* 89, no. 12 (1980): 1–37.

Kim Ch'anghyŏn. "Ch'ungsŏn wang ŭi t'ansaeng kwa kyŏrhon kŭrigo chŏngch'i." *Han'guk inmulsa yŏn'gu* 14 (2010): 101–51.

———. *Koryŏ hugi chŏngbang yŏn'gu*. Seoul: Koryŏ Taehakkyo Minjok Munhwa Yŏn'guwŏn, 1998.

———. "Koryŏ Hyŏnhwa-sa pi punsŏk." *Mokkan kwa munja* 9 (2012): 69–101.

Kim Chongguk, "Kōrai bushin seiken to sōto no tairitsu tōsō ni kansuru ichi kōsatsu." *Chōsen gakuhō* 21 and 22 (1961): 567–89.

Kim Ch'ungnyŏl. *Koryŏ yuhaksa*. Seoul: Koryŏ Taehakkyo, 1984.

Kim Hodong. "Koryŏ musin chŏnggwŏn sidae sŭngnyŏ chisig'in Chinul Hyesim ŭi hyŏnsil taeŭng." *Minjok munhwa nonch'ong* 13 (1992): 1–28.

———. *Mongol cheguk kwa Koryŏ: K'ubillai chŏnggwŏn ŭi t'ansaeng kwa Koryŏ ŭi chŏngch'ijŏk wisang*. Seoul: Sŏul Taehakkyo Ch'ulp'anbu, 2007.

———. "Mongol cheguk kwa Tae Wŏn." *Yŏksa hakpo* 192 (2006): 221–53.

———. "Mong-Wŏn chegukki han saengmongin kwalli ŭi ch'osang: Isa K'ellemech'i ŭi saengae wa hwaltong." *Chungang asia yŏn'gu* 11 (2006): 75–114.

Kim Hyewŏn. "Koryŏ hugi Sim(yang) wang ŭi chŏngch'i kyŏngjejŏk kiban." *Kuksagwan nonch'ong* 49 (1993): 30–58.

———. "Wŏn kansŏpki ipsŏngnon kwa kŭ sŏnggyŏk." In *14-segi Koryŏ Sahoe Sŏnggyŏk Yŏn'guban, 14-segi Koryŏ ŭi chŏngch'i wa sahoe*, 39–93.

Kim Hyŏngsu. "Ch'ungsuk wang hu 8-nyŏn (1339) kamch'alsa pang kwa Ch'unghye wang pogwi." *Han'guk chungsesa yŏn'gu* 11 (2001): 99–123.

———. "Koryŏ Ch'ungsuk wang 12-nyŏn (1325) kyosŏ ŭi chaegŏmt'o." *Pokhyŏn sarim* 24 (2001): 1–47.

Kim Inho. *Koryŏ hugi sadaebu ŭi kyŏngseron yŏn'gu*. Seoul: Hyean, 1999.

Kim Kapchu. "Chosŏn chŏn'gi sawŏnjŏn ŭl chungsimŭro han pulgyogye tonghyang ŭi ilgo." *Tongguk sahak* 13 (1976): 47–85.

———. *Chosŏn sidae sawŏn kyŏngjesa yŏn'gu*. Seoul: Kyŏngin Munhwasa, 2007.

Kim Kidŏk. "14-segi huban kaehyŏk chŏngch'i ŭi naeyong kwa kŭ sŏnggyŏk—Kongmin wangdae kaehyŏgan ŭi punsŏk ŭl chungsimŭro." In *14-segi Koryŏ Sahoe Sŏnggyŏk Yŏn'guban, 14-segi Koryŏ ŭi chŏngch'i wa sahoe*, 446–506.

Kim Kwangch'ŏl. "14-segich'o Wŏn ŭi chŏngguk tonghyang kwa Ch'ungsŏn wang ŭi T'obŏn yubae." *Han'guk chungsesa yŏn'gu* 3 (1996): 290–343.

———. "Ch'unghye wang ŭi wangwi kyesŭng." *Yŏksa wa kyŏnggye* 28 (1995): 87–120.
———. "Hong Chabŏn yŏn'gu—Ch'ungnyŏl wangdae chŏngch'i wa sahoe ŭi ilch'ŭngmyŏn." *Yŏksa wa kyŏnggye* 1 (1984): 1–40.
———. "Koryŏ Ch'ungnyŏl wangdae chŏngch'i seryŏk ŭi tonghyang—Ch'ungnyŏl wang ch'ogi chŏngch'i seryŏk ŭi pyŏnhwa rŭl chungsimŭro." *Ch'angwŏn tae nonmun chip* 7, no. 1 (1985)
———. "Koryŏ Ch'ungsŏn wang ŭi hyŏnsil insik kwa tae Wŏn hwaldong—Ch'ungnyŏl wang 24-nyŏn susŏn ijŏn ŭl chungsimŭro." *Yŏksa wa kyŏnggye* 11 (1986): 37–72.
———. "Koryŏ Ch'ungsuk wang 12-nyŏn ŭi kaehyŏgan kwa kŭ sŏnggyŏk." *Kogo yŏksahakchip* 5 and 6 (1990): 181–209.
———. *Koryŏ hugi sejokch'ŭng yŏn'gu*. Seoul: Tonga Taehakkyo Ch'ulp'anbu, 1991.
Kim Pogwang. "Koryŏ Ch'ungnyŏl wang ŭi k'esik'ŭ (*kesig*) che toip kwa kŭ ŭido." *Sahak yŏn'gu* 107 (2012): 125–68.
———. "Koryŏ sidae naesi ŭi unyŏng kwa munban kwanjik." *Yŏksa wa hyŏnsil* 75 (2010): 127–63.
Kim Sanggi. *Sinp'yŏn Koryŏ sidaesa*. Seoul: Sŏl Taehakkyo Ch'ulp'anbu, 1996.
Kim Sŏngjun, "Yŏdae Wŏn kongju ch'ulsin wangbi ŭi chŏngch'ijŏk wich'i e taehayŏ: T'ŭkhi Ch'ungsŏn wangbi rŭl chungsimŭro." *Han'guk yŏsŏng munhwa nonch'ong* 1 (1958): 211–65.
Kim Tangt'aek. "Ch'ungnyŏl wang ŭi pogwi kwajŏng ŭl t'onghae pon ch'ŏn'gye ch'ulsin kwallyo wa 'sajok' ch'ulsin kwallyo ŭi chŏngch'ijŏk kaltŭng: 'Sadaebu' kaenyŏm e taehan kŏmt'o." *Tonga yŏn'gu* 17 (1989): 195–232.
———. "Ch'ungsŏn wang ŭi pogwi gyosŏ e poinŭn 'chaesang chi chong' e taehayŏ: Sowi 'kwŏnmun sejok' ŭi kusŏng punja wa kwallyŏnhayŏ." *Yŏksa hakpo* 131 (1991): 1–29.
———. "Koryŏ Hyŏnjongdae kwagŏ ch'ulsin kwalli ŭi chŏngch'ijŏk chudogwŏn changak." *Yŏksa hakhoe* 200 (2008): 231–48.
———. *Koryŏ ŭi muin chŏnggwŏn*. Seoul: Kukhak Charyowŏn, 1999.
———. *Wŏn kansŏpha ŭi Koryŏ chŏngch'isa*. Seoul: Ilchogak, 1998.
Kim Yŏngmi, "Koryŏ sidae pulgyogye t'ongje wa yullyŏng—sŭngnyŏ haengdong kyuje rŭl chungsimŭro." *Sahak yŏn'gu* 67 (2002): 1–30.
Kim Yongsŏn. *Koryŏ kŭmsŏngmun yŏn'gu*. Seoul: Ilchogak, 2004.
Kim Yongsŏp. "Koryŏ sigi ŭi yangjŏnje." *Tongbang hakchi* 16 (1975): 67–115.
Kim Youngmi. "Buddhist Faith and Conceptions of the Afterlife in Koryŏ." *Seoul Journal of Korean Studies* 21, no. 2 (2008): 193–220.
Kim Yun'gon. "Koryŏ kwijok sahoe ŭi che mosun." In *Han'guksa* 7, edited by Kuksa P'yŏnch'an Wiwŏnhoe, 27–86. Seoul: Kuksa P'yŏnch'an Wiwŏnhoe, 1981.
———. "Sinhŭng sadaebu ŭi taedu." In *Han'guksa* 8, edited by Kuksa P'yŏnch'an Wiwŏnhoe, 142–74. Seoul: Kuksa P'yŏnch'an Wiwŏnhoe, 1981.
Ko Hyeryŏng. "Ch'oe Hae (1287–1340) ŭi saengae wa sasang." In Yi Kibaek Sŏnsaeng Kohŭi Kinyŏm Han'guk Sahak Nonch'ong Kanhaeng Wiwŏnhoe, *Han'guk sahak nonch'ong*, vol. 1, 877–99.
———. *Koryŏ hugi sadaebu wa sŏngnihak suyong*. Seoul: Ilchogak, 2001.
———. "Wŏn kansŏpki sŏngnihak suyong ŭi il tanmyŏn—Ch'oe Mundo rŭl chungsimŭro." *Han'guk chungsesa yŏn'gu* 18 (2005): 137–71.

Ko Pyŏngik. "Koryŏ Ch'ungsŏn wang ŭi Wŏn Mujong ongnip." *Yŏksa hakpo* 17/18 (1962): 675–85.
Ko Yusŏp. *Songdo ŭi kojŏk*. Reprint. Seoul: Yŏlhwadang, 2007.
Ku Sanu. "14-segi chŏnban'gi Ch'oe Hae ŭi chŏsul hwaldong kwa sasangjŏk tanmyŏn." *Chiyŏk kwa yŏksa* 5 (1999): 33–86.
Kwŏn, Cheeyun. "The Scripture of the Ten Kings from Haein-sa: An Overgrown Underworld Pantheon in the Koryŏ Dynasty." *Pigyo han'gukhak* 12 (2004): 1–43.
Kwŏn Hyosuk. "Chuin pakkwin myo . . . 600-nyŏn twi myojisŏk i saja ŭi chinsil palk'ida." *Kŭllobŏl ik'onomik*, June 7, 2013, accessed February 10, 2016, www.g-enews.com/ko-kr/news/article/life_005/201306070759540050403_1/article.html.
Kwŏn Sŏnu. "Koryŏ Ch'ungnyŏl wangdae Kim Panggyŏng mugo sagŏn ŭi chŏn'gae wa sŏnggyŏk." *Inmun kwahak yŏn'gu* 5 (1999): 93–134.
Kwŏn Yŏngguk. "14-segi chŏnban kaehyŏk chŏngch'i ŭi naeyong kwa kŭ sŏnggyŏk—sahoe kyŏngjemyŏn ŭi kaehyŏk ŭl chungsimŭro." In 14-segi Koryŏ Sahoe Sŏnggyŏk Yŏn'guban, *14-segi Koryŏ ŭi chŏngch'i wa sahoe*, 409–45.
Kyŏnggi kŭmsŏk taegwan. Kyŏnggi-do: Kyŏnggi-do, 1992.
Lakoff, George, and Mark Johnson. *Metaphors We Live By*. Chicago: The University of Chicago Press, 1980.
Lamotte, Étienne. *Le Traité de la Grande Vertu de Sagesse de Nāgārjuna (Mahāprajñāpāramitāśāstra) avec une nouvelle introduction, tome III, chapitres XXXI–XLII*. Louvain: Institute Orientaliste, Université de Louvain, 1970.
Ledyard, Gari. "Yin and Yang in the China-Manchuria-Korea Triangle." In *China among Equals: The Middle Kingdom and Its Neighbors, 10th–14th Centuries*, edited by Morris Rossabi, 313–53. Berkeley: University of California Press, 1983.
Lee, Ki-baik. *A New History of Korea*. Translated by Edward W. Wagner with Edward J. Shultz. Cambridge, MA: Harvard Yenching Institute, 1984.
Lee, Peter H. *The Columbia Anthology of Traditional Korean Poetry*. New York: Columbia University Press, 2002.
Lee, Peter H., et al., eds. *Sources of Korean Tradition*. Vol. 1, *From Early Times through the Sixteenth Century*. New York: Columbia University Press, 1997.
Legge, James, trans. *The Chinese Classics, Vol. III, Part II, Containing the Fifth Part of the Shoo King, or The Books of Chow; and the Indexes*. London: Trübner & Co., 1865.
———. *The Chinese Classics, Vol. IV, Part II, Containing the Second, Third, and Fourth Parts of the She-King, or the Minor Odes of the Kingdom, the Greater Odes of the Kingdom, the Sacrificial Odes and Praise-Songs; and the Indexes*. London: Trübner & Co., 1871.
———. *The I Ching*. 2nd ed. New York: Dover Publications, 1963.
———. *Li Chi: Book of Rites, An Encyclopedia of Ancient Ceremonial Usages, Religious Creeds, and Social Institutions, Edited with Introduction and Study Guide by Ch'u Chai and Winberg Chai*. Vols. 1 and 2. New York: University Books, 1967.
Levering, Miriam. "Ta-hui and Lay Buddhists: Ch'an Sermons on Death." In *Buddhist and Taoist Practice in Medieval Chinese Society: Buddhist and Taoist Studies II*, edited by David W. Chappell, 181–206. Honolulu: University of Hawai'i Press, 1987.
Liu Xihai. *Haidong jinshi yuan, 8 juan, buyi 6 juan, fulu 2 juan*. Taipei: Yiwen Yinshuguan, 1966.

Lusthaus, Dan. *Buddhist Phenomenology: A Philosophical Investigation of Yogācāra Buddhism and the Ch'eng Wei-shih lun*. New York: Routledge, 2002.
Ma Qichang. *Han changli wenji jiaozhu*. Hong Kong: Zhonghua Shuju, 1972.
McBride, Richard D. *Domesticating the Dharma: Buddhist Cults and the Hwaŏm Synthesis in Silla Korea*. Honolulu: University of Hawai'i Press, 2007.
McCann, David. *Early Korean Literature: Selections and Introductions*. New York: Columbia University Press, 2000.
Min Hyŏn'gu. "Cho In'gyu wa kŭ ŭi kamun (chung)." *Chindan hakpo* 43 (1977): 5–32.
———. "Cho In'gyu wa kŭ ŭi kamun (sang)." *Chindan hakpo* 42 (1976): 17–28.
———. "Koryŏ hugi kwŏnmun sejok ŭi sŏngnip." *Honam munhwa yŏn'gu* 6 (1974).
———. "Koryŏ hugi ŭi kwŏnmun sejok." In *Han'guksa*, vol. 8, edited by Kuksa P'yŏnch'an Wiwŏnhoe, 13–59. Seoul: Kuksa P'yŏnch'an Wiwŏnhoe, 1981.
———. "Koryŏ ŭi nokkwajŏn." *Yŏksa hakpo* 53/54 (1971): 55–98.
———. "Wŏlnam-sa chi Chin'gak kuksa pi ŭi ŭmgi e taehan il koch'al." In *Koryŏ hugi pulgyo chŏn'gaesa yŏn'gu*, edited by Pulgyo Sahakhoe, 11–57. Seoul: Minjoksa, 1986.
Morihira Masahiko. *Mongoru hakenka no Kōrai: Teikoku chitsujo to ōkoku no taiō*. Nagoya: Nagoya Daigaku Shuppankai, 2013.
Moriyasu Takao. "Shiruku rōdo tōbu ni okeru senka: Kinu, seihō ginseng, kanfu kara ginchō e." In *Chūō Ajia shutsudo bunbutsu ronsō*, edited by Moriyasu Takao, 1–40. Kyoto: Hoyū Shoten, 2004.
Munhwajae Kwalliguk Munhwajae Yŏn'guso. *P'aju Sŏgongni Koryŏ pyŏkhwamyo: Palgul chosa pogosŏ*. Seoul: Munhwajae Kwalliguk Munhwajae Yŏn'guso, 1993.
Naitō Shunpo. "Kōrai jidai no takabō ni tsuite." *Chōsen gakuhō* 8 (1955): 65–82.
Nivison, David S. *The Ways of Confucianism: Investigations in Chinese Philosophy*. Edited with an introduction by Bryan W. Van Norden. Chicago: Open Court, 1996.
No Myŏngho et al. *Han'guk kodae chungse komunsŏ yŏn'gu (sang): Kyogam yŏkchu p'yŏn*. Seoul: Sŏul Taehakkyo Ch'ulp'an Munhwawŏn, 2000.
No Yongp'il. "Hong Chabŏn ŭi 'P'yonmin sipp'alsa' e taehan yŏn'gu." *Yŏksa hakpo* 102 (1984): 31–61.
O Ilsun. "Koryŏ hugi t'oji pun'gŭpche ŭi pyŏndong kwa nokkwajŏn." In 14-segi Koryŏ Sahoe Sŏnggyŏk Yŏn'guban, *14-segi Koryŏ ŭi chŏngch'i wa sahoe*, 270–92.
Ōyabu Masaya. *Gendai no hōsei to shūkyō*. Tokyo: Shūei Shuppan, 1983.
Pae Sanghyŏn. *Koryŏ hugi sawŏnjŏn yŏn'gu*. Seoul: Kukhak Charyowŏn, 1998.
Paek Inho. *Koryŏ hugi pu-Wŏn seryŏk yŏn'gu*. Seoul: Sejong Ch'ulp'ansa, 2003.
Pak Chonggi. "11-segi Koryŏ ŭi taeoe kwan'gye wa chŏngguk unyŏngnon ŭi ch'ui." *Yŏksa wa hyŏnsil* 30 (1998): 148–72.
———. "14-segi ŭi Koryŏ sahoe—Wŏn kansŏpki ŭi ihae munje." In 14-segi Koryŏ Sahoe Sŏnggyŏk Yŏn'guban, *14-segi Koryŏ ŭi chŏngch'i wa sahoe*, 13–35.
———. *Chibae wa chayul ŭi konggan, Koryŏ ŭi chibang sahoe*. Seoul: P'urŭn Yŏksa, 2002.
———. "Koryŏmal waegu wa chibang sahoe." *Han'guk chungsesa yŏn'gu* 24 (2008): 173–207.
Pak Kyŏngan. *Koryŏ hugi t'oji chedo yŏn'gu: 13/14-segi chŏnje ijŏng chŏngch'aek ŭi ch'ui*. Seoul: Hyean, 1996.
Pak Yŏngje. "Wŏn kansŏpki ch'ogi pulgyogye ŭi pyŏnhwa." In 14-segi Koryŏ Sahoe Sŏnggyŏk Yŏn'guban, *14-segi Koryŏ ŭi chŏngch'i wa sahoe*, 509–54.

Pak Yongun. "Koryŏ hugi *bishechi* (p'iljajŏk pich'ikch'i) e taehan yŏn'gu." In *Koryŏ sidae kwan'gye kwanjik yŏn'gu*, 237–64. Seoul: Koryŏ Taehakkyo Ch'ulp'anbu, 1997.
———. *Koryŏ sahoe wa munbŏl kwijok kamun*. Seoul: Kyŏngin Munhwasa, 2003.
———. *Koryŏ sidae taegan chedo yŏn'gu*. Seoul: Ilchisa, 1980.
———. *Koryŏ sidaesa, sang/ha*. Seoul: Ilchisa, 1987.
———. "*Koryŏsa*" *paekkwanji yŏkchu*. Seoul: Sinsŏwŏn, 2009.
Pak Yujin, "Koryŏ sidae sŭngnyŏ ŭi hyŏlchokkan sasŭng kwa kŭ ŭimi." *Han'guksa yŏn'gu* 142 (2008): 69–103.
Palais, James B. "Land Tenure in Korea: Tenth to Twelfth Centuries," *Journal of Korean Studies* 4 (1982–83): 73–205.
Pelliot, Paul. "Les Mots Mongols dans le *Korye sa*." *Journal asiatique* 217 (1930): 253–66.
———. "Notes sur le 'Turkestan' de M. W. Bartold." *T'oung Pao*, 2nd ser., 27, no. 1 (1930): 12–56.
Petech, Luciano. "Tibetan Relations with Sung China and with the Mongols." In *China among Equals: The Middle Kingdom and Its Neighbors, 10th–14th Centuries*, edited by Morris Rossabi, 173–203. Berkeley: University of California Press, 1983.
Puggioni, Tonino. "The Life and Times of Yŏm Sŭng-ik." In *Korea: Language, Knowledge, and Society, Proceedings of the 3rd Biennial Conference, Korean Studies Association of Australasia*, edited by Gi-hyun Shin, 164–79. Canberra: Australian National University, 2003.
Pulgyo sahakhoe. *Koryŏ chung-hugi pulgyosaron*. Seoul: Minjoksa, 1986.
Pyŏn T'aesŏp. "Koryŏ chaesang ko: Samsŏng ŭi kwŏllyŏk kwan'gye rŭl chungsimŭro." *Yŏksa hakpo* 35/36 (1967): 110–38.
———. *Koryŏ chŏngch'i chedosa yŏn'gu*. Seoul: Ilchogak, 1977.
Pyŏn Tongmyŏng. *Koryŏ hugi sŏngnihak suyong yŏn'gu*. Seoul: Ilchogak, 1995.
———. "Sŏngnihak ŭi ch'ogi suyongja wa pulgyo." In Yi Kibaek Sŏnsaeng Kohŭi Kinyŏm Han'guk Sahak Nonch'ong Kanhaeng Wiwŏnhoe, *Han'guk sahak nonch'ong*, vol. 1, 930–56.
Rashīd al-Dīn Ṭabīb. *The Successors of Genghis Khan*. Translated by John Andrew Boyle. New York: Columbia University Press, 1971.
Robinson, David M. *Empire's Twilight: Northeast Asia under the Mongols*. Cambridge, MA: Harvard University Asia Center, 2009.
Rogers, Michael. "*P'yŏnnyŏn t'ongnok*: The Foundation Legend of the Koryŏ State." *Journal of Korean Studies* 4 (1982–83): 3–72.
Rossabi, Morris. "Khubilai Khan and the Women in His Family." In *Studia Sino-Mongolica: Festschrift für Herbert Franke*, edited by Wolfgang Bauer, 153–80. Wiesbaden: Steiner, 1979.
———. "The Reign of Khubilai Khan," In *The Cambridge History of China*, vol. 6, *Alien Regimes and Border States, 907–1368*, edited by Herbert Franke and Denis Twitchett, 414–89. New York: Cambridge University Press, 1994.
Rotman, Andy, trans. *Divine Stories: Divyāvadāna, Part I*. Somverville: Wisdom Publications, 2008.
Ryu Hongnyŏl. "Koryŏ ŭi Wŏn e taehan kongnyŏ." *Chindan hakpo* 18 (1957): 25–46.
Seidel, Anna K. "Imperial Treasures and Taoist Sacraments: Taoist Roots in the Apocrypha." *Tantric and Taoist Studies in Honour of R. A. Stein*, vol. 2, *Mélanges*

chinois et bouddhiques, no. 21, edited by Michel Strickmann, 291–371. Brussels: Institut Belge des Hautes Études Chinoises, 1983.

Sharf, Robert H. *Coming to Terms with Chinese Buddhism: A Reading of the "Treasure Store Treatise."* Honolulu: University of Hawai'i Press, 2002

———. "How to Think with Chan Gong'an." In *Thinking with Cases: Specialist Knowledge in Chinese Cultural History*, edited by Charlotte Furth, Judith T. Zeitlin, and Ping-chen Hsiung, 205–43. Honolulu: University of Hawai'i Press, 2007.

———. "Ritual." In *Critical Terms for the Study of Buddhism*, edited by Donald S. Lopez Jr., 245–70. Chicago: The University of Chicago Press, 2005.

Shultz, Edward J. "Han Aninp'a ŭi tŭngjang kwa kŭ yŏkhal." *Yŏksa hakpo* 99/100 (1983): 147–83.

———. *Generals and Scholars: Military Rule in Medieval Korea*. Honolulu: University of Hawai'i Press, 2000.

———. "Twelfth-Century Koryŏ Politics: The Rise of Han An-in and His Partisans." *Journal of Korean Studies* 6 (1988–89): 3–38.

Shurmann, Herbert Franz. *Economic Structure of the Yüan Dynasty*. Cambridge: Cambridge University Press, 1967.

Sin Ch'ŏnsik. *Sangch'on sŏnsaeng ŭi saengae wa sasang*. Seoul: Kyŏngin Munhwasa, 2003.

Song Ch'anghan. "Ch'oe Hae ŭi ch'ŏkpullon e taehayŏ: Songsŭng Sŏnji yu Kŭmgangsan sŏ rŭl chungsimŭro." *Taegu sahak* 38 (1989): 121–43.

Sŏng Hyŏn. *Yongjae ch'onghwa*. In *Kug'yŏk taedong yasŭng*, vol. 1, edited by Minjok Munhwa Ch'ujinhoe. Seoul: Minjok Munhwa Ch'ujinhoe, 1971.

Sŏnggyun'gwan Taehakkyo Taedong Munhwa Yŏn'guwŏn, ed. *Koryŏ myŏnghyŏnjip*. 5 vols. Seoul: Sŏnggyun'gwan Taehakkyo Taedong Munhwa Yŏn'guwŏn, 1986.

Song Lian et al., eds. *Yuan shi*. Beijing: Zhonghua Shuju, 1976.

Song Pyŏnggi. "Nongjang ŭi paltal." In *Han'guksa* 8, edited by Kuksa P'yŏnch'an Wiwŏnhoe, 59–91. Seoul: Kuksa P'yŏnch'an Wiwŏnhoe, 1981.

Stiller, Maya Kerstin Hyun. "Kŭmgangsam: Regional Practice and Religious Pluralism in Pre-modern Korea." PhD diss., University of California, Los Angeles, 2014.

Sudō Yoshiyuki. "Kōrai makki yori Chōsen shoki ni itaru nuhi no kenkyū." *Rekishigaku kenkyū* 9, no. 1 (1939): 6–45; no. 2 (1939): 57–76; no. 3 (1939): 23–66; no. 4 (1939): 64–94.

———. *Kōraichō kanryōsei no kenkyū*. Tokyo: Hōsei Daigaku Shuppankyoku, 1980.

———. "Kōraichō yori Chōsen shoki ni itaru densei no kaikaku." *Tōa gaku* 3 (1940): 115–91.

Tackett, Nicolas. *The Destruction of the Medieval Chinese Aristocracy*. Cambridge, MA: Harvard University Asia Center, 2014.

Takahashi Tōru. *Richō bukkyō*. Tokyo: Hōbunkan, 1929.

Teiser, Stephen F. *The Ghost Festival in Medieval China*. Princeton: Princeton University Press, 1996.

———. "The Growth of Purgatory." In *Religion and Society in T'ang and Sung China*, edited by Patricia Buckley Ebrey and Peter N. Gregory, 115–46. Honolulu: University of Hawai'i Press, 1993.

———. *The Scripture on the Ten Kings and the Making of Purgatory in Medieval Chinese Buddhism*. Honolulu: University of Hawai'i Press, 2003.

To Hyŏnch'ŏl. *Koryŏmal sadaebu ŭi chŏngch'i sasang yŏn'gu*. Seoul: Ilchogak, 1999.

———. *Mogŭn Yi Saek ŭi chŏngch'i sasang yŏn'gu*. Seoul: Hyean, 2011.

Tokiwa Daijō. *Shina bukkyō no kenkyū*. Vol. 2. Tokyo: Shunjūsha, 1941.
Twitchett, Denis. "The Fan Clan's Charitable Estate, 1050–1760." In *Confucianism in Action*, edited by David Nivison, 97–133. Stanford: Stanford University Press, 1959.
Vermeersch, Sem. "Buddhist Temples or Political Backgrounds? Kaesŏng Temples in Relation to Court and Aristocracy." *Bulletin de l'École française d'Extrême-Orient* 94 (2007): 195–227.
——. *The Power of the Buddhas: The Politics of Buddhism during the Koryŏ Dynasty (918–1392)*. Cambridge, MA: Harvard University Asia Center, Harvard University Press, 2008.
——. "Royal Ancestor Worship and Buddhist Politics: The Hyŏnhwa-sa Stele and the Origins of the First Koryŏ Tripitaka." *Journal of Korean Studies* 18, no. 1 (2013): 115–46.
——. "Views on Buddhist Precepts and Morality in Late Koryŏ." *Journal of Korean Religions* 7, no. 1 (2016): 35–65.
von Glahn, Richard. "Monies of Account and Monetary Transition in China." *Journal of the Economic and Social History of the Orient* 53, no. 3 (2010): 463–505.
Walraven, Boudewijn. "Beyond 'Confucianization.'" *Sungkyun Journal of East Asian Studies* 7, no. 2 (2007): 1–24.
——. "Buddhist Accommodation and Appropriation and the Limits of Confucianization." *Journal of Korean Religions* 3, no. 1 (2012): 105–16.
Walsh, Michael J. *Sacred Economies: Buddhist Monasticism and Territoriality in Medieval China*. New York: Columbia University Press, 2010.
Wi Ŭnsuk. *Koryŏ hugi nong'ŏp kyŏngje yŏn'gu*. Seoul: Hyean, 1998.
——. "Nongjang ŭi sŏngnip kwa kujo." In *Han'guksa* 19, edited by Kuksa P'yŏnch'an Wiwŏnhoe, 225–90. Seoul: Kuksa P'yŏnch'an Wiwŏnhoe, 1996.
Wilkinson, Endymion. *Chinese History*. Rev. ed. Cambridge, MA: Harvard University Asia Center, 2000.
Wu, Shu-hui. "On Chinese Sacrificial Orations *Chi Wen*." *Monumenta Serica* 50 (2002): 1–33.
Xiao Qiqing. *Yuandaishi xintan*. Taipei: Xinwenfeng Chuban Gongsi, 1983.
Yampolsky, Philip B. *The Platform Sūtra of the Sixth Patriarch*. New York: Columbia University Press, 1967.
Yang Hŭich'ŏl. "'Che mangmae ka' ŭi ŭimi wa hyŏngsang." *Kugŏ kungmunhak* 102 (1989): 241–61.
Yi Chaech'ang. "Characteristics of Traditional Meditation Schools in Late Koryŏ: Focusing on Chigyŏm, Iryŏn and Ch'ŏnch'aek." In *Buddhism in Koryŏ: A Royal Religion*, edited by Lewis R. Lancaster, Kikun Suh, and Chai-shin Yu, 139–71. Fremont, CA: Asian Humanities Press, 2002.
Yi Chongbong. "Koryŏ sidae ŭi yangje." *Kuksagwan nonch'ong* 82 (1998): 197–233.
Yi Chŏngju. "Kongyang wangdae ŭi chŏngguk tonghyang kwa ch'ŏkpul undong ŭi sŏnggyŏk." *Han'guksa yŏn'gu* 120 (2003): 115–56.
——. *Sŏngnihak suyonggi Pulgyo pip'an kwa chŏngch'i-sasangjŏk pyŏnyong: Chŏng Tojŏn kwa Kwŏn Kŭn ŭl chungsimŭro*. Seoul: Koryŏ Taehakkyo Minjok Munhwa Yŏn'guwŏn, 2007.
Yi Chŏngnan. "Chungnyŏl wangdae Kyeguk taejang kongju ŭi kaehon undong." *Han'guk inmulsa yŏn'gu* 9 (2008): 103–43.

Yi Chŏngsin. "Wŏn kansŏpki hwan'gwan ŭi haengjŏk." *Han'guksa hakpo* 57 (2014): 85–115.

Yi Hyŏnjong. "Waegu." In *Han'guksa* 8, edited by Kuksa P'yŏnch'an Wiwŏnhoe, 204–34. Seoul: Kuksa P'yŏnch'an Wiwŏnhoe, 1981.

Yi Ikchu. "Ch'ungsŏn wang chŭgwinyŏn (1298) kaehyŏk chŏngch'i ŭi sŏnggyŏk—kwanje kaep'yŏn ŭl chungsimŭro." *Yŏksa wa hyŏnsil* 7 (1992): 113–45.

———. "Koryŏ Ch'ungnyŏl wangdae ŭi chŏngch'i sanghwang kwa chŏngch'i seryŏk ŭi sŏnggyŏk." *Han'guksaron* 18 (1988): 155–222.

———. "Koryŏ-Wŏn kwan'gye ŭi kujo e taehan yŏn'gu—sowi 'Sejo kuje' ŭi punsŏk ŭl chungsimŭro." *Han'guksaron* 36 (1996).

———. "Koryŏ-Wŏn kwan'gye ŭi kujo wa Koryŏ hugi chŏngch'i ch'eje." PhD diss., Seoul National University, 1996.

———. "Myojimyŏng charyo rŭl t'onghae pon Koryŏ hugi kwanin ŭi saengae—Kim Pyŏn (1248–1301) ŭi sarye." *Han'guksa hakpo* 23 (2006): 123–64.

———. *Yi Saek ŭi salm kwa saenggak*. Seoul: Ilchogak, 2013.

Yi Kaesŏk. "Tae Monggoguk-Koryŏ kwan'gye yŏn'gu ŭi chaegŏmt'o." *Sahak yŏn'gu* 88 (2007): 39–92.

Yi Kanghan. "1270–80 nyŏndae Koryŏ nae ŭngbang unyŏng mit taeoe muyŏk." *Han'guksa yŏn'gu* 146 (2009): 75–117.

———. "Koryŏ Ch'ungsŏn wang ŭi chŏngch'i kaehyŏk kwa Wŏn ŭi yŏnghyang." *Han'guk munhwa* 43 (2008): 267–300.

———. *Koryŏ wa Wŏn cheguk ŭi kyoyŏk ŭi yŏksa: 13–14 segi kamch'wŏjin kyoryusang ŭi chaegusŏng*. Seoul: Ch'angbi, 2013.

Yi Kibaek, *Han'guksa sillon*. Rev. ed. Seoul: Ilchogak, 1990.

Yi Kibaek Sŏnsaeng Kohŭi Kinyŏm Han'guk Sahak Nonch'ong Kanhaeng Wiwŏnhoe. *Han'guk sahak nonch'ong: Yi Kibaek sŏnsaeng kohŭi kinyŏm*. Vol. 1. Seoul: Ilchogak, 1994.

Yi Kinam. "Ch'ungsŏn wang ŭi kaehyŏk kwa sarimwŏn ŭi sŏlch'i." *Yŏksa hakpo* 52 (1971): 55–102.

Yi Kyŏngsik. *Chosŏn chŏn'gi t'oji chedo yŏn'gu: T'oji pun'gŭpche wa nongmin chibae*. Seoul: Ilchogak, 1986.

———. "Koryŏ hugi sawŏn ŭi chungsu/chungch'ang kwa kyŏngje munje." *Munhwa sahak* 27 (2007): 759–95.

Yi Ponggyu. "Koryŏmal sadaebu ŭi sasang ŭl yuhyŏnghwahanŭn han tokpŏp: Kubŏpp'a wa sinbŏpp'a ŭi taebi, To Hyŏnch'ŏl, *Koryŏmal sadaebu ŭi chŏngch'i sasang yŏn'gu*." *Chŏngsin munhwa yŏn'gu* 23, no. 1 (2000): 219–26.

Yi Pyŏnghŭi. *Koryŏ hugi sawŏn kyŏngje yŏn'gu*. Seoul: Kyŏngin Munhwasa, 2008.

———. "Koryŏ hugi sawŏn ŭi mangp'yehwa wa t'oji munje." *Munhwa sahak* 26 (2006): 228.

———. *Koryŏ sigi sawŏn kyŏngje yŏn'gu*. Seoul: Kyŏngin Munhwasa, 2009.

Yi Sangbaek. *Yijo kŏn'guk ŭi yŏn'gu—Yijo ŭi kŏn'guk kwa chŏnje kaehyŏk munje*. Seoul: Ŭryu Munhwasa, 1949.

———. "Yubul yanggyo kyodae ŭi kiyŏn e taehan il yŏn'gu." In *Chosŏn munhwasa yŏn'gu non'go*, 1–170. Seoul: Ŭryu Munhwasa, 1947.

Yi Sŏngmu. *Chosŏn ch'ogi yangban yŏn'gu*. Koyang-si: Han'guk Haksul Chŏngbo, 2001.

Yi Sugŏn. *Han'guk chungse sahoesa yŏn'gu*. Seoul: Ilchogak, 1984.

———. "Yŏmal Sŏnch'o t'osŏng ijok ŭi sŏngjang kwa punhwa—Andong Kwŏnssi rŭl chungsimŭro." In Yi Kibaek Sŏnsaeng Kohŭi Kinyŏm Han'guk Sahak Nonch'ong Kanhaeng Wiwŏnhoe, *Han'guk sahak nonch'ong*, vol. 1, 957–83.
Yi Sukkyŏng. "Koryŏ Ch'ungsuk wang Ch'unghye wang kwa sangin ŭi kwan'gye chinch'ul." *Han'guk inmulsa yŏn'gu* 4 (2005): 89–116.
———. *Koryŏmal Chosŏnch'o sap'aejŏn yŏn'gu*. Seoul: Ilchogak, 2007.
———. "Yi Chehyŏn seryŏk ŭi hyŏngsŏng kwa kŭ yŏkhal—Kongmin wang chŏn'gi (1351–1365) kaehyŏk chŏngch'i ŭi ch'ujin kwa kwallyŏn hayŏ." *Han'guksa yŏn'gu* 64 (1989): 43–82.
Yi Sŭnghan. "Koryŏ Ch'ungsŏn wang ŭi Simyang wang p'ibong kwa chae Wŏn chŏngch'i hwaltong." *Yŏksahak yŏn'gu* 2 (1988): 23–73.
Yi T'aejin. *Han'guk sahoesa yŏn'gu: Nongŏp kisul paltal kwa sahoe pyŏndong*. Expanded ed. P'aju: Chisik Sanŏpsa, 2008.
Yi Usŏng. "Koryŏ ŭi yŏngŏpchŏn." *Yŏksa hakpo* 28 (1965): 1–23.
———. "Koryŏjo ŭi 'i' e taehayŏ." *Yŏksa hakpo* 23 (1964): 1–26.
Yŏ-Wŏn kwan'gyesa yŏn'gut'im, ed. *Yŏkchu Wŏn Koryŏ kisa*. Seoul: Sŏnin, 2008.
Yü, Chün-fang. "Chung-feng Ming-pen and Ch'an Buddhism in the Yüan." In *Yüan Thought: Chinese Thought and Religion under the Mongols*, edited by Hok-lam Chan and Wm. Theodore de Bary, 419–77. New York: Columbia University Press, 1982.
Yun Kiyŏp. "Chosŏnch'o kunso chongp'a sosok ŭi Chabok sach'al silt'ae—Chabok sach'al 19-sa ŭi yŏnhyŏk kwa pyŏnch'ŏn ŭl chungsimŭro." *Kukhak yŏn'gu* 28 (2015): 135–74.
———. *Koryŏ hugi ŭi pulgyo: Sawŏn ŭi pulgyosajŏk koch'al*. Seoul: Ilchogak, 2012.
Yun, Peter. "Mongols and Western Asians in the Late Koryŏ Ruling Stratum." *International Journal of Korean History* 3 (2002): 51–69.
Yun Yonggyun. *Shushigaku no denrai to sono eikyō ni tsuite*. Keijō: Keijō Imperial University, 1933.
Zaborowski, Hans-Jürgen. *Der Gelehrte und Staatsmann Mogun Yi Saek (1328–1396): Studien zu seiner Biographie*. Wiesbaden: Harrassowitz, 1976.
Zhao, George Qingzhi. "Control through Conciliation: Royal Marriages between the Mongol Yuan and Koryŏ (Korea) during the 13th and 14th Centuries." *Toronto Studies in Central and Inner Asia* 6 (2004): 3–26.
———. *Marriage as Political Strategy and Cultural Expression*. New York and Bern: Peter Lang, 2008.

INDEX

A

academicians, titles of, 189n66
agency, 10, 146n30
"aid and remedy" (*pibo*), 14, 49, 59, 65–66, 133
altars to the spirits of soil and grain, 89, 108, 140
Amdo (Duosima), 124
An Chŏn, 91, 95, 176n63, 179n89
An Hyang, 145n21
An Pyŏngu, 195n23
Andong Kim descent group, 186n25. *See also* Kim Panggyŏng
Andong Kwŏn descent group, 6, 83, 144n17, 145n25. *See also* Kwŏn Chun; Kwŏn Kŭn
Anhwa-sa, 158n68, 172n30
Anji, Prince of, 165n16
Ansan Kim descent group, 115, 117
anti-Buddhist movement, 5–6, 136, 156n39; and Confucianization, 10, 42–44; and corruption, 11, 138, 155n34; driven by social concerns, 10–11, 146n31; fiscal crisis thesis, 44–45
appointment bribes, 101, 182n129
Aqutai, 188n57
arable land, 49, 150n28, 156–57n47, 159n69
Ariq Böke, 84, 85
Asad, Talal, 146n30
asceticism, 38–40, 153n62
Avataṃsaka Sutra (Huayan jing), 38, 154n13
Ayurbarwada (Renzong), 123, 188n57, 190nn77,79

B

Baizhu, 124
Bakkula, 29
banquets, 96, 97, 167n48
Baoen Guangjiao Monastery, 66–67, 68, 70, 167n39
baoyin levy, 175n55
Baraq, 85
Bayan, 98, 125, 191–92n101
Benavides, Gustavo, 146n36
bichēchi (*p'iljajŏk*), 62, 89, 95, 103, 164n11, 178–79n88, 179n89
Birge, Bettina, 184n9
board of personnel (*chŏllisa*), 120, 136, 173n36, 185n12, 190n74. *See also* personnel authority
board of recruitment (*sŏnbu*), 190n74. *See also* board of personnel
Bodhidharma, 32–33
Book of Rites (Li ji), 108–9, 184n7
Bossler, Beverly, 109
Bourdieu, Pierre, "strategy of distinction," 146n33, 147n38
Boyantugusi, 191n84
Bresson, Alain, 147n38
bribery, 96, 101, 122, 186nn26,29
Brook, Timothy, 147n44
Brown, Peter, 150n26, 193n129
Buddha, 28, 29; relics of, 21
buddha nature, 31, 32, 153n68
Buddhaśrī (Jiguo Imperial Princess): and Ch'ungsŏn's consorts, 71, 115; marriage to Ch'ungsŏn, 99, 181n117; plan to remarry, 117, 188n57; and the removal of Ch'ungsŏn, 102, 103, 183n138

227

Buddhism: abandonment of, 105–6, 119–20, 127–29, 131; and commerce, 11, 146–47n36; corruption of, 11, 13, 42, 51–52, 54–55, 138, 146n35, 148n3, 155n34; criticism of, 42, 45, 136; as "dark and mysterious," 37, 39, 40, 42, 56; decline of, 11, 13–14, 56, 141, 147n44; eulogies in, 22–27, 152nn43,48; and family greatness, 78–79; and the fiscal crisis, 42, 44–45, 47–48, 138; management of death, 3, 4, 7, 15, 24–25, 56, 105, 108, 119–20, 131–32; and moral principles, 58, 59, 60, 105; and the privatization of wealth, 141; reformist movement in, 53, 162n94; religious fervor in, 11; scriptures, 18–19, 107, 149n22; social function of, 52, 161n88; and the state, 157n62; transmission of, 32–33; wastefulness in, 5, 12, 42, 44; and the Yŏnbok-sa controversy, 134–36, 138–39, 140. See also anti-Buddhist movement; memorial monasteries; monasteries; salvation and wealth; Sŏn Buddhism

Bulughan, empress, 188n57

bureaucratic service (sa), ideals of, 12, 81–82, 104, 111, 114, 118, 119, 131. See also regular bureaucracy

C

causality, 31–33, 153n78

censorate (ŏsadae), 91, 92, 96, 102, 113, 179n95, 181n109

Ch'a Sin, 97, 98, 101, 182n130

Ch'a Tŭkkyu, 91, 97

Chabok-sa monasteries, 47–48, 157nn56,57

Chabui, 180n108

Ch'ae Ch'ungsun, 17, 21–22, 24, 149nn17,21

Ch'ae Hajung, 123, 192n116

Ch'ae Hongch'ŏl, 45–46, 123, 156n42, 192n116

Ch'ae Mo, 118–19, 188n62

Ch'ae Sangsik, 52, 65, 161nn87,88, 162nn91,96

Ch'ae Songnyŏn, 115

chaech'u (officials in the chancellery and security council): under Ch'ungnyŏl, 93, 95–96, 102, 183n134; Ch'ungsŏn's reform of, 102, 183n134; and the definition of sejok, 171n5; members of, 98, 176n65; prayers for great khan, 84–85; role in political affairs, 171n12; special office, 95–96; state funerals provided for, 5, 143–44n10, 184n3; taxation of 172n30; and Wŏnjong's favorites, 87

Chaghatai *ulus*, 85, 88

Chahyo-sa, 3, 7, 8

Ch'ang, King, 192n114

Chang Ch'ungŭi, 185n12

Chang Kwangbu, 185n12

Chang Sunyong, 69, 168n56

Changan-sa, 49, 158n65

Changwŏnsim (monk), 140, 195n25

Ch'anyŏng (monk), 127, 128, 192n114

charitable funds, 20, 149n23

chastity, 107, 108, 109, 184n9

chemun (eulogies), 22–27, 152nn43,48

Cheng Hao, 121

Cheng Yi, 121, 145n18

Cheng-Zhu learning, 121, 189n73

Chigong (monk), 57

Chikchi-sa, 49, 158n63

Chikusa Masaaki, 151n31

Chin Ch'ŏk, 96, 179n94

Chin Sŏnggyu, 148n3

Chindo (island), 172n28

Chinjong-sa, 75, 76

chinsin (truth-body), 22

Chinul (monk), 51, 53, 54. See also Susŏn-sa

Cho, Lady (consort of King Ch'ungsŏn), 71

Cho, Lady (wife of Yu Yŏngjae), 185n19

Cho Chŏk, 123

Cho Chŏngsuk. See Cho In'gyu

Cho Chun: land-reform memorials, 45, 49–50, 159n69, 160n79; member of P'yŏngyang Cho, 64, 65; member of reformist group, 5, 43, 83, 156n37

Cho Ch'ung, 100

Cho Ch'ungsin, 63, 165n21

Cho Chwaho, 177n70

Cho Hyu, 194n5

Cho In'gyu (Cho Chŏngsuk): amassed fortune as palace favorite, 118, 163n3; appointments and titles, 62, 91, 95, 97, 103, 164n13, 176n61; daughter of, 62, 102, 116–17, 118; death and funerary

inscription of, 63–64, 163–64n8, 165n21; descendants of, 64, 166n25; exile of, 71; family background, 61, 104, 163–64n8; as hostage of great khan, 88; house of, 181n118; Mongolian language skills, 61, 180n101; offering hall of, 64, 73; posthumous name, 63; relationship with Mongols, 61–62, 117, 164n10; remained in office under Ch'ungsŏn, 101, 182n130; royal message for Susŏn-sa, 176n65; sons of, 62, 163n3, 165n16; sons-in-law of, 103, 188n59; target of anonymous letter, 103
Cho Ryŏn, 62, 63, 64, 165n16
Cho Sŏ, 62, 63, 64, 165n16
Cho Tŏgyu, 64, 65
Cho Un, 166n25
Cho Wi, 62, 165n16
Cho Yŏngin, 185n19
Cho Yŏnsu, 62, 72, 165nn16,21, 166n34, 169n69
Ch'oe, Lady (wife of Kim Ryun), 106, 119
Ch'oe Ch'am, 101–2
Ch'oe Ch'iwŏn, 22, 151n34
Ch'oe Ch'unghŏn, 84, 115
Ch'oe Hae: on Buddhist methods of managing death, 55–56, 58; commemorative text for Sŏnwŏn-sa, 36–37, 120, 149–50n24; criticism of Buddhism, 37–43, 44; funerary inscription for Wŏn Sŏnji, 143n10; letter to monk Sŏnji on Mount Kŭmgang, 37–40, 45; "Lotus in the Rain" (Uha), 155n23; record for Kanjang-am, 40–41; reflections on Buddhism, 36–37, 59
Ch'oe House, 173n36, 176n64
Ch'oe Munbon, 92
Ch'oe Mundo (Ch'unhŏn): abandonment of Buddhism, 119–22, 125; failure to take literary examination, 121–22, 189n69; funerary inscription by Yi Chehyŏn, 120–22, 189n67; Mongolian language skills, 121; mourning for parents, 120, 122, 189n65; *sajok* credentials, 121–22; service in Dadu, 189nn69,70,71
Ch'oe Munjin, 36, 154n4
Ch'oe Nubaek, wife of, 185n19

Ch'oe Piil, 120
Ch'oe Sagŏm, 189n69
Ch'oe Sajŏn, 100
Ch'oe Sawi, 17
Ch'oe Seyŏn, 99–100, 181nn118,119
Ch'oe Sŏ, 119; daughter of, 119
Ch'oe Sŏngji: bribes collected by, 122; career in regular bureaucracy, 121–24, 189n68; and Ch'ungsuk's edict, 124–25; control of recruitment and promotions, 121, 122, 190n74; disloyalty of, 122, 123; donations to Sŏnwŏn-sa, 36–37, 55, 65, 122; financed restoration of Ch'ŏnhwa-sŏnsa, 74, 120, 122; funerary inscription for, 36, 123, 124, 154n4, 191n86; as Lord of Kwangyang, 120–21; management of death, 120; retirement of, 124, 154n2; *sajok* credentials, 122; supporter of Ch'ungsŏn, 123
Ch'oe Sŭngno, 44, 49
Ch'oe U (Ch'oe I), 52, 54, 120, 189n67
Ch'oe Ŭi, 173n36
Ch'oe Ŭng, 100
Ch'oe Yuŏm, 117
Chogye sect, 66
Chŏlla circuit, 91, 131, 175n56, 179n95, 187n31
Chŏn, Prince (Wŏnjong), 84, 86, 171nn10,12. See also Wŏnjong
Chŏn Oryun, 195n16
Chŏn Paegyŏng, 195n16
Chŏng Ch'ong, 136
Chŏng In'gyŏng, 86, 97, 173n37
Chŏng Mongju, 43, 44, 126, 137, 192n114
Chŏng Obu, 86, 91, 97
Chŏng Sach'ŏk, 136
Chŏng Sado, 126
Chŏng Sŭngo, 95; son of, 97
Chŏng Tojŏn, 5, 43, 135, 136, 137, 156n37
Chŏngan Im descent group, 115, 117
Ch'ŏnggye, Mount, 64, 165n22
Ch'ŏnggye-sa, 64, 73
Chŏnghŏn, 127
Chŏnghwa, Court Lady, 169n68, 190n81
Chŏngjong, King, 149n22
Ch'ŏngju Yi descent group, 117
ch'ŏngnyŏm (honest and upright), 9, 84, 104, 113–14, 119, 131

Chŏngo (Muoe), 67–68, 72, 167nn44,45,47,50
Chŏngsun, queen consort, 117
Ch'ŏngun-sa, 70, 168n63
Ch'ŏn'gyu (monk), 140
Ch'ŏnhwa-sŏnsa, 36, 74, 120, 122
Ch'ŏnsu-sa, 49, 158n68
Ch'ŏnt'ae sect, 66, 68
Ch'ŏrwŏn Ch'oe descent group, 117
Chosŏn dynasty: Buddhism under, 133, 147n44; founding of, 13–14, 43, 137
Chu Chŏ, 17–19, 21, 22
Ch'unggyŏng (Honwŏn), 25
Chunghŭng-sa, 192n116
Ch'unghye, King: consorts of, 145n27, 184–85n9; faction of, 125, 191–92n101; succession of, 125, 129
Ch'ungji (Sŏn master), 25, 152n43
Ch'ungmok, King, 193n123
Ch'ungnyŏl, King (Prince Sim): arranged son's marriage to Mongol princess, 98–99, 180n108, 181n111; attempt to strengthen the throne, 94–96; attending officials in Dadu, 90, 93, 95–96, 100, 174n48, 181–82n123; death of, 117; establishment of *bichĕchi*, 95, 178–79n88, 179n89; establishment of falconry offices, 89, 90; fiscal problems under, 93; as hostage in Dadu, 89–90, 174–75n50; inner circle of, 89, 101, 174n43, 183n138; machinations against Ch'ungsŏn, 102; marriage of, 88, 173n37, 174n41; and Minch'ŏn-sa, 168n61; and Myoryŏn-sa, 70, 72, 168n60; negotiations with Qubilai, 94, 95; nontraditional support network, 81–82, 83–84, 89–93, 96–97, 103, 170n3, 171n3; palace favorites, 92–93, 94–96, 97–100, 163n104; regular bureaucracy under, 91–93, 94–95, 111, 176n63; reinstatement of, 103; renaming of government offices, 102–3; retirement of, 69, 100; royal ancestral shrine of, 110; as Simyang Prince, 61, 86, 87, 169n68, 178n78; status of, 89, 174n42; support for Gammala, 180n108, 181n117; supporters at the Mongol court, 188n57

Ch'ungsŏn, King: abolition of personnel authority, 101–3, 189–90n74; adoption of Kwŏn Chae, 8, 145n27; assumption to throne, 100; attempt to limit men from nontraditional backgrounds, 100–101, 171n3, 182n123; Buddhism under, 66, 67; bureaucratic reforms, 82, 101–3, 170–71n3, 182n133, 183n138; conflict with Ch'ungsuk, 124; consorts of, 71, 110, 115, 116–17, 184–85n9, 187n48, 188n55; death of, 124; edicts on merit subject status, 100; exile to Turfan (Xigaze), 123, 124, 125, 191n84; falconry officials under, 175n56; favorites of, 145n21, 182n123; forced to abdicate, 69, 102, 103, 117, 183n138; list of ministerial families, 110, 114–15, 117–18, 187n44; marriage of, 71, 98–99, 180n108, 181n111; moved his father to Purŭn-sa, 69; and Myoryŏn-sa, 70, 72, 168n61; named Wang Ko as heir apparent, 123, 190n81; network of supporters, 101–2, 115, 122, 182n131, 190n75; noble titles of, 169n68, 180n109; purge of Ch'ungnyŏl's favorites, 99–100, 181n117; and the P'yŏngyang Cho, 62, 71; relations with regular bureaucracy, 102, 111, 118, 190n76; relations with Yuan court, 103, 123, 183nn138,144, 190n80; residence in Dadu, 103, 122, 123, 181n109, 183n144, 190n80; retirement of, 123, 190n80; return to the throne, 115, 117, 188n57; Wang Yuso's plot against, 187n47

Ch'ungsuk, King: consorts of, 145n27; death and funeral, 125; edict rewarding bureaucracy with commemorative arches, 124–25; granted title to Lady Hŏ, 107; house arrest in Dadu, 113, 123, 191n87; invitation to Ŭisŏn, 66; and Myoryŏn-sa, 70–71, 72; nominal enthronement, 123; palace favorites, 129; regular bureaucracy under, 111; release and return to Koryŏ, 124; rivalry with Wang Ko, 71–72, 123, 166n38, 191n88; visit to Kwŏn Chun's house, 145n21

Ch'unhŏn. *See* Ch'oe Mundo

circuit commissioners, 91, 92, 96, 100–101, 176n63, 179n95, 186n26, 187n39
classicism, 18, 89, 109, 110, 122, 125. *See also* Confucianization; Neo-Confucianism
commemorative steles, 16, 148n3. See also under *individual monasteries*
Commentary on the Greater Perfection of Wisdom Sutra, 28–29, 152n58
concubines, 184–85n9
Confucianization, 10, 42–44, 127, 145–46n29; Chosŏn, 133. *See also* family shrines; Neo-Confucianism
consanguineous marriage, 115, 117, 148n5
Consolidated Army Command (Samgunbu), 156n37
"conspicuous consumption" (Veblen), 150n25
corruption: Buddhism and, 11, 13, 42, 138, 146n35, 148n3, 155n34; under Mongol rule, 55; myth of, 48–49, 51–55
council of princes and nobles (*quriltai*), 98, 180n108, 181n117
cultural competency, 20, 150n25
Cunda, 28

D

Da Yuan, 171n18
Dadu: envoys to, 97, 180n101; hostages in, 88, 89; Koryŏ sovereigns' tours in, 113, 186n38; Mongol court, 85, 117, 123, 188n57, 191n83; Tianyuan Yansheng Monastery, 66, 67, 166n36; tribute women, 89, 116. *See also under* Ch'ungnyŏl, King; Ch'ungsŏn, King; Ch'ungsuk, King
Dahui Zonggao, 152n48
darughachi, 62, 85, 93, 94, 117, 164n13, 178n81
Daxue yanyi (Extended Meaning of the Great Learning), 128, 192–93n117
death management: classicist methods, 125, 131, 193n129; Buddhism and, 3, 4, 7, 15, 24–25, 56, 105, 108, 119–20, 131–32; early Christian, 193n129; by elite families, 105–6; by Lady Hŏ, 106–8; mourning period, 106–7, 108, 120, 125, 126, 185nn12,13; vegetarian feasts, 22, 23, 25, 36–37, 71, 105, 120, 147n1, 185n11

Deuchler, Martina, 104, 145–46n29, 146nn31,34, 148n5, 155n24, 187n44; "strategies of distinction," 10, 146n33
Dharmaśrī, 190n77
Dharmodgata, 38, 154n13
"dialectic of asceticism" (Teiser), 153n62
distinction: Bourdieu on, 146n33, 147n38; Bresson on, 147n38; Deuchler on, 146n33; wealth and, 12–13
Divyāvadāna, 153n61
Documents (Shangshu), 194n14
dragon cult, 193n3
Duncan, John, 146n34, 155n32, 171n12

E

El Temür, 191–92n101
eunuchs: barred from high office, 91, 97, 99; interest in wealth and power, 11, 112; in king's inner circle, 83, 99, 172n21, 182n123, 190n75; as men from nontraditional backgrounds, 12, 81, 83, 91; as palace aides, 177n70, 180n101; purge of, 99, 181n117; restoration of monasteries, 75, 169–70n77
evil destinies, 24, 39, 152n39, 154n15
Extended Meaning of the Great Learning (Daxue yanyi), 128, 192–93n117

F

falconry, 83, 90, 91, 92, 97, 103, 178n82, 179n89. *See also* falconry offices; O Sukpu
falconry offices, 89, 90, 92, 96, 101, 175n53, 175–76n56, 178n86
family records, 63, 74, 129
family shrines (*kamyo*), 133, 136, 189n73; built by Ch'oe Mundo, 120, 122; legislation of, 131; promoted by Chŏng Mongju, 126; of Yun T'aek's family, 4, 126–27, 128, 131
Fan Zhongyan, 20
fields of merit: Buddha as, 28, 29; Buddhist monasteries as, 19–20; in China, 152n51; explanations of, 30; and the guarantee of salvation, 8; miracles accruing from, 19, 21–22, 29, 33; moral principle and, 58, 59, 60, 105; *saṅgha* as, 28–29, 55, 152n58; seed metaphor, 27–29, 30–33, 35; and the virtues of

fields of merit (*cont.*)
  giving, 29, 35. See also salvation and wealth
filial piety: and actions of giving, 35; and classicist methods of managing death, 125–26; emphasized in stele inscriptions, 75, 76; and monastery building, 16, 18–19, 148n3
fiscal crisis thesis, 42, 44–45, 47–48, 51, 156n39
five blessings (*obok*), 6, 9, 145n19
Four Books, Zhu Xi's commentaries on, 6, 145n18
Fukaya Toshigane, 173n35
funerary inscriptions, 5, 6–7, 143–44n10, 145n23. See also Ch'oe Hae; Hŏ, Lady; stele inscriptions; Yi Chehyŏn; Yi Kok; Yi Saek
funerary portraits: commissioned by *sejok* families, 7, 132; housed in family shrines, 128; and monastery construction, 17, 149n15, 158n68; and monastery endowments, 49, 156n35; portrait halls for, 18, 63–64, 70, 74, 76, 149n15, 159n78; Ŭisŏn's, 77–78. See also memorial monasteries

G

Gammala (Prince of Jin), 98, 99, 166n36, 181n117; son of, 124
ganying (sympathetic resonance), 22
Gao Zhaoyi, 151n34
Gernet, Jacques, 11, 146n36, 149n24
Ghost Festival, 26
Gómez, Luis O., 153n71
grant land (*susajŏn*), 87, 101. See also grant ordinances
grant ordinances, 90–91, 93, 96, 100, 176n57, 182n124, 195n23
"grazing land" (*pangmokso*), 182
"great families" (*taejok*), 12, 59–60, 63, 110; great-family credentials, 74–76, 77, 78–79, 105, 110

H

Ha descent group, 163nn102,104. See also Ha Wŏnsŏ
Ha Wŏnsŏ, 56–57, 163n104
Ha Yunwŏn, 185n13

habitus (Bourdieu), 150n25
Haein-sa, 49
Haeju Ch'oe, 117, 119
Hallim Academy, 82–83, 101–2, 103, 112, 120, 170n3, 189n67, 190n74
Han Kimun, 148n3, 157n56, 161n85, 162n96
Han Ko, 137
Han Sanghwan, 46, 156n45
Han Ugŭn, 156nn39,45,46
Han Yu, "Origins of the Way" (Yuandao), 36–37, 42
Hanyang, 134, 135
Harghasun, 117, 188n57
hereditary elites. See *sejok*
Hindu (Xindu), 96
History of Koryŏ (Koryŏsa): biographies, 170n77, 179n95, 192n112; on *chaech'u* posts granted to former slave, 98; on donation of land for Hyŏnhwa-sa, 150n28; on the dragon cult, 193–94n3; on grant ordinances, 90; on mourning customs, 185n13; on Myoryŏn-sa, 168n60; on ranks of palace aides, 177n70; "Treatise on Law," 159n75
History of Yuan (Yuan shi), 180n109
Hŏ, Lady, 106–8, 184nn3,8, 186n22; funerary inscription for, 108–10, 111, 119; posthumous title of, 119
Hŏ Chae, 110
Hŏ Hŏngsik, 149n15
Hŏ Kong, 87, 110, 115, 118, 173n36, 174n46, 186nn22,26; daughter of, 117
Hŏ Kwan, 118
Hŏ Kyŏng, 110
Hŏ Su, 110
Hŏ Ŭng, 136, 195n16
Hoeam-sa, 48, 194n9
holchŏk. See *qorchi*
Hong Chabŏn, 61, 101, 116, 182n129
Hong Mun'gye, 115–16, 118, 119, 187n51
Hong Pogwŏn, 178n78
Hong Sŭnggi, 177n70
Hong Tagu, 94, 95, 96, 177n77, 178nn78,84
Hong Yŏngt'ong, 128
hongbok togam (directorate of expanding merit), 135, 194n11
Hon'gi (Cho In'gyu's older brother), 65, 166n27
Hongsŏ (monk), 67

Hon'gu, 167n52
Honwŏn, 162n97
hostages, 88–89, 174nn40,48
Huiyi Luguo Imperial Princess, 156n35, 194n11
Hŭngbok-sa, 27
Hŭngch'ŏn-sa, 156n45
Hŭngwang-sa, 49, 50, 158n67, 160n80, 172n30
Hwabi (consort), 145n27
Hwang Hŭi, 137
Hwangch'ŏn Cho, 117
Hwangnyŏ Min descent group, 117. See also Min Sap'yŏng
Hwaŏm sect, 52
hyangga (native songs), 23
hyangni (hereditary local elites): descent groups, 75, 163n8, 170n80; and new scholar-officials, 53, 82, 162n91; and reformist movement, 53, 55; support for monasteries, 51, 55
Hyegŭn (Sŏn master), 26
Hyesim (abbot), 51–52, 53, 162n97
hyŏn (mysterious), 8, 14, 19
Hyŏnhwa-sa: as act of filial piety, 18–19; Buddhist scriptures installed at, 18–19, 149n22; construction of, 17; endowment for, 20–21, 49, 150n28, 151n30, 158n66; as a field of merit, 19–20, 21–22, 150n25; mystery of, 21–22; name of, 19; relic stupa at, 21; rituals performed at, 26; stele commemorating, 16, 17–18, 21, 24, 148nn2,3, 150nn28,30
Hyŏnjong, King: and the construction of Hyŏnhwa-sa, 17, 20–21; construction of Pongsŏn Honggyŏng-sa, 148n12; filiality of, 18–19, 22; and the Khitan campaign, 17, 148n8; regulations concerning monks, 159n75; reign of, 159n75; relocation of family remains, 17–18; relocation of remains of T'aejo, 17, 148n11; rise of, 16–17. See also Hyŏnhwa-sa
Hyŏnsŏng-sa, 99

I
I Ching (Yi jing), 112
icchantika, 31, 153n67
Im Chŏnggi, 179n95

Im Yŏn, 86, 87, 116, 172n21; daughter of, 118
Im Yugan, 172n23, 174n48
Im Yumu, 86, 87, 115, 176n58; father of, 116
In Hu, 94, 97, 98, 101, 180n101, 182n130
In'gyŏng hyŏnbi, 145n26
Injŏl hyŏnbi, 145n26
Injong, King, 149n15
inner-circle politics: under King Ch'ungnyŏl, 83, 89, 99, 101, 115, 171n3, 174n43, 183n138; under King Ch'ungsŏn, 122, 182n131
intermediate existence, 25
interpreters bureau (*t'ongmun'gwan*), 93
Inye Sundŏk, 145n26, 158n68
Iryŏn, 162n97; *Memorabilia of the Three Kingdoms* (Samguk yusa), 23

J
Jaini, Padmanabh S., 153–54n79
Japan: Mongol invasions of, 87, 88, 94, 96, 179n96; pirate raids, 138, 162n98, 195n23
Jing, Duke of Song, 194n14
Jingde chuandeng lu (Jingde era record of the transmission of the lamp), 153n72

K
Kaegug-nyulsa, 78
Kaegyŏng, 85, 86, 172n26; great well of, 194n3
Kamŭng-sa, 106, 184n5
Kang Cho, 16, 17
Kang Hoebaek, 134–35, 194nn7,8
Kang Hoegye, 194n7
Kang Kamch'an, 100
Kang Yung, 111–12, 114
Kang Yunso, 85–86, 91, 92, 172n20, 174–75n50
Kanghwa Island: distribution of salary land, 173n34; pirate raids on, 162n98; resistance to the Mongols, 84, 85, 94. See also Sŏnwŏn-sa
Kangjong, King, 52
Kanjang-am (Hermitage for Reading the Tripiṭaka), 40–41, 75
keshig (household guards), 89–90, 103, 163n104, 174n47; of the khan, 117, 121, 178n78, 189n69; shifts, 175n51
Khitan campaign, 17, 148nn8,11

Kilsang-sa, 51, 160n80. *See also* Susŏn-sa
Kim, Lady (mother of Yun T'aek), 4, 126, 143n8
Kim, Lady (wife of Ch'oe Sŏngji), 36, 120, 154n4, 162n94, 189n69
Kim Chajŏng, 86, 91, 97–98, 180n101
Kim Ch'anghyŏn, 148n3, 178n88, 182n131, 183n144, 190n74
Kim Chasu, 135–36, 137, 194nn13,14
Kim Ch'o, 42, 45, 136, 137
Kim Chŏn, 136
Kim Chujŏng, 95, 178n86
Kim Chun, 84, 85, 87, 171n12, 172nn20,21
Kim Chunggu, 52
Kim Hodong, 163n99, 164n13, 171nn14,18, 173n37
Kim Hon, 117
Kim Hwŏn, 112, 113, 120, 154n4, 187nn39,42
Kim Kaemul: exile of, 111–12, 113; funerary inscription for, 112–13, 114, 186n32; funerary inscription for Lady Hŏ, 108–10, 111
Kim Kapchu, 157nn59,60
Kim Koeng, 112, 186n32
Kim Ku, 93
Kim Kwangch'ŏl, 171n5, 178n88, 190n80, 191n84
Kim Kwangjae, 169n75
Kim Kyŏngjik, 193n123
Kim Mun'gwi, 192n116
Kim Panggyŏng, 94, 95, 99, 100, 177n77, 178n84, 186n25
Kim Po, 126
Kim Pogwang, 175n51
Kim Pyŏn: death ritual and epitaph, 106–8, 184n2; family of, 117; gravesite of, 107, 184n8; as hostage in Dadu, 89, 174nn40, 48; merit subject status, 180n98
Kim Ryun, 106, 107, 109, 119, 123, 184n5
Kim Sim, 122–23, 190nn77,78
Kim Sŏ, 89, 174n48
Kim Sŏngjun, 181n117
Kim Sun, 186n25
Kim Sŭngmu, 186n26
Kim Tangt'aek, 164n9, 172n21, 179n89
Kim Ŭigwang, 95
Kim Wije, 192n116
Kim Yong, 126
Kim Yongsŏn, 169n74, 189n73

Kim Yŏngŭi, 78
Ko Hyeryŏng, 144n13, 189nn70,71
Ko Yongbo, 75
Kohŭng Yu descent group, 105
Kojong, King, 84; daughter of, 176n65
Kŏjo-sa, 51
Kökejin, Empress Dowager, 99, 102, 188n57
Kŏndong-sŏnsa, 56–58
Kongam Hŏ descent group, 110, 114–15, 117–18, 119, 186n22. *See also* Hŏ, Lady; Hŏ Kong
kongjŏn (public land), 50, 51, 156n46, 159–60n79
Kongmin, King: abolished and revived three-year mourning period, 126; accession to the throne, 129, 193n123; advised to abandon Buddhism, 127–28; attempt to restore Yŏnbok-sa stupa, 139–40; consort of, 156n35, 194n11; established directorate of expanding merit, 194n11; and the funeral of Kwŏn Chun, 3; honored at Sillŭk-sa, 27; lit incense for his father, 168n63; reforms of, 127; reign of, 163n102; rewarded filial piety, 126
Kongnam Hŏ descent group, 104
Kongyang, King (Wang Yo), 127, 193n1, 194nn7,11; definition of virtue, 138; restoration of Yŏnbok-sa, 133–39, 140, 141, 194n9
Koryŏ: capital of, 134, 168n54, 194n11; fiscal crisis of, 138, 195n23; loss of taxable population, 86–87, 172n27; under Mongol rule, 62, 81, 84–85, 88, 164n13, 171n14; royal ancestral shrine, 89; relations with the Yuan, 84–85, 88–89, 171n18; sovereignty of, 85, 89, 124; surrender to the Mongols, 81, 84; as tributary state and princely appanage, 88–89, 97, 164n13, 174n45. *See also individual kings*
Kukch'ŏng-sa, 49, 67–68, 158n68, 167nn48,49
Kŭmgang, Mount (Mount P'ungak), 37–40, 45, 49
Kŭmju, 4, 143n8
Kŭmsan Kim descent group, 143n8
Kŭmsin, Mount, 17

Kwak Ye, 95
Kwangdŏk-sa, 185n12
Kwangjong, King, 49
Kwangju Pak descent group, 75, 170n80. *See also* Pak Swaenoooldae
Kwangmyŏng-sa, 54, 168n63, 194n3
Kwangyang, Lord of, 37, 162n98. *See also* Ch'oe Sŏngji
kwŏn (the powerful), 58, 59, 101. *See also kwŏnmun; kwŏnmun sejok*
Kwŏn Chae (Wang Hu), 145n27
Kwŏn Chun: death and funeral of, 3; funerary inscription for, 3, 6–7, 8; grave of, 143n1; memorial monastery Chahyo-sa, 3, 6, 8; posthumous title, 3; *Record of Filial Deeds* (Hyohaeng rok), 6; *sejok* credentials, 7–8, 145n25; wealth of, 7, 145n21
Kwŏn Han'gong, 122, 123, 190n74, 191n88
Kwŏn Kŏŭi, 185n13
Kwŏn Kŭn, 83, 139–41, 144n17
Kwŏn Pu, 6, 144n17
Kwŏn Tan, 102, 144n17
Kwŏn Wan, 134
kwŏnmun (gates of power), 10, 83, 116, 146nn31,34
kwŏnmun sejok (powerful hereditary elites), 82–83, 146n31
kyŏl (measure), 150n27, 151n30
kyŏng (measure), 151n30
Kyŏngi (state preceptor Wŏnhye), 67, 71, 72, 167n44
Kyŏngjong, King, 16
Kyŏngwŏn Yi descent group, 7, 115, 117, 145n25

L

land privatization, 45, 138, 161n86, 195n23
land registers, 45–46, 156n42
landed estates, 11, 13, 53, 138, 156n42, 157n60. *See also* grant ordinances
"legitimation thesis," 20, 148n3, 157n62
literary examination, 5, 61, 62, 82, 112, 121, 122, 189n69
Lushi Monastery, 166n36

M

Mahāparinirvāṇa Sutra, 27–28, 31
Mandŏk, Mount, 53

Manŭi-sa, 65–66, 68, 166nn27,33
marriage alliances, 60, 88, 97, 98–99, 115, 148n5, 173–74n37
Maudgalyāyana, 26
Medicine Buddha, 68–69
memorial monasteries: considered wasteful, 4, 7; versus family shrines, 4, 126; and great-family credentials, 74–75, 77; injunction against excessive construction, 157–58n62; private, 165n24; and the royal cult, 149n15, 158–59n68. *See also* Chahyo-sa; funerary portraits; Hyŏnhwa-sa; Myoryŏn-sa; Susŏn-sa
memorial rites, 52, 70, 74, 161n85, 169n75
Mencius, 134–35, 194n8
merit subject status, 46, 66, 74, 96–97, 100, 110, 156n47, 179n97, 180n98
metaphors, 20, 22, 150n26; seed-and-fruit metaphors, 8, 27–29, 30–33, 35, 153n78, 153–54n79
military rule, 51–53, 82, 84–86, 87, 161n86
Min Chi, 118–19
Min Hyŏn'gu, 163n8, 173n35, 186n22
Min Sap'yŏng, 106, 184n5; family of, 117
Minch'ŏn-sa, 168nn61,63
ministerial families, 110, 114–15, 117–18, 187n44
miracles, 19, 21–22, 25, 29, 33
Mokchong, King, 16
monasteries: construction and restoration of, 56, 64, 72–73, 75–76, 78, 165n24; donations for state prayers, 52, 161n86; endowments for, 49, 149–50n24, 161n85; graveside, 151n31; illegal seizure of, 66; landholdings of, 11, 13, 45–46, 48, 49, 156n42, 157n60; number of, 47, 157n52, 168n54; patrons of, 55; as places of aid and remedy, 14, 49–50, 65–66, 133; regulations regarding, 15, 133, 147n1; relationship with the state, 49–50, 147–48n1, 159n72; royal gifts to, 49–51; survey of property in 1397, 46; taxation of, 46, 156n46, 172n30. *See also* memorial monasteries; portrait halls
monastic reform, 46–48, 157n56
moneylending, 149n24

Möngke, 84
Mongol court, power relations at, 117, 123, 188n57, 191n83
Mongol invasions, 61, 156n42, 172n27; of Japan, 87, 88, 94, 96, 179n96; surrender of Koryŏ, 81, 84
Mongol princesses, 169n65. *See also* Buddhaśrī (Jiguo Imperial Princess); Qutlugh Kelmish (Qiguo Imperial Princess)
Mongol rule: and Buddhist institutions, 13, 105; in China, 182n133; establishment of Tongnyŏng Directorate General, 86, 164n9; and the identity of the Koryŏ elite, 12, 58, 131, 139; Koryŏ as princely appanage, 89, 97, 164n13, 174n45; and the myth of corruption, 55; P'yŏngyang Cho and, 60–62, 164n13; and reduction in tax base, 172n27; and the rise of men from nontraditional backgrounds, 91, 176n60, 177n70. *See also* Qubilai Khan
Mongolian language skills, 61, 76, 180n101. *See also* translators and interpreters
monks: Chinese, 32, 107; criticism of, 39, 91; involvement in politics, 11; regulations regarding, 45, 47, 159n75; social backgrounds of, 74, 162n95. *See also* monasteries
moral principle, 57, 84, 105–6, 109, 119; Buddhism and, 58, 59, 60, 105. *See also ch'ŏngnyŏm* (honest and upright); filial piety; virtue
Morihira Masahiko, 164n13, 171n14, 174nn42,45
Mount Kaji branch of Sŏn, 68, 167n52
Mount Kŭmgang Record, 38. *See also* Kŭmgang, Mount
mourning period, 106–7, 108, 120, 125, 126, 185nn12,13
Mubi, 99–100, 181n115
Mūlamadhyamakakārikā (Treatise on the middle), 31–32
Mun Kongwŏn, 185n19
Mun Ŭng, 96, 179n94
Munhasŏ, 102
Munjong, King, 49, 50, 145n26, 149n22, 158n67. *See also* Hŭngwang-sa

Muoe, State Preceptor, 68, 72. *See also* Chŏngo
Muqali, 172n29
Musong Yun descent group: abandonment of Buddhsm, 127–29, 131; family shrine of, 126–27, 128; great-family credentials, 130–31. *See also* Yun Kusaeng; Yun Sojong; Yun T'aek
Myohye, 65
Myŏngjong, King, 162n96
Myŏngsun Palace, 69
Myoryŏn-sa: abbacy of, 67; commemorative stele by Yi Chehyŏn, 70, 72, 73–74, 168n60; control by P'yŏngyang Cho, 55, 65–66, 167n45; as memorial monastery, 70, 168n63; restoration of, 67, 68, 70, 70–72
Myrobalan tree, 29

N
Na Yu, 97
Nāgārjuna: *Commentary on the Greater Perfection of Wisdom Sutra*, 28–29, 152n58; *Treatise on the Middle*, 31–32
Nam Ŭn, 136
Namjŏn Pumok, 128
Namp'yŏng Mun descent group, 185n19
National Museum of Korea, 143n1
Neo-Confucianism: and controversy over the restoration of Yŏnbok-sa, 137; and the corruption myth, 55; and female chastity, 184n9; growing influence of, 53, 55, 184n9, 192–93n117; mourning and funerary practices, 5, 185n12, 189n73; and the reformist sociopolitical clique, 5, 43, 144n13; and the regular bureaucracy, 83–84; Tohak (learning of the Way), 6, 144–45n18. *See also* Confucianization; family shrines; Zhu Xi
new scholar-officials, 42–43, 53, 55, 82–83, 113, 118, 146n31, 186n22
No Chinŭi, 177n77
No Chun'gong, 185n13
No Kyŏngnyun, 187n39
No Sung, 131
nuns, 168n54; regulations regarding, 147n1, 159n75

INDEX   237

O

O Cham, 115, 124
O Han'gyŏng, 102
O Ilsun, 173n35
O Sukpu, 91, 92, 176nn61,66
Ŏnyang Kim descent group, 117–18. *See also* Kim Pyŏn
offering halls. *See* portrait halls
office of royal sacrifices (*taesang*), 3, 4
office of the royal seal (*chŏnbusi*), 111, 186n28
official titles, 67, 91, 93, 163n6, 164n11
Ögödei *ulus*, 85, 88
ortoq merchants, 175n55
ŏsadae (censorate), 91, 92, 96, 102, 113, 179n95, 181n109

P

Pae Kŭngnyŏm, 156n37
Paek Hyoju, 178n82
Paek Ijŏng, 144–45n18
Paek Munbo, 128
Paek Munjŏl, 95, 96, 178n82, 179n94
Paengnyŏn-sa, 53, 67, 167n50
Pak Ching, 75
Pak Ch'o, 42, 45, 136–37
Pak Chonggi, 161n86
Pak Chŏnji, 101
Pak Hang, 91, 95, 176n63
Pak Hŏjung, 66, 166n34
Pak Hwang, 145n23
Pak Kyŏn, 75
Pak Kyŏngnyang (Pak Sŏn), 118, 122–23, 188n59
Pak Ryŏ, 182n123
Pak Swaenooldae, 75, 76
Pak Ŭi, 90, 98, 101, 176n56, 182n130, 188n59
Pak Yongun, 178–79n88
palace aides (*naeryo*), 93, 95, 97, 177n70, 180n101
palace attendants (*naesi*), 39, 91, 145n23, 177n70
palace favorites (*ch'ongsin*): of Ch'ungnyŏl, 92–93, 94–96, 97–100, 163n104; of Ch'ungsŏn, 118; of Ch'ungsuk, 129; grant land awarded to, 87, 90–91, 93, 96, 100; purge of, 99; in service of imperial princess, 93, 177n76, 182n124; as the "wealthy and powerful," 177n72; of Wŏnjong, 88
palace guards, 90, 163nn102,104, 175n51. *See also keshig*
Palais, James, 160n79
Pang Sinu, 75, 169–70n77, 182n123, 190n75
Pang Usŏn, 63, 165n20
panjŏng (half allotments), 173n35
paper currency, 13, 147n43, 167n39, 194n11
P'ap'yŏng Yun descent group, 110, 130. *See also* Yun Sŏnjwa
peasants, 53, 101, 162n93, 182n126
pedigree, 108–10, 186n22
Perfection of Wisdom Sutra, 149n22; commentary, 28–29, 152n58
personnel authority (*chŏngbang*): abolition of, 101–3, 189–90n74; and the *bichēchi*, 178–79n88; Hŏ Kong and, 87, 173n36, 186n26; and nontraditional appointments, 95; opposition to reformists, 128; power over recruitment and promotions, 101, 122, 129, 173n36; restoration of, 123, 189n74; transmitter of, 183n141. *See also* board of personnel; royal transmitters
pibo (aid and remedy), 14, 49, 59, 65–66, 133
p'iljajŏk (*bichēchi*), 62, 89, 95, 103, 164n11, 178–79n88, 179n89
pimyŏng. *See* funerary inscriptions
piracy, 138, 162n98, 195n23
Platform Sutra, 32
po (family records), 74, 169n74
Pŏbye (monk), 134
poetry exchanges, 165n22
Pogwang-sa, 75, 169n77
Poje-sa, 172n30
pokchŏn (field of merit), 8, 19. *See also* fields of merit
political cliques, 123, 144n13, 178n87, 190n80, 192n101
Pomyŏng-sa, 21
Pongsŏn Honggyŏng-sa, 148n12
Pongŭn-sa, 159n72
Pŏpkyŏng (abbot), 21
Pŏpsang sect, 52
portrait halls, 18, 63–64, 70, 74, 76, 149n15, 158–59n68

powerful families, 58, 59, 93, 124, 146n31, 170n3; Ch'ungnyŏl's network of, 82–83, 171n3
Powŏn-sa, 49, 158n64, 158n66
pratyekabuddhahood, 29
principle (ri), 57, 59. See also moral principle
pugok, 76, 83, 97, 170n81, 176n56
P'ungak, Mount (Mount Kŭmgang), 37–40, 45, 49
Purŭn-sa, 68–70, 72–73
P'yohun-sa, 48
P'yŏngyang Ch'ae descent group, 115, 117
P'yŏngyang Cho descent group, 60–64, 165n16; accusations and public disgrace, 60, 71, 163n3, 169n65; and the bichēchi, 164n11; and Buddhist methods of managing death, 58, 59–60; control of Myoryŏn-sa, 55, 65–66, 167n45; criticism from other elite families, 73, 77; great-family credentials, 63, 65, 73–74, 74–76, 105, 110; and Manŭi-sa, 65, 166n27; as ministerial family, 115, 117, 187n44; and rivalry between Wang Ko and Ch'ungsuk, 71–72, 166n38; ties with Mongol court, 60–61. See also Cho Chun; Cho Ch'ungsin; Cho In'gyu; Cho Yŏnsu; Hon'gi; Ŭisŏn

Q

Qaidu, 85
Qaishan (Wuzong), 122, 188n57
Qiguo Imperial Princess. See Qutlugh Kelmish
Qinglian Monastery, 165n22
qorchi (holchŏk), 90, 95, 101, 174nn48,50, 182n124
Qubilai Khan (Shizu): and Cho In'gyu, 61, 117; and Ch'ungnyŏl, 94, 95; death of, 98; divine edict of, 171n14; invasion of Japan, 179n96; and the marriage of Prince Sim, 88, 173n37; monastery for, 70; succession struggle of, 84–85; and Wŏnjong (Prince Chŏn), 84–86, 88, 171n10
Qurumshi, Prince (Turyŏn'ga), 86, 172n29

Qutlugh Kelmish (Qiguo Imperial Princess): and Cho In'gyu, 61, 117, 164n10; commissioned monastery and portrait hall, 70, 168n60; death of, 99; exile of Hong Mun'gye, 116; marriage to Prince Sim, 88; memorial monastery of, 168n61; punishment of Ch'oe Seyŏn, 181n118; retainers of, 69, 94, 97, 180n101, 182n130; Temür's comment on, 180n108

R

rank land law, 45–46, 100–101, 156n38, 156n45, 173n35
"reclaimable land" (kanji), 87, 173n35
Red Turban incursion, 13, 44, 138, 184n5, 193n2
reform and corruption myth, 51–55
regular bureaucracy: and the attempt to enthrone Wang Ko, 123; under Ch'ungnyŏl, 91–93, 94–95, 96, 98, 111, 176n63; under Ch'ungson, 101–3, 111, 118, 190n76; under Ch'ungsuk, 111; and classicist methods of managing death, 122, 125–26; as "honest and upright," 9, 84, 104, 113–14, 118, 119, 131, 187n39; prohibition orders, 125–26; social identity of, 111; and the term sadaebu, 82–84, 111. See also bureaucratic service, ideals of; chaech'u
remonstrance officials (nangsa), 91, 92–93, 95, 100, 156n45, 190n76, 195n16. See also Kim Hwŏn; Yi Saek
Renzong (Ayurbarwada), 123, 188n57, 190nn77, 79
"respected families" (mangjok), 59
retreat societies, 51–52, 53, 54, 67, 71
Robinson, David M., 178n78, 191n84
Royal Confucian Academy (Sŏnggyun'gwan), 42, 44, 120, 137
royal edicts (sŏnji), 91–92, 176nn64,65, 188n62
royal historians, 182n123
royal transmitters, 95, 103, 178n87, 183n141, 186n26
royal treasury (t'angjang), 47, 48, 76, 87, 173n33

S

sadae (serving the great), 171n14
sadaebu, 82–84, 104, 111, 118; families, 125, 146n34. See also regular bureaucracy
sajik (altars for soil and grain spirits), 89, 108, 140
sajok (families of officials), 56, 57, 58; Buddhist management of death by, 131–32; family of Ch'oe Ch'unhŏn, 121–22; status of, 104, 106, 111–12, 113. See also "great families"
sajŏn (private land), 156n46, 160n79
salary rank land (nokkwajŏn), 87, 96, 156n38, 173nn34,35. See also rank land law
salvation and wealth: Buddhism and, 8, 11, 15, 23–24; requirement of moral principle, 58, 59; role of rituals and metaphors in relationship, 19, 20, 24, 27, 33; separation of, 12–13, 14, 35, 58, 81, 131
Sambyŏlch'o (Three Elite Patrols), rebellion of, 86, 87, 88, 112, 172n28, 177n77
Samgak, Mount (Mount Pukhan), 192n116
Samgunbu (Consolidated Army Command), 156n37
Samhwa-sa, 40
saṅgha: as field of merit, 28–29, 55, 152n58; purification of, 50
Sangwŏn, 61
sarim (forest of officials), 83, 84, 111, 113
Sarimwŏn (Sarim Academy), 101, 102, 103. See also Hallim Academy
Sa-skya sect, 170n85
Sautrāntikas, 153–54n79
scholar-officials (shidaifu): argued for moral principle, 105; Buddhist offerings by, 40–42; changing attitude toward Buddhist death ritual, 42–44; Ch'oe Hae's reflections on, 40–41; Confucianization of, 42; identity crisis of, 58; in Song, 151n31. See also new scholar-officials
Seal of the Branch Secretariat for the Eastern Campaigns, 88–89, 96, 174n42
seed and fruit metaphors, 8, 27–29, 30–33, 35, 153n78, 153–54n79

sejok (hereditary elites): and Buddhism, 8, 125; Buddhist management of death by, 7, 105, 108; conflict with the "powerful," 10, 104, 146nn31,34; and elite credentials, 7–8; ideals and practices of, 7, 12, 114, 118–19, 124; kwŏnmun sejok (powerful hereditary elites), 82–83, 146n31; meaning of, 83, 171n5; as sadaebu families, 83, 146n34; wealth of, 7, 118–19
seven seven rites, 25
Shidebala, Yuan emperor (Yinzong), 71–72, 123, 124, 191nn83,84
Shijing (Classic of Poetry), "Splendid Are the Flowers," 72, 169n70
Sillŭk-sa, 27, 152n54
silver, 87, 90, 93, 172n30, 173n33, 175n55; utensils, 71, 149n22
Sim, Prince. See Ch'ungnyŏl, King; Wang Ko
Sim Chiŭi, 185n19
Sim Inbong, 134
Sim Yang, 96, 179n94
Simyang (Shenyang) Prince (noble title), 169n68, 178n78, 188n57. See also Ch'ungnyŏl, King
Sin Chŏng, 125
Sin Ton, 128, 193n3
Sinbok-sŏnsa, 75, 170n78
sinhŭng sadaebu (new scholar-officials), 146n31. See also new scholar-officials
Sinjo (monk), 66, 167n51
sinmunsaek, 95. See also bichēchi
slaves: barred from high office, 97, 98, 180n101; conversion of commoners to, 101, 182n126; descendants of, 111; entry into officialdom, 92, 177n70; in monasteries, 44, 47
Sŏ Hŭi, 100
Sŏ Kŏjŏng, Anthology of Korean Literature (Tongmunsŏn), 22
Sŏ Pongnye, 137
Sŏ Ton'gyŏng, 52
Sŏ Ung, 185n12
Sŏk Ch'ŏnbo, 187n47
Sŏk Ch'ŏn'gi, 187n47
Sŏk Ch'ŏnyŏng, 187n47
Sŏk Chu, 115, 187n47
Sŏl In'gŏm, 174n48

Sŏl Konggŏm, 89, 95
Sŏn Buddhism: Mount Kaji branch, 68, 167n52; sects of, 66, 68
Son Ki, 113
Sŏn learning, 54, 162n96
Sŏnch'ang (monk), 128
Song dynasty: eulogies, 109; war with Mongols, 85, 88
Sŏng Hyŏn, 168n54
Song Lin, 115, 188n57
Song Pangyŏng, 115
Song Pun, 89, 90, 95, 96, 115, 118, 176n58
Sŏng Sŏngnin, 192n114
Song Songnye, 176n58
Songak, Mount, 148n11
Songdo, 85, 134, 168n54
Sŏnggyun'gwan (Royal Confucian Academy), 42, 44, 120, 137
Sŏngjong, King, 16, 49
Sŏngmalch'ŏn'gu (Shimotianqu), 93
Sŏnhŭng-sa, 75, 169–70n77
Sŏnji (monk), 37–40
Sŏnjong, King, 145n26
"sons of the yurt" (kŏmnyŏnggu), 93, 177n76, 182n124
Sŏnwŏn-sa, 54, 65, 120, 162n98; commemorative text by Ch'oe Hae, 36–37, 120, 149–50n24
Sorim-sa, 78
sosang (first death anniversary sacrifice), 25
southern branch (namban), 177n70
southern capital, 64, 128, 192n116
special office chaech'u, 95–96
śrāvaka, 31
state funerals (yejang), 184n3
stele inscriptions, 63, 70, 73, 75, 76, 105, 166n25. See also Ch'oe Hae; Chu Chŏ; funerary inscriptions; Yi Chehyŏn; Yi Kok; Yi Saek
Subi (consort), 145n27
Sukchong, King, 145n26, 158n68
Sundŏk (consort of King Yejong), 158–59n68
Sunjong, King, 145n26
Sunyŏng Palace, 168n61. See also Minch'ŏn-sa
Susŏn-sa: abbots of, 128, 162n97; appeal to military leaders, 52–53; celebration of completion, 162n97; community of, 160n83; endowments and donations, 52, 53–54; as memorial monastery, 54; property and income, 51–52, 160n84; as reaction to Buddhist establishment, 53–54; restoration of, 51–52, 160nn80,81, 162n94; retreat society, 51–52, 53, 54; royal message for, 176n65; scholarship on, 52, 161n88; Sŏn learning at, 54, 162n96
sympathetic responses, 22, 24

T

T'aego Pou, 127–28, 192n116
taejehak (academician title), 189n66
T'aejo (first king of Koryŏ), 17, 148nn5,11
T'aejo, King (Yi Sŏnggye), 46, 49, 156n45, 157–58n62, 158n68, 159n79. See also Yi Sŏnggye
taejok. See "great families"
T'aejong, Chosŏn King, 46–48, 157nn57,59, 193n1
taesang (office of royal sacrifices), 3, 4
Taeun-sa, 51, 159nn72,78
Takahashi Tōru, 155n34
Tamjin (Song master), 54, 162n96
Tamna, 180n101
Tamuk (monk), 40
Tang dynasty eulogies, 109
Tangsŏng Hong descent group, 104, 116, 117–18. See also Hong Mun'gye
T'anmun, 49
Targi, 123, 188n57, 191nn83,84
Teiser, Stephen, "dialectic of ascetism," 153n62
Temüder, 123, 190n79, 191n83, 192n101
Temür (Chengzong), 98, 117, 180n108
tenant farmers (ch'ŏgan), 91, 176n59
three evil destinies, 24, 152n39
Three Jewels, 25, 27, 30
three obediences, 184n7
Tianshi Dao (Way of the Celestial Masters), 38
Tianyuan Yansheng Monastery (Dadu), 66, 67, 166n36
To, King, 123
To Hyŏnch'ŏl, 144n13
To Sŏnggi, 99
Tohak (learning of the Way), 6, 144–45n18

INDEX   241

tŏk. See virtue
Tŏkcha Palace, 69. See also Purŭn-sa
Tongnyŏng Directorate General, 86, 164n9
Tosŏn (monk), Record of Secrets (Milgi), 46–47, 134, 157n48
translators and interpreters, 12, 61, 93, 97. See also Cho In'gyu; Yu Ch'ŏngsin
traveling expenses bureau (panjŏnsaek), 172n30
Treatise on the Middle, 31–32
tribute women, 89, 116, 174n46, 187n48
Tugh Temür, 192n101

U

U, King, 128, 185n13
U, Superintendent, 24
U Inyŏl, 128
Ŭibi (royal consort), 70, 188n55
Ŭich'ŏn (monk), 67, 162n96
Ŭijong, King, 145n23
Ŭisŏn (monk): abbacies held by, 65–67; encomium by Yi Kok, 77–78; friendship with Yi Kok, 165n22; fund-raising and monastery construction, 66–69; and Manŭi-sa, 65–66; and the P'yŏngyang Cho, 62, 64, 65, 166n34; restoration and abbacy of Myoryŏn-sa, 65, 67, 70–72
ulus, 85, 88; Great Yuan, 85, 89, 97, 174n37, 177n76
ŭm privilege, 60, 62, 74
Unam-sa, 44, 155–56n35, 157n49
Unmun-sŏnsa, 49
Uran (Yulan) Bowl, 26, 30
Üs Temür, 98

V

Veblen, Thorstein, "conspicuous consumption," 150n25
vegetarian feasts, 22, 23, 25, 71, 105, 147n1; described in Ch'oe Hae's record, 36, 37; hundredth day, 185n11
Vermeersch, Sem, 146n35, 148n3, 150n28
virtue (tŏk): definitions of, 138, 139; in five blessings, 145n19; of Lady Hŏ, 109, 111; royal, 134–35, 194n14; in tomb epigraphs, 112, 119, 124; and wealth, 6, 9, 138–39, 141. See also ch'ŏngnyŏm (honest and upright)

W

Walraven, Boudewijn, 145n29
Wang Cha, 190n81
Wang Chakchegŏn, 194n3
Wang Chŏ, 193n123
Wang Hu (Kwŏn Chae), 145n27
Wang Hyo, 145n23
Wang Hyŏn, 117
Wang Ki (King Kongmin), 129. See also Kongmin, King
Wang Ko (Sim Prince): attempt to enthrone, 71–72, 123, 124, 166n38, 169n68, 191n88; conflict with Ch'unghye, 125, 192n101; invited Ŭisŏn to serve as abbot, 66–67; named as heir apparent, 123; relationship to royal family, 169n68, 190n81
Wang Kŏn, 194n3
Wang Samsŏk, 113
Wang Uk, 16, 148n12
Wang Yo (King Kongyang), 133–34, 193n1. See also Kongyang, King
Wang Yŏng, 187n48
Wang Yuso, 115, 122, 187n47, 188n57
Way, the, 76–77, 79
Way of the Celestial Masters (Tianshi Dao), 38
Way of the wife (pudo), 109
wealth: and bureaucratic service, 7, 81–82, 111, 131; donations to monasteries, 7, 8, 54, 56, 65, 75, 77; and power, 93, 177n72; and principle, 57, 105–6; privatization of, 66, 138, 141; and religion, 11–14; and virtue, 4, 6, 9, 119, 138–39. See also land privatization; salvation and wealth; sejok
Weber, Max, 146n36
Wi Tŭgyu, 177n77
Wi Ŭnsuk, 195n23
Wihwa Island coup (1388), 66
Wŏlmyŏng (monk), 23, 151n36
Wŏn Kyŏng, 90, 101
Wŏn Sŏnji, 143n10
wŏndang (memorial monasteries), 149n15. See also memorial monasteries
Wŏnhye (Kyŏngi), 67, 71, 72, 167n44
Wŏnjong (Prince Chŏn), 84, 86–88, 97, 171nn10,12, 172n26, 178n84
Wu, Emperor of Liang, 57

Y

Yampolsky, Philip, 153n77
Yang Kyu, 100
yangban, 43, 101, 151n30, 155nn29,32, 173n35
Yao and Shun, 18
Yao Sui, *Muan ji*, 174n44
Yejong, King, 158n68, 185n13
Yesün Temür, 124, 169n69
Yi Chagyŏm, 159n68
Yi Chayŏn, 8, 145n26
Yi Chehyŏn: commemorative inscription for offering hall at Sŏnhŭng-sa, 169–70n77; commemorative stele for Myoryŏn-sa, 70, 72, 73–74, 168n60; and credentials of great families, 74; father of, 102, 113, 187n42; funerary inscription for Ch'oe Ch'unhŏn, 120–22, 189n67; funerary inscription for Kim Kaemul, 112–13, 114; inscription for Kaegug-nyulsa, 78; as member of conservative clique, 5; and Neo-Confucian learning, 6, 144–45n18; preface to funerary inscription for Ch'oe Sŏngji, 123, 124; and the proposal to turn Koryŏ into a branch secretariat, 124; on rank land conversions, 173n35; reforms of, 127; restoration record of Kŏndong-sŏnsa, 56–58; tablet for Hŭngbok-sa, 27; tomb epitaphs by, 110, 119; views on Buddhism and the construction of monasteries, 59, 105
Yi Chijŏ, 95, 97, 98, 101, 176n59, 179n89
Yi Chin, 102, 113–14, 118, 187n42, 187n51
Yi Ch'ŏm, 24, 25
Yi Chonbi, 95
Yi Chŏng, 90, 98, 175–76n56, 180n102
Yi Hon, 95, 190n74
Yi Hye, 25
Yi Ikchu, 170–71n3, 171n14, 178n84, 180n108, 181n117, 182n131, 183n138
Yi Ikpae, 95
Yi Imjong, 40
Yi Inbok, 3, 6–7, 8–9
Yi Injŏng, 93, 95, 177n71
Yi Kaesŏk, 164n13
Yi Kanghan, 182n133
Yi Kibaek, *Han'guksa sillon*, 170n1
Yi Kinam, 170n3, 178n88, 183n138, 187n44

Yi Kok: on Buddhism and moral principles, 105; bureaucratic career of, 165n21; and credentials of great families, 59–60, 74; encomium for Üisŏn's funerary portrait, 77–78; funerary inscription for Cho In'gyu, 63–64; funerary inscription for Yun Sŏnjwa, 9; *Kyŏngsa Kŭmson mit'a-sagi*, 169n75; memorial project for, 27; memorial record for Pogwang-sa, 169n77; poems of, 165n22, 189nn69,71; record for Baoen Guangjiao Monastery, 66, 167n39; restoration record for Purŭn-sa, 68–70, 72–73, 168n54; restoration record for Sinbok-sŏnsa, 75; stele inscription for offering hall at Ch'ŏnggye-sa, 73
Yi Kongbo, 182n123
Yi Kyŏngsik, 173n35
Yi Punhŭi, 95, 176n65, 178n84
Yi Punsŏng, 91–92, 95, 176nn63,65, 178n84
Yi Pyŏnghŭi, 150n30, 160nn80,81, 151n30, 158n67
Yi Saek: on Buddhism and moral principles, 105; and credentials of great families, 59–60; criticism of Buddhism, 44; father of, 9; follower of the monk Ch'anyŏng, 128; funerary inscription for Yun T'aek, 126, 128, 129–30; inscription for Chinjong-sa, 76; as member of conservative clique, 5; opposed overthrow of Koryŏ, 43; and Sillŭk-sa library project, 27
Yi Sangbaek, "Yubul yanggyo kyodae," 155n34
Yi Saon, 122–23, 190n78
Yi Sŏnggye: coup of 1388, 44–45, 66, 156n37; as founder of Chosŏn dynasty, 137–38; as reformist leader, 128; and the restoration of Yŏnbok-sa, 139–41, 195nn29,30. *See also* T'aejo, King (Yi Sŏnggye)
Yi Sŏngsŏ, 44, 155–56n35
Yi Sugŏn, 144n11, 163–64n8
Yi Sŭnghyu, 40, 55, 74–75, 96, 102, 154n18, 179n94
Yi Sungin, 27
Yi Sŭngno, 193n123
Yi Usŏng, 186n22

Yi Yangjik, 149n23
Yi Yŏnjong, 40–41, 154n17
Yŏhŭng Min, 46
Yŏm Kyŏngae, 185n19
Yŏm Sŭngik, 61, 95, 101, 163nn4,6, 176n61, 182n126
Yŏmyang-sŏnsa, 75
Yŏnbok-sa, 54, 134–39, 193n2, 195nn29,30; nine wells of, 134, 194n3; restoration record by Kwŏn Kŭn, 139–41
Yongam-sa, 68, 167n51
Yŏngch'wi, Mount (Vulture's Peak), 18, 149n21
Yongsu-sa, 160n80
Yŏngwŏn-sa, 68, 167n52
Yongjia Xuanjue, "Song of Realizing the Way," 77, 170n84
Yonjang-sa, 162n98
Yose, 53. *See also* Paengnyŏn-sa
yu. *See* classicism
Yu Chŏnghyŏn, 135
Yu Ch'ŏngsin, 75, 76, 97, 98, 101, 124, 170n81
Yu Kyŏng, 173n36, 179n89
Yu Paeksun, 137
Yu T'ak, 75, 76
Yu Yŏngjae, 185n19
Yujŏm-sa, 48
Yulan (Uran) Bowl, 26, 30
Yulan Bowl Sutra (*Yulan peng jing*), 30
Yun Chaun, 130
Yun Hae, 130, 193n126
Yun Hoejong, 130, 134, 194n5
Yun Hŭngjong, 130
Yun Hyang, 137
Yun Hyojong, 130
Yun Kilson, 99
Yun Kŭngmin, 110
Yun Kusaeng, 4, 127, 128, 129, 130, 131, 192n112
Yun Kwan, 110
Yun Ŏnju, 169n65, 183n142
Yun Sojong, 5, 127–28, 129–30
Yun Sŏnjwa, 9, 123, 130
Yun Su, 90, 175n56, 178n86
Yun Sup'yong, 130, 143n8
Yun T'aek: abandonment of Buddhism, 4, 126–27; bureaucratic career, 129; burial of, 4–5; deathbed instructions, 3–4, 6, 15; family shrine, 4, 126–27, 128; funerary inscription for, 126, 128, 129–30; indifference to wealth, 3–4, 7–8; as palace favorite of Ch'ungsuk, 129; retirement, 129; *sajok* credentials, 129, 130; support for Wang Ki, 129, 193n123; titles of, 3, 4, 143n3. *See also* Musong Yun descent group
Yun Yangbi, 130

Z

Zhang Daoling, 38
Zhenzong (Song emperor), 18
Zhou, Duke of, 194n14
Zhou Dunyi, 121
Zhu Xi: commentaries on the Four Books, 6, 145n18; *Family Rituals*, 4, 5, 126, 128, 131–32, 193n129; writings of, 121
Zongmi, commentary on Yulan Bowl Sutra, 30